Bitter Sweet – Road to Life

Bitter Sweet – Road to Life

The Endless Story That Everyone Should Read

AL DUHAN

iUniverse, Inc.
Bloomington

Bitter Sweet – Road to Life
The Endless Story That Everyone Should Read

iUniverse books may be ordered through booksellers or by contacting:

iUniverse
1663 Liberty Drive
Bloomington, IN 47403
www.iuniverse.com
1-800-Authors (1-800-288-4677)

ISBN: 978-1-4759-4620-8 (sc)
ISBN: 978-1-4759-4621-5 (ebk)

Printed in the United States of America

iUniverse rev. date: 08/27/2012

Preface

The Story you are about to read will capture your heart when you follow this young boy through his footsteps on the road to life. His parents fleeing from the turmoil in the early nineteen hundreds from the Soviet Republic never had a chance to capture their belongings. They were forced to leave their wealth and just grab what they had with them. His Dad was born on the ship just days before arriving to America and never knew that he was not an American Citizen. The family settled and worked on a farm in Yonkers New York until they could afford to own their own. This boy is just one of three brothers and three sisters that settled on a large farm in Brookfield Connecticut. This farm is located along the Housatonic River with Six hundred acres of land starting from the Lillanoha Bridge, then south to Sandy Hook. It has a large home, two large barns, a large pond, many fruit trees and a vineyard. This could have been a paradise for most families. This little boy is me, Al and this place is not a Paradise but the closest thing to Hell, as I have lived and is explained it this episode "Road to Life".

Written in every day street language with little education, not professionally altered and self edited to help many young kids from self-destruction while on their way to Their "Road of Life"

Notice

The material contained with-in this brochure, or C D is copyright protected by the Owner, Author. Therefore, the contents or any part of cannot be used for any reason other than the personal privilege given to the party (s) for reading entertainment only. Contents cannot be copied, shared or traded without written consent from the owner. I reserve the right to imply civil liabilities against anyone that shall willingly and deliberately breach the trust I have extended. Some names and places have been changed to protect the innocent and to avoid ambiguities. Any names found in similarity are purely coincidental.

My mind goes back, searching for my mistakes. I have always wanted things to be right and believe that I have always tried. I am not perfect and believe that I never appeared to be. I now believe that my biggest hang-up was possession and merely wanted to own what was mine or what I believed was mine. When I was a child I was never allowed to have anything and even things I found on a dump were taken from me. I never had possession of anything except my mind. I never allowed anyone to take this from me and have tried to protect myself because, I learned as a child that no one else would care. "Love! What is love?" Is it possession, ownership or a power to compel you into desperation, or is it something that you would like in return for things that you had offered? Is it the fulfillment of happiness or just another avenue to loneliness? I believe now that it is none of the above and you must earn it. You will find that love is not free and is only a temporary gift that demands more than wealth. Your first desires may be confused with love and are merle sexual fantasies that cannot be separated but combined analytically and not unilaterally, and then it will be all of the above. Fortunately, everyone will not experience this in the same equation or proportion.

We could plan our future, but never guarantee the results because we are not a product of our environment, but a product of the changes that we may encounter. Our lifestyles are not permanent and can be altered with devastating effects in moments, and we must then prepare ourselves for the ramifications of past obligations and future endeavors. We are here for a life sentence, which has not been predestined and is not equal in proportion or quality with the habitants in which we share. Our future is not based upon equality or professionalism, but merely where we were placed in the road of life. Our past is our future, which we cannot change or hide, and these are the roots of the foundation that we shall be forced to build upon. We may fight to build a future that is satisfying and meets the status quo, but we must learn to accept the present while building better bridges for a planned future. This may only be in dreams and may never reach maturity, while a simple factor may change the outcome. There is no guarantee for the poor, handicapped, unhealthy or the underprivileged and only the fortunate will prevail.

"I Do Till Death Do Us Part." This is the understatement of a lifetime.

"I will, until my life changes and my desires differ from the status quo." Then I will realize that I am my own. I may change my life but not that of others, as is told in the story that you are about to read. This union was my first real endeavor and the beginning of a foundation that was only in dreams that I waited so long, but soon to find that they were in parallel with previous encounters and adventures. The second was when I adopted a little girl that called me "Daddy" when she was nine months old. She was my pride and joy, because I was so very proud and thankful to have this privilege. I became very excited that my future was becoming a reality, and a foundation was no longer just a myth to further my desires. I was then gifted in marriage and a long awaited son, but I did not realize that my opening statement would change my life forever.

The following story is true and based on facts but has been formatted for easier understanding. The language may have been changed, but the subject remains in the contents. The names and places of some have been changed and names used in this edition are of random source to protect the living. While parts have been altered to avoid ambiguities and legal provocations, I reserve the rights to freedom of speech, my beliefs and opinions.

I was just fifteen years old when I found that my tortured childhood had altered my life and interfered in many of my decisions. I was very shy and always gave in to avoid hurting other's feelings. I was never allowed to state my mind without devastating circumstances, and will bear this burden forever. Your dreams you will forget, but nightmare you will regret.

I was raised on my father's farm that bordered the Housatonic River, where we owned six hundred acres of property along this river. For most people this might have been a paradise; but for my brothers, sisters, and I, this was the closest thing to hell, but we did not know the difference and thought that life should be this way. We had no close neighbors and our house was more than one half mile from the road. There were heavy woodlands around our home and it was not visible from the road or neighbors. Between our home and river were all pastures and hay fields. The river was not far from our home and I can still remember when I was just two years old and almost drowned, but there are many things that I remember as a child. I remember things that happened when I was four and five which caused me imperil consequences and has affected my ability to comprehend life as it should be. One day the police came to our home then took our hired hand with them and I never did see him again. He came to this country in the same boat with my father and grandfather from Europe in nineteen hundred four. My parents are Russian and Slovak and in Russia my grandfather was a high-ranking official in the Parliament with the Soviet leadership, but had to save his family and escape the revolution. During the turmoil he did not have the opportunity to recover his assets and barely escaped with their lives. My father was born on the ship two days before they entered America. I did not understand much then, but I did wonder why our helper that came with my parents was made to live in the barn with the cattle. I don't know what he ate or if he ever cleaned up. He worked every day and we very seldom spoke with him, although he appeared to be a nice person. His name was Botchik and he worked every day except Sunday. In the summer, he would wash in the pond and that was the only time I saw him clean himself. My grandfather did speak with him often and explained why the police came to take him away. My grandfather was very good to us children and saved us from harm several times. He was the one that explained what happened with Botchik.

This one afternoon after Dad went to town with Mom, my sister Mary Ann went to the barn for bread. Botchik was there and asked her to look at something. She didn't answer, but then he zipped down his trousers and took out his penis. She was stunned from his actions and did not know why he did this so she didn't reply. He then grabbed her and almost took her to the floor, but being wiry she was able to escape. She was afraid and ran very quickly to the house. Just at that time Mom and Dad drove in. They were in a horse-drawn wagon because we did not own an automobile. Botchik ran toward Dad, fast because he thought my sister would speak to my father before he could. Mary Ann quickly grabbed Mom while Botchik was talking with Dad. Mom told Mary Ann to tell Dad what happened. I was told that Dad panicked and beat him until blood covered most of his body. I was told that he was all bloody, but did not see the fight, because I was just born. Mary Ann was just six then and I never heard her speak of it but it was the day before the police came and took him away. That very same year we found that some thieves were stealing our calves and pigs, so Dad started to keep watch. One night he caught someone stealing a pig. It was dark and he could not see whom it was. He yelled, "Halt!" several times but the intruder still ran with the pig. My dad fired the shotgun twice at the ground behind the intruder. But the pellets ricocheted off of the ground and struck the legs a woman, whom was the thief. She later died in the hospital, but I could remember that my father felt very badly and was never the same thereafter. We then went through some very difficult times in the next few years. This was the beginning of the Second World War, when everything was rationed and many products were hard to get. Everyone was trying to make money the best they could. We could not get much sugar and what we did get was used to cure meats in brine, so we would eat our oatmeal or cornmeal without it. We had that for breakfast almost every day, and would have pumpkin or squash mixed with it. Mom did make us better food when she could get it, but we did not have much money. We had to sell all of the milk and the meat when they butchered an animal, so we would have to eat what they did not sell. I know Mom loved us very much because she would always try and give us something that she would make and we did like that.

We would pick berries and fetch apples, and then she would make pies. She was always with us kids and cried when things were bad, but she always told us that she hoped things would get better. I remember my mother did cry a lot and never knew why. Maybe it was good that we did not eat very much, because we did not have inside toilets and would have to go outside to a back house. It was about three hundred feet away. In the winter at night we would have to run out there bare-footed and sit on a cold wooden seat. In the summer it did not smell good and we would have to leave quickly, but we got smart and found a pail to urinate in, then kept that in our room. Later, we did get beaten for that because we poured it out the window and it made stains on the side of the house.

This is a brief summary of the torture and cruelty that I endured as a child, when I was just a little boy. I remember that my father and mother started to fight a lot and my father would beat her until she would cry. We were very sad then and could not help, but just before I was five years old, my father and mother had a very bad argument and he beat her very badly.

Losing Our Mother

All of us kids went to help her and made him stop hitting her. The next day my father left and my uncle (mother's brother) came to our home with some other people that we had never seen before. My older brother (six), my sister (one), and I ran outside to hide because we thought they were going to harm us. We were afraid and just watched from behind a bank of dirt, because we did not know where our father was. We watched while they threw out all of our dishes and small furniture then broke them in a big pile. They then drove the big truck over all of it and crushed it, but we were even more scared to come and ask why. Shortly after they all left, we looked for our mother but could not find her. She did not come to see if we were all right and we did not see her go with them. But she must have known that our father would be here soon. We were crying and waiting for our father, but he did not come until many hours later.

I had two older sisters and an older brother whom were in school. They came home from school before my dad came home. My brother Mike, whom was with me and I explained what happened, then started to cry. We did not watch our one-year-old sister, so she wandered away and we did not find her until late that night. She was found four miles away and a neighbor brought her back. This was like the end of the world to all of us. I did not know what my father meant, but I was led to believe that my mother was sick and went away for a while, but a short while later my dad brought a young woman to live with us.

She was a neighbor's daughter and was nineteen years old. This is when I understood that my dad wanted her more than our mother and that he would marry her. She did not like our mother and always told us that our mother was evil and we should never talk to her if she came to the school. She told us to throw stones at her, so from the very beginning we did not like this new woman. Well, we were right and this was the beginning of hell on earth. We had about one hundred cows and sixty of them milking. We all milked cows every morning and I started milking when I was four. My brothers and I would have to round up the cows, bring them to the barn and lock them in stanchions. We did not have any shoes and there was frost on the ground so our feet became very cold and hurt. We would have to run fast to try and keep them warm. We would have to feed the animals, milk them and clean their stools (crap) before we would go to school. We had to walk more than one mile to catch the bus and five miles if we missed it. I started school when I was five and we did not have nice clothes to wear, nor did we have boots to wear in the winter. Our shoes were too big so we had to stuff paper in them and wrap rags around our feet so they wouldn't fall off. We had crow manure on us and many kids would not play or want to sit next to us. We did not have under-clothes and sometimes just wore a wool sweater that would itch and was too big for us. My brother Mike is allergic to wool and our stepmother would make him wear wool as punishment. I remember one hot day in my first year of school when I switched my shirt with my brother. I wore the wool sweater to school and the teacher instructed me to go to the locker, which was in our schoolroom to remove my sweater. I did not have anything under it and would not take the sweater off, because I was too modest to explain this to my teacher in front of all the other students. She called me over to her desk and beat my knuckles with a ruler, but the pain was not as bad as the embarrassment would have been.

We could not afford to get school lunch and would bring our own. Sometimes mustard and sugar sandwiches, but I was able to find some friends that were also farmers and they would share their food with me. I liked having these friends because they would help me in a fight when other kids tried to hurt me, because they hated me for smelling and dressing awful. When we got home we had a lot of work to do, it was the same as in the morning and we also had to split wood, then carry it in to the house. We were never allowed to play and would be punished vary badly for it. Our new stepmother would notice when we didn't obey her and beat us with a cat of nine tails. This would bring blood, and then hurt for several days. Then, on most Sundays, she would force us to kneel on hard split wood under our knees for hours and we weren't allowed to talk. After the first few months she hated us kids and loved to hurt us. My father did not like the way she treated us, but instead of helping he stayed away. I did not know where he went; I just knew that he was not there to protect us from the evil that he brought into our lives. We were so very lucky to have our grandfather live with us. He was forced to live in the attic, but if he was not there I am sure that our stepmother would have hurt some of us kids very badly. My grandfather at one time did grab her and tell her that if he caught her hurting any of us again that he would kill her. After this he was not allowed to come into the living quarters of our house, but he always watched. My grandfather was eighty years old and worked very hard on our farm. He raised a garden that was very large and he grew almost everything that we needed. He would break up stones larger than a car with just a sledgehammer, crowbars, and wedges. He would work every day except Sunday, because he was very religious and prayed every day but prayed the most on Sunday. He always prayed in his foreign language and I could not understand it all. When I became a little older I asked him about the story that I heard. I asked if someone was killed in our house. He did not want to answer, but knew he had to tell me. We were in the garden and he sat on a log and did not answer for a while, but I could see he was in deep thought. He reached for my hand and pulled me closer. He said, "I don't think you will understand." He spoke more Russian than English, but we could speak our native tongue enough to understand him. He said, "A long time ago, before you were born, I was in the barn while Stefan and Anna (he meant our father, Stephen, and Mother) was away, something happened." I was excited and asked, "What? Tell Me?"

He replied, "It was dark and very late. Elaine (my oldest sister) was just one and one half years old. I could hear screaming from the house, so I grabbed the oil lantern and ran to the house."

Murder or an Accident

"We had another man whitewashing the barns that stayed overnight in the barn sometimes. When I entered the house, he had Elaine on the floor with her clothes pulled off and it appeared as if he was attempting to get on top of her. I became furious and swung the lantern at him. The lantern had a large flat base and it struck him in the head. It split his head open."

I asked, "Did he die?" and Zeda shook his head "yes". I asked again, "What did you do then?" and he answered, "I dragged him outside." I said, "Then what?" and he replied, "I buried him over the bank where we bury the dead animals." I did not question him any longer because I noticed tears in his eyes. I just squeezed his hand and went back into the house. I thought, *what more am I going to find out about my life?* We never had any friends and no one ever came to our house. When our aunt and uncle came we would put our hands over our eyes and thought they couldn't see us. We were afraid of them because we would very seldom see them. I don't know why, because they were good to us and brought us candy or cake. The only real friends we that had was a black family that lived across the river and we did go there before we had our new mother. They were the Randall family. There was Ben, his wife, three sons, and a daughter. We would walk across the big steel bridge to go see them, but it was made with three inch squares and our feet would get caught so we had to make sure we stepped in the right spot. We were bare-footed and the metal was very hot in the summer, so we had to run fast not to burn our feet. This was a long way and took a long time to get there, but there was a short cut across the river so we tried to swim there and this is where I almost drowned but I was pulled out with no problems. One day there was just Mike and I trying to swim across and Mike got pulled under by the rip tide. I couldn't find him so I screamed. Pauline, the daughter of our friends, was in the water on the other side and heard me. She swam right over and found Mike, but he was not breathing and his lungs were full of water. She grabbed him by the legs, then shook him upside down vigorously and water kept coming from his mouth. She laid him down, and then blew in his mouth and he started breathing again. He was very sick for a while, but we did not tell our parents what had happened.

We were very happy to have this family as friends. Ben would put me on his lap and tell me stories. He had a lot of comic books that he showed us, and told us stories about Briar Rabbit, plus a lot more. We were very lucky because the two brothers took us to the city dump, that wasn't very far away and we found so many good things. We found shoes, clothes, and many toys. This was like a shopping center for us and we found two bicycles that we were able to make one from. We did not have a front tire but we rode it on the rim anyway. This family was also poor, but we loved them for what they were. I was very happy one day when I found a doll. She was very pretty. She had long black hair and her eyes were big and dark. She was only a rag doll, but I did love her and she made me happy to have her, so I took her home with me. The bike was large and I couldn't reach the pedals, but I would push it up the hill and coast down and that is how I learned to ride. We also found some blankets and took them because we were very cold in the winter. I also found a small blanket and it was near the doll, I believed it was hers so I kept it for her. My oldest sister told me I shouldn't have the doll, because she said boys didn't play with dolls. I didn't care, I loved her so I found a place to hide her, then I would sneak down there and play with her. I took an old barrel that was broken and made a safe place for her where nobody went.

When I was seven I had to use the tractor to mow hay and plow the fields. I was very small and could not reach the clutch and I would have to stand on the clutch, and then pull up with my hands, because I was not heavy enough to make the clutch go down. One day I ran out of gas with our tractor and needed gas to finish the mowing. I checked our spare gas can and when I shook it I thought there was some gas in it, but it would not pour. Not knowing any better I lit a match to see if there was any gas. The gas can exploded in my face because I had my face close to it to see. I could not see from one eye and my face burned very bad. Lucky my stepmother was in the milk cooler where she seen what happened, then quickly ran to me and asked how I was. She noticed that my right eye was all white and no pupil showed. I was crying from pain and she told me she would take me to a doctor. We did not have a car and my dad had the only truck, so she saddled a fast stallion horse "Midnight" and road me about five miles to the doctor's house.

His name was Dr. Wright and he was very old and I do believe he could not see either, because he told her to spank my ass and put Vaseline on my face, then put me to bed. The pain was getting worse and I couldn't see from either eye now, but only movements of a gray like fog. She then put me back on Midnight, and road me about ten miles to the Danbury Hospital. I was taken straight to the emergency room, which I will never forget. They first placed a very bright, hot light right over my eyes and this hurt like I never knew. Two nurses held me down while the doctor peeled the scabs from my eyes. I was screaming with pain, but I do remember the doctor telling someone, "I don't think we could save this eye." I was very afraid of what was happening, but I could not understand why life was so cruel. *Why* was there so much pain in my life? I did not know how to die, but I did know that life was hard to bare. I was in the hospital for a long time and after a few days the doctor removed the bandage from my left eye. I could not see well in the beginning, but in a short time I could see with it. The right eye still needed more scraping or whatever they did, but it did not hurt as much as the first time. After this time whatever they did I was told that I had a fifty/fifty chance to see with right eye again. I still had a lot of burns on my face and around my right eye and it did hurt when they peeled the skin off. They removed the bandage several times to apply medication and I knew that the light did bother my right eye. I told this to the doctor and he stated that this was a good sign. Finally they removed the bandages and by the end of the day I could see images from my bad eye. The light did hurt in the beginning but it got better with time. They then told me that I would go home the next day. I was not too happy to leave the hospital, because I still remember that I could be punished for being so stupid and I didn't want any more pain for a while. While I was in the hospital I thought about things that I thought were not right. *Why do the other kids in school smile and laugh? They all appear to be happy and why do they have nice clothes and shoes?* I thought that the whole world was like us and that was how it should be.

I am in the second grade now and found I am very lucky. I missed a lot of school last spring because of my burns but we had two new girls in my class now. They are Brooke and Bridget Hayward. I am told that they were the daughters of the movie star Rita Hayward. I don't know much about movie stars because I have never seen a movie, but these girls were very nice to me. I sat next to Bridget because I remember she had blond hair and Brooke was a brunette. I was behind with my homework and she helped me. She was the only girl that had ever offered to help me and Brook was also very nice, so I loved having them in my school. I remember that they both were very intelligent and appeared to be older than they said, but Bridget was almost two years younger than me and knew all about my schoolwork. She answered my questions without ever hesitating. It was that same year that we moved to another school, so I never seen them again.

Danger on the Farm in Brookfield

I am eight years old now and during the summer we always had packs of wolves come on our property and they would attack our cattle, so I was ordered by my father to carry the sixteen-gauge shotgun. This was to shoot the wolves when they came on our property, because they always came in packs of eight or more. I was already familiar with this gun because my older brothers would let me fire it. It did hurt my shoulder, but it was fun anyway. By this time we all were very good shooters and we could hit a woodchuck at a hundred yards, but my brother Mike was the best shot of us all. We also had other rifles, a 38/40, a 30/30, and a 12-gauge shotgun. Our dad always would let us use these guns because he said we might have to protect ourselves some day. He would also share target practice with us to teach us how to handle a gun safely and this became part of our normal duties on the farm. We also had many other wild animals come on our farm that were dangerous. We had many snakes, but I don't know all their names, rattlesnakes, water moccasins, copperheads, black snakes, milk snakes, and many more. I believe that very few people have seen a milk snake. They were long and light green with some yellow. They would follow a cow and actually suck milk from its udder. We watched them run away and while traveling downhill, they would bit their tail and roll like a wheel. We also had fox, red and gray, rat coons, mink, jack rabbits, and bobcats. We could only ride the horses after we changed the grassing area because it was too far to walk. We had names for our horses; the stallions were named Midnight, Black Beauty, and Flicka. I loved riding and it would take us an hour sometimes to round up the cows. There was one time that I had a problem, there was a place in the far pasture that was about three hundred feet long and one hundred fifty feet wide and was surrounded by a stone wall. The wall was about four feet high but had a few places that were lower from age and falling. It was filled with briars and weeds and by accident my horse jumped into there and we landed into a nest of snakes.

The horse jumped and threw me off and I landed on the nest of snakes. It looked like there were hundreds of them all curled and ready to strike. I just jumped and ran, but I don't think my feet touched the ground very much and jumped the wall. I was so afraid and told my father. He said he could not understand why I was not bitten. He had seen the snakes and said they were mostly copperheads. We went back and got a lot of gas and burned the whole area. I never went near there again, but I did have nightmares. Summers were very hard for us because we had to work from five a.m. until seven p.m. and there was never time for anything except work. Our daily chores were milking all the cows and cleaning their stables. Then we would have to mow hay, heap it with pitchforks, load the wagon and take it to the barns to unload it. We also had to plow the garden and the hay fields, then plant new crops. We had four acres of corn that had to be planted in the spring and harvested in the summer. This was all done by hand and we would bundle it and take it to the chopper to make silage. This was to feed the cows and pigs in the winter. We also had to plant and cultivate our garden, which was very large. Before winter we had to cut wood and haul it in with our horses. We then split most of it for our wood stove, which we used for heat all winter and heated our water. We did not have any running water in our house and would have to carry it from an outside pump. In the winter we were always cold because we only had the one stove for heat and during the night our stepmother would close the door. My brothers and I would sleep together to stay warm and I believe my sisters did also.

On Sundays we would have to weed the gardens and pick the cutting worms off, then put them gas to kill them. We did have a big pond but were forbidden to go in. I did go in once when my stepmother wasn't there but a snake chased me to the shore. Dad told me that they couldn't bite you while you are in the water, but it did bite me on my heel when I reached shore. I had to step on it with my other foot to kill it because it would not let go. It hurt very badly but I did get beaten anyway because I went in.

John Wayne and our Hereford Steer

Later that year my dad and two friends bought two thousand head of White Face Hereford Steer from John Wayne's ranch in Texas. They had them all sent to New Milford by rail, then trucked them to our farm. All of us were very busy before they arrived, because we had to fix all the fences and install electric fences where needed. This was still during the war and we were butchering them to sell. We butchered dozens a day for weeks along with all the other work we had. I had to tan and roll the hides and then someone came to buy them. This went on for a year or more until my dad stopped butchering, and then covered all traces and evidence of what we were doing. I did not know why, but the FBI came and talked with Dad. They were all looking and asking for some kind of records, but I knew that Dad had burned them. They came back with shovels and a crew of men and found what they were looking for. They placed handcuffs on Dad and took him with them. I did not know what was going on but I found out that what we had been doing was called the Black Market, because of the war and rationing. I did not understand this because these were our animals and people needed food. I thought he would come right back but I was told he would be in jail for at least one year.

Right after they took Dad away our lives became terrible. All we could do was work and there was never time for fun. We were constantly being punished for just about anything. We were always hungry, but would get beat if we took any food, and I remember always going to bed hungry. My brother and I would have to round up the cows and bring them to the barn every morning, even when there was a heavy frost and our feet became very cold. We never had shoes to wear and had to keep the ones just for school. In the summer after we cut the hay, there were sharp twigs that always cut our feet, especially between our toes. That hurt very much but we were not allowed to complain about it. What my brother and I hated the most was when the bulls chased us. They would put their heads down and come storming towards us. We would have to run as fast as we could and luckily we always beat them to a fence.

We both tore our trousers from going through the fence so fast, so for punishment our stepmother forced us to wear skirts to school. We were very ashamed to go into the school like that, but the teacher made us go to class while laughing at us. Our first teacher, Gladys Randall, hated us kids and always loved to embarrass us in front of the other students. To top it all, they gave us girls' names, which I will not repeat because it hurts to hear them even now. One day I had the nerve to report this to the principle, but somehow he contacted our stepmother and I was beaten for telling anyone. We were not just beaten but mentally tortured, then made to kneel on split wood most of the Sunday afternoon. Our knees hurt very badly, but if we complained, we would get struck with the cat-of-nine-tails. No one knows how bad we were treated or how many nights we were sent to bed without food.

Our Field Trip to New York

One day our school was having a field trip to New York and Mike and I really wanted to go, so we did not tell her about it. Some way she received information about it, but we decided not to tell her and told her we didn't know when they were going. We told her that it was in a few weeks and she said we were lying so she shaved our heads so that we wouldn't go. It was this week and we both went anyway. Shaving our heads was worse than the beatings, but this did not stop us and we did go to New York.

Mike and I were the only ones that went, and we felt sorry for our sisters and brother, John. First, we went to the Empire State Building and went to the top. I could not believe what it was like to be way up there. I could barely see the cars and the wind was very strong. I could feel the building swaying but was not afraid. I think it was because we were so high and you lose perspective. After that, we took the bus to Radio City Hall and watched the Great Caruso with Mario Lanza. The stage was beautiful and it is amazing how they could make it disappear into the floor. This was so very exciting for me and I couldn't believe this was our world. The only places that I had ever been were to school and the hospital before this. The next place we went to was the Planetarium. This looked as if we were in a different world. We saw different galaxies, distant stars, and even a lightning storm. It really appeared as if we were out in the open. Then, last but not least, was the Museum of Ancient History. I never knew that we had these large animals on earth before, and we hadn't studied this in school yet, but I really wanted to. I can really say that this was the most exciting day of my life and it was even nice to ride on the Greyhound Bus.

Living Through a Nightmare of Fear

While Dad was gone, things got very bad and were unbearable. We barely survived the fall and winter but spring came and things weren't bad enough. The wind started blowing very hard and we heard this loud noise like a train coming towards our home. It then turned very dark and we all ran for the house. We went to our wine and potato cellar, then hid in there until the noise stopped. We could also feel the wind come through the house and into our cellar. The floors above us shook and things fell on us while the noise was unbearable. I was very scared and could see everyone else was also. It lasted for about twenty minutes or so and then the noise stopped. It became silent and it felt as if I was in a vacuum.

It became more scary when we went out to see what had happened. The wine cellar was underground and separate from the house. When we entered the basement, we could see that the stairway to the house was broken and twisted, but we were able to go up them. When we entered our house, we could see that it was lifted up and turned on the foundation. We quickly looked outside and there was nothing else standing. We ran out and found that all of our barns were torn down, ripped apart and scattered all over. Our apple orchard was missing. Trees were torn from the roots and were scattered all over. The horses and many of our cattle were locked in their stalls. The horses escaped, but the cows couldn't. We quickly took the tractor to pull the barns apart and cut the throats of the cows that we could get to. We couldn't save them, but tried to save the meat. This was the worst thing that I've ever seen and it made me sick and worried about what would happen to us. I have never seen so many dead animals and it was so hard removing them from the rubble. I wondered why they were all killed and we were spared. With my life as it was and Dad away, I became very confused and just hated life as it was.

It took several weeks, before we had time to think about what had happened and found out it was a tornado. It appeared strange, because our farm received the most damage, because in the surrounding area the damage was minimal. Our pond that was near the barn had most of the water sucked from it, and fifty feet along either side of our farm nothing was touched. This was a direct hit on our farm and livelihood. I wondered if I was possessed by Satan or if we all were. Our pigpen, which was just a short way from our barn, was not touched. We still had them, our horses, that had escaped and only a few cows left. We were lucky we did not have the entire herd of steer then, because they were taken away shortly after Dad was arrested. After all this, I knew my life would not get better and provocations from some strange power were preventing my family from achievement. All of our lives were interrupted and it became very difficult to comprehend these circumstances. We all tried our best just to survive and we knew that this world was not for us. We all just felt sorry for each other and Florence was also in the dumps. But we were all too young to know what to do and without Dad we were lost.

My Introduction to the Church

One day I was called to the principal's office. I was afraid to talk to him because I was afraid of almost everyone. I felt that I might be scolded for something or for being so sad. When I entered his office, he was not alone. I just sat in the chair across from him and waited for what was to happen. The other person was a lady and she moved her chair closer to me and asked what was wrong. I just asked why! Why do you ask? She said, "Your name is Alvin, right?" I replied, "I like Al better."

She said, "OK, Al, your teacher said that she believes there is something wrong. Could you please tell us?"

I looked at the principle, and then put my head down. I did not answer because I was still afraid of the reason they wanted to know anything about me. I was old enough or in school long enough to know that no other kids were treated as badly at home as I was, or my sisters and brothers. I knew I couldn't tell her about the way we were tortured at home and that Dad was in jail. I was too afraid that our stepmother would find out again.

I did not look up, but I could see that she walked towards the principle, then came back to me. She reached for my hand and asked if I would come to her room with her. I did not answer, but I did get up and followed her. When we reached her room, she seated me in a chair then sat right in front of me. I looked at her and I may have been crying, when she said, "Al! I know there is something wrong and I want you to please tell me," and without stopping she said, "I also know it is about your home life. I promise I will never tell anyone about anything we say here, and it will be our secret."

I said, "I don't know you, and I have never seen you before."

She replied, "I'm a counselor, and it is my job to help children such as you."

She appeared to be very nice and earnest, and I did believe her. I said, "I can't tell you about that, I mean what happens at home because I will just get beaten again."

She said, "No, you won't. I assure you no one will ever know about this. I am here to try and help you, so please trust me." She kept talking, but I don't think I heard much of what she was saying, but I heard her mention God and church.

I remember that from my mother when she came to see me last year. She mentioned God many times and I started thinking about the last time I had saw her. She had told me that God would help me and make me stronger. She also said that God helps everyone who needs him. I knew something about God because my grandfather had always prayed to him and my sisters also told me things about Him. She interrupted my silence and said, "I want you to go to church with us on Wednesday." When I asked when and what time, she told me that it was a short ways from here and it was after school.

I told her, "I can't. I must go home right after school because I have too much work to do every night and I will get beaten if I don't go home."

She asked, "Please, could I speak to your parents?"

I said, "No. I will get beaten for that also."

Then she asked, "Will you ask them and let me know?"

I said, "I will try. When will you be here again?" When she said that she was always there, I said, "Oh, I didn't know that." She then walked me back to my room while talking to me, but school was over so I just got my things and got on the bus. On the way home I talked to my brother, Mike, and he also must have spoken to this lady because he knew what I was asking him. We both agreed to ask Dad if we could go. Our stepmother disagreed, but after a long conversation with Dad, he said OK. But he said, we would have to walk home. It was seven miles from the church to home, but we did stay Wednesday night. We went to church, which was a catechism and it was beautiful. There was a statue of Jesus, Mother Mary of God and hundreds of candles that lit the complete area with different colors. There was also the Grotto just behind the church, while equally as beautiful where we walked and said prayers. This night was so nice and I felt so much better while I was there. I learned some hymns and a lot about Mother Mary and Jesus. The walk home was very long and scary. Our road was just dirt with all woods on both sides and we heard so many weird noises, so we ran as fast as we could. We were happy to be home but we still wanted to go again.

Living in Bridgewater

Shortly after Dad came home, we moved to another farm. This one was much smaller and had about two hundred sixty acres. I did like it because we had neighbors who were not too far away and only had to walk less than one half mile to school, but it was scary. There was a cemetery that we had to pass and I was afraid when I was alone. I heard very strange noises, so I ran very fast and always wanted someone to go with me. But it wasn't long before I was walking through it and looking at all the names on the gravestones. Life became a little better but we had much more work to do again. We did buy about two dozen more cows and once again sold milk. My father also bought a sawmill, since we did have a great amount of forest. We got the sawmill operating, and then between the milk and lumber revenue, we made some money. My dad bought a car and another truck, they were old, but they ran good and the car even had a radio which we never had before.

I was almost nine years old when we moved here and became very close friends with one teacher, Stanley. He called me into his room one lunch hour and asked me about my home life. I was afraid to tell him the truth and told him that it was all right. I was afraid to say any more, but he told me that we could keep this confidential and no one would find out. I then felt more secure and told him about the beatings and how we would have to kneel on split wood. He listened to me and tried to educate me in ways to avoid this treatment. I did follow his advice because it was better and I believe that I became my step mother's favorite. I was in second grade and doing very well. I believe that I was smarter than the other students in my class. The second and third grade classes were in the same room. Stanley surprised me when he allowed me to skip second grade and put me into third grade. I was very proud and this made me work even harder.

Stepbrothers and Stepsisters

I will include just a small summary of the next five years. Things weren't too bad until my father went away for a week, which he did often. My step mother bared three children and we were treated badly over a problem with our stepfamily because they were always right. They always received the best food, were always able to eat first and we had to eat the leftovers. If we said anything bad to those kids, we would get beaten very badly. When Dad came home, he noticed the welts on our whole bodies from being beat with a cat-of-nine-tails. Our grandfather told him that if he did not stop this torture then he would. My father was so mad that he grabbed his rifle and chased her through the barn. He fired six shots at her but did not hit her. I believe he just wanted to scare her and things did start to get better. The weather started to get colder and we had to get everything ready for the winter.

While working outside without a jacket, I caught the strep virus and became very sick, but no one knew what to do. I was given honey, lemon, and when that didn't help; they gave me a lot of cod liver oil. I really hated that and I told them that I was having a lot of trouble breathing and my legs and arms hurt all the time. I was getting very weak and could not walk up the stairs without stopping halfway to rest. The first doctor that examined me said that I was just overworked, but I didn't feel that way and I just wasn't getting enough air to breathe. I knew it wasn't that, and I told Dad that something was very badly wrong. I was getting worse, so my dad finally called another doctor and he told my dad to take me to the emergency room. The doctor told my dad that I had acute bronchitis with a strep virus and had to be admitted to the hospital. I was given an antibiotic and took many tests before I was diagnosed with acute rheumatic fever, which developed into a severe heart condition. Two of my heart valves were badly damaged. And the other two were also infected. The blood was bypassing and my blood pressure was very low. I also had no blood flowing through my tendons, which caused all my joints to become inflamed and swollen. At this stage, this was life threatening, so they placed me on oxygen and into intensive care. For six weeks or more, I was ordered not to leave the bed and not to walk or be excited. I hated this because I had to use the bedpan, but after several more tests and strong antibiotics, I was allowed to go home. I was also confined to my bed at home, but I could go to the bathroom. I missed many months of school, but I did do school homework and studied for exams. Florence started to treat me better and would bring me books to read. She even bought me candy, but my big surprise was when my favorite teacher, Stanley, came to see me. He said that he would get my schoolwork to me and would make sure that my sister brought my homework to me every day. I don't remember how long I was in the hospital, but I know that I was confined to total bed rest for many months. I missed almost the full semester and was asked to take several tests and exams to pass that school year. I did, and my lowest report was in the high eighties.

My grandfather did spend a lot of time with me while I was confined to bed. He taught me many card games along with cribbage, which he liked the most. My grandfather told me that my dad told him the doctors wanted to replace two of my heart valves with plastic ones. But after the doctors stated that I would need surgery several times in my life to replace them, and that there was only a fifty percent chance that I would survive all this, but my dad decided not to allow it. Today I am glad that he made that choice. I was always very smart in school and by the time I was in the sixth grade, the teacher would use me as an example. I was elected to make most of the school posters for events such as scrap drives and school activities. I also made speeches in front of class, which was hard because I was very bashful, and it took a while, but I did a very good job.

Moving to New Milford

When I finished sixth grade, we moved to New Milford. Dad bought another farm, again with more than two hundred acres. This was a very nice place also. It had a very large house that used to be the Leavenworth Hotel, a trading post for the travelers and wagons that would stop to rest here. Somehow we ended up with about fifty or more cows and installed milking machines. Dad also said that we would bring the sawmill here, but it never did come. I think he sold it or traded it for more cows. In seventh grade I made all of the posters for the scrap drives that were published, and in eighth grade I drew the posters explaining how a bill is made and passed through Congress. I narrated this event before a live audience on graduation night and thought that my life was getting better. I started to notice that most of the kids that hated me, started to like me now, but I believe that they were jealous. I was receiving a lot of attention and for the first time in my life, I had a new suit and shoes. I couldn't believe how nice I looked and I was so proud that finally I was being noticed. But the biggest surprise was when my stepmother took me to the tailor to buy the suit. It was dark navy blue and it had a white collared shirt with a necktie to go with it. I now believe it was because I almost died with my heart problems, but I was happy to look nice. I always thought I was ugly, but looking in the mirror I thought, well, maybe I'm not.

That summer I was not allowed to do any heavy work and did just what I thought I could. The next two years went by as before and we had so much hardship. John was burned very badly and they wanted to remove his leg. Dad had an accident with the tractor and it nearly killed him. Both of my older sisters left home and John went into the United States Marines. Mike left home when he was fourteen. I was home with just my youngest sister, Arlean, and it appeared that the whole world had changed. I was lonely and did not know what to do most of the time. My sisters and brothers were all that I really had. I was fourteen and wanted to run away, but did not know where to go. My dad and Florence did not get along very well, but I tried to manage the farm and sawmill with just Florence and Dad. She had five children now, two girls and three boys. Shortly after her last one was born she placed him with the state, because she could not handle him and the problems caused by cerebral palsy. Florence also had an accident where she cut off three fingers from her right hand. That made it very busy for us on the farm again, but I did feel very sorry for her and realized that she never had a life.

Dad and I became very busy after he received several contracts from the town. He bought another truck and hired two men. With the extra money he made, he finally bought a new car. It was very nice and it was all black with shiny chrome. I was happy for my dad and once again I thought things were better. Shortly after he bought the car, he was struck by a Light & Power utility truck. This rolled his car over into a tree and my dad was hurt and could not walk so they took him to the hospital. I was in school then and did not know this until I came home. When Florence came home from the hospital, she explained that dad had an accident and he may have fractured his back. We did not know the extent of his injuries until the next day. The doctor explained that Dad suffered with a fractured vertebra, just above the lumbar section. He was put into a body cast and after a few days, sent home. The fracture caused damage to a nerve and he had a great deal of pain in his stomach. He had trouble eating and getting around and when he was able to get up, someone would have to lift him because the body cast was very heavy. I knew it would be a long time before he would be able to work. I ran the farm the best I could and we kept the hired men busy with the tree work. The engine went bad in our tractor and my dad told me to call his friend Lee.

Lee owned the Ford dealership in town and would visit Dad often. He sent a mechanic to look at the tractor, but after inspecting it he told my dad that the engine was shot and could not be fixed. I told my dad not to junk the tractor because I would try to fix it. Lee laughed at me and told dad that it could not be fixed without installing a new engine. I was the most mechanically inclined of all of us kids and I was the one who kept most of our equipment running. The main problem with the tractor engine was the crankshaft. The connecting rods were knocking, which meant that the crankshaft was damaged. I removed the crankcase and connecting rod bearings first. Then I found that the rod bearing spun on the crankshaft and inside the connecting rod. I knew that my dad would not allocate any money for this and I would need all of the parts, but I removed the engine to inspect it anyway. This was very hard because it was very heavy and I knew that I could not lift it myself. So I disassembled it in the tractor so that only the block and crankshaft were left. I worked on this for about a week and started the engine. It ran very well and I was driving it when Dad came out. On Sunday, Lee for the Ford garage came and after seeing me

24

driving the tractor, he wondered if we had bought a new engine. My dad told him that I had rebuilt it. Lee was amazed and said that if I ever wanted a job, to please come to him. I had just turned fifteen years old and could not leave my dad alone.

Time went by and my dad was getting around much better. We only had a few cows milking now and weren't making much money, so Dad started working again and shortly after, he received contracts with the town again, and we became busy.

I don't know why, but it seems there were always hardships and tragedies in my family. My dad received word from the U. S. Marine Corp. that John had been rushed to a hospital in critical condition in Korea. They gave a date that he would arrive in Camp Pendleton in California and be placed in the hospital there. We didn't know what was wrong, but he was told that John had a very slim chance to survive. He was diagnosed with three types of meningitis with two of the brain. Dad rushed to go there and stayed as long as he could, but John was still in a coma. There was nothing he could do there so he came home. He said John's body was swollen twice the size of normal and he had to wear protective clothing to see him. The doctor told Dad that he had less than one chance in a hundred to come out of the coma. Now all we could do was pray and wait for more news. We all felt very bad again and it was very hard to do anything right because for several weeks we just waited for some good news. My dad did call and it was always the same bad news. He was still in a coma. We all tried our very best to keep going, but we never knew when more disaster would affect our lives.

Our Auto Race Track

My dad always talked about building a stock car racetrack on our property and we had a perfect spot for one. Dad filed for all of the permits and they were granted. Then he had several meetings with some people that I didn't know, but I heard the conversations. They were discussing building an oval quarter-mile track and a smaller one in the middle. We would have stock car races on Saturday nights and Sunday late afternoons. On Wednesday nights and early Sunday afternoons, we would have motorcycle races. The lot size was about twenty acres and had a large slope on one side, but the rest was very flat. The grade of the slope was close to what was needed for the bleachers and right next to it was another flat spot for the concession stands. I used the small dozer and bucket loader to strip the topsoil, and then piled it for sale. I then leveled the parking lot and the area for the tracks. We hired a contractor with a D 8 Bulldozer to grade for the seating area, but the hard part was installing a cement block wall halfway around the track. The footings had to be four feet deep and the wall height four feet above ground.

My dad, Mike, and I, with one mason, completed it in a few weeks, and then built the concession stands. We built two, eighteen hundred square feet each and we used the lumber we had left over from our sawmill. When we finished with all the grades, we started to haul in the clay and this must be four inches thick. We had about one half of the clay laid and leveled when Dad came to us and said there was a stop work order issued and we had to stop all work on the race track. He did not explain why, and said he would later. I never knew why and he would not tell me why the racetrack came to a halt, but I knew something was bothering him. He was not himself after this and would walk around the farm.

The only thing he told me was that all of our money was tied up in the racetrack. I walked the racetrack many times and hoped that someday we could finish it. I became very sad again and felt sorry for my father because he had not recovered completely from his accident and was still having problems, but he wanted to keep busy. He would take the tractor hauling logs, moving stones, and working the farm. I did not try and stop him, but later I would be sorry that I had fixed the tractor. We had a brook running through our property a short ways from our barns and it was in a valley. Behind the barns were two banks that a dam could be built between. So my dad decided to build a dam and make a pond. This pond would be the size of two acres and would be good for the farm.

My dad started to clear for the dam using the tractor to move stones. One day while he was working alone, he got stuck with the tractor in the mud. He spent a long time trying to get out but he buried the rear wheels. The rear wheels had four inch V spikes for traction. Dad took some logs and tried to place them under the wheels. This was hard to do alone, so he left the tractor running in gear with the throttle about one quarter and got off the tractor. He tried to jam the logs under the spikes but he log caught quickly and he couldn't move quickly enough, being in the mud. He was caught by the log, forced under it, and the only thing that saved his life was the soft mud. He did break some ribs, punctured his lung and was back in the hospital again. This took a very long time to heal and he could not do anything. I had just started my junior year in school and was forced to quit school to run the business.

Quitting School

My dad called me and said that we had received a phone call about John. Some family said he had wandered there and they had been trying to find someone who knew him. They said that they had been calling everyone to find who he was. Dad was very happy and asked me if I would go get him. They told Dad that he may have some kind of amnesia, but John did remember he was in the marines. When I got there he did remember me and was very happy to see me. By the time we arrived home or shortly after, his memory came back and we were all happy to have him home again. We had a family gathering and the next day I took him to the veteran's hospital in West Haven for evaluation. They did examine him and he received medication for his severe headaches. He then filed for medical assistance and was discharged from the marines. He purchased a 1948 Chevy and lived with us for awhile. He still complained about severe headaches and started drinking alcoholic beverages. He started to go to New York State where the drinking age was eighteen, while twenty-one here in Connecticut. My brother did go with him at times but he would always get into trouble with someone. One Friday night, when Mike and I went with him, he was drinking and instead of taking us home, he headed for Hamilton, New Jersey to see his friend who had taken care of him when he had amnesia. Mike and I weren't drinking very much but couldn't convince him not to go. We also had a friend with us who was very drunk and sleeping in the back seat. We made it to Norwalk and we hit a tree at a very high speed.

I was in the back seat and Mike was in the front. Mike was thrown through the windshield and stopped when his head hit the tree. I hit the front seat with my face and was thrown through the windshield that Mike had already broken. Mike's face was all cut up and I smashed my face and nose. I was knocked out and came to on my way to the hospital. My face was crushed and I also hurt my knees but I didn't know it until I tried to walk. My nose was crushed and I needed complete bone replacement, which they did with plastic. I was in surgery for many hours and had to stay awake during the complete operation because I would have drowned on my own blood. I remember they popped my eyes from my eye sockets. I was drugged, but still very scared. My complete face was black and blue and all swollen. I couldn't believe how much it hurt. I was very happy that it was in the summer because I didn't want to miss any more school. We had the car towed back to the farm but it was too damaged to do anything with it. I had to go back several times because I always had problems breathing after that. John just hurt his chest and the passenger who was asleep didn't get hurt.

This was probably the worst break of my life because I was only fifteen years old and wouldn't be sixteen for several more months but my brain was impregnated with so many unwanted memories. I kept trying to look forward, but I could only imagine more downfalls and wondered what I had ever done to deserve this life. I became very depressed and knew then that I must also leave. I did not believe I owed anything to my parents and believed that things would never get better if I stayed. I did stay until the dam was completed and my dad was able to work again. I called Lee from the Ford garage and he told me to come right away. I started as a mechanic right away in service with tune-ups and many small items. After working with long-time mechanics, I knew that I was gifted beyond normal to understand the functions involved with mechanics. I was employed there only a short time when a customer ordered a new nineteen fifty-five Thunderbird. It was a shiny black convertible. It was delivered to us on a car carrier. We noticed that there was an oil leak in the rear of the engine and a knock on deceleration. The master mechanic, Lou, who was a friend, was in charge of this type of complaint and it was under factory warranty. Lou told Lee that the knock was caused from improper ignition timing. When hearing this statement, I approached Lee and told him that was not my first choice and I doubted that prognosis.

I explained that the engine knock and the oil leak were related. This had nothing to do with engine timing and I explained my beliefs. This engine being new from the manufacturer had accidentally left out the top half of the rear main bearing insert. This would explain the knock and the oil leak. Lee listened to me but did let Lou work on his theory.

After two days with no results, Lee then ordered Lou to remove the oil sump and check the rear engine bearing as I had suggested. Lou was upset but did obey the command and when the sump and bearing cap were removed, my prognosis was correct. The top half of the insert bearing was missing as I suggested. I was not surprised but I knew that I would be on Lou's shit list. Lee remarked with amazement and asked how in the world did I know, because this had never happened in all the years that he had been in the automobile

29

business. I replied, "Review the complete scenario with all the possibilities in your mind and then use the simple common denominator (common sense)."

After this, Lou would not speak to me but only to schedule my work. I did not like this feeling but I did accept the praise from all of the other workers. Suddenly everyone was asking me questions about problems they had and finally I was someone because someone did look up to me. Within the next few weeks I knew I would leave here because I did not need this feeling of guilt and I knew that I had interrupted the balance that had been present before I came.

My First Two Weeks Notice

I was only sixteen years old and I knew that I must find myself. Where am I? Who am I? Was I wrong to state my opinion? In my heart I knew that I was smart and never possessed fear of challenge. I then applied to work at a textile factory at the Robertson Bleachery. I really did not want to leave, because I loved mechanical work and I knew I was good. Another reason was that two houses away lived a girl who I thought was very good looking and we were becoming a little friendly. I thought this would end any chance of a relationship. I didn't know why but the first time I saw her she attracted my attention and I wanted to get to know her. I gave my two week notice and was accepted at the textile plant.

Lee invited me to dinner which he had done several times and he does like me. I think people mostly liked me because of my sad, shy and collective personality, but Lee's wife, Eleanor, seemed to love me. She could not have children of her own and said that she would adopt me. This was a very good feeling to have. I have had several conversations with her about my past and since Lee knew my father, they did have knowledge of some of my past childhood. They were very sad about my decision, but after all was said, they both agreed with me. Lee did tell me that I should consider an education in mechanics and reiterated that I was the most unusual person he ever had employed. He said I was eager to learn and starved for knowledge. He followed with the statement that he could see that I was fighting to be someone. I believe that Lee was right because I fought all my life and found nothing to change that now.

My First Love

While sitting at Lee's house, I could see the girl next door walk by and I really liked her but I was way too bashful to approach her, but always wanted the opportunity. I had looked at other girls before and really wanted her but came to the conclusion, why would she want me. I was just a poor farmer until now. I never had anything and I only have a 1937 Ford coupe to drive. I feel that I must appear better before I lose the chance with this girl. In the conversation that I did have with her, I discovered that her name is Dorothy. She had long black hair and a very light complexion. Her eyes were large and dark. I never had a girlfriend, and if I do get the chance, I know that I would prefer her.

The Devastating 1955 Flood

Once again my life was interrupted. I was in the second week of my notice and woke up to a great storm. There was water everywhere, but I was able to drive to work and see that the water was rising to flood level. We watched the river rise and heard the news that a large dam had broken in Massachusetts, which would create massive flooding. We watched the town get flooded and the water rose fifteen feet in a few hours. The center of this town is very high and we don't have to worry but I could see many buildings and homes go under water. The textile plant was half under water and I knew I wouldn't have a job there now.

The news was stating that Winsted, Torrington and Waterbury were being washed away. Winsted lost one half of the city in just hours and all of the roads were closed to New Milford. Some were flooded, bridges were washed out, and roads were undermined and missing. We were contained and couldn't leave town. We could not do much at the Ford place, so I offered to help with evacuations and saving people. I rode in the amphibious boat with Paul Halgowich, a friend, and went across streams that were now raging rivers, to help people across. We installed ropes across, then attached safety ropes to us, and brought many people to safety.

When the rescue operation was completed and I couldn't help any more, I drove gravel trucks to Torrington to repair roads. The roads were very bad and in places, they had to install bailey bridges. This was being performed by the Army Corp. of Engineers. I was proud to be able to help people, even if I was not getting paid for the rescues. I was getting paid for driving trucks. We were in the third week of the flood and we were told that this was the worst flood in history.

Once again my life took a turn and I had no other options but to stay at Ford because the textile plant would be closed for at least six months to a year. I didn't mind staying because we were very busy, and I had the opportunity to a new challenge. Automatic transmissions were fairly new and very few mechanics could understand them. Lee offered to send me to school but I stated that it was too late and I believed that I would learn much faster on my own. Lee asked me if I thought I could do them. I answered sarcastically that I could do anything and in my heart I did believe that I could. We were towing in dozens of cars a week with automatic transmissions filled with water and sand. We only had two other mechanics who could rebuild them, but they could only do Ford products. I was working with Tom first because he was the transmission man, and we did get along well. We do not have to remove and replace these because we have other helpers for that.

After working with Tom all day, I knew that I would not require any more experience from him, and I could do them alone. I told Lee I wanted my own bench and to be left alone. He agreed because we were getting far behind and at this pace we would not get the sludge and water out in time. I worked all day on this one fordamatic and I hoped I did not make any mistakes. I wouldn't know until the next day. The first two days I only did two transmissions but this was equal to Tom and Lou. Two weeks later, I was doing two to three a day on average, but I could do them in my sleep by then. Tom and Lou still did one a day and at times complained to Lee that the ones I did might not work. I had no problems at all. We were not gaining on the amount of work we had and Lee said that he could not find any more help. I volunteered to work late every night and Sundays, but I had just found out that our neighbor's car had gotten flooded and the engine would not start. I really wanted to fix this car to impress Dorothy and get to talk to her again. I asked Lee and he told me that he would appreciate it if I did not. He stated that I was the fastest and best transmission rebuilder that he had, and he wanted me to stay with what I was doing. I missed a chance that I had been waiting for, and said to myself maybe I am not supposed to meet her because it is not written in my future. I still saw her walk past every day, and was getting used to the time, and tried to make sure that I waved to her as she went by. I had developed a name for being the best transmission rebuilder in town. This reinforced my own theory that I was good and maybe I could have my own business some day. The gentleman who owned the Thunderbird heard the story of my prognosis and asked me how I had known, when Lee's top mechanics hadn't known. I answered shyly that it was a lucky guess. He snickered and told me that I was very modest. I thanked him and he said his name was Kurt and that he was the president of the Colonial Bank. He added that if I ever needed anything, not to hesitate to come and see him. I could see every day that most of the employees did not like me and thought I was getting too much attention. They made statements that I was a show-off and Lou said that I was a ringer. I did not know what that meant but I did not think it was good. Although I loved my job, I was not happy and just worked all the time. I had changed my lunch hour so I would not go to the restaurant the same time as the other workers. I was getting my way with Lee on rebuilding other types of transmissions and I was rebuilding different models. I was already hearing complaints that I was tying up a lift that was needed and that this place was a Ford garage.

Why is it that every time I reach out, everything goes wrong, and why do the workers here not like me? I have never refused to help them and I have never put them down or questioned their ability. I have always tried to be nice and wish that I could speak with someone who could help me understand what I am doing wrong. Do I have to act stupid to keep friends and do just as they do? Why can't I be myself and do the best that I can? I do believe that I must be wrong somehow and do not know how to correct it. I know I interrupted the balance that was here before I came and I will allow it to resume. I need to find myself. Was I wrong to state my opinion? I know I am very smart in mechanical diagnostics, so why can't I speak out? I know now that someone younger than their co-workers cannot be smarter and get along. I really don't want to leave because I do love mechanics and I would like to have my own business someday.

My mind goes back to when I was in first and second grade. This was the hardest time and I really did not know what was going on or why I was alive. I did not ask to be born and was not sure that I wanted to live. The times that are very strong in my mind are as follows. One day a school worker approached me and asked if I would like to go to church. I did not know what that meant, but I associated it with the prayers that we recited in the morning. She told me that I would like it and it would probably help me. I did not know how she knew I needed help or what kind of help I needed. My real mother came to the school to talk to us children and did mention that she would like to take us all to church with her. I would have done that but I remember that Florence told us all that she would beat us if we even talked with her. I asked my mother if I could come and live with her. I do not remember how she stated it, but the answer was no. I was very sad and did not hear all that she had to say. I did know that she cared because it was hard for her to come this long way on a bus to see us. I just couldn't understand why I couldn't live with her. She always loved me and was always good to us. She then told me that if I needed help I must pray for it. During our conversation she mentioned the words church, God and prayers several times. I was told that there was a God, that He created the earth, He helped people, and led them into temptation. Since I was three or four years old, I was tempted to do anything to get away from this, but there was never anyone there to lead me. I thought that we lived so far into the woods that He could never find me. I told this lady that I would like to go, but she would have to explain it to me.

By this time, I knew when Dorothy walked by, and I wanted to know more about her. I had planned this several times, but I did not have the guts. I always thought that she would not like me and my fantasies would be over. This day I told myself that I must and she was walking towards the garage, so I timed it to meet and walk with her. The restaurant was just two hundred feet from the garage, and I would only have that time to do something. I did meet and walked alongside of her. Then I said, "Hi, Dorothy. My name is Al. How are you? I notice that you walk here almost every day."

She answered, "Yes."

I waited, but she did not say any more. I did not know what to say next, and waited for some words to come out of my mouth. There were a million things that I wanted to say, and finally I said, "Would you care to join me for a soda or something? I am going to lunch and would love to have you come."

She answered in a low, pleasant voice, "I would love to, but I can't right now. I would be late for work, because I start work now."

She did not say any more, and I wanted to shout something, but nothing came out. She kept walking and I knew I had the chance to ask for a later date, but I didn't know how and I was afraid that the answer might be no. I think I was afraid that I would be let down and did not want to face that now.

I reapplied at the textile plant and was going for an interview. I knew that I had a job because the supervisor was a customer and he confirmed that I did. I gave Lee my final notice and after all of the conversations we had, Lee and Eleanor did understand. I did see Dorothy walk by several times and I waved to her. She waved back, but never gave me reason to think that she would be interested. I finally gave up, but hoped that sometime in the future we could meet. I still had two more weeks before I started at the textile plant. Lee told me that a sports car was coming in for some clutch work, and asked me to handle it. It was a 1954 Jaguar that had won the Grand Prix in France. It was very nice and was specially built. The clutch was specially designed for racing and would be expensive to replace, and would take a long time to get. Lee told me that he would try to sell the owner a new Thunderbird, and I do believe that he did. Lee did order the T bird and said that the Jaguar might be traded in. I do not know how much money was involved, but I fell in love with it and told Lee that if he did trade it in, I wanted the first choice to buy it. He told me that the car belonged to this man's son, and that he would have to ask him. This man was seventy years old and I didn't think that he would care. The owner's son was out of the country and it might be some time before we got an answer.

The gentleman with the Jaguar did not get back to me, and I wanted to be here when he came back. I told Lee to please call me if he did trade it in, or wanted to sell it. I went home thinking about Dorothy and had this feeling that I never had before. I could still see her dark eyes. My mind went back to when I was a child and had found the doll in the dump. I had a similar feeling then, and wondered if there was some kind of connection. I fell asleep thinking about my doll and felt bad that I had left her in that barrel on our old farm. I made up my mind to meet with Dorothy and ask her again, because the last time she had said that she would love to. I met with her while she was walking and asked her again. She replied "You know where I live, so why don't you come over. I said I would and then asked how about Saturday. She said that would be fine because she would be home all day. I was so excited that I went back without lunch.

The Car We Named Zhasha

While my brother John started living with us again, he bought a 1951 Ford convertible and he wanted to customize it because while he was in California, he noticed many customized cars and went to see them. He explained to me his ideas of what we should do. I did have some knowledge of what he was explaining because I had seen them in magazines. I was modifying a Mercury 8CM engine before he came back and it was almost completed. We decided to install it in the Ford. We totally stripped the complete car then welded all the seams to make the body appear to be just one piece. We removed the crease in the hood and the recess in the trunk. This made the body appear as if it was all one piece. Then we removed the body mounts to lower the body on the frame. We changed the grill and side molding with parts from a Pontiac and when we finished with everything, it was something you had never seen before. We painted the front and the lower half jet black and the top half from the door and the trunk off-white. We redid the complete interior with fur and the doors with two-tone black-and-white leather. We installed the best sound system we could find and it really was awesome. I then installed the Mercury motor that I had modified and knew it was the fastest car around. The first time I drove it, it would just spin the wheels so we knew we needed bigger and wider tires. When I drove it, I noticed everyone had to look and I was very proud because this was my engine that I rebuilt from scratch.

I had not seen Dorothy all week and decided to go to her house on Saturday. I did not like going there with my car because it was an old ford and didn't look very nice. I drove into her yard and she was standing at her door so I went to her. She asked me what I did all week, because she hadn't seen me around at all. I told her that I had been very busy building a new car. She asked me what I meant and I told her I would show it to her someday. I apologized about my old car but she didn't seem to mind. I asked her if she wanted to go to Al Pats and she said that she would love to. We both had a small late lunch and I asked her if she wanted to go anywhere. I don't think she even heard me because she was singing to the music from the jukebox. There were very few people and she asked me if I wanted to dance. I said, "Not here. I don't know how to dance." She said, "Well, let's do something."

I just dropped the subject and asked her what she wanted to do. She was singing in tune with the jukebox and I don't think she heard me, but the more I looked at her, the more I fell in love with her. She was everything I ever wanted and I could see the doll came to life. The jukebox was loud so I raised my voice and asked her again if I could take her somewhere. She answered that she had promised her friends to go out with them, and followed up with, maybe next Saturday. I do know where you work and I will probably bug you to death for a ride. I said, that I would love for her to bug me, but this is my last week here". She said "that sounds normal, every time I find a friend, they move". I told her that I wasn't moving, that I was just changing jobs, and that I was starting at the Robinson Bleachery Textile Plant. She told me to stop at her house any time because she was home every weekend during the day, or to stop in the morning during the week, because she didn't start work until eleven. I told her I would stop in when I drove by, and then I took her home. She looked at me with a big smile and I walked her to her door. I did not go in, but I told her I was happy to take her to the diner. I left to go home and had trouble going to sleep, because I could still see those big eyes looking at me.

The Ford was completed, but not registered. It was very fast, but I didn't care to drive it with the wrong plates and for some reason, I did most of the driving. John didn't like to drive much since his illness but I didn't mind because he started drinking a lot again. I told him I was not going anywhere the next day, because it was Saturday, and I wanted to stay home. I stayed in bed longer than usual and just took it easy all morning. Later in the afternoon I went to see Dorothy and we went to Al Pats for lunch. We talked for awhile and she played the jukebox. We did have a lot of fun and when we arrived back at her house I had coffee. Then we talked along with her mother. She told me she wasn't going out that night and wanted to stay home. I did not ask why and told her I would see her during the week. On Sunday I just rode around looking for a better car, and I went to most of the car dealers, because I didn't think I would hear any more about the Jaguar. The dealers were closed on Sundays, but I did look at the cars they had and I didn't find anything I wanted. I really wanted a Ford convertible but I didn't see one so I asked a few people and they said there are much larger auto dealers in the Waterbury area, so I decided to go there.

I would be starting at the textile plant this week, but I wouldn't make as much money per hour as I had with Ford. I will be working many more hours and have a lot more overtime. John still went out when he was off work and asked me to go to a different place in Brewster, New York that he had found. It was a restaurant and a nightclub and he said that everyone went there. I decided to go with him and found it was a fun place. The drinking age was eighteen and I was only seventeen, but I did have a little to drink and they did not ask my age. I did not drink very much and I didn't like beer, but I tried a seven and seven and it was pretty good. While we were there, John met someone, his name was Frank, and he appeared to be nice, and hung around with us all night. This was the first time we had met him, but he was very friendly and paid for our food. We stayed until almost closing time and Frank asked John if we would give him a ride to his motel. It was on our way home and we agreed. We got into the car and were heading to the motel, then home. We drove about two miles from the 6-22 Diner where we were pulled over by police. We knew we weren't breaking any laws and John only had one or two drinks all night. There were two police cars and four police officers. They ordered us out of the vehicle and put handcuffs on all of us. I didn't know what was wrong and was afraid to ask because they were very mean. They slammed us around and it was evident that they wanted to show off their authority and hurt us. One cop grabbed me and ordered me into the back seat of the cruiser.

I did ask him why they were doing this and he did not answer, but just shoved me into the back seat. I hit my ankle on a sharp object in his car that was part of the divider from the front seat. I told the cop, "You hurt my ankle, and why are you doing this to us?"

He punched me in the back of the head and said, "Shut up and get in."

The back of my head and neck hurt very much where he had struck me because it was at the base of the skull and neck. I was afraid to ask why he was doing this and just kept quiet. I said to myself, "Why is this happening to us? I'm just a kid and have never hurt anyone or did anything wrong." I knew that the only thing that gave him that power was the gun, badge and the other cops with him. I knew that if we were alone I would kick the shit out of him. I could see he was just a scrounge-looking punk just waiting for the day he would get what he deserved. They took us to the barracks, put us into separate rooms, and started questioning or interrogating me. They said that Frank was an escaped convict that we were harboring, and we were going to jail. I told them that I never had seen Frank before and I could say the same for my brother, John. He made me take off my shirt and struck me with what appeared to be a rubber hose. I said that he could beat me all he wanted, but that I couldn't tell him what I didn't know, and that I wouldn't lie for him or anyone else. They stopped and let me put on my shirt, but my back burned from the beating. I found later that they had used this hose because it doesn't leave marks for very long and they are gone before you go to court. I was then left alone in this room for an hour or more before they said that I could leave. They still had my brother, John, but would not let me go see if he was all right. I could not go to the car and was ordered to wait in the front waiting room. It was almost daylight when John came out and we were allowed to go to our car. He told me that they had arrested him after he threw one of the cops against the wall and three others had to help pull him off. John was still wearing his dog tag from the marines because of his illness, and that was why they released him on his own recognizance. He was ordered to return to appear in court for a hearing on charges of criminal behavior and battery against an officer of the law. I couldn't believe this because the cops should have answered to these charges and not us.

This is our law and we must learn to live with it. John and I went to our car and found it all torn apart. The seat covers were ripped off and the seats were cut with a sharp blade. The floor covering was ripped out and the visors were broken off. There was more damage but we couldn't see it until we arrived home and it was daylight. The wrecker that was used bent our bumper and ruined the grill with dents and scratches. On top of all that, we had to pay for the towing. When John went to court I went with him and brought pictures of the damage to our car. The cop tried to make us look very bad and said that the car was in that condition when they pulled us over, but take a guess who the judge believed. I did not complain about the beatings or the strike to my neck that still hurt because I know the cops would say that we were beat before they stopped us and I know whose side the judge would take. They did dismiss the battery charges but I left the court very angry. I could see the shit-eating grin on the cop's face and said to myself, "It is not over because I will be back." I felt that if this happened to us it could happen to anyone and this had to be stopped because if the courts can't uphold the law, then I must.

My dad had a 300 Savage rifle with a three by nine scope that I used for target practice a lot and I could shoot the balls off a fly at one hundred yards away. I had in my mind to go back and shoot him in the lower spine. I did not want to take him out, but just put him to his knees so he no longer could torture innocent people. I'm sure he did this for fun and it appeared that the courts condoned their actions. I went as far as to go there in the daytime to execute a plan but decided not to bring myself to his level because I am not the coward that he is. I was still very angry and decided not to go to Brewster again, but just forget what had happened because my plan was still tempting. I took a long time and a lot of money to repair the car, but we did it, and it looked like new again. I heard in the past that there are cops like that, but could not believe that they do stoop this low. I knew it would be very hard to ever trust another cop again, and had to be extra careful because I would expect this treatment from all of them now. After this we did not go there, but went to Wingdale and Putnam Lake. I did learn to forget what had happened to an extent because the policeman, Bruce Nearing, in New Milford, was very nice and fair to everyone. I don't go to New York State much and when I do, it is to dance and have fun.

I don't dance much but John has taught me how to dance the California Bee Bop. I must do it good because a lot of people like to watch me, but when I notice them watching me I stop because I am still very shy. I still hope to go out with Dorothy and I think about her a lot. I don't have any close friends and it would be nice to have someone to talk and share things with.

My First Auto Accident

By this time, John had a girlfriend, but he always asked me to drive him around and I didn't mind because I loved driving that car. One Friday night, I drove them to New York State and I was driving on Route 22, a four-lane highway, when another car pulled alongside me and challenged me to a race. I tried to ignore them, but they would pull in front of me and then slow down and I would have to pass them. They would then fall way back and pass me at a high rate of speed then slow down again. John noticed what was going on and asked me to lose them. The car was on my side so I accelerated and went way ahead of them, but they could not catch me. I noticed lights ahead and slowed down below the speed limit, but the car I was racing did not see this and ran into the back of my car at a high rate of speed and forced my car into a lot of parked cars. There were two police officers there. One ran for his car and tried to catch them while the other policeman was directing traffic and had seen everything. This turned out to be a carnival and there were many people there. My car damaged several cars and was a total wreck. The policeman came back and said he could not catch them and that they must have pulled off the road. Both of the officers observed the complete episode and knew I was not at fault in any way. I was asked to show my driver's license, but did not have one yet. I told them I left it home and would bring it back the next week, but I did go to the motor vehicle and got my operator's license, then called the number to the officer. I then was called to appear in court in Watertown, New York, which was a few hundred miles away. Since I was not at fault, I did not appear and never heard any more. We had our car towed home and could not fix it, but we kept my engine that was not hurt. John then bought a 1953 Mercury so we put my engine in that and started to redo it the same as Zhasha.

My two weeks were over and I was to start work at the textile plant on Monday. Lee asked me to come to dinner at his home again and I did. I spoke with Lee and Eleanor and they tried to make me change my mind, but finally did agree with me. He reiterated that I was gifted beyond anyone he had ever employed and I should pursue a mechanical education and stay in the automobile field. He did ask again if I would reconsider if he spoke with his employees, but I did not agree. I said if it was any other circumstances, I would, but I do have my pride and self-respect. I also told him that I was hired and had to start work on Monday. They wished me luck and said that I could always come back. I thanked them and said I would stop to visit them when I could. I left there and was very sad but I knew I had to leave. I walked to Dorothy's house, but she was not there because she was working. I went to see Beatrice. Dorothy's mother seemed to like me and always asked me to come over. We had coffee and talked a lot about why I quit work with Lee. I stayed for awhile then went home to work on the Mercury. I stayed home all weekend working on the car and did not go to see Dorothy at all.

I had to get ready to start work at the textile plant on Monday. Sunday afternoon I went to my sister's house to see the kids and Marianne, who is having problems with her husband. She found out that he is dating another woman and she is very upset about it. He has not brought much money home and the kids don't have much food or toys, so I try to help. I do not care to see kids neglected and it reminds me of my own childhood. The kids love to see me, and Debbie called me Daddy once. That made me very sad. Marianne also had two more sons, their names are Conrad, Junior, but we call him Timmy, and Danny. They also were sweet kids and they are very well-mannered. I would go there whenever I had a chance and would bring them something. I then visited my sister, Elaine, who lived in Danbury. She is also enduring marital problems. I believe this was the result of them both leaving home young to escape the torture. They married the first men they dated. That is also why I want to be careful about marriage. My youngest sister, Arlean, plays the guitar with me at times. She plays very well and I'm glad that I taught her how to play. She has the best voice I have ever heard and I hope she pursues a career in music. I know that some people came to talk to her about it but her boyfriend, Frank, asked her not to go, because he was afraid that he would lose her. It is too bad because every place she played, the people just loved her.

The Robertson Bleachery

At this time, I was employed at the textile plant and had been training to operate the back end, or feed end, of the number 6 frame. This was fairly new, and it was nearly 100 feet long. It was the finishing stage of the textile. The front end, or the finish end, of this machine was very complicated and required training by the manufacturer to successfully operate. I was full-time on that machine and would have loved to be the main operator. Frank, who was in charge, was very hard to get along with and loved to push around his weight, I just did the best I could and said as little as possible. I believed that I got along with him better than most operators did. This Monday I would be transferred to the night shift and work seven p.m. until seven a.m.

My First New Car

Since I had Saturday off, I decided to go to Waterbury and look for a new car. While searching the newspapers, I found a 1955 Ford Crown Victoria convertible. I drove there early and found it was a new leftover, but it was beautiful. It was a two-tone, dark blue and white, with a blue convertible top. It had an automatic transmission, a stereo radio system, and all the accessories. It was really the car of my dreams so I paid cash for it, but could not register it until Monday. I went early that morning after receiving the registration and drove my car back. I had to leave my old car there, but Dorothy's father said he would go back with me and drive it home. I was surprised because I found he worked with me on the night shift. I waited until Dorothy was home from work, and then drove to her house. I went to the door and Beatrice let me in, and as always, asked if I wanted coffee. I said sure, and asked where Dorothy was. She must have heard me because she was there before Beatrice could answer. She did not see my car so I sat with them and had a coffee. I then asked if she wanted to see my new car. She said yes, then got up and grabbed my hand. I did not finish my drink, but I was happy that she was that interested. She was surprised and all in one sentence said, "Oh! It's beautiful and you must take me for a ride."

Without hesitating I said, "I would love to, but I will be working the night shift all next week."

She interrupted and said, "Why? Can't we go right now?"

I said, "Hop in." We drove around town with the top down and the music up loud.

We had a lot of fun, then went to Al Pat's Diner. While we were there, I asked again if we could go out this Saturday night. She told me to stop in during the week and she would let me know. When we arrived at her house, I walked her in, and went into the kitchen. I wanted to talk with her mother, because I couldn't understand why she didn't say yes or no about us going out. Beatrice and I sat while Dot went to her room. While we were talking, Beatrice asked if I liked Dorothy, and I told her that I did, very much, but that I didn't think that she wanted to go out with me. She replied, "Well, I hope she does, because she needs someone more respectful."

I asked, "What do you mean?"

She said, "I didn't like her last boyfriend." When I asked her why, she said that she would tell me some day.

Dorothy came into the kitchen so we changed the subject. She said hi to me, and then asked her mother if we had been talking about her, with a smirk and a shrug. I laughed, thinking she was cute. She walked straight towards me and said, "Well, are we going out?"

I said, "When?" Then she replied now, we went to the car and I asked her where she would like to go. She said that she was hungry, and suggested Al Pat's. I still had the top down and was proud that everyone could see us together. We both had a snack then she put change in the jukebox and started dancing. I was surprised because I thought she was bashful. She grabbed my hand and asked me to dance with her. I told her that I was too shy in front of all those people, and that I didn't know how to waltz.

She said, "Why don't we go to the Bog and I'll teach you?" I said "what's that?", and she said it was a nightclub in New York. I said, "New York?" and she said, "Yeah, just over the state line."

We left then and she showed me how to get there. When we walked in, everyone appeared to know her and she was friends with the owners. We sat then, ordered a drink, and she had Martha, the owner's wife, make her one special. She said it was much weaker than usual. We sat for awhile, then she took my hand and said she wanted to dance. I told her that I didn't know how to waltz, just Be Bop. She said, "Come on, I'll show you." She put both arms on my waist, and then told me to watch her feet, follow her, and watch her feet. I put my hands on her shoulders and we started to move. It wasn't too hard and I seemed to do well, so I pulled her closer and placed my hands around her waist. I was so happy that I didn't know what my feet were doing. I just knew that I was holding her close to me.

She pulled back away from me and said that I was squeezing her too hard, so I loosened my grip, but I still held her close. We danced for about five or ten minutes, then sat again. Just then the owner, Bill, came over and said hi to Dot. Dorothy introduced me as her friend. Then more people came in, so Bill went back to the bar. It seemed that everyone who came in said Hi Dot, or Dorothy, and I became a little jealous and wanted to leave. I never associated much with crowds and was shy and nervous. I ordered another drink and felt better because we were alone again. Everyone started dancing so Dot took my hand and pulled me to the floor, but in the corner. I was surprised because she held me tighter than I had been holding her before. I really loved every bit of it, and it felt that my dreams were coming true. Before now, Dot and I had been out several times, but only for a ride or to Al Pat's Diner. This was the first time I really held her close and it made me realize how much I really loved her. After finishing our drinks, she said that we could leave if I wanted to. I asked if there was any place she wanted to go. She said, "Not really, I just want to go home, but I want to talk to you before I go in the house."

I said, "Okay," and we drove to her house. I drove into her driveway and turned off the headlights. There was a street light just behind us and I could see her very well. We just looked at each other for a minute, and then she said, "You probably want to know what I want to talk about.

I answered, "Yes," without hesitation and then let her talk.

She looked at me with a look that I hadn't seen before and said, "You and me."

I was nervous and asked, "What do you mean?" At this time I didn't know if this was love or infatuations, but I knew it was exciting and adventurous. She was still looking at me and I could see she was not that shy and timid girl I thought before and I could feel my body tremble.

She moved closer to me, put her arms around me, and kissed me on the cheek. Then she said, "Thank you for a very nice evening."

I said, "We didn't do anything."

Then she replied, "I really had a nice time and this is the first time I've been out in a while." She stopped talking and kept looking at me. After a deep breath, she said, "Al, I think you are a fantastic person, you have always addressed me as a lady and shown respect. I could see that you liked me and I believe that you want to know me more. I could see it in your eyes and the way you are with me. You really treat me better than anyone ever has. I won't say that you don't have a chance because I would be lying, and I have been watching you ever since I first seen you next door. I was sad when you left and felt that I would never see you again. I am also interested in getting to know you better, but I must tell you: I had a boyfriend that, pause, that hurt me, and I know I could not love anyone right now. I can't explain now and if by chance we do get together I will tell you the whole story." She stopped talking and she appeared to become very sad or annoyed. I didn't know what to say, so I reached over and pulled her close to me. I just held her tight until she looked at me and said, "I'm very sorry, but I can't get serious with anyone right now. I also want to make sure I find the right one this time. I am not telling you I want you to leave, and I do want you to come as before because I still want to go out with you as a friend."

I just looked at her and didn't know what to say. I don't think I was sad or happy, but I believe some tears came to my eyes. She noticed it and held me again, then kissed me on my lips. I held her very tightly, and she put her arms around me and squeezed me very tightly. I choked up and my eyes filled with tears. I think she knew because our faces were together, and she must have felt it. She pulled back to look at me and our lips went together, but I could see she wanted to stop. I let go then and she slid back a little. I held my head down so she wouldn't see the tears, but she picked up my chin and said, "Don't be sad."

I said, "I'm not sad, I'm very happy that you went out with me and this was the best time of my life." I let go of her hand while she moved over to her side. She opened her door and I went to meet her. I took her hand and walked her to her door, but before we got there she asked me if I would take her to a drive-in movie. I said, "I would love to, but I work every night except Saturday and Sunday."

She said, "Well, I'll see you during the week and will let you know."

I said, "Alright," then turned around and walked to my car without looking back, but I heard the door close behind her. I drove home very slowly, but couldn't understand the feeling I had and didn't know if it was from being so tired, sad, or happy. But I did know that the knot in my stomach got bigger, so I went into the house and went straight to bed. I just couldn't wait until I saw her again. I could still feel her lips on mine and I knew I waited for that for a long time. I was still thinking about taking her to the movies and must have passed out. I awoke early and was thinking about what she said, and I didn't know why I hadn't thought about it the night before. Now it is bothering me: "We can only be friends. I can't love anyone now."

I decided not to go see her today because, while brushing my teeth, I could see I looked horrible. My eyes were swollen and red, and I knew I was still tired but too excited to sleep any longer. I made some coffee and could still feel that knot in my stomach and in my lower groin, but didn't know what it was. I had never been in love before, and I wondered if it was because of what she had said. I said I never loved anyone before but I did and still love my mother, but it never hurt like this.

My Only True Friends

I looked out the window and forgot I had my new car. I felt better and wanted to take a ride in it. I waited until lunchtime and went to Al Pats. I met a girl that I knew from school and gave her a ride home once when she was hitch hiking. She was a cute little blond and lived by the lake in a very nice house. She knew my name and her name was Sparky. I sat at a table and she came over and sat with me without asking. She said, "Hi, Al. What are you doing?"

I said, "Just having a coffee," but while looking at her, I did like her for some reason. She had always been nice to me in high school and went out of her way to see me. I wouldn't have minded having her as a friend, because I didn't have any female friends. I said, "I suppose you want a ride home?"

She said, "How did you know?"

I just said, "I don't mind, and I feel like having company anyway, because I was riding around.

She replied, "Well, I don't have to go home now." Just then the waitress brought my coffee, so I ordered her a Coke. We talked about school and things we had been doing, and then we walked to the car. I did not open the door for her and just went to mine. She was surprised and said, "You got a new car! Oh, I love it," while she was getting in. The radio was already on loud and I did not turn it down and she said, "I love your radio, it plays so loud."

I drove towards her house and asked her, "Where would you like to go?" and she said, "Anywhere with you."

I said, "Don't get cute."

Then she asked, "Why are we going towards my house?"

I said, "I don't know," then turned around and rode around town for a while. I did not go past Dorothy's house because I didn't think it would be right. I didn't want her to be mad at me. I decided to take Sparky home and headed back to her house. On my way up the hill, there was a girl walking.

Sparky said, "Could you please stop? I have to talk to her."

I stopped and the girl said, "Hi, Sparky," then looked at me and said, "My name is Jeanne."

Sparky didn't wait at all and said, "His name is Al and he is all mine."

I just laughed and said, "You know how to be a smart ass, don't you?" I was just going to take Sparky home, but there was something about this new girl that attracted me. She had long black hair, big dark eyes, and a pure complexion. I said, "Jeanne, are you just going to stand there or are you getting in?" Sparky slid over close to me, and I mean, *right* against me. I said, "You know, I have to breathe," and she moved over about an inch. I asked, "Where do you want to go?" Sparky said she wanted to go home.

I said, "Do you have to go home now?" and Sparky said, without hesitation, "Why? Do you want to take me somewhere?"

I said, "I would like to take both of you to just ride around." Then I asked Jeanne, "Do you want to go with us?" but Sparky tried to answer for her so I interrupted and said, "Jeanne, dear, would you like to go with us?" and she laughed and said, "Yes, I would love to." Sparky didn't waste any time and said, "That's enough of the 'dear' stuff," but Jeanne and I just laughed. I noticed that Jeanne was looking at me a lot and I could see she was really beautiful. I had a sensation and I didn't know what it was, but I thought it had something to do with her eyes and the way she looked at me, because I believed she felt the same. I could see she was very young and I removed that from my mind. It was a lot of fun having them both with me and they seemed like real good kids. I asked them where they would like to go and Sparky said, "Anywhere with you, dear."

I said, "What happened with that 'dear' stuff?" and then said, "What about the Lark Drive In?" They both agreed and liked to go there because it was a fun place. They had loud music outside and carhop service. The food was also very good and I did like going there.

While we were there and in-between songs when I could hear something, Sparky asked, "Well, when are we going out?"

I said, "We are out," and Sparky said, "No! I don't mean this way. I mean *out* out. Don't be smart, you know what I mean."

I said, "No, I don't know what you mean, because you do know I do have a girlfriend."

She said, "That has nothing to do with me."

I said, "It does with me but you might be able to twist my arm." She grabbed my arm and I said it wouldn't take that much. I did that because I didn't want to give them the impression that I wouldn't go out because I wanted them to be my friends. I knew if Dorothy and I didn't make it, I would be interested in going out just to have fun.

Jeanne kept staring at me with that look of uncertainty, and I believe she was searching my thoughts. I believe that I did look at her more than I should have. She also had long, black hair and very dark eyes, which seemed to attract me. Every time we looked at each other, I could see something there. She gave me a smile and a certain look, which I took as an invitation. Well, it was getting late and I just took them to Sparky's house. When Jeanne got out, she stood looking at me as if she wanted to say something, and I winked at her, but Sparky didn't see me. Jeanne smiled, then said thank you to me, and Sparky said, "See you later, Sweetie." I just shook my head and left but I was glad that happened because the knot and the pain I had in my groin was gone. For some reason, I really liked these girls. Sparky was nice, but I knew that I could never love her. I think that I could like Jeanne more, and she is more my type. It was easy to talk around them, and I liked having them around. Oh well, maybe I was just confused, and searching for love because when I got home I could only think about Dorothy, and what she had said. I knew that I wanted to be with her tonight. My mind had a couple of hours break today and I did feel better. I had been trying to understand the situation with Dorothy, but I was confused and I said to myself, "Give her a chance, you just met her and have gone out with her twice." Well, maybe I could take her to the drive-in theater Saturday night and I was really looking forward to it. If we could be alone, maybe she could tell me everything, But I felt that the hurt that she carried towards that other guy could get them back together. I would be let down again, and I did not want any more let downs.

It was Monday afternoon and I had to go to work that night, so I decided not to go to Dorothy's house, but I would stop in the morning after work. It was two o'clock. I did all my laundry, the dishes, and cleaned all day. I was going to town to see if Sparky or Jeanne was around, but no luck. But I wanted to talk to someone.

I had finished my training and had been there just a short time. I operated my machine very well, and also got to know the proprietors well. I have had the opportunity to repair their cars for them. Fred, who is head of operations, told me that we were behind on production. He said that I had learned the operation very fast, and asked if I would be willing to operate the main end of the frame. This would place me in charge of the second shift. I had not trained to operate the main end, but I thought that I could do it. I did spend all week studying this machine, and watched Frank. I told him that I would love to, and I'm not afraid to try, but he said he would stay with me in the beginning. I did not mind, and was looking forward to it, because I would receive an increase

I my salary. I was just starting my first day on the main frame, and Fred came in when I started, to make sure that I would be able to perform what he had expected.

Frank left the machine in operation and I just had to take over. This night we had a special sample to run, and it had to be run slowly, because it was a very heavy material. It had a braided rope woven in about six inches apart. This would take about two hours, then I would change to a large batch of Mini Check and Octavia. Fred stayed for an hour and saw that I had no trouble and that I appeared calm and sure of what I was doing. This was only skin deep, because I was scared to death, but put on a good show. I am very good at hiding my true feelings. I was happy that Fred did not tell me to run the mini check at a low speed. After we finished the sample, we ran the stringer through and took a small break. I wanted to talk with Toots, that's Dorothy's father's nickname. The operator for the feed end was Marty and I knew his father from buying gas from him at his gas station. Toots also said that he knew my father well, and I did not know if that was good or bad.

We got started on the new batch and I had reset the heat and the setting for this application, then started running it. I started to run at eighty yards per minute, which was faster than Frank, and after an hour or so, I realized that I could run much faster. When you increase the speed, you must increase the heat simultaneously. I watched it very closely, and reached speeds in excess of one hundred yards per minute. At that speed, I could not take my eyes off the cloth for even a second. I had trouble eating lunch and didn't bother to try. Toots came to talk to me, and I enjoyed our conversation, but he noticed that I could not stop to talk much. He asked me if I was running it too fast. I said, "I'm not having any problems." He nodded and left, but didn't say much about Dorothy.

My First Clash with my Superiors

At seven o'clock, Frank came in to relive me but before he came in, I reset the machine to operate at sixty y. p. m. (yards per minute). This is what he usually did. I did not stay around, because Frank didn't think that I should have been offered this position without any experience. He didn't say too much and I did not offer to indulge,. but he asked in a sarcastic way, "Well, how much did you run?"

I said, "Quite a bit," and left. I got home at seven thirty and shortly after, the phone was ringing. It was Fred from the plant and he was yelling so loud that I didn't need the phone to hear him. He was screaming something like I had ruined thousands of yards of material. When I asked him why, he said that no one could produce that quota in one night, especially without experience. I asked him to please calm down and I was getting angry. I knew enough about this operation to know that there was no way that anyone could say I had ruined anything until it had run through the folders. I knew that hadn't happened yet. I told him that I would be right down. I went straight there, and met with Fred. I could see Frank grinning as we went to the folders that were just set up, and watched.

A folder is a machine that takes the material off of the roll, folds it in one yard strips up and down in front of the inspectors, all of whom are women. After it's inspected, the inspector steps on a pedal and a new fold will come up. It is then folded in piles and taken away. I watched while they ran several hundred yards, and so far there were no complaints. Fred looked at me without saying anything and went to his office. This was the cloth that I had ran at less than one hundred y. p. m., and they wouldn't get to the faster run for a few more hours. There were twelve folders and they only worked on the day shift. After Fred left, I asked the girls if they had found any problems. They were excited, and said, smiling, "Less than Frank's." I think they like me better than Frank because I showed respect for everyone. I thanked the girls and asked one of them to call me at home before Fred does, if there were any problems. I then went to Fred's office, told him that I was going home, and to call me if he needed me. He still didn't speak., he just nodded his head, and I left without talking to Frank.

Since there was no one yelling at me, he didn't know what to say. I went home, then went to sleep, and I did not get any phone calls, so I didn't know what to expect. I woke up at five o'clock, and got ready to go to work. I normally would have lunch at this time, but the phone did ring, and it was Fred. He asked me if I could come in early because he wanted to talk to me.

I was nervous and wondered what he wanted. I hoped that there was nothing wrong, but I believed that I had not ruined any material. I had been so careful, and watched every second. When I entered Fred's office, he had the owner of the mill there, and I was scared to go in. The owner's name is Charley and I had met him a few times, so I addressed him first. Then Fred asked me to sit, which I did. He stated that he did not want me to run this machine at that speed ever again. I quickly replied, "Did I ruin that much material?"

He said, "No," and continued, "That is not the reason we are asking you this."

I interrupted, "Well, how much cloth did I ruin?" This morning I was told that I ruined hundreds of yards"!

Charley entered the conversation and said please listen to what he has to say. I apologized, then shut up. Fred then said that he had other operators, and every time this happens, they get negligent and we lose a lot of material. Truthfully, he said, he couldn't believe that the returns were much less than normal, but that was not the reason. I then, very softly said, "Could I please speak?" Charley said yes, and I said, "Frank, What did you tell me and why am I on the night shift? You told me that we were way behind on our quota. I put my heart and soul into this to help get caught up. I very much appreciate you giving me the opportunity to operate this machine, but do you think it's easy to run it that fast? I never took my eyes off the material for a second, and I couldn't even eat my lunch. I don't walk around like Frank does, and I do take pride in everything I do." Charley tried to interrupt me, but I kept going, because for the first time in my life, I was going to defend myself. "Sure, I could do less." Charley interrupted again, so I stopped.

He spoke very softly and said, "You have us wrong, please listen to all we have to say. You don't have to take that chance. After you have more operating time, then we would like you to do more. We have both been talking here for hours because we both can't believe that you did this with no experience, while we've had men here who went to school to learn. The day person on the other end has been here for years and still can't operate this end. We have never questioned your ability to operate anything in here, but you must realize, if something does go wrong, running at that speed, a lot of damage could happen in minutes. We would place you on any piece of equipment in here, but this is the hardest and most intricate piece of equipment we have, and it is hard to find operators who stay. Furthermore, I do know your last employer, and had several conversations about you. He is not happy that you left, but he said he understood why you did. We don't know why you left, and won't ask, but we do know that you could have made a lot of money there."

I stopped him and said, "I will tell you. Due to circumstances beyond my control, I lost the ability to better myself and go further into the field, but most of all, I could not be myself and do not want to put on a false front to get along with my coworkers." I was so hurt, upset, flattered and proud that I had finally spoken my piece, but I didn't know if I should cry as usual, or laugh. I turned without saying anything, and walked out. I went to my station and was fifteen minutes late. I must have defended myself properly, because neither Charley nor Fred came to my machine or said any more. I was surprised that I had spoken with authority, because in past experiences if anything like that happened, I always felt as if I would have to leave. For the first time, I felt that I was standing on stronger grounds.

I ran my machine just under one hundred y. p. m. all night and in the morning, Frank came to relieve me. He was polite, but I did not care to converse with him, and I expected Charley or Fred would speak to him first. I believe that Frank thought that I had ruined some material, and must have talked with Fred yesterday morning during all the fuss. Well, I was happy that things were back to normal, and I didn't have to worry. I do understand the concern from Fred and Charley, because they are good people.

I was happy that our night shift chemist was Dorothy's father, because I left right at seven o'clock, and when I got to the gatehouse, he was clocking out. Charley had just walked in, he was talking to the guard, but turned to say, "Good morning, Al." I replied, and walked out, because I really wanted to talk with Toots. I walked to the cars with him and he asked what in hell had happened last night. I said, nothing, I just did too much work. Toots said that he had heard that I may have ruined a lot of cloth and might get fired. I replied, "Hell, no! They're looking for twenty more like me." I laughed and asked him who told him. He said he heard Frank talking to Marty. I said, "I figured it would be Frank." Then I ended the conversation because I wanted to talk about Dorothy, not Frank. When we got to the cars, Toots asked me "what I was going to do now". I told him I planned to go home.

I had not stopped in the past few days to see Dorothy, and did want to see her today, because I was so upset before. Toots asked me if I wanted to stop at his house for coffee, and I told him I would love to. I followed him to his house and walked in with him. I did not see Dorothy and thought that she was still asleep. Toots told Beatrice what had happened at the plant. She said she was sure I knew what I was doing, and invited me for coffee. We spoke a little, then she remarked that Dorothy had asked if I stopped by, and she had told her no. I finished my coffee, and started to get up, and she said, "Don't leave now, Dorothy will be down in a little while." I said ok, and my heart started beating faster. I didn't know what to say because it had been four days since I had seen her. I was drinking the second cup of coffee when she walked in. She had not combed her hair yet and was still in her nightgown, but my heart stopped when she spoke.

She said, "I'm sorry I look this way, but I just woke up."

I replied, "What do you mean, you look beautiful."

She smirked and went to the cupboard to get breakfast. She turned and said, "How come you didn't stop in?"

I said, "It's a long story, but I did miss you." She smirked again, but said no more, then sat with a bowl of cereal and had breakfast. I felt that I may be intruding and started to get up. I said, "Well, I'd better leave now." Dorothy stopped me by saying "You don't have to leave now", I took that as an invitation and asked about Saturday night. She said she didn't know, but would let me know tomorrow for sure.

I stopped in the next morning and she said "I haven't seen you all week, and I already made plans. I told her I would stop in on Friday. Then she said that I didn't have to stay away all week. I told her that I had been very busy. Doing the same work every day was getting boring and I felt that I had no future here. Charley was on my side and I did respect his authority. I really did like him and he always spoke highly of me. I saw Fred every day and sometimes he would ask me questions that concerned the operations. That made me proud because I had saved the company a lot of money due to my ability to understand the complexities and functions of our equipment. The most challenging encounter that I had was when the main frame heating system shut down and the warning "no pilot light" went on. I would have had to shut down for the night and wait for an engineer the next day.

Copies of the blueprints were in the control cabinet, and I reviewed them very carefully. I always have test equipment in my car from the garage, because I have electrical hobbies at home. While tracing the electrical system, I discovered that one of the multiple contactors had lost continuity in the pilot safety circuit and this automatically shut down the complete system. Without this gate of safety, raw propane gas would flow into the heating system and could explode. I removed the contactor and double-checked it. It was a sealed unit, but I was able to pry it apart, and then found that one contact was corroded and was not making contact. I studied the reason for failure and noticed that this contactor had a one quarter inch hole for air expansion, because in normal use there is a potential temperature change within the contactor and the ambient temperature change would create a vacuum. The area where the main control panel was located was highly contaminated with lint from all the fabric. My prognosis was that the contactor inhibited lint that burnt between the hot contacts and caused the failure. I repaired the problem and double-checked the complete system, and then I got a green light and started the pilots, then shortly after the main flames went on. I made a report to explain the unauthorized system repair, then restarted the frame and continued through the night. When Fred came in, I approached him and explained the situation. He wanted to shut down the system and call an engineer. He seemed to be upset and I said, "Fred, please read my report first." He did and I waited for him to talk to me. I also explained that there was a back up shut down system incorporated into this system and that there was no reason for alarm. He said ok and that he would call the company and report this failure. I went home then and got some sleep. Later I went to Al Pats for a good meal. I had not been taking good care of myself and was getting run down.

At seven o'clock I was back at work. Frank had been very nice since that big problem and was very nice today. I read the day's work order and started to set up the frame. Frank had finished a batch a short time before, and I had a new batch to start. He did not shut the system down. The pilots were normal but before adjusting the heat, I opened the ignition system. I wanted to be sure everything was ok. I reached in and felt the contactors and they appeared to be normal. There are eight of these contactors and that is why I was concerned. I did not mention this to Fred because he said that he would call the manufacturer.

Without noticing, Charley walked up behind me and put his hand on my shoulder. He asked, "What are you doing? Is there anything wrong?"

I was still startled and replied, "No, I'm just making sure that everything is all right." He just looked at me while I replaced the cover and I just stood there waiting for what was next.

He finally asked, "What makes you do these things?" or something like that.

I answered, "I don't know. I guess it's my machine when I'm running it and I feel obligated to keep it running. Ain't that what I'm being paid for?"

He laughed and said, "No, this is not your responsibility, but I did read your report after talking with Fred and why did you write it?"

I answered, "I did not want a problem like the last one and felt that was the best way to explain."

Charley said, "After reviewing your report, I don't believe we need to call the manufacturer because you seem to have it under control."

I replied, "There are eight of these contactors. They may have the same problem and I would say that this is a manufacturing defect. I think you should discuss my report with them because the contactors are not protected from debris, such as lint. They may have an improved version." He agreed.

When I got out of work, I went to see Dorothy. I just walked into her house and she was just getting out of bed, so I had breakfast with her. She seemed to be in a good mood and asked why I didn't stop every morning for coffee. She said, "There is coffee ready and you won't have to make it at home."

I said that I would love that, and I will when I can. "But, while I'm here, did you find out about Saturday night?"

She said, "You didn't stop in, and I forgot to call them, but I will try and break it."

I said, "I will stop before you go to work and that will give me time to make plans if we don't go out."

I left to go home, thinking about what I was doing, because this was the second time she had made plans and it appeared that she would rather be with them. She did tell me that she went to the Bog last Saturday and it appeared that is the only place she wanted to go. I went home and fell asleep wondering about what was happening because I knew I would break any plans to go out with her. When I awoke, I went to Al Pats and drove past Jeanne's house, but did not see her and I felt I needed someone to talk to. I went to work but I had a lot of long runs, which gives me time to think about Dorothy. I hoped she could break her plans this time.

On Saturday morning I realized that I had been thinking about going to the drive-in with Dorothy all week. I may be wrong, but I didn't think she was very excited about going with me. I had my heart set on going with her, but I may be let down, so I won't go there until later in the day.

I drove to Al Pats and Jeanne and Sparky were walking away towards their home. I drove up to them and stopped. They both ran over then got into the car. Sparky sat close to me, then gave me a small kiss. I asked Jeanne, "Do I get a kiss?" She just smiled.

Sparky said, "Hey!" I interrupted her and said, "Come on, you're both my friends. Can't we be fair?"

Sparky said, "Boy, you like to tease, don't you?"

I said, "Don't get sexy." Then I got off the subject. They both started singing with the radio and I looked at Jeanne. I did notice that she was looking at me a lot and at one time when our eyes met, I could feel a magnetic attraction between us. I think I liked this feeling, but Dorothy always came to mind. There is something about Jeanne I like. I believe it is her pure complexion, dark eyes, and long black hair. She is very well mannered and takes good care of herself. I felt that I wanted to spend some time with them and asked if they had to go home. They both said no, so we rode around the lake, and I invited them for a soda at Al Pats. When we got there, I handed them all my quarters, because I knew Sparky would ask for some. These girls love the jukebox and could spend the day here just singing with it. I started to think about Dorothy and I wanted to go see her. I took the girls home and thanked them for a very nice time. When Jeanne got out she had time to look at me while Sparky was getting out. Her eyes were wide open and I had that feeling again. I could see that she was interested in some way and I seem to enjoy it. Jeanne appears to be very young, maybe sixteen, and I'm sure this will not go anywhere but she is a very sweet girl and I would still love to have her as a friend.

I drove to Dorothy's house and pulled into her driveway, then went in. She was sitting on the couch, reading a book, or maybe a letter. I just looked at her and waited for her to say something. She looked up and said, "Well, I did break my date, but I want you to take me to the Bog."

I said, "Why? Why do you always want to go there?"

She replied, "I told you, all my friends are there."

I did not answer right away, and thought that if she would rather be with her friends, then who am I? I answered, "I made plans to take my friends to the drive in with us, because I thought you would want to go. So if you do want to, you could call me at home."

I started to walk out and she called me back and said that she would go with us. I was happy she was going with me, but still wondered about the connection with the Bog. I wished that she would never go there, because I believe it was more than her friends. I went home to change, then went back to pick her up. My friend, Jacky and his girlfriend went with us and they sat in the back seat. The movie, "Splendor in the Grass", starring Natalie Wood was playing. Dorothy looked so much like her. I was very happy to have her with me, because she sat real close and held me very tight. Everything became just as I dreamed and I was so happy. I held her and kissed her a lot through the first movie, but when it was over and my friends went to the concession stand, she moved away from me. She started crying, so I tried to pull her back to hold her, but she resisted. I asked what was wrong, but she said I wouldn't understand. I said, "Please let me try". I still had my hand on her and tried to pull her over again, but she said, "Will you please take me home?"

I did not say any more, but just waited for my friends to come back and told them I must take Dorothy home. I took them home first, and then went to Dorothy's house. She was still crying so I walked her to her bedroom. I kissed her good night and said "If you want me at all, I will need to know the truth." Beatrice was still awake, so I went to the kitchen and had a coffee with her. I couldn't understand what was wrong and why Dot wouldn't tell me. I went back into her bedroom and she was half asleep, but she turned to face me. I could see in her eyes that something was very wrong. She was still crying, but said that she was very sorry to have ruined my night. I just looked at her, but didn't know what more to say. Just a short while ago, I was in heaven. I told her how much I loved her and she appeared to be happy also, but something happened in her mind that she couldn't handle. Just in seconds my whole life changed again and I became lost. She turned and looked at me again. I could see she was trembling and she pleaded for me not to be mad at her. I sat on the bed next to her and placed my hand on her face. She reached up with both hands then held my hand very tight and said, "Will you please stay here with me?"

I said, "Yes, Honey." I stayed until she fell asleep. I went home and had trouble getting to sleep and when I awoke, all I wanted to do was go to her house to see her.

On my way there, I thought that maybe I should not go and try to forget her. But it seems that something happened last night that made me love her even more. I did go there and she appeared to be much better. She was still in bed, and had her face buried in the pillow, but she did look up at me. I asked her how she was feeling because I didn't know what else to say. My brain was twisted and I was very confused and didn't know how to handle what was happening. I thought about her always wanting to go to the Bog and I believed that she was still attached to her old boyfriend. I didn't like going there, but if I didn't I would never be able to help her and never know the truth. I felt the least I could do was help a friend, because who else did she have to turn to? I didn't want to stay here, because I couldn't understand what she was going through and it hurt me so much to see her cry. I kissed her on the cheek and she apologized again. It appeared that she didn't want to talk so I walked to the door to leave.

While I was walking out I heard her say, "Will you please come back later?" I did not answer and acted as if I didn't hear her. I drove straight home very sadly and didn't want to see anyone. I picked up my guitar and started to play, but could only think about the songs she always sang and that made me sad.

I decided not to see her at all this week and stayed home when I wasn't working. I did practice with my guitar a lot to keep me busy, but this did not take my mind off of her. I couldn't stay away any longer, so I stopped in on Friday before she went to work to see her. I walked in and she acted as if nothing had happened, but asked me if I would take her to the Bog the following night. I said "I would stop in during the day and let you know". I couldn't believe that she could forget what had happened. We talked for a few minutes and then she had to go to work so I gave her a ride there. It was only a block away, but by the time we got to her job I told her I would take her to the Bog.

I picked her up early, then went to Al Pats before going to the Bog. She was in a very good mood and was a clown on our way there. We spent most of the night dancing and I noticed that she held me much closer than anyone else she danced with, which made me happy because I thought she was telling me something. I had a few more drinks and became lightheaded, but I did not like this feeling. It did give me more nerve but I wanted to leave, because I did not like all these guys asking her to dance. But things were not too bad, because at least she was with me. Earlier I had heard her ask if Cat was there and she asked, "Do you know if he's coming tonight?"

The person said, "No, he's not here," and "I don't know if t he's coming." I wondered who that was and later she asked someone else. I searched my mind and could only believe that this Cat was her old boyfriend. I realized that this must be the guy she wanted to hurt and wondered if her close dancing with me intended to be a way to hurt him? I was sure word would get around about us dancing so close and I was the new kid on the block. I was not comfortable at this point and wanted to leave. I danced one more dance with her and held her extra close, then put my hands on her butt and pulled her even closer. Because I wanted to give them something to really talk about. Then I asked her if we could leave. She agreed and was very nice on the way home. She made me laugh and would come close and tickle me under my ribs, where I was very ticklish. I got my arm around her and pulled her close to me. Then she held me very close the rest of the way home. She became very silent and did not say any more until we were almost to town, then she asked if we could stop at Al Pats. I said, "Sure," and pulled in and we sat in the parking lot. She was still quiet and I was still thinking about this Cat, but I did not ask any questions.

We went in and I noticed that Jeanne was there. She was with two other girls that I did not know. I walked past her and said, "Hi," while going to a seat with Dorothy. Jeanne walked up to me before I sat and asked if I'd seen Sparky. I don't think she was looking for Sparky, but wanted Dorothy to see her talking to me, because she was acting very cute as if she knew me very well. I told her that I hadn't and then sat with Dorothy. Dorothy did not wait long to ask me who she was and then, who Sparky was. I told her Sparky was just a friend from school and I gave Jeanne a ride home when she was walking. Sparky asked me to stop because she had to talk with her and I gave her a ride to Sparky's house. I dropped the subject, but I think she may have been a little jealous, which made me happy. While sitting with Dot I noticed that Jeanne changed seats with the girl that she was with and she was facing me now. I tried to avoid eye contact with her, but I could feel that same feeling again and I noticed that she was staring at me a lot. Dot had her back to Jeanne and didn't notice anything or say anymore about her.

We left Al Pats and sat in her driveway for a while. She sat close and held me close, then just looked into my eyes. I could see she was troubled, so I pulled her closer to me, then kissed her while saying, "You do know I love you."

She looked at me and said, "I know you do and I'm happy that you do, but you must forgive me because I can't promise you my love right now." Tears came to her eyes and she thanked me for a very good night.

She slid over to her door, then opened it and ran to her house. I noticed that Beatrice was watching from the porch and invited me in for coffee. I said, "It's after midnight, isn't this late to be up?"

She said, "Hell, no," and I went to the kitchen with her mother. She made a fresh pot of coffee and we sat and talked, but the first thing she asked was, "Well, how do you like my daughter?"

Without thinking, I said, "I love her."

She replied, "Well, I'm happy for her and I hope she realizes what she has with you." I asked her why and she answered, "I do not like the guys that have brought her home. Sometimes they would not bring her home until two a.m. and it appears that they were all drunk. I find beer cans on my lawn when they leave and they are very noisy."

Al Duhan

So I asked, "Does she still go with them?"

She said, "No, not for a long time, because she had a serious problem with them. If she doesn't tell you, then someday I will, but I can't tell you now." I didn't want to talk about that anymore so I left.

Sunday I took Dot to Al Pats and asked her about that but she said, "I only went out with one of them and his friends were the nutty ones." I tried to believe her, but I still felt there was a problem there.

I Knew that I had to talk to her mother again and I did stay late one night. Dot went to sleep and I went to the kitchen with Beatrice. I asked her if she knew who this Cat was and she said, "Yes, that's her old boyfriend". This helped me to put the puzzle together and I didn't want to hear anymore, so I went home. Now I knew why she always wanted to go to the Bog and I wondered what her plans were for me. I had trouble trying to sleep, but I felt that my only chance to make it through this so uncertain relationship was to enforce my common denominator. When I left her house, I thought about this Cat and why she was so involved with him. If she wanted him instead of me, why didn't she say so and I would leave. But I sensed that there was more to this story. I did love her very much and would keep trying until I found the truth or where I was in this triangle.

I went to her house before she went to work and sat at the table. I asked her where I stood in her life. I did not get a straight answer and got the impression that she didn't want me now, but she wants me to wait until she gets her life straightened out.

She followed with, "I don't want to lose you, but if I do I will know that it will be my own fault and I will have lost the one I love the most."

I said, "Dorothy, I do love you with all my heart, but I have to know what to do. There are other girls that are asking me out and I must know what I'm doing." I waited for an answer, but she got up and walked towards her bedroom. I stood up and she stopped, and then turned to looked at me. She came to me and held me very tightly, then started crying very hard again. She appeared to have trouble breathing, so I just held her until she stopped crying.

I said very quietly, "I really need to know the truth, because it is not fair for me not to know where I stand. I could see you have a problem and I believe that you should let me help you." I laid her down in her bed and she buried her face in the pillow. I said very firmly, "I will do all I can to help you, but I cannot promise that I will keep loving you." I let her go, then walked out the door and left. I really didn't want to leave, but I knew I had to find myself. I was so lost for answers and wondered if my love for her was worth it, because I'd probably

64

lose her anyway. My brain was numb and I was too hurt to cry. I was not feeling sorry for myself, but I did think, "*Why do things always have to be this way in my life*"? I felt very lost and was so deep in thought that I drove past my driveway. I finally made it home and spotted my guitar. I picked it up and started playing it. I had just learned a new song, "It's Only Make Believe" by Conway Twitty. I remembered it because it explained my relationship with Dorothy.

I stayed home all week and only went to work. I did not talk with many people and did not try to see Jeanne or Sparky. I did think if she was older, she could help me break this bond that I had with Dorothy, which I believed I would be forced to do anyway. I was only working forty hours a week and had lots of time. I was still one of the highest paid employees and had enough money to do almost anything that I wanted. I missed the auto business and asked Dad if I could use one of the concession stands to repair some cars. He agreed, so I fixed up the shop and brought the tools that I would need. I still had all my tools from the Ford place, but I still needed a welder, air compressor and painting equipment, etc. I started to love fast cars and wanted to make mine faster. One time Dot had left me at the Bog, I drank too much and I was challenged to a race, so I agreed. I won the race only because of my driving skills. I could see his car was faster, but he could not handle the corners as well as I.

When I reached town, I went to Al Pats for coffee and noticed that Sparky was there. She came over to me and asked, "What's the matter? You're not being yourself and I haven't seen that smile yet."

I said, "Nothing, I guess I'm just tired and I gave her a small smile."

She said, "Come on, now. I know it's more than that, did you have a fight with Dorothy again?" I said I hadn't, but she did not believe me. She then asked very sincerely, "When are you taking me out?"

I said, "I don't know, but I may surprise you soon." I was still hurt over Dorothy and wanted to see who brought her home. It had been an hour since she left and I wanted to drive past her house. I hadn't expected her to be home yet, but when I drove past she was just going into her house. She did notice my car and without looking, I knew she turned around and watched me go by. I did not stop and drove straight home as if I hadn't seen her. When I arrived at home the phone was ringing so I answered it. It was Dorothy. She wanted to tell me what happened, but I was very hurt and wanted to forget about it. I had been hurt throughout my life and at this point I couldn't handle any more.

I said, "Please leave me alone, I need some time to see where I am and what's happening with my life now." I did not say anymore and we were both silent. I could hear her breathing, but she still hadn't said a word. I said, "I talked with Sparky tonight and she asked me out. I said I would, but I know I couldn't love her, because I never want to love anyone again because love hurts too much." There was silence again. Then I said, "I'm lost and I believe this may help me find my way. I am very sorry for hurting you and making you cry, but that by far was never my intentions."

She finally interrupted me and I could hear she was crying again. She said in a broken and shaky voice, "Al, would you please come here? Please?" After hearing that, I completely fell apart. I could feel my face and throat swell and could not answer. I held the phone and could still hear her crying, so I just hung up, because I wanted to put some water on my face. I had a bottle of Vodka in my cupboard that a friend had given me a long time before, so I went to get it. I took a big swallow and it nearly choked me to death. I had more trouble breathing, so I drank some water. I did not know it was that strong and I went to lay down. My mind was spinning very fast and I was more confused now than ever, but the phone rang again.

It was Dorothy again and she said hysterically, "Please don't hang up." I said I wouldn't and tried to talk to her, but nothing would come out. She didn't answer me so I asked if she was still there.

She spoke in a very low and sad voice and said, "Al, I tried to tell you that I have problems and I've never told you what they were or how it has affected me. I know what it is to live in pain and never want to wake up again. I told you this is my problem and I don't know how to tell you, but most of all I believe the truth may hurt the both of us. Furthermore, I love you too much to drag you into this. I will tell you that I have never kissed anyone as I did you or let anyone ever put his hands on me as you did. It was hard at first, but I became to really love it and I will tell you now that if I ever do more than that with anyone, it will be only with you."

After this, my heart was in my throat and I couldn't talk. She kept talking and said, "I'm probably no good for you and really believe that you could do better. If you do find someone else I will understand, but this is by no means what I want. All I ask from you is to please give me a little more time."

I interrupted and said, "Dorothy, I'll give you all the time that you want, but where is it getting us? I have been doing all I can, but all you tell me is that we could be friends and you can't love anyone." She started crying again, so I hung up and left the receiver off the hook. I decided that I wouldn't see her for a while, so I would just stay home and work on my car.

I knew that Ford had made a thunderbird engine that had a three hundred twelve cubic inch, cylinder displacement and I planned to strip it down and modify it to the limit. Then I knew mine would be the fastest car around. I would also redo my car as I did Zhasha before. My shop was complete and I started to work on my car. I ordered the engine and all racing parts and waited. During this time, I did not go out very much because I had several people asking me to do some customizing on their cars, but mostly painting and I was happy to do that. I was making extra money and it kept my mind off the confusion with Dorothy. I still saw her but it was just on a friendly basis. I didn't know why she was like that and I believed she should really want to be with me. I didn't believe any of her friends had ever treated her as I did, but somehow she appeared to love me in her own way. I told her I would wait for her, but I would date other girls. I did see Sparky and Jeanne, but became busy when my engine parts arrived. I then worked on my car and engine most of the time. I really thought Jeanne was beautiful, but I became afraid of her age. She was a lot of fun to be with, so I would still like to be her friend.

I still take them with me and always have fun. I think that was the only times that I laughed. I had stopped to see Dorothy and things hadn't really changed. She had only asked me to go out with her once in the past two weeks and it was always to the Bog. I told her I was too busy in my shop, but I would some time. I knew she had polarized my mind and for some reason I could never love anyone else. I waited until Saturday, and then went to her house because I missed her so much. I said I would not ask her, but leave it all up to her, so late Saturday afternoon, I went to see her. I went to her house and the door was open, so I just walked in. She was sitting on the couch and reading something. I asked her what she was reading and she said it was just a love story. I commented that "I thought you didn't like love stories", and she said, "What do you mean? I love them." I sat in the chair next to her and she asked what I had been doing. I said that in my spare time I played my guitar. She said, "You play guitar? What do you play?" I told her I played love stories and she laughed and said, "How do you play love stories on a guitar?" I said "I meant love songs". She then said, "Are you here to take me out tonight and how come you don't come here very much anymore? Don't you like me anymore?" I just asked her where she would like to go, but I should have known.

I was hungry so I asked her if she had eaten. When she said no, I asked if she wanted to go to the diner, because if I was going to drink, I wanted to have a full stomach. She asked if she could change first and then we left. I was not in a very happy mood because I didn't want to go there, but I missed her and at least I was with her now. I did not talk much and Dorothy asked if I was all right. I said, "I am just tired", but part of this was that if I didn't like it there, I could say I was not feeling well and wanted to leave. After I had a few drinks, I did feel better and we were dancing. She was being very funny and had everyone laughing. I was starting to have fun and tried to make the best of the night. She pulled me to the dance floor and we danced a lot. I couldn't dance well, but the more I drank the better I got and I was doing the California Be Bop. The very next dance, she pulled me very close to her and I just knew I would never stop loving her. I held her very close so I could feel all of her body against me. When she looked at me, I kissed her and she seemed to enjoy it. I was very happy and everything went very well until around eleven o'clock when three guys and two girls came in. They walked past us, and then said hi to Dorothy. The third and single guy asked her where she had been lately. She said that she had been staying home a lot and he told her she should get out more often, that it was good for her. She smiled and said, "Yeah".

I was surprised she didn't introduce me to any of them because she did have the chance. I could see a different look on her that I had not seen before. Her mood changed and she was not being a clown anymore. She asked me to dance and I did, but I really didn't want to because I felt shy in front of all her friends, although it was easy to do this dance with her tonight, because all she did was hold me very close and rub her body against mine. She told me that this dance was called the Grind and that it was popular here, but I said to myself, I could see why young girls get into trouble. This would tell me that a girl was looking for something more than a dance. But who was I to complain, because, I loved it more than anything else I've done. I noticed that the guy who had talked to her was staring at her a lot as we danced. I did not like facing him but I did notice that Dorothy tried to keep her back to him. When we sat down, I took the seat that was facing him and did not want her to be looking at him. We stayed about another hour and she did not have any more conferences with him, although she did dance with one of the guys who had a girlfriend. I did not try and stare at her, but I noticed that they did talk a lot. Shortly after that dance, she asked me to take her home. She did not want to stop anywhere and we went straight to her house. On the way, I could only think that there was something wrong and I was in the middle of it. When we got to her house I turned the lights and motor off, because this would tell her not to leave yet. I asked her what was the matter and she said nothing. I think she felt that I knew something was wrong. She slid over to me and put her arms around me. At that time I felt that I must know how she felt, but most of all, how I felt. She was holding me very tight and had her head on my shoulder. I pulled my head back and placed my hand on her face and turned her head.

I then placed my lips against hers and held her tight. I felt her try to pull back as if she wanted to stop, so I released my grip to let her know that she could have moved away. She then clenched us together and kissed me like never before in my life. I felt like I was made of butter and was melting in her arms. All the pain and worries that I had have disappeared and I thought that I had found my true love. We stayed that way for a long time when she finally pulled back and asked if I was satisfied now.

I told her no and pulled her back in to the same position. This time we did not kiss that long, but this was the closest I had ever been to heaven and I never wanted this to come to an end. She pulled back away from me and moved in her seat so she could face me. Before she could say anything I said, "I love you. I really do love you so very much." She stayed silent for a second and I waited for her to say that she loved me also, because it would be hard for me to understand anything different. She looked at me with big eyes and said, "You don't love me. We've only been out a few times, but what I did with you just now was to show you that I do care about you a lot and you are the best friend that I have. I hope you can see that and I'm sorry, because what I gave you tonight is all that I can offer for now. I really must have time to understand my own life and solve the problems that I have first. I'm sure in time, I will explain everything to you because you do mean a lot to me, but I can't right now." I was silent because I didn't know how to take this statement. I told her I hoped that I wasn't being pushy and she said that she had loved every minute of it. It was after one o'clock a m and she had to go in, so I walked her to the door. I told her that it was the best and most exciting night of my life that I understood and appreciated her being candid. She walked into the house and I left.

I drove home very slowly and was having problems trying to decipher and comprehend what was happening. My heart was pounding and I think I was trembling. I did not have a knot in my stomach but I felt weird and felt that I would not want to live without her. I could only remember while she was in my arms and our lips were together. But now I am not able to think straight. I am very confused about her statement that she only did it for me. In other words, she wouldn't have if I didn't push the issue. When is it going to sink in that she only wants me for a friend and maybe just a ride to find who she's really looking for? "You don't love me and you're the best friend I have." I waved that back and forth in my head and still could not evaluate the meaning. I knew in my heart and soul how much I loved her and didn't want to be anywhere else when I was with her. I went home, but could not go to sleep and did not ask her if she wanted to do anything tomorrow. She did not ask me to stop in to see her either. I started to play my guitar and played "Young Love". That was one of her favorite songs and I had tears in my eyes while playing it. I did not play my favorite song, "It's Only Make Believe."

I didn't think I could handle it right then and somehow I did fall asleep. It was nine o'clock Sunday morning, I had just awaken and needed a coffee, because my lips were numb and my throat was dry. I was looking back on the happiest and saddest time in my life. I thought that I might have been a little too pushy, so I decided not to see her today. I was told that absence makes the heart grow fonder and maybe if I don't push myself on her, she would respect me more. If I didn't go there so much maybe she would miss me as I missed her. I thought I would go out with the other girls and hoped she would find out. This would tell me whether or not if she really had any feelings for me.

Jeanne

I went to the diner first and there was no one there, so I drove up towards Sparky's house. On the way, I saw Jeanne walking and thought she might be going to Sparky's. I stopped to ask her if she wanted a ride, but she just hopped in and said hi. I asked her if she was going to Sparky's and she said no, it was such a nice day that she thought she would go to the town park. This was less than a mile from her house and I said I would take her there. We drove into the park and she told me that I would need a pass to be able to get in. They have a gatehouse with a guard and he checks your pass, which you must have on your windshield. I drove to the gatehouse and was surprised to see Red Pottenburg there, because he was a guard at the textile plant and a customer at the Ford place, so we greeted each other then talked for a moment. I told him that I was bringing Jeanne here and he told me to park by the gatehouse. He said that if it wasn't so busy, he'd let me park anywhere I liked. I said I know that and I'll come back to talk.

Jeanne and I walked to the beach. Then she went into the rest room and came out in a one piece bathing suit. She walked up to me and I said, "Wow, you're beautiful." She blushed a little and said "I know you're kidding". Then I said, "Well you are something very nice for sore eyes." She said that she was going into the water. I said, "All right, I'm going to talk to Red, but if anyone bothers you, just call me and I'll come running." She snickered and thanked me. I left her then, but I kept her in my sight at all times and just loved that much beauty all in one package. I talked to Red for about an hour while she was in the water with another girl. It looked as if they were having fun, but I did want to get back there. I walked back to the beach, then sat on a bench. She knew I was watching her, but I didn't care. She finally walked up to me and I could not take my eyes off of her. She looked young and I wanted to find out her age, but she was so cute, I just wanted to hug her, if you know what I mean. She sat next to me on the bench and asked "why were you watching me". I said, "I couldn't help it. I was looking after you and I did bring you here, didn't I?"

Smiling, she said, "You don't have to look after me, I'm a big girl now." I laughed and said "you're just a kid" and she snapped at me, "I am not. I'm

71

almost eighteen." I said, "I knew I could get you to tell me your age", and I was surprised, because she didn't look it. We just stood there and looked at each other without talking. I was looking into her eyes and she was searching mine from one eye to the other. I wanted to reach out and put my arms around her, but I didn't have the courage' although I don't think she would have stopped me. I was very excited, but I was scared and thought about Dorothy. I asked her if I could get her a hot dog and soda, because I noticed that they had a hot dog stand. She said she would like a pop. I said, "Coke?" She said that was fine and that she would walk over with me. I got a hot dog and talked her into a French fry because I don't like to eat alone. I asked her where she was going when we left there and she said, "Anywhere with you." She quickly added that she was just copying Sparky and that I could take her there if I wanted. I asked, "Were you really just copying her?"

She said, "Well," then paused, "you already have a girlfriend."

I said, "Maybe not." I did not elaborate but said, "I don't mind taking you to Sparky's house." We drove towards Sparky's house and she sat on the seat with both knees on the seat facing me. I knew she was staring at me so I said that I hope to see you again. She said "I'm sure you will." Sparky came right out and asked "where in hell have the two you been". Jeanne and I both explained but I do think that she is a little jealous. I said, "I don't know why you are asking all these questions, because I was on my way up here to see you." She said, "Really?" She went around to get into the car. Jeanne went into the house to change into dry clothes and Sparky asked me where we were going. I said nowhere, and she asked if I would take her to the Lark.

I said, "I really can't. I just came up to see if you were going to be around during the week." She told me that she is always around. I knew she liked me and could not see why she did. I was never very nice to her and never led her on. Just then Jeanne came out and stood by the car. Without hearing our conversation, she asked "where are we going now". I did not answer and thought to myself, I can't change my mind now. I said to Jeanne, "I thought you had to go home." She answered not until nine. I said, "I would have given you a ride back home, but I do have to leave." They both said no please, stay a little while. I waited then said, "All right, I'll take you to the Lark, but no hanky panky."

Sparky said, "You're taking all the fun out of life." We did go to the Lark, but didn't stay long and got back at six thirty. Sparky gave me a kiss on the lips and said she would see me during the week. I told her I would call her and left to take Jeanne to her house. I stopped in her driveway and she told me that she had a lot of fun. She thanked me and I said "I might see you during the week". She said "I will be looking forward to it". I think she knew that I liked her and I thought about how it would be to hold her in my arms. I knew that I was still longing for love that I was not getting from Dorothy. I watched her walk towards her house and for the first time, I knew that I could leave Dorothy. Jeanne was not that young kid I had feared, but a beautiful young lady.

On the way home, I stopped at Dorothy's. It was only seven o'clock and she was in the kitchen sitting at the table. She said they had just finished dinner, but she would make me something if I was hungry. I told her no thanks, but thanked her for asking. I told her she looked very nice. She said, "Thank you," then followed with, "I need you to do me a favor. Bill, at the Bog called me and asked if I knew anyone that could play some music, because they are having a party with some special guest at three o'clock Sunday. I told him that I would ask you, because you played the guitar very well."

I said, "But you never heard me play."

She said, "You told me you were good, and I know that you put your heart and soul into everything you do."

I said, "You could say that again."

She laughed and said, "Will you? Will you, please?"

I said, "No. I can't, because I have never played on a stage before."

She said, "Please do it for me."

I did not want to, but I saw such a change in her and the way she thought about me made me believe that she did love me. I said to myself, I think if I give her some time, we could be together. Not just in mind, but in body and soul. I said, "Let me go home and practice some things that I could play, that will last for an hour."

She said, "You won't have to stay up there for the whole hour." I did not say any more and walked out. Dorothy came running after me and said, "You didn't say goodbye or anything. Are you mad?"

I said, "No. I'm just thinking if I could do it." She put her arms around my neck, hugged me and picked her feet up off the ground. Then she said, "I knew you would do this for me." She gave me a big kiss on the lips and went back into the house. I went home and played a few instrumentals that I had written. I was sure that I could play for just one hour, even if I had to repeat or mock a few numbers. I really didn't want to do it, because I thought that I would fall apart in the beginning. But I needed the experience and I didn't want to let her down.

I went to work and thought about my promise, because I knew I would have to do it now. I had been there about two hours and Fred came over and asked for me to come to his office when I had a break. I said sure and went to his office with him. I walked in and sat in Charles' chair and Fred asked, "Have you heard any rumors about a union?"

I said, "No. Why?"

He said, "There are some workers who have talked to the T.W.U.A. (Textile Workers Union of America) because a union her now would probably close this place. Things are slowing down and there would be too much confusion." He asked, "Would you be in favor of a union?"

I said, "I don't know that much about a union." Fred went into some detail explaining it, and I said, "I don't like quotas." I agreed that a union might harm my position. He asked for me to keep my ears open and to let him know if I heard anything. I told him that not many people like me here and that most likely they wouldn't tell me anything.

We talked for awhile and he mentioned that Joe, our maintenance man, was leaving and asked if I would be capable of handling that department. He continued, "We are getting slow and we have already cut back in the Bleach House. We are only running one shift in some of the areas. We will also be cutting the shifts to eight hours and there will be no more overtime."

I really didn't know what this all meant and for the first time I believed that my life was becoming impetuous. I know that I responded impulsively by telling Fred that I'd try anything he wanted. I knew I could handle the electrical part, but I had little experience with the mechanics in that type of operation. I reiterated that I'd do what I could and Fred tried to reinforce my ability by telling me that if I could rebuild automatic transmissions, then this job would be a cinch. Fred then asked me how well I knew Joe. I said I knew him pretty well, that he was a friend and I had helped him a few times. Then he asked me to see if I could try to get Joe to stay a little longer, I told Fred I'd try. I went back to my frame and finished early, but I could see what Fred meant about us slowing down. It was just a short while ago that we were so busy and I can't believe things could happen so fast. I was worried about the union and really did not understand the complexities. I decided I would walk the floor throughout the plant, because I wanted to see what was involved in the new assignment. Some of the workers were looking at me and I'm sure they were wondering what I was doing in the Bleach House. One worker asked if I was lost and I replied nicely, "No. I'm being transferred to maintenance." He asked why, but I did not tell him. I just said it was to help Joe and I kept walking. I looked around and it didn't seem too bad, although I did have some questions. I went home and did not practice on my guitar because too many things were happening all at once and I was too tired. I woke up one hour early so I could speak with Fred. I went into his office while he was walking out. I told him that I did walk through the Bleach House and it seemed that everyone there wanted to throw things at me. He said that he understood and told me to come to his office before I left, because Charley wanted to talk to me. I felt better because Charley is a lot smarter than me and I respected his ability to communicate. I finished the work on the frame and started talking with all of the help on the shift. This was just on my floor which is one third the size of the Bleach House. I didn't have problems with the people that I worked with on my floor and I tried to get information about the union. The conversation did come up and most of the people were in favor of it. I did not participate in any way, nor was I asked. It appeared that all of the common workers were for the union. They said that they would get better pay and more benefits. I did not know and did not say anything. Charley and Fred walked in while I was still with all of the employees. They walked up to us and said good morning. They announced that there was a meeting at seven and that all employees were required to attend. They motioned for me to follow them and I went into their office.

Charley spoke first and said, "Fred has explained your conversation with him to me, which we have discussed. We are making many changes to the operation and will discontinue some of the products that we now have. The Southern and Overseas plants are underbidding us and we must meet that criterion. Fred is going out to meet with all of the employees to discuss with them their new hours that will take effect this Monday. You are here now because we want to offer you a proposal and need an expeditious response. This is our offer: your temporary hours will be eleven a.m. through eleven p.m. Monday through Friday and some Saturdays for equipment repairs. This will be only until Joe leaves and you get familiar with the new system. Then you will be on a straight seven to seven shift and your position will detail maintenance and head assistance to cover this floor. That means that if anyone has a problem, they will come to you for assistance. We have also placed you on salary and you will receive a raise in pay. Fred and I do have the confidence that you are more than applicable for this position."

I responded, "I will accept, but I do have a problem. Almost everyone in the Bleach House has ill feelings against me and that may create a problem.

He said, "Let us handle that, because Fred and I will have a conference with them and the first one that creates a nuisance will be fired". I asked if I could please be at that meeting so that I could be properly introduced?

He said, "I don't see why not." Then our conversation ended and Fred came into the office.

I reiterated to him, "I will do all that I can." Then we shook hands and I left. I worked with Joe and he showed me all that I had to know. I found it was less complicated then I thought *and you sit on your ass most of the time.* I told Joe what Fred had asked and he said that he could not stay, but he did say that he would give me his phone number in case I needed help. I thanked him and went home, because I had to get ready for my recital at the Bog.

My First Recital

I have not practiced at all and must this weekend before Sunday. The recital is scheduled to be at three p m and I want to be there at two, so I went to Dorothy's at noon. I think that she was more nervous than I was and was helped me get everything that I needed into my car. I told her I wanted to go to Al Pats before I went there because I did not want to drink on an empty stomach and I knew I would have a few when I got there.

We arrived at the Bog and there were more people than I expected. We sat for a while and talked with Bill, the owner and he thanked me for doing this at such a short notice. I told him it was a privilege and that I was looking forward to it. I set up stage, Dorothy and Bill both helped and I was able to use the existing sound system. I used their Sound Distribution Center which included speakers and pre-amps, then was able to use my personal amplifier, which had a reverberater and could produce echo chamber effects. When I was all set up I tried it out at a very low volume. I could tell that this increased my d b gain at least by one hundred percent. That made me happy because this would be the best system that I had ever used. I wanted another drink because it may have helped me calm my nerves. Everyone was there that they expected and I was so very excited. I prayed that I could make it through, then went on stage and everyone was looking. I practiced an opening that was kind of loud and I thought appropriate. I ran the pick over the strings while in the cord E and moved the trem-bar. This combination was wild. My opening was a combination of Duane Eddy and my own.

I had told them that all of my numbers would be instrumental and I would not sing. I started to play with the sound. The balance was perfect and the reverberation was awesome. This came out perfectly, but I think that the windows were vibrating and some people stood up and walked closer to me while clapping and shouting. Then they sat again, but I could see that they were happy when I looked at them. I looked at Dorothy most of the time, she was all smiles and I was so happy watching her, because I thought we would be together forever after this. She gave me thumbs up and clapped when I stopped. I also looked at Bill and his wife, Martha. They were together looking at me and Bill had his thumbs up. I could see the clock and noticed it was time to play some soft music. Without stopping, I dropped into some slow romantic waltz music. I played for twenty minutes, then sat on the stage. Bill was there in record time with a mug of vodka 'n Seven, which he knew I drank. Everyone started their dinners and I took a break to sit with Dorothy. She wanted to sit on stage with me, but I convinced her to sit where she was. I told her she was my moral support, but the real reason was that I wanted her to be there for my closing. I had to be able to see her and her reactions. My break was over and I was back on stage again. I started to play some soft dinner music and really didn't know the difference but they all enjoyed it.

After dinner I did a few more mixed combos loud and soft, then took my last break. Dorothy came to the stage and told me that she was very excited and never realized or dreamed that I could play that well. She hugged me in front of everyone and sat where she had been, so that I could see her. Everyone had finished and some drinks were served to them. Martha also brought me vodka 'n Seven, which I needed for support. Then I started with a combo using my reverberation and trem-bar. I again gave it all I had and this got all their attention. By now I knew that they all loved my performance and I was not afraid anymore. I really wanted to sing this song, but I didn't think that I would have the nerve. Well, I do now and I spoke loud and said, "I am dedicating this song to my very close friend "Dorothy". Her birthday is in a few days and this is for her." I played a few chords and sang her favorite song, "Young Love" and gave it all that I had. I could see the look on her face and the gloss in her eyes. When the song was over, they all clapped and we sang "Happy Birthday, Dorothy".

It was after three and I was exhausted. I put my guitar down and a lot of people yelled, "Please, one more!" I was lucky that this was a young crowd and I don't think there was anyone older than thirty. They would not let me say no and Martha came to the stage and asked if I could please play one more. I said I had planned on doing one more song. I walked to the end of the stage and said, "Does anyone here want more?"

I think everyone yelled at once, "One more! One more, please!" At that moment I was thinking that if anyone was watching from outside they would have thought that this was rehearsed.

I yelled out, "Alllllllll Riiiiiiiiiiiiight! I sang one for Dorothy, now I want to sing one for me." I did not think that was appropriate, but it came out and it was too late to change it. I then sang the song, "So Help Me I'm Falling in Love with You". Tears came to my eyes, so I held my head down as if I was looking at my guitar. Then I played one more instrumental, put my guitar down and faced the audience. I said, "Thank you for having the courage to be able to sit through this. This was the first time that I've ever performed on stage or in front of anyone. Thank you."

I turned and thanked Bill and Martha. They both came to the stage while I was walking down along with Dorothy and said, "You were great. We must say, you were the best entertainer we've ever had and would like to ask you if we could get you back again." I said that I would love to and we all sat at a table, because no one had left yet.

They were all still drinking and I had three or four more drinks that had no effect at all. I thought that I was in a trance and could not believe that I had done that well. Bill offered to pay me and I refused to accept it. I said, "I should pay you for the opportunity."

Dorothy said to Bill, "I told you that he was the best." We sat around for a couple of hours and I put my instruments back in the car. When I went back in Bill and Martha told me I did not have to pay for any drinks when ever I came here. I said "Thank You".

We sat there for a while longer and Dorothy told me that I really surprised her. She said, "You really are the very best and should really do this more because everyone here loved you." I told her I had always thought of making it my career, but I didn't know how to get started. Then I told her I was exhausted and wanted to go home. She asked me if she could please stay because she had promised Bill and Martha that she would stay to help them clean up and get ready for the night crowd. I asked if I could go home and come back to pick her up later. She agreed and thanked me for letting her stay. I walked out to my car, while she followed me out and hugged and kissed and thanked me again. I was totally flattered that I did so well and was very proud of myself. I knew I loved performing and wanted to do more, but between the excitement and the alcohol I really was exhausted. I just wanted to go home and get some rest. I thought about this all week and believed that this would bring us together. I thought I would never have a problem again, because she would see the real me and if she had any love for me before, this would be enough to fulfill her desires. I was counting on it on the way home. Then I laid down and fell asleep. When I woke up it was nine thirty. I didn't want to be this late, because I wanted to leave earlier and spend some time with Dorothy. So I rushed back to pick her up.

My Big Let Down

The place was packed when I got there and there was no parking places. I had to take a place in the far parking lot. I did not like to leave my car where I couldn't see it, especially here. I walked in the door and looked for Dorothy. I walked halfway through the crowd and noticed she was in the far corner with several other people. There were more guys than girls and she appeared to be happy. She noticed me and her laughter stopped but she came to greet me. I held her in my arms, but she pulled away from me and said, "Come sit with us." There were no empty seats and we sat with two other kids. She introduced me to them as her friends and explained to them that I was the guy that had played here earlier. They said, "I heard you were great". You must come play for us one night."

Dorothy did hold my hand under the table, but while looking at her it appeared that she had more to drink than I had ever seen before. She acted differently and it was not like her norm. I also noticed her speech was different and she was talking slower. Then a cold sweat came over me and I was lost for thoughts again. I looked at the band and by now they all knew that I was the guy that had played here today. Within the next twenty minutes, a lot of people came up to me and said that they had heard about my playing. I was flattered, but worried more about Dorothy. I noticed that I did not make friends with the band and got a few dirty looks. Dorothy did not say much, she only bragged about me but did not let go of my hand at all and I thought things may be alright.

Bill noticed that I was there so he brought me a drink where I was sitting and said, "You should keep her as your promoter." I felt like a celebrity, but I did want to leave. The band took a break and I asked Dorothy if she was ready to leave. She hesitated and then said, "Let me say goodnight to my friends." I said it was alright, so she went back to the same corner and stayed for a few minutes.

While she was gone someone came up to me and said, "What, are you looking to take my job?" He did not sound very pleasant.

I asked, "Why?"

He said, "I heard that you played here today."

I said, "No, Buddy, I'm not taking your job. I did this as a favor." Then Dorothy came back and was ready to go. I turned my back on him and walked her to my car. I told her I did not like to leave my car so far from the door and that was why I wanted to leave. On the way home, I tried to be very friendly and act as if everything was alright. I thought that she may have been excited about me and that was why she had more than usual to drink. On the way home she sat close to me, but not right next to me. I reached over and put my arm around her and pulled her over. She came right over and put her head on my shoulder. She seemed very tired and I did not push the issue, because I was happy to have her next to me. We reached town and I asked if she wanted to stop at Al Pats. She replied in a half-asleep voice, "No, I just want to go home." I drove to her house and shut off the lights and the engine.

She stayed where she was, so I turned her a little more by moving closer to the door and lifted her head. I put my lips to hers and pulled her closer and she didn't stop me or respond at all. I felt bad because this was to be the day that would make my life complete and here I was with a dead girl. I tried to arouse her with my kisses, but it didn't seem to work. She would just open her eyes, look at me and then close them again. I did not think she had enough alcohol to do this and I had to believe that she was that tired, because I never seen her drink very much. After all, I did go home and get some sleep while she was going all day.

I kissed her, caressed her body and one time by accident my hand went to her breast. I quickly moved it and didn't think she even knew. I asked if she was going to sleep. She said she wasn't and I asked her if she wanted to go to her house. She replied very slowly, "No, I want to stay here." I believe that this girl was dead tired and needed some rest. She seemed very content so I kept kissing her and never wanted to let her go. I kept caressing her and again placed my hand on her breast. This time I left it there and she made no attempt to stop me. I knew she was awake and tried to get her to respond, so I gently squeezed it. I tried to feel the shape, because I had never felt a girl's breast and wanted to explore. I was moving my hand around and squeezing it very gently for a while. I don't know how long but she did not move. Finally, she put her hand over mine and pressed my hand harder to her breast. I was happy that she was not mad, but she pulled my hand down slowly and said, "Could I go into the house now?"

I said, "Sure" and I will walk you in. But while we were still in the car, I asked her if she was mad at me for what I had done. I continued, "You know, that was the first time in my life that I ever did that. Thank you for not being mad at me."

She said, "Actually, I liked it." This made me happy and I felt much better. I walked with her to the house and she had trouble walking in, so I half carried her. She went straight to the couch and I stayed with her. I asked if she was alright. She said, "I am very dizzy and I feel very sick." I asked if there was anything I could do to help and she said she just wanted to go to sleep. Beatrice was still up, so I went to the kitchen and had a coffee with her. She asked how the night went.

I told her "Very well and everyone liked my playing, but I think Dorothy is exhausted from the excitement and she stayed to help Bill and Martha clean up". I went back to see her and she was still on the couch and I asked her how she felt again.

She said, "I'm getting very sick and I never felt this way." I thought she must have had too much to drink and was going to vomit, so I should leave her alone. I told her if there was anything she wanted or needed to please call me.

"I'll be right here," I said, I love you and kissed her goodnight. I told her mother that she may be getting sick and to please watch her. I said, "I don't think she drank very much and I don't know why she's sick. I wasn't gone for that long and she only had a weak drink the time I was with her." I went back once more to see her and it looked like she was sleeping so I went home. I was a little puzzled, but knowing that she let me put my hand on her breast did give me some confidence. I did not tell her about the remark that the band player made because I thought it could only complicate things more. I thought to myself, *I hope this just blows over, because I don't want people mad at me there. It seems like it is the only place she wants to go.* I went home and had trouble sleeping, but I did fall asleep.

I woke up at eight o'clock but I stayed in bed thinking about the night before and how excited I was. Her breast felt so nice, but the fact that she let me and pulled my hand tighter makes me feel that this was the closest we had ever been. I thought about my recital and was happy about that also. I waited until ten o'clock and I was going to see her then. I didn't want to be away from her any more than I had to and went straight to her house. I met Beatrice and asked her how Dorothy was. She told me that she was still in bed and wouldn't talk much. She just said she was sick and wanted to be left alone. Beatrice said I could go in and see her if I wanted. I said I would like to, and then I walked in to her room. She was in bed all bundled up, but it was very warm out and I couldn't understand that. I sat on the end of her bed and asked, "Are you awake?"

She turned toward me and said, "Yes, but I don't feel good. I don't know what to do." She was pure white. I kissed her on the cheek and asked her if she wanted anything. She said, "If you go anywhere, would you bring me some ginger ale?"

I said, "Yes. I'll go and get it now."

She said, "No, not now. I want you to stay here." She turned to look at me. When she turned I could see that her eyes were dilated and she did not look well. I thought to myself that it was not from drinking and something else was wrong.

While we were talking I asked her, "How much did you drink after I left?"

She said, "I didn't drink very much." Then she hesitated. "I had two drinks with you. I didn't have any more until much later and Bill makes my drinks weaker for me, but someone gave me one just before you came. I was fine until you came in."

I said, "You mean it's my fault?"

She said, "No! No! I mean, that is when I started to get very dizzy." I asked her if she vomited. She said, "I think so, but I was too weak and I was going to pass out. My mom took me back to bed and I don't remember any more." She looked like she wanted to go back to sleep so I said I would go get her soda. I left to go to the drug store on the corner and picked up some ginger ale, then went back to her house. She looked like she was almost asleep so I left her alone. I told Beatrice that I talked to the druggist. He said it is better to drink it at room temperature and let the fizz out, so I poured a glass, and then left it by her bed. I was confused and thought something else was wrong. I didn't know what or why I thought that, but I could see something in her eyes. I had been with her when she had drunk more than that and I had not seen that look before. One thing about Dorothy I knew was her eyes. I didn't want to stay there because I needed some time to think. I told her mother that I was going home and to please call me if she needed me. I felt hurt that she felt that way and was thinking that I should ask someone about this. I couldn't think of anyone to call, but I knew that Joe was a boozer. Joe worked with me and I thought that I would call him. He answered the phone.

I said, "I have a problem and hope you can help me. I don't know anyone else that I could call."

He said, "Go for it Buddy." I then explained the situation and he quickly said, "Someone slipped her a Mickey." I asked him what that was and Joe explained it in detail. I asked how much it would take and he said one glass could knock you out. I asked what happens. He said, "At first you get weak, tired, and you don't know who or where you are. Then you pass out." I thanked him very much and thought that she had all those symptoms, but she did not really pass out. I wasn't sure about anything and went back to see her. When I got there she was awake and still very faint, but could talk better. I thought about what Joe said and that she would have passed out if she had a Mickey. I then thought *what if she did not drink it all?* This could be what happened. Without using pressure, I asked her about the last drink that she had. I asked if Bill made her that last drink and she said someone else had brought it to her. I asked "Did you drink it all?"

She said, "I think I had a few sips and I don't think I drank much because it was very strong." She raised her voice and said, "Why are you questioning me?"

I said, "Honey, I'm not. I just think that you may have gotten a bad drink with something in it that made you sick. I don't like to see you this way, but I'm sorry. I just want to help you."

She smiled and said, "I know," and I asked her to do me a favor. She asked me what it was and I said, "I want you to drink this whole bottle of ginger ale, because it will flush your system." She said she would try to.

I filled her glass that was empty and she asked, "How do you know about this?" I said I had heard about it before and a lot of liquid could only help. I did not want to tell her that I suspected it was a Mickey. I wanted to see what happened first because Joe said he thought that it would take a few days to wear off. I stayed around for a while and she drank another glass of soda. I waited until she fell asleep and I had to go home. I got to hate the Bog and would like to burn it. I thought for a while and decided to go to the Bog because I wanted to talk to Bill. I started to drive there and thought, *this may cause more problems.* I did have Bill's phone number on the card in my wallet, so I turned around and went back home. I called him and told him the story that I suspected someone slipped her a Mickey and I thought it must have happened just before I got there.

He said, "We think a lot about Dorothy, but she is hanging with a bad crowd. There are about six of them that come here from Watertown and I do not like them. They are here almost every Saturday or Sunday night. They like to push people around and they are very rowdy. They're not nice to anyone and I do not make much money with them because they only buy one drink, just to get in. I am sure that they have their own stuff in the car." I thanked him very much and hung up. I thought for a while and forgot to ask Bill what time they arrived, so I called him back. He said about a half hour before you came in. This did support my theory, but I became concerned and I knew I would have to make up my mind after this. If Dorothy still wanted to go there I would have to break our relations. I thought, *Once again, from Heaven to Hell in just a few hours. It appears that I am getting myself into more problems, my lifestyle is changing. I'm drinking more than ever and I'm making enemies. I can't think well at my job and I'm sacrificing my future to be what I want. I have never had this much happiness and yet never this much sorrow.*

When I was a child, I thought of the hurt, sorrow and pain, but it was constant and I was used to it. I thought that was what life should be and I didn't know the difference. But the pain that I feel now was worse than going with rags on my feet, the beatings with a cat of nine tails, kneeling on split wood and the constant mental torture. That pain would go away and just leave scars on your skin, but this would leave scars on my heart forever. I searched my mind for answers and came to the conclusion that it must be my fault. I felt now that I would help Dorothy until she felt better. I had been in love with her for nearly two years now and believed that my life was worse now than before I met her. My life was becoming too uncertain to keep up to the changes with her. I was starting to think more about Jeanne and Sparky now, because I always had fun with them and they have never hurt me. I knew I should start dating someone, but my mind would always go back to Dorothy.

I took a ride to Al Pats and just had a coffee, because my stomach was too upset to eat. There was no one here that I knew so I drove towards Sparky's. I went slowly past Jeanne's house and she came running out. I stopped to let her in and she said, "Were you looking for me?" and I said, "How did you know?" She replied "I was just hoping". I could see that same look again and without thinking, I said, "I love having you with me." She had a beautiful smile and slid over right next to me. I was a little scared and told her I just told Sparky I was on my way, but she asked, "Do we have to go there?" and I said I had promised her, but I would like to go with you alone if we could.

She said, "I would love that." Then we did go to Sparky's. She had company that had just arrived, but she was going to ask me to take her to the Drive-in Theater. I said I would next time and Jeanne and I left.

I asked Jeanne where she would like to go and she said, "Anywhere with you, and I'm not copying Sparky this time." She was sitting close to me, so I put my arm around her and pulled her closer. I knew now that I was waiting for this to happen. She asked me about Dorothy so I told her we were breaking up and she said that Dorothy didn't deserve me anyway. We went to the lark and had a lot of fun. Then she asked me if I would take her to the Drive In theater and I said I would love to. That made me very happy and I believe that she knew it, because we could be alone. At the Drive In theater she sat right next to me and I knew she liked me, but for some stupid reason I started to think about Dorothy. I was staring at the movie, but I noticed that she kept looking at me. I turned to look at her and when I looked at her and into those big, dark eyes in the dark, they looked like mirrors and at that one instant I could not take my eyes off of hers. I was intrigued and could see the reflection of a new life in front of me. I was afraid to move because I didn't know what to do.

A New Love in a New World

She put her arms around me and put her lips against mine. Her lips were wet and warm and she moved in a way that I will never forget. She did not stop and I did not have the power or will to try. She stopped, then looked me straight in the eyes again and repeated. I knew that the night was hers and I could not stop her, nor did I want to. We were very cuddly the rest of the night and had lots of fun, while we talked about everything. I could see that she was very intelligent and I had a very enjoyable evening. I wasn't supposed to be with her alone, so I had to pick up Sparky to bring her with me, then take Jeanne home. I drove fast because I thought what if Sparky wasn't there? Then Jeanne would get into trouble. We arrived at Sparky's house early and Jeanne asked me not to say much to Sparky about the night. She said just to tell her we had a lot of fun and that it was a great movie. I prayed that Sparky would not ask me what the movie was about.

When we arrived, Jeanne called her home and they offered to pick her up. I don't think that I knew what love was and if that was love, then Jeanne was full of love. This night stayed on my mind for days and at that time and I was very happy. The strong hurt I had with Dorothy was gone and I thought that I would fall in love with Jeanne. I did not see Jeanne all that week and only saw Dorothy once in the morning. I wanted to talk to Jeanne but I could not call her at her home. Her father was very strict with her and she did not want him to know that she went out with me alone. I drove up her road a few times but she wasn't around. I decided that I wanted to go out with her again, but this time I would try to be free from thoughts of Dorothy. I finally met Sparky. She was with another girl name Marguerite, who was cute and very small, but she seemed to have a great personality. I picked them up and gave her a ride to the school and kept Sparky with me. I wanted to ask Sparky about Jeanne but did not want to hurt her feelings. She was the one that got Jeanne and I together. We rode around and I asked her if she would like a soda. She said, "Yeah, why not?" I stopped at Al Pats and just like all girls, she asked, "Do ya have any quarters?" I reached into my pocket and found none, so I gave her a dollar to get change.

I did not have to ask what they were for. What else, the jukebox. She came back with the change and I said, "Put it in the jukebox." She was hopping and half-dancing on her way over through the people. Totally no scruples and just a dumb ass kid, but I loved her like a friend. I was upset that she didn't mention Jeanne's name but I was lucky because she played the right song, and it was the third or fourth one.

She said, "Do you know this is Jeanne's favorite song?"

I said, "No," and asked her, "Where is she, anyway?"

Sparky said, "Oh, you didn't know? She was grounded this week."

I said, "Why? Not because of me, I hope!" She said it wasn't. She told me Jeanne had a fight with her father because she can't go out after eight o'clock during school days. I said I thought that was a good idea because school is important. I tried to find a way to get her out that Saturday, so I said, "Well, if she has no one to take her out this weekend, I'll take her out on Saturday.

Sparky jumped and said, "Oh, no way. You're taking me out Saturday night."

I followed quickly, "I did not say Saturday night, I said Saturday."

She said, "Well, I said Saturday night and will you please take me out?"

I said, "You know, I did tell you I have a girlfriend and I am in love with her."

She was a little snappy and said, "Well, you took Jeanne out. Do you like her more than me?"

I said, "Hell, no. She's a pain in the ass. All she did all night was throw popcorn at me. That's not a date." Sparky said that sounded like her. Then she asked me if I was still going out with Dorothy and I told her we were having problems.

She remarked, "Well, it's not my fault you have a dumb girlfriend. I told you that you should dump her."

I said, "Boy, you have the nerve to talk because Dorothy is the smartest girl that I know and just because she has problems doesn't make her dumb. But if I don't go out with her, then I will take you out."

She said, "My girlfriend's parents are leaving for the week and she will have the house to herself. It is on the lake and it is very nice." I asked her what she planned to do there. She said "the girl would have her boyfriend there also". I didn't know if that would be good or bad, but I told her that I would let her know Saturday.

I gave her my phone number and said, "Call me at nine." Then I suggested for her to give my number to Jeanne just in case she gets in trouble and needs help, because when I was with her I forgot to. Sparky thought that was kind of me. Friday late morning before Dorothy went to work, I stopped at her house. I was trying to forget her, but I knew deep in my heart she was number one in my life and what I was doing was just a cover-up for my failure. I knew I was forcing myself towards Jeanne, but I did like her and would have loved to take her to the Drive In Theater again.

Dorothy in Canada

I was glad that I did stop to see Dorothy, because she had a chance to go to Canada for two weeks with her relatives. I said, "Oh, my God, go. It will do you good."

She said, "Do you want to get rid of me?"

I said, "Of course!" Then I said, "No, I will really miss you, but you should go. Don't worry about me, because I'm sure I'll be here when you get back." I asked, "When are you leaving?" She said she would be leaving Monday and I said, "I will see you over the weekend."

She asked, "Do you want to go out tomorrow night?" And this was the hardest choice I had ever made.

If I followed my heart I would have gotten on my knees and begged her to go out, but I said, "Oh, I'm sorry, I made plans."

Her face dropped and she said, "Okay, what about Saturday?" I said I would stop in Sunday to see her before she left. I thought that my refusal to take her out would be on her mind while she was gone and I would be the last guy to see her before she left. I said, "I'll see you Sunday." But if she wanted to go out I would go with her, but she would have to ask me then. I was finding that the other girls wanted to go out with me more when I kept rejecting them. I did not like playing hard-to-get, but I didn't think a girl wanted someone who throws themselves at them. I gave her a hug without a kiss and left. I was sure that she noticed my change of heart and this had to bother her, even if she didn't love me. I went to work and thought all day about what I should do. Then I decided that I would take Sparky out. I still loved Dorothy with all my heart, but I did accept this as a failed love affair. I did not go out after work and just stayed home to play my guitar. This made me very sad about Dorothy, but I did not call her.

I called Sparky Saturday morning when I awoke and she answered the phone. I asked her what time she wanted me to pick her up and she screamed, "You're really taking me out?" I asked her "why, don't you want to go out with me"? She replied, "Oh, yes, yes, I do." She calmed down and I agreed to pick her up early. I went to my shop and finished some work that I was doing to my car. I repaired most of the shop and finished some work I was doing on my car. I repeated most of the customizing that we performed on Zhasha, John's Ford. It became time to pick her up so I got dressed, not fancy but casual. I left to go to her house, but couldn't pass Dorothy's house without stopping in for a moment, so I walked in. Beatrice was in the kitchen, but I did not see Dorothy. Beatrice asked if I would join her for coffee and I said I would love to.

I did not see Dorothy and did not ask where she was. I did not stay long, but did wonder where she went. Beatrice did ask me where I was going, and I replied that I had a date, but I don't think she was surprised. I drove to Sparky's house and she was watching for me, then came running right out. I couldn't believe that she looked so nice. Her hair was pulled back so I could see her complete face and she wore a skirt with a white blouse. For the first time I could see that she is not a smart ass kid, but a beautiful young lady. She hopped in, then slid over close to me and this time I did like it. I put my arm around her and held her close for a minute. I could see she was excited and that did make me happy, because I never showed her the affection as I did Jeanne. I asked her where she wanted to go, and she replied as usual, "Anywhere with you." I really didn't want to go to a party, but if I did have to I wanted a few drinks first. I decided to go to the Bog and this should cause a lot of rumors, or I may even find Dorothy there with someone because I was sure she didn't expect me to go there, especially with Sparky.

We arrived at the Bog and we went in and sat at the booth where Dot and I always sat. I was surprised that she was not there, because I did think she would be. Sparky and I did dance a few times and I could see she danced very well. She was asked to dance several times, but she rejected and I liked that because it told them that she was with me. I was proud of the way she handled it and she would not drink very much and she did not finish the first one that I brought her. We stayed for about two hours and Dot never showed up, but I did have several drinks. She said that this was her first time here and that she never went to these places. I knew that there would be talk, but Dot could not think that I was cheating, because why would I bring her here? We left and Sparky did want to go to her friend's house party so we went. On the way I was very quiet and she asked me what I was thinking about. I said it was nothing, then she followed with, "Is it Dorothy?"

I said, "No, she's going to Canada for two weeks and she's leaving on Monday," but that made me think about her. I didn't elaborate any further, but I knew she must have wondered why I wasn't out with Dorothy tonight.

I knew I had to ratify my absence and said, "I was just looking at you because you look so nice."

Mistake Or Good Judgment

We drove into the driveway and there was just one car there. I walked in with her and there was no one around. Then some girl yelled out from another room, "Is that you, Sparky?"

Sparky said, "Yes," and the girl said, "Help yourself to some drinks." But we didn't want anymore and she led me into a bedroom. The lights were bright and she just pushed me onto the bed, and then hopped in herself. I just laid there and she came close to me, she turned towards me then pulled me close to her. The lights were too bright, so I asked her to just leave the one on that was on the dresser next to the bed.

She then laid with me again and worked her arm under me and held me very closely. I got my arm around her and our lips went together. She pulled away, and then said, "You know, you're amazing and different." While looking at her I felt that she was about to question me and I did not want that now. I pulled her tight and our lips stayed together for a long time. She pushed me over so her face was on top of mine and kept kissing me while holding my head against the pillow. This was a new experience for me and I could feel my heart beating faster and my body getting warmer. I knew that I was trembling and wondered if she could feel it. I started to hold her tighter and could feel her tongue moving on my lips and against my teeth. I held her even tighter and broke into a cold sweat. I knew that I had lost all control and did not want to stop. My mind was searching for answers, because I had not had sex before and I believed that this was the feelings that took control of me. I became worried and wondered if this was what she wanted. She finally stopped and lifted her head and smiled while looking at me. I looked at her and could see she was leaving it up to me and it was my move. At that moment I felt that I loved her more than anything in this world and never wanted this to end. If you asked me this before I went out with her tonight, I would say you're crazy. I did not know what to do, so I pulled her close again and started kissing her as before. I turned more to my side because I needed more air and I was sweating more. My hand was on her back and she reached back and held it very tightly. I could feel her tremble as she squeezed my hand harder. I knew

I couldn't explain how I felt or what I thought, but I was very excited. She was very restless and was moving her tongue faster in my mouth while still moving her lips all over mine and caressing my body. She took my hand while we were still kissing and pulled it in front of her and placed it between her legs.

I felt that she did not have anything on under her dress then she released my hand and put her hand between my legs and held me. I left my hand on her because this was the first time that I did this and it was very exciting. She felt warm and soft and I felt I may have Russian hands and Roman fingers. I wanted to go further, but I knew then, that no matter what I do next would change my life forever, yet at this moment I wanted so much to continue. I knew while I had my hand on her and exploring, that I was getting very excited and was responding to the movement of her hand on me also. For some reason I thought about Dorothy and felt a strange feeling come over me. I thought that I shouldn't be doing this and she felt the chill come over me. I slowly moved my hand and then hers, because I knew that if I continued I would be indebted to her. She would own me and there would never be a Dorothy if my life again. Plus, I would lose any chance with Jeanne. I thought that I may be stupid and may regret it, but I did believe that I was not ready for this now, not tonight. I knew Sparky for a long time and never wanted to go out with her, so I wondered, *why do I love her tonight? Is this love or the power that sex has upon us? Is this the power that ruins so many lives and why so many girls have unwanted babies, along with so many divorces? If I do this tonight, what will this do to her? Will I be someone I can be proud of?* Before I could continue I needed these answers and I didn't have them now. I became very cold and choked up, and then tears came to my eyes. I was more afraid for her than myself and knew that I was still in love with Dorothy. I knew that I would not want to marry Sparky if something happened. She lifted my head and was looking at me while wiping my eyes. She said, "Don't be sad. I understand."

I said, "Do you really understand?"

She answered, "Yes, because this is just you and your pride. I know how much you wanted me and I know how much it took for you to stop."

I then tried to reiterate the thoughts that went through my mind and said at that time, "I never wanted anything more in my life than I wanted to make love to you, but what would it do to you after I left, because I am still in love with Dorothy?"

She responded, "This could only make me respect you more and you thought more about me than you did yourself." I was still choked up, but I pulled her to me and held her very close.

Then I told her this was far from being over because she was the first girl that I was ever intimate with and I would cherish these moments forever. No matter what happened, there would always be love in my heart for her. "I may find I made a big mistake tonight. But only time will tell."

I was not planning on spending the night here but there was no other place that I would rather be more. It seemed to have lasted a lifetime, but we were there just an hour or so. We both fell asleep holding each other, but she fell asleep before I did and I had the chance to really look at her. Her blond hair was really long, it was spread all over the pillow, on her face and she was a beautiful girl. I guess I was just so wrapped up with Dorothy that I never noticed. She was totally natural and I never seen her wear any makeup. I knew what took place tonight had changed me and I must reevaluate my priorities.

I awoke before her and was very quiet not to awake her or anyone else. I looked at her while standing by her bed and she looked so nice cuddled up with her hair all over her face. I was careful leaving the bed and looked for a piece of paper and a pencil. There was a pen stuck on the refrigerator and I had a piece of paper in my wallet. I wrote in big letters, "Love you. Please call me" and my phone number. I was able to leave before anyone awoke and went home. I made coffee, then sat on my bed and searched my mind. The more I thought about it, the more I wished I stayed there with her, because I didn't believe that I was fair to her and I should have not walked out on her. I could still see her in my mind on her bed and feel where my hand was and wished I had never left. I was not sure where I was with Dorothy and may have left someone that would really love me. I did fall asleep and awoke late, but I promised Dorothy I would see her before she left, but I didn't want her to see me in this condition. I had a lot of pain in my groin and didn't know why, because I had not had this much pain since I was a little kid, which I will explain later. I even had problems trying to pee, so I went back to bed. I did not sleep long and was thinking about Sparky and for some reason my feeling became very strong to be with her. Dorothy didn't appear to be that important right now and I thought that I did make a mistake by leaving the night before. I waited for her to call and I decided to write Dorothy a letter. I really needed to find myself now and more than ever, because I appeared to be falling back, and my life was changing at a pace that I could not keep up with. I finished the letter without saying much, because I didn't know how much to write and still no phone call. I picked up my guitar and started to play some of my instrumentals and was doing alright until I played Dorothy's favorite song again.

I became sad and wanted to see her. I still hurt too much to go there now, so I went into my work shop and saw that I was getting behind on my work, but just left it and decided to just take a ride to town. I drove around, then past Jeanne's and Sparky's house, because it was three o'clock and this was when I would find them walking. I did not see anyone, so I went to Al Pat's for coffee and sat for a while. I drove around town once more, then went slowly past Dorothy's house. Before I got there I noticed her standing on the porch, so I drove in as if I was going there anyway. She appeared happy to see me and grabbed my hand and we went to the kitchen. She poured me coffee and asked why I was dressed up so nice. I just answered that it was Sunday and I had a nice jacket on. During our conversation, I found that she babysat for her sister last night, with whom she was going to Canada with. She did not ask me anything about last night and I did not offer my whereabouts. She was in a funny and good mood, but I felt guilty about the episode with Sparky and felt she would hear about it at the Bog.

Dorothy was singing and had the radio very loud. Her dad came into the kitchen and yelled, "Turn that damned thing down!"

Dorothy just got up, turned it off, then grabbed my hand and said, "Let's get out of here." We walked past the living room and she said goodbye to her mom as we walked out. I said, "Where would you like to go?" and she said sarcastically, "Anywhere but here and let's never stop."

I said, "We must stop for gas." She said "Don't get smart". Just then I pulled into Al Pat's but she said, "No! I don't want to go here. Let's go somewhere that no one knows us." I didn't say anymore and drove to the Lark Drive In where I took Sparky and Jeanne.

On the way I said, "I was surprise that your dad yelled at you like that."

She said, "Oh, that's nothing, because he always treats me that way and we just don't get along." This answered my question why he never came and sat with us. The music started playing and she became in a much better mood. I pulled her over and she came without hesitation, and then kissed her on the lips. She slid back towards her side and stopped. Then she said, "You know something? You're good to me."

I replied, "I'm sorry, but that's just me."

She said, "Don't be sorry. It's beautiful." I then asked her about her job and she said, "I quit yesterday." I asked her why? and she said "they wouldn't give me time off to go to Canada". The next statement put my heart back into my throat. She said, "I will be eighteen when I get back and I could work at the Bog. Martha asked me if I would and I said I would let her know when I get back." I could feel the blood draining from my face and my smiles were gone. She asked me what the matter was.

I didn't know what to say and hesitated, but finally I asked, "Why do you want to work there? There are always fights and drunks around. You may get hurt."

She interrupted me and said, "Honey! I can handle myself and I could make a lot of money just on tips." I dropped the subject and did not ask anymore. I was still thinking that she called me "Honey". This was the first time and it meant a lot to me. I believed I still had a chance with her, but only if she didn't take that job. She did not say she wouldn't and I was worried about it. I had recently been told about a problem that happened to her there, and I knew that if she did take that job, our relationship would deteriorate. This was forced to the back of my mind and I never wanted to reveal it. I thought she noticed the change in me, so she moved close to me and put her head on my shoulder. This was the first time she came over on her own. We stopped at a traffic light and she turned to me and kissed me. This was the Dorothy that I had always hoped for. I drove the long way home along the lake. This would put me past Sparky's and Jeanne's houses, but I had no intentions of seeing either one. I was just wishing that when she returned from Canada we could get married. Then she wouldn't have to work at all.

We drove into her driveway and I noticed another car there. She said it was her sister, the one she was going to Canada with. I was properly introduced and we were all laughing and being funny. Her name was Charlotte and I was happy that she was there because she said the magic words. She looked at Dot and I, then asked, "Well, when are you two getting married?" I wanted to say, "As soon as she gets back." I left it up to her to speak first and she said with emphasis, "I'm never getting married." I didn't know how to take that or liked what she said and asked myself, *Why can't she be like Jeanne or Sparky?* They were ready to leave so I did kiss her good-bye, but it did not affect me as before. I didn't feel any warmth from her and instead of hugging me she made that remark. I had a complete different feeling and thought I may never want to see her again. Everyone applauded, then they left, but I was still very hurt after that remark and I believe she is telling me something. After that statement, I believe that her actions today were not candid but just to influence me to wait for her return so she may have a taxi service. I must refrain myself from being naïve and not listen to my heart.

My Job and My Life, Falling Apart

Things got very rough at work and I heard that they might vote in a union. I was told that I might have been part of the problem, because I made foreman in such a short time. I was offered the position of Chief Engineer in charge of maintenance, but it appeared that everyone there hated me. I went back to Fred and Charlie and said, "We must have a meeting with the employees before I could consider". We did schedule a meeting for the following week, and I would be allowed to speak. I did sympathize with the employees, because I had been there just over a year and made it to where I was, while some of them had been there on the same job for forty years. Before we could conduct this meeting, the plant went on strike. I had to fight to get in and I was threatened so I walked across the train tracks to the back entrance. I stayed there for almost a week without leaving. The week there was terrifying and I ran as many machines as I could, plus the maintenance. The strike ended on Friday and I was happy, but not knowing what was ahead.

Searching For Love

I awoke late and it was after ten o'clock. I cleaned up and went to Al Pat's for breakfast, but there wasn't anyone there I knew, so I went back home and cleaned the house. I waited until the afternoon and became very lonely. I remembered what Dot said, so I decided to look for Jeanne. It became very cold now and was nearly freezing out. I drove up Lake Road and went very slowly past Jeanne's house, but she was not around. I went past Sparky's house and found the same. Again I went past Jeanne's, turned around and went up Lake Road again. I drove further this time because I was deep in thought and didn't want to go back home. I drove down past her house again and went to the stop sign to go back to town. There was still some snow on the ground from last night and I believed they didn't want to come out. I started to turn towards town and Jeanne came running to my car.

I let her in and she said, "Boy is it cold." Then replied, "I was looking out the window when you went up, and I knew you were looking for someone. But what took you so long, were you looking for Sparky?"

I said, "No way. I just wanted to give you time to get ready and come out." She asked me how I knew she would. I replied, "I didn't. This time I was just hoping."

She said, "Why? Did you miss me?"

I said, "You bet I did," and asked her where she was going.

She said, "With you of course," and I told her that was wonderful because I wanted to see her. Before we got to Al Pat's she asked if we could go somewhere else because she didn't want her father to know she went out. I suggested the Lark and she said that would be fine. As we drove away, she came over and hugged me, saying, "Boy, did I miss you." She put her face in front of me and started kissing me. I did not push her away, but I did have trouble seeing through her hair.

She stopped and started laughing, so I asked, "What in the hell is so funny?"

She said, "Boy was my father mad at me, he could only see me now." We stopped for a stop light and she started kissing me again, but I moved away and she said, "He grounded me for a week for going to the Drive-in Theater without asking him."

I said, "With me?" and she said, "Oh, he doesn't know who." I said "how did he find out, it was me". She replied Oh! Sparky told him but he doesn't know it was you."

I said, "Really, she ratted on you?"

She replied, "Not really. Sparky has no boundaries or goals and goes anywhere she wanted, but sometimes forgets that I can't." I asked her "why did you tell me that it wasn't because of me". "Well, it wasn't, because the biggest thing was when I told him it was none of his business. He slapped my face and told me to go to my room. Then he said 'I don't want to see you",' and I replied "I don't care" so he grounded me. I was surprised because I was never grounded before." We drove into the Lark and she started hugging me, saying, "I am so happy to be here with you. Let's just talk about you and me." We ordered some food and while we waited, she asked me, "Where's Dorothy?"

I said, "In Canada with her sister." She asked if I was still going with her and I said, "Yeah, she wants to get married when she gets back." Jeanne was snappy and sarcastic, and then said, "To who? Not you, I hope." I said I was just kidding, but I was very sorry that, because things had happened between us that made me want to be with you, "besides, If I didn't care about you, I would not be here now."

She came back over and held me again, so I asked her when she was getting married, and she replied, "Well, you haven't asked me yet." I laughed and said, "You're a real screwball, but I like that."

She said, "Why? You don't like me?"

I said, "I drive up and down the road in the freezing cold, looking for you because I don't like you.

She said, "I am very happy that you do like me. I love being with you." She said, "By the was, I have a job at the phone company, my mother got me in". I will just be working some nights and weekends until three p.m. if that's alright with you.

I asked, "What does this have to do with me?" She said it was just in case I came to look for her. I said, "Well, I was planning to take you out every night this week."

She said, "Good, because I don't start until next week."

I said, "Damn you! I can't even tease you, because you always win."

She then said, "Do we have to stay here? I would like to be alone with you for a while before I have to be home." We left there and I told her what I told

Sparky about her just throwing popcorn at me all night. She said, "Yeah, she told me that, pause, why did you say that?"

I said, "Well, I didn't want to hurt her feelings because of all the times she asked me out, and I would never go out with her. I just felt sorry for her and the other night was the only time I ever kissed her.

Girls Like to Talk

Jeanne looked at me strangely and said, "That's not all you did with her."

I said, "Oh? What else did I do?"

She said, "Well, you stayed in bed with her all night."

"Yeah? What else?"

Jeanne was very quiet and said, "Well, she left the rest up to me."

I said, "Boy! You girls like to talk! What do you think I did?" She looked down and said, "I didn't know". I said, "Do you think I had sex with her?" She again said "I don't know". I said, "Could I ask you a question?" She said "Yes", and I replied, "What are you doing going out with me?"

She said, "I was hoping it wasn't true, because I want you to like me." This was a bad subject for both of us and I didn't like to see her so sad and confused. I knew what Sparky wanted her to believe and she didn't deserve this. I took the back road home and pulled into a parking place. I felt that I had to prove to her what did happen that night. It was almost seven o'clock and I asked her what time she had to be home. She said, "At least by nine."

Maybe Getting Careless

I just looked at her in the dim light from the street lamp and she was more beautiful every time I looked at her. I said, "What would you like to do?"

She answered, "I just want to be with you." She was not sitting close to me, but not close to the door either. I reached my hand to her and she took it and slid very close to me. We held each other tightly while our lips met and this was when I realized I was falling in love with her. We stayed that way for a long time without saying a word, only stopping to look at each other at times. I did look at her and could see those big, dark eyes searching for answers. I could see and feel the innocence in this young and beautiful girl, with no idea what was out here. In the wrong hands her life could be ruined, but I knew it wouldn't be by me.

I started kissing her very sexually and doing things with her that Sparky did to me. I put my tongue in her mouth and moved between her teeth and on her gums, because that is where it is sensitive. I tried to pull her tongue into my mouth to suck on it and she did let me, then she did it without fear. I pushed her away and started to kiss her neck and nibble on her earlobes, then went back to her lips. I could feel and taste that she was sweating as she pulled away then she asked if she could remove her sweater. I helped her take it off, because it was very heavy wool and I knew it must have been very hot. But I also knew that this girl had never been this far before. I just looked at her and knew this innocent girl did not have a clue of what she was doing. I pulled her over and said, "I know that I could really love you," but I knew I shouldn't have said that.

She replied, "I do love you very much." It was too late to retract, so I just went back to where we were. She felt so good without her sweater, and I could feel her body against mine, while our sweat was running together. Her neck was wet, but I liked the taste of her. We changed the position that she was sitting in to face me and I had my arms around her while caressing her body. Then I would go close to her breast, because I wanted to see if she would let me put my hands on them. Her blouse was loose and I put my hand inside and had my hand on her stomach. I caressed it, then moved my hand up towards her breast and lifted them. She quickly moved her hand down forcing mine away, but did not stop kissing me, so I knew she was not angry. I did not want to give her a break, because I felt that I had to prove a point and she might realize what I was doing. I started to kiss her neck again and placed my hand under her blouse and onto her stomach again. I rubbed her stomach and back to her breast again, but not long enough for her to stop me. I wished I hadn't because I had to control myself even more now. When I touched them I could feel her muscles tighten, so I stopped and just held and kissed her.

I turned her around and pulled her closer and just held her tight. She pulled back so I could look at her and I knew how much she meant to me now. Then again, I said, "I know with time, I could really love you," but, "I think you should go home now". Then I emphasized "This was the most exciting time in my complete life. Thank you for that and you are everything that I thought you were."

She replied, although her voice was shaky, "This was mine also and I know now that there is no other place I would ever want to be. Thank you."

We sat apart for awhile to dry off and I said, "I am still troubled about what Sparky wanted you to believe and it was not fair to you. I believe she wanted you not to like me, because she really wants to go out with me. I will tell you the truth and you can put it into proper perspective. I went much further with you than anyone else in my life and I gave it all I have to push you to the limit. But I could see that you are very much as I am. I believe Sparky is traveling down a dangerous road and just wanted me to be another notch in her belt."

I pulled out and started to take Jeanne home and she said, "I don't have to go home yet. Can't we stay a little while longer?"

We did stay and during our conversation I asked her, "Would you please tell me the truth? At any time tonight, did you really want to make real love to me?"

She answered, "No!"

I said, "What more would I have to do?"

She replied, "Well you did push me to the limit and I loved every minute of it. I let you go this far only because I thought that you do love me and I did love you, but while in your arms tonight, I know now that I really do love you. But there is nothing you could have done except to force me, and I know I would never go out with you again."

She kept talking and I did not hear all she said. My mind drifted back to Sparky, whom I am now angry with. This episode that Jeanne experienced and the statement just made by her, brought back the memory of the conversation that I had with Beatrice, Dorothy's mother. I had promised her that I would never reveal this, but it is on my mind now. Jeanne told me that she only had a few small school dates where she experienced some kissing, but she got the nerve to exploit me from Sparky. Sparky explained everything that there is to know about sex and what guys like the most. I told Jeanne that I believe Sparky is starving for affection and this was the only way she could get it. But I knew that she was your friend and I didn't want to interfere with that. I assured her not only did I not have sex with Sparky, but I had never had sex with anyone. "You said you love me and yet all we have done so far is sit in a car and hug and kiss. This can tell me that this may only be sexual infatuation. The only thing we have demonstrated is that we could be lovers through sexual desires and don't know any more about each other. You also mentioned that you listened to Sparky to learn about sex, which I believe was just to try and satisfy or entice me into liking you more."

She interrupted me, "Could I please say something?" She said, "Yes, I did listen to Sparky, but not to learn about sex, but to learn how to avoid it when someone like you tries to go too far. I also felt that you were testing me tonight, because this happened right after I told you about what she said, and this was not the usual you. Well, could I ask, how did I do and did I meet your expectations?"

I said, "Honey, more than you could imagine and if we accomplished anything tonight, it was to open the door of opportunity to explore real and true love. But you mentioned that I tried to go too far. That was not my intention and I would never want to lose your trust. But I felt that I had to prove to you the truth concerning that unfair statement."

We drove into her driveway and it was just before ten o'clock. I asked her if she would get into trouble. She said, "No, but I may have to introduce you to my father."

I said, "Oh, no, not tonight. Just look at me and could we make it for tomorrow?"

She said, "I think so, but you are coming anyway, aren't you?"

I said, "Yes, and I would rather meet your parents then." I got out and opened her door, then walked her to the door.

She asked, "What time?"

I said, "How about two o'clock?" She said that would be fine, then she went in.

I left and was driving home when all of this hit me. I could only think about the conversation I had with Beatrice. This was also what Dorothy wanted to tell me someday. I believe she was too embarrassed to tell me and since I didn't mention it she felt comfortable. She must realize that this is why I don't want her to work at the Bog. It had become time that I reiterate the problem as I was told, but this came second-hand from Beatrice that was told to her by Dorothy. I could only believe that this was the truth, but I reserved the right to believe that the content my not be complete. I will have to wait to hear it from Dorothy.

Dorothy's Revelation:
The Night of the Jackals

One night, while dancing at the Bog, I danced with this guy nicknamed Cat and I started dating him. I had only been with him here at the Bog and have not gone out with him to other places. He was one of a gang and all his friends looked up to him as a leader. Several girls were also involved and always hung around with him. He has always treated me well and boasted to his friends about how beautiful I am. This night he kept offering me drinks and telling me, "Come on, drink up." I only had two drinks that Bill or Martha made for me and they were always made weaker for me. While we were dancing, someone made a drink for me and Cat told me to drink it. I did not want it, but they made fun and embarrassed me, so I did. Shortly after that I felt strange, dizzy, and wanted to fall asleep. Cat and his friends coached me into his car and we went to where I believe was his house. On the way he did not drive, but was with me in the back seat and kept trying to feel my breast. I was very dizzy and weak and couldn't stop him. He then put his hand between my legs so I squeezed my legs together and he couldn't do anything. But when we arrived at his house there were other couples there. He grabbed me and started to take off my shirt, but I stopped him. He shoved me back into a recliner and pulled off my jeans, while his friends held me down. The other guys and girls were watching and laughing, but I held onto my underpants. I knew what was happening and I did not have the strength to fight them off, but I did not let go of my underpants. The other guys and girls had their hands on my breast and were digging their fingers into them. While they were holding me down, Cat tore my underpants off and tried to stick his fingers into me. It felt as he was pushing very hard and it hurt so I tried to scream, but nothing would come out. They were still pulling on my breast and one guy took out his penis and was stroking it in front of me. Cat then got on top of me and tried to stick his penis into me. Just then I was able to scratch at his hand and went for his eyes. Then somehow I was able to scream and I did as loud as I could, but they would not stop. The others told Cat to stop, because someone would hear her and they'd get into trouble. Just then I was able to escape and run out of the house while I kept screaming. I was dressed with my torn blouse and somehow I was not as drunk as before, although I was very dizzy, weak, and sick. I kept screaming, "Help me, someone," as loud as I could. This appeared to be a busy neighborhood, but no one came to help. Two of the girls and Cat ran out after me and tried to quiet me, but I kept screaming, "Keep him away from me." I heard the girls tell Cat to leave me alone and they would handle it. I asked one of them to get my clothes. I started screaming again. "Get my clothes now and I ran down the road to where I could see more lights. One girl came after me and told me to please wait, that she would bring my clothes. I did, then she brought me my jeans and shoes and I asked her where my purse was, then someone ran it out to me. I started running down the road and no one followed me, so I started to walk.

It took all I had to continue, but I made it to a gas station that was still open. I spotted a pay phone and called my father. He asked me where I was and I had to ask the man in the office. Then I went back and told him where I was. As soon as I hung up, I became very sick, but I did make it to the rest room before I started vomiting. I could not stop and believe that this is what they call the dry heaves. I was still too sick to go outside, but I didn't want to miss my father. I did make it out and spotted a Coke machine. Lucky I had my purse for the phone and the Coke, but as soon as I drank it, I started to vomit again and ran back into the rest room. It seemed as if I waited for hours, but he finally got there. I did not tell him what happened, because I thought he would go there and get hurt. He is just a small man and not a fighter. I was still very sick and my vagina and breast hurt very badly. All the way home I was very sick, but I knew now that someday I would have to find a way to tell him. When I arrived home, Mom was waiting but I did not tell her what happened on the phone. I tried to get out of the car and my legs felt like rubber. She came running out and we made it into my bedroom. She undressed me and helped me into the shower while I explained that I was raped. I smelled of alcohol and vomit and was happy to wash it all off. My mom was alarmed that I was bleeding from my vagina, but I was too weak and tired to care. I laid down and must have passed out and awoke late in the afternoon, but I was still very sick. Mom made me drink ginger ale and I stayed in bed until that night, but I did get up only for an hour or so. I explained what happened to my mom and she said I was bleeding. I was still sore there and my breasts were all scratched and hurt. She checked me and said that I stopped bleeding, but I should try and rest. The rest of the story is self-explanatory.

In reviewing her revelation, I hope that you understand why I was reticent and not forthcoming, to accept the criterion that has impaired my ability to be comprehensive. I have spent weeks searching for answers and if I find them, I will be able to accept the consequences. Was this provoked because she is imperturbable or did she fall into the wrong hands? Why was she drinking alcohol at a bar at the age of sixteen when state and federal laws prohibit this abuse? It hurts me to think about it and I must restrain myself from being reminiscent. I have come to the conclusion that if I do find the answers, it will be because of my relations with Jeanne. But I am afraid now that I am leading Jeanne on for my own satisfaction and using her, because I made a promise to Dorothy made me indebted to her. She has given fair warning that she could not love anyone until her personal problems were solved. I could have left then, but I really felt that she was everything that I ever wanted and now wonder if I should attempt to reconcile or incorporate her problems into my own life. I have been true, decent and pure and should I accept a second-hand girl for my beloved wife? But until I hear the truth from her, I believe that I must feel this way. I would have been satisfied with this episode, but the dilemma of extended circumstances has me concerned. Ever since I have known her, her main concern was going to the Bog and there must be reasons beyond my comprehension. I know I must find if this is a continued affair, vengeance, or both. I do understand that I incorporated these problems and must dispose of them in their proper perspectives. But I must realize that it was not I that has kept us apart, but her own mistakes and they appear to continue. At this time, I do believe that she will never vanquish her past encounters, then I will lose her anyway. Without Jeanne, I will have completely failed and once again, be alone.

Parental Permission

Today is Sunday and I hope that Jeanne does call me to meet her father. I also hope that they like me and let me date her, but she is almost eighteen years old and I know she would find a way, even if they didn't. I would rather have it turn out that they do like me, because I really want to be with her as much as I could. I was very nervous and thought I would go to breakfast first. I went to Al Pats and had a coffee, but could not eat. It was still early and I thought I would go to church, which I hadn't done in a while. I went to Saint Francis Church and felt very good to be there. It made me feel clean and want to do right. I went back and waited for Jeanne to call, but I decided to go there early. I had not seen Sparky nor had I tried, but I would have gone out with her again. Because in my heart, she is just a little girl and I knew how girls liked to brag about who they went out with, especially when she tried to keep me from Jeanne. I had just arrived at her house, Jeanne saw me drive in and met me at the door.

She said, "What are you doing her so early?"

I said, "I'm nervous and want to meet your parents now."

She said, "I haven't told him yet, because he didn't ask me where I went last night."

We walked to her door and her father said, "Who is it Jen?"

I told her to tell him that I was there to introduce myself, so she said, "It's Al." Then we walked in and she explained it to him. I was very nervous, because I had never had to do this before. I walked into the living room where he was watching television, but he did turn to looked at me.

I said, "My name is Al, and I am pleased to meet you."

He said, "My name is Robert and the same here," but without pausing, he said, "So you're the guy that's been taking my daughter out and may I ask, how long has this been going on?"

I said, "Two weeks ago, we went to the drive-in theater. Yesterday we went to the Lark Drive-In Food Stand and I have taken her there before with Sparky. Other than that, only when giving Sparky a ride home and when she asked if I would pick up Jeanne, because she was walking, so I did take her to Sparky's."

He then looked at Jeanne and said, "So he's the one that took you to the drive-in.

She answered, "Yes, he is."

He then said to me, "And why didn't you come here to pick her up?"

I replied very diplomatically, "This was not planned and the original plan was to take Sparky, then she asked me if Jeanne could come with us and I said sure. When we got to Sparky's house, she decided not to go, but I'm sorry that I did not come here and ask permission, but that is why I am here now"

He followed with, "I haven't seen Sparky get anything right yet."

I said, "I have not seen her lately and I heard a rumor that does not agree with my lifestyle."

He said, "I know what you mean and I tried to tell Jen not to hang with her."

I interrupted him and said, "From what I have seen, you could really trust your daughter, because she is a real lady."

He said, "Thank you, and I want to keep her that way."

I wanted to tell him that he could check my credibility with Lee at Ford and the owners at the textile plant, but I didn't have to. There was a football game on and he asked if I would like to stay and watch the game. I said "I would rather take your daughter out to lunch".

He looked straight at me, eyes wide open, "Boy, you're persistent, aren't you?"

I said, "Not really, I'm working a lot of hours at the plant, just trying to keep it running. Right now, I am loaded with obligations and don't get out much."

He asked, "What do you do?"

I said, "I'm an engineer."

He asked, "What kind of engineer?"

I replied, "Electrical and mechanical, I do all the repairs in the plant."

He said, "How in the hell old are you? You look like a kid."

I said, "I am a kid. I'm nineteen."

He said, "At least you're honest and respectful." Then he looked at Jeanne and said, "Why aren't you dressed?" Jeanne ran to get her sweater and Bob looked at me and said, "I want her home by nine o'clock."

I said, "You can count on it."

Jeanne was almost out the door when Bob walked over and said, "Thanks for coming to introduce yourself. You're a gentleman."

I said, "Thank you very much."

Then I walked with Jeanne to the car. I walked to her side, opened the door for her and waited until she got in, then shut the door. I did not know if Bob was watching or not, but I would still do the same. I got into the car and Jeanne said, "Boy, you made a good impression on my father. He seems to like you and doesn't mind me going out with you."

I said, "It pays to be honest. I really don't like to lie, because one small lie could lead to much larger ones."

I was just sitting in my car thinking about her father when and she slid over and sat right next to me and said, "What are we doing sitting here?"

I said, "I'm sorry, I'm just happy."

She said, "Oh, I'm so very happy also." Then we drove out. We were driving away from her house and she already had her arms around me. I seemed to like her more every time we went out. I asked her where she wanted to go and she said "to Al Pats, because I want everyone to see us together. She made me feel so proud and I had every reason to be proud with her. She was playing the jukebox and was so much fun to be with, because she never talked bad about anyone. We stayed there for about an hour, and then just drove around. We went to Danbury then to Rogers Park. There was a large pond there and we watched the kids ice skating. She kept holding me and said "I am so very happy to be with you". Then continued "I had thought about this ever since you the time that you took me to the lake at the town park. I really hoped that you liked me then and wished that someday you would go out with me". I told her that I also wanted to get to know her better and would have loved to take out with me. But I did tell her that I have problems, but I did not care to elaborate now and get off the subject.

I just pulled her over and kissed her then and said, "I should take you home early because I don't want to abuse the privilege your dad has granted us."

She said, "Please, not this early. Can't we stay here for a while longer?" We were at the far end of Rogers Park and most everyone had left. I looked at her big eyes while they were studying me, looking from one eye to the other. She was the only girl who did that and I could see that she was earnest. I couldn't think of anything, but to just hold her closer and keep kissing her. Our bodies were close together and I loved this very much. We loved each other as before, and then I took her home. I was very tired and told her that I would be working a lot this week and most of the nights also, but I would call her.

Brains or Seniority, You be the Judge

Monday morning, I had just arrived at work and when I walked in, Fred was waiting for me. He asked me to come to the office. We discussed what the main events were and the order we would execute them, but in our conversation he mentioned that things were really slowing down and the union might force them to lay off and shut down some departments, because the new union is not helping. They want more overtime, more benefits and they complained about people like me getting the best job here. I said that wasn't true, that I only do what I was asked to do. He said "I know that, but most employees had been here for years on the same job". I replied "it isn't my fault, if they had any brains they also could have done better". Then I asked him "who do you have here that could run the number six frame if I wasn't here". He agreed, but said "that isn't how the union looks at it". I was screaming mad and said, "Fred, we must have a talk with all the employees and I want to be there, Please!" Then he promised that he would arrange it.

We finally had the meeting and after Fred and Charley explained everything, it did not appear to resonate to the workers the importance of this meeting and it made me very upset. I walked in front of Charley and Fred and said, "Don't you assholes know that we are doing everything that we could, just to keep this place in operation?" "I myself tried to quit because I have a much better job waiting for me, but is there anyone here who can handle all the maintenance or operate all the equipment in the finishing department? I don't see anyone raising their hands, so if I quit, the Bleach House will be closed in a month and all of you will be looking for a job." I lowered my voice, "Do you understand?" Some did say yes and I just walked back to the office.

I looked back and Fred and Charley had followed me. They closed the door behind them, while they were laughing and said, "Boy! That was some speech; we never knew you had it in you, because you are always so quiet and low-profiled."

I started laughing and said, "I really got pissed off, they are all idiots."

I went back to work and had to run the frame, because Frank quit. This put everything on my shoulders and I knew I couldn't take it much longer. I knew that I would have to leave here soon but would give ample notice.

At six o'clock I called Jeanne and explained what happened. She wanted to go out, but I explained that it may not be until the weekend. I finished work at eight o'clock and went home to make something to eat. Then it dawned on me that Dorothy would be home in two days. I never thought about her, because I was too wrapped up with Jeanne. While in bed, I remembered that her birthday was soon. I knew I had to get her a present, because I knew she would be calling me to take her to the Bog. I really hoped she changed while she was there and if she does take that job there, I knew that I would break off with her. I would feel that she is looking for someone other than me.

Today was very hectic at work, but we are slow and I am leaving at five o'clock. I called Jeanne and she answered on the second ring. I asked her why she always answers the phone and she said because I thought it was you. She explained that her father never answers it and her mother works the second shift. I told her I didn't ask for a speech, and then laughed so she knew I was just joking. I asked her, "How's chances for going out to dinner with me?"

She said, "I'll go ask my dad." She did, and said that she would have to be back early. I went straight there, walked to the door and thanked Bob. Jeanne grabbed my hand and walked with me to the car. She said "my father likes you because you have manners and appeared to be very intelligent". She slid over and started hugging me as we drove off. We had a nice dinner, and then went next door to the garage parking lot. She then asked if we could go somewhere more private. I could see now that she had become very much involved with me and I wondered if I was making a mistake. I don't know why, but for some reason, the image of Dorothy always appears in my mind and I become confused.

Jeanne spent most of her time saying how much she loved me and that she could never accept losing me. I told her she should always prepare herself for the worst. She asked, "Why? You might leave me?" I held her in my arms and said it would hurt me very much and I would suffer for a long time. I pray to the Lord to give me the strength, courage and wisdom that will render me the right decision and that he should lead me through these difficult times. We must ask for help from a power that is greater than our own. She appeared to be confused, but kept holding me.

I said, "Honey, when I'm with you, I feel as though we are one and belong together. To change the conversation, I told her that the shop was closing soon and if not, I might quit anyway. She is always very understands.

Back From Canada

Wednesday afternoon, the snow really started coming down and the wind was blowing harder than usual. We were very slow at work and Fred told me we would be closing soon. I didn't worry about a job because Bob and Chape from Sega's Redi Mix already had tried to hire me. I had told them I would be there in the spring. I left work at seven and stopped to see Beatrice. She was happy, but didn't ask where I had been. I told her I was dating another girl. She was very frank and said that she couldn't blame me. I changed the subject and asked when Dorothy would be home. She said there was a very bad storm, so they had started later, but they should arrive by nine pm tonight. I finished my coffee and told her I was going home to shower, but to please call me when she gets here. I waited until nine o'clock with no phone call, so I decided to go there and wait. Beatrice sat with me and had coffee while we waited, but still at ten o'clock there was no word. I became very restless and worried, because I did not think this over and I had this awful feeling in my heart. I didn't know if it was love or fear of a mistake that I might be making. I was really lost and confused. I was thinking about Jeanne while we were parking and knew then that she was all I ever wanted. But now I am not sure.

Pure Love or Total Mental Destruction

Just then, we heard a car drive in and Beatrice went to the door. and yelled, "They're home." My heart went into my throat and I couldn't get up to help. Dorothy was the one to come in and was not carrying anything. She came running towards me, so I stood up to greet her. She jumped up and put both arms around me and started kissing me. I was in shock and just put my arms around her to hold her up when I noticed she was crying.

She said, "Oh, my God did I miss you, so very much. and I couldn't wait to get home."

Her sister said, "My God, that's all she talked about." Dorothy looked at me and I could see the tears in her eyes as she said, "Did you miss me?" I just said of course, but a lot of things had happened. She then burst out crying and then asked what, so I told her the plant was closing. She interrupted and said "I really didn't think you would be here waiting for me. She was squeezing me, but when I heard that I couldn't handle it and started crying myself. I thought about Jeanne and really choked up. I walked outside not knowing what to say or do, because I knew I just couldn't hurt Jeanne.

Until now, I thought it was over with Dorothy and never thought this would happen. But now that I am with her, I knew there was so much love trapped inside me for her. The cold air enabled me to breathe better and Dorothy was standing there waiting for me to make a move. I put my arms around her and picked her up and kissed her like never before. I let her down while she stepped back and said, "I love you so very much and missed you more than anything in this world." I started crying again, because I could not believe this was happening. I don't know how to accept it and this is the first time she ever said she loved me.

I became totally lost and uttered, "What in the hell are you doing to me? One day you don't want me and the next you love me." My heart was beating very fast and I needed time to think about what I was doing. I didn't know what to say or do, so I just held her in my arms. I could feel she was crying harder and all I was doing was making things worse. I did think about her life and thought, *How much more could she take?* I knew how much I did love and wanted her, and it had been nearly two years that I had been waiting to hear those words.

Then someone came to the porch and yelled, "What in the hell are you two doing out there?" We did not answer nor did we feel the cold, but she looked up at me with her big crying eyes and said, "I am so very sorry, but I never realized what I was doing to you. You can leave if you want."

I didn't know what to say, so I just held her and finally said, "I came here in this storm to see you and now you tell me I can leave." She said "I didn't mean it that way, I just didn't want to hurt you anymore.

Just then, something happened and my mind was completely free of thought, while looking at this little girl standing in this freezing snow crying and pleading to me because she loved me. While looking at her, I could see all the beauty that I longed for so long and I knew now that her love occupied my heart. I knew then, that there was no more room for anything else. I melted into her arms and waited for her next move. She said, "Could we go into my bedroom? I'm getting very cold now."

I said, "Yes, Honey." So we sneaked in and laid on her bed.

While she was holding and kissing me, she asked, "Did you really miss me?" I just kept kissing her and didn't reply. She didn't respond to my refusal, but instead asked, "Will you please stay here with me tonight?" I asked where and she said, "Right here in bed with me." I paused and said yes, that I would love to. We were still dressed in our heavy clothes, so we took off our wet jackets and shoes and hopped in bed.

She pulled the blanket over us and I asked, "Won't anyone get mad?"

She said, "I'm old enough to do what I want and I'm sure my mother will be happy." I did not answer because I knew she was right, and her sister had left already. We laid here for a long time while kissing and caressing each other's bodies. While laying here I thought about what happened to her and wondered if she got over it, or if it would become a new problem between us. I knew that I must find that answer and this must be an invitation to heal my thoughts.

Encounters of the First Kind

I didn't think that anything I did would be sinful and she should realize that I was a man with feelings also. After loving for a while, I put my hand under her blouse and was caressing her stomach, then up towards her breast. I could feel her tighten, and then grab my hand to stop me. I rubbed her stomach and she said, "Please, I can't do that. Could we please wait because I am afraid?" I said "I just wanted to see if you could get over what happened to you and just wanted to help. I pulled away and we looked at each other with just the light from the street lamp.

I said, "I really do love you so very much and want to know if you would always have this fear." She did not answer me, so I asked if I could just put my hand on them. She pulled me closer and just kissed me, then took my hand and placed it over her blouse on her breast. I felt them both for just a short while, then she removed my hand. I said, "They feel so nice and I have never felt any before now." We just laid together while saying sweet nothings and I put my hand under her blouse again. I stopped when I came close to her breast and she pulled my hand away and sat up. I was afraid she was leaving but instead she removed her blouse and took her bra off. I could not believe this was her, but when I put my hands on them, I knew she was someone that I really loved. I kissed them lightly and she pulled my face closer.

I said to myself, *I finally have my life's dream.* I had my hand on her leg and could feel her skirt was pushed up so I started rubbing her legs softly. I moved my hand further every time and finally between her legs. She jumped and pulled her legs together and said, "Please, could we wait," while looking at me with big, scared eyes.

I said, "Honey, you must trust me. You know I will never hurt you or do anything to upset you. I'm just afraid of what happened to you and I'm sure I could help. I know what you went through and I would never attempt to do anything you did not agree to".

She said, "I'm sorry, but I hope you understand." I said "I do, but you must give us both a chance". "I'm not saying that we should make love now, but just trust each other" She said, "Thank you. I do trust you with my life, and I'm sorry."

We were close together again and this time she took my hand and placed it between her legs. I just held it there tightly without moving, because I could feel her muscles tighten. I kept kissing her then on her neck and earlobes. I started to move my hand softly and she did not try to stop me, then moved her legs to allow me more room. I was very happy because I felt now that she could get over her problem, and I believed that I discovered the difference between love and sex. I was here in total freedom and knew she wanted me to be here with her. I did not have any guilt, but was very content and discovered that she had also found contentment. She laid there very comfortably, so I left my hand there and we both fell asleep.

We must have fallen to sleep around three a.m., but I don't know why I woke up at six thirty and went to work. I did not awake Dot because I knew she needed the sleep. I had a very bad day because I was very hurt about what I would tell Jeanne. I couldn't keep my mind on my work and Marty asked me what was the matter. I told him I was sick, so Fred let me go at two p.m. I just wanted to go home, but I had this problem with Jeanne. I knew I would rather die than hurt her and knew that I had to call her. She was just getting out of school, so I decided to meet her at her house. I drove there and she was just walking to her house. She watched me drive in and came running over. She looked at me and asked, "What's wrong?" because I appeared very tired and worried.

I said "I don't feel well and Fred allowed me to leave work early". She replied, "I'm so sorry, but I'm very happy to see you." I looked at her and never hurt this bad and thought *this beautiful little girl has so much love to give, but what am I going to do?* As bad as I felt, all I could do was grab her and squeeze her as I cuddled her. There was no one there, so she let me lay on the couch. She squeezed alongside me but I fell asleep. I heard Jeanne say, "Al, my dad will be home shortly." I apologized and walked towards the door, but she grabbed me and asked, "When can I see you again?"

I said, "I will pick you up Saturday," then drove out. The nap made me feel better, but instead of going home I wanted to see how Dorothy was doing, so I went there. I couldn't believe it, because she was still in bed.

She heard me come in and yelled, "Come in here," so I went in. She held her arms up for me to come to her and as I went to kiss her, she pulled me onto the bed. I asked her how come she stayed in bed all day. She replied, "I was really tired and had nothing better to do." She said, "What time did you leave this morning?"

I said, "Just after six."

She said, "You must be dead tired." I said "I am and I don't feel very well". She helped me take off my jacket and shoes, then covered me then she went to help her mother with things. I must have fallen asleep right away and she came in and kissed me and said, "Are you hungry? because we just made dinner."

I said, "I'm not hungry, but I do want to get up now." I went to the kitchen and we talked about her trip, but I did not stay very long and went home. I fell asleep again and slept until ten p.m. I took a shower and was hungry after the long day, so I drove to Al Pat's. I found that my personal life was starting to affect my ability to be rational. I was very confused and didn't know what to tell Jeanne besides, "I am not sure of who I really want now." My complete life was in a ramshackle. My job was falling apart and no one appeared to like me there except the management. I didn't know why because I tried so hard to do what's right. Sometimes I thought I should just leave because I believed I was becoming a gypsy, but where would I go? I had never been out of my home state before. Fred and Charlie asked me to please stay and help remove all the equipment, because it was being moved to the Derby textile plant. I agreed that I would terminate the electrical and gas supply and have the equipment ready for removal. I went home and thought about Christmas, because I must get Dorothy and Jeanne a present.

Sudden Death

I called Dorothy and told her I was going shopping and wanted to go alone, but she pleaded to me that she wanted to go with me. I asked "how could I buy you a present if you are with me". Then she asked "do you have to buy presents for anyone else" and I said "yes", so she said, "Well, I'll help you pick them out and you don't have to worry about me."

I said, "Yeah, great. Do you think I wouldn't get you a present?" Well, here we are shopping, but I will admit that we were having a lot of fun. We finished shopping, but I knew I would have to still go shopping for her and Jeanne. We stopped at a restaurant in Danbury, then went to her house. Beatrice was waiting and I could see she was very happy. She was talking with Dorothy and I heard them talking loud while I was in the bathroom.

Beatrice said to her, "I told you that you were stupid for not listening to me before. You know that Al's the best thing that ever happened to you."

She did not stop and kept picking on Dorothy and just as I walked out Dorothy screamed at her, "Mom, why do you always do this to me? I do have a mind of my own, so please let me think for myself." She was still screaming, "I hate you, I really hate you sometimes." I was speechless and just stood there, then Dorothy looked at me and said, "You might as well leave, can't you see that I'm too stupid for you?" She then ran into her bedroom crying and I never seen her this way, as a matter of fact, I never seen anyone this way before. Her eyes were wide open and she turned pure white.

I was upset and didn't know what to say, so I just sat for a minute and Beatrice said, "I don't know what's wrong with that girl," but I did not answer. I went into her bedroom and never knew things could happen this fast. I laid in bed with her and just held her without saying anything, but I could feel her trembling. Dorothy told me that her mother was always doing this to her and now I could see the problem. She stopped crying and turned to face me with big, scary eyes. I had never seen her this way before.

She said, "Do you know why I hate her? I can't do anything right and I always have to please her. Sometimes I hate you too, because she thinks you are some kind of God or something. 'Well,' I told her, 'I don't need a God to live with,' then she turned away from me. She put her face in the pillow and wouldn't answer me. I sat on the end of the bed and felt as if I was punched in the mouth. I waited for her to turn and say something, but she stayed with her face buried in the pillow.

I said, "The problems you have with your mother are not relevant to out affairs, but I won't be back until I know the truth." because I don't deserve this and I believe that there is more that I should know". I left quietly and went to my car.

I went home thinking that she had serious problems with her mother and her mother was killing her own daughter without knowing it. I believe that I may be too prudish and should change but I always wanted to be myself, but I found now that my only problem in life was with Dorothy. I did not find myself prudish with anyone else and I was far from being provocative, because I always yielded to others to avoid hurting feelings. I did not blame this all on Dorothy, because she had mentioned that her mother was always running her life and blamed her for the rape. She had always forced Dorothy onto me and never let her have her own mind, which has been our problem right along. I could see even more that she needed help, but I didn't know how I could help in this situation. I finally fell asleep and awoke early. I worked until noon and finished with the electrical, then went home to change. I wanted until two p.m. for a call from Dot but with no luck. I was very worried about her, because I had never seen her this way before. Just minutes before, she was so happy and loved me so much. I went to Al Pats for lunch, because I didn't have any food there and I had not been taking good care of myself lately. I was losing weight and I was always tired, but I just had a coffee and couldn't eat. I drove to Jeanne's house, hoping to see her. The I realized they may be in the middle of lunch. As I drove in, Jeanne came to the door and I met her there. The door was open and I heard, "Who is it, Jen?" and I asked, "Is that your mom?" She said yes and I said I wanted to meet her. She was in the kitchen doing dishes and Bob was not there, so I sat with Jeanne. Her name was Betty and when she came into the room, I stood up and said, "Good morning. My name is Al."

She replied, "I know who you are. I hear enough about you from Jen and now I'm starting to hear it from Bob.

I said, "Thank you," and she said, "I know more about you than you think," and I know many people that you work with". I said, "Oh, my God. What do they say about me?"

She remarked "do you really wanted to know. I answered "Yes"! And she said, "At first, they thought you were a brown nose always getting everything you wanted and a lot of people were mad."

I said, "Why? I always treat everyone equal and I am always polite."

She said, "It's not that, they just couldn't understand why you got the jobs you wanted, when there have been people ahead of you for years." I said "I believe that I met their qualifications and I thought that Fred and Charlie knowing my last boss helped, but I was asked to take these positions. I was not as if I forced this on them". She answered, "I also know Lee and I am friends with Eleanor. They care about you very much and said you are very intelligent. I replied, "I like them both very much also, and I still visit them." She asked, "May I ask why you left there?"

I said, "Yes, because, I could not be myself and I was interrupting the balance that was there before me. I felt like I was in an environment where I couldn't get ahead."

Bob walked in while we were talking and said, "Betty, why are you questioning him?"

I said, "No, she not. I'm asking her these questions." We continued, and I asked, "Well, what do they think of me now?"

She replied, "Well, once they got to know you, they thought you were a great person, maybe a little shy but showed respect to everyone." I asked if that was it, and she said, "No, they said you appear to be very intelligent and do your job very well, but you try and do too much."

I said, "I'm glad to hear that."

Jeanne interrupted and said, "Mom, he's here to see me, not you." Betty said, "Come on, I do have the right to know the guy you're going with," then said, "Okay, I'll leave you two alone." I told her that it was a pleasure talking with her and to please let me know if they say any more. Jeanne pulled me to the couch and I sat with her and Bob. I told Bob about all the problems we were experiencing at work, and I felt sorry for all the other workers that had been there most of their lives. I reiterated that the place was closing and most likely this month, but they offered me a job at the Derby plant, where I would be a supervisor. I continued, I would probably have to move there, and Jeanne interrupted and said, "You're not leaving me, are you?"

I answered, "No way. Besides, I don't care to stay in the textile field.

Bob asked, "What do you think you will do?" I answered that I already had a job waiting, and I would be driving a tractor trailer for Sega Redi Mix. He said, "Bob and Chape?"

I said, "Yes, but I just want to do this until I go on my own. I have been working on a home course in electronics and may get a job with Litton Industries in California."

Jeanne jumped up and said, "Dad, I'm going with him."

He just said, "My dear, after college, then you can decide."

Jeanne said, "Al, can't we leave now?" so I told her to ask her dad. He smiled and said yes. She took my hand and kissed me in front of her dad, and then we left. I walked to the car with her and thought, *What a great family this is.* Because of my own life, I didn't know there was anything wrong with Dorothy's family until I met Jeanne. I was always happy and carefree with her and her family. Jeanne said, "What are you thinking about?"

I said, "You and your family are always no nice to me." She sat close and hugged me, but I did not have that warm feeling as before, because I was still very confused. My life was becoming impetuous again and I couldn't keep up with it. She turned to face me and said, "Al, what's wrong?"

I said, "I don't know, I just don't feel well. I haven't been eating well or taking care of myself at all. I may be coming down with something. I am only twenty years old and I feel I've lived a lifetime. It appears that everything is always up to me and I don't know if I have the answers.

She said, "I don't know what you are talking about. This is not you." I put my arm around her and drove into a parking area. It was very cold out so I left the engine running, then I pulled her close, but I did not see that sparkle in her eyes. I kissed her, but I could feel she was holding back and I knew that I hurt her feelings.

I pulled her tighter and told her, "The only time my life is worth living is when I am in your arms." I felt very sad for her and my eyes clouded over. Then I said, "I feel content. Thank you for making my life worthwhile."

She looked at me and said, "Thank you, I needed to hear that because I don't think you know how much I love you," and I said, "Honey, I do." We became like old times again, but for some stupid reason I was still worried about Dorothy, but I knew I must break the bond that ties. This girl had shown me so much happiness and we had never had any cross words. Being in her arms, I wanted to fall asleep so I didn't have to worry, but the girls may be right when they told me that Dorothy didn't deserve me. But I didn't see it that way. If she had a decent family it would be different. Her father didn't care and her mother was killing her without knowing it, so who did she have to turn to? I may be too reticent or naïve, but I was afraid to speak out because of my childhood. I knew I must overcome it, but I thought I'd come a long way so far. I had never received and love before now and I didn't want to lose any that I get. I guess I was silent for too long and Jeanne said, "Al, what's wrong?"

I was really lost for words, because I knew she was right, so I said, "Honey, I told you that I don't feel well and if I didn't want to be here, I would tell you, but there just no other place in this world that I would rather be. You are the only girl who had kept me happy, it is Saturday night and where am I? You asked about Dorothy and I said she was a problem. I want to tell you a story and you tell me what to do." I explained to her about the rape, what her mother does to her and her father doesn't even talk to her. "I am very afraid she may retrogress and kill herself or her mother. She has no one to ask for help and pleads to me. I'm afraid that I can't help her anymore, but if something does happen, I will feel very responsible, because I may be able to avoid it. Besides, you have such a wonderful family and can't imagine what it is like living in hell all the time because I know, I was there."

Jeanne was very solemn and said, "I don't think this should be your responsibility, but knowing you I do understand, but why don't she move out?"

I said she really didn't have anywhere to go. In all our conversations, I had learned that she wanted to hurt the guy that raped her and I was afraid of what she'd do. "But I should find out before she does and I promise that if I can't solve it soon, then I will stay out of it."

She held me tighter and said, "I just never want to lose you because I love you so very much." I said, "Thank you for being so understanding, because if it was the other way around, I don't think I would be."

When we returned to her house, she took me to her bedroom, because she wanted to show me some drawings that she made for a school project. They were so nice I couldn't believe she did it and I told her so. I asked her if she knew anything about music and said, "Yes, I had two years of music in school. Why?" I told her I played the guitar and wanted to write some songs. She said, "I'll help you if you want." I said I would love it, if you did. She then said, "I remember you played in New York for Dorothy. Where is she, anyway? "Is she Still in Canada?"

I said, "No, she came home last week," and did not elaborate any further. To change the subject, I said, "I will bring my guitar here sometime and we could get together." We then went to the living room and she told Bob and Betty that we were going to write some songs together.

They asked, "Why?" and she said that I played the guitar. Bob said, "Are you bringing it here?" and I said yes. He said, "Oh, good, I want to hear you." I went straight home and expected a phone call, so I waited up until midnight with no luck. I said to myself *It may be better if she never calls me again.* I fell asleep with the phone close to my bed and awoke at 9:00 a m with no calls.

I stayed home most of the day and did some cleaning, but I worried about Dorothy and hoped nothing happened to her. I was just walking out when the phone rang.

I thought it was her, but it was my dad. He asked me if I could meet him later and I said that I would be there. I called Jeanne and told her that I had to meet my dad, but would call her right after. She always had the right words to make me feel good, so I asked her if she wanted to take a ride with me. We went to Al Pat's and had a nice lunch, then I asked her if she wanted to meet my dad. We drove to the farm and I introduced her to my dad. She said, "I am pleased to meet you and Al has told me a lot of things about you."

He replied, "He also told me things about you," and she quickly asked him what. "He said you were a beautiful girl and I could see that he was right." She smiled and thanked him. He then said, "You're Bob's daughter, aren't you?"

She replied, "Yes, I am."

He said, "I know Bob very well."

Then I interrupted them, because I was afraid he would mention Dorothy because he is also a friend of her family. I knew he was planning to build a housing development and he wanted to show me the plans, so I said, "Let's go."

We reviewed them and it looked very well planned. He wanted to walk the site with me, so I asked Jen and she said sure. We then drove to the site that would become the new Mountain View Terrace development. We walked to the top of the hill and he pointed out the main road and the avenues. He said he would need my help running the bulldozer. I said, "Sure, call me when you're ready."

When we finished with dad I asked Jen where she wanted to go and she said, "Anywhere with you, but we could go somewhere to be alone."

I said, "Yes, I want to go to a different world with you. She said that would be great." I drove up behind the textile plant, because no one ever used this road and there was no one there now. We took off our jackets and she sat with her legs away from me as we did before. The light was dim, but I could see her beautiful shape, which made me want to hold her even tighter.

I started kissing her neck and ears again and put my hand under her blouse. I slowly lifted her breast, but she pushed my hand down, so I said, "I promise I won't try anything else and you can trust me to behave." She then said, "Okay, but just for a second." Her bra was tight so she lifted it up for me, but I wished I hadn't done that. I felt them all over and became very excited, because they were so firm and yet so soft. I said to myself, *I better stop now*, because I was trembling.

She said, "What's the matter, don't you like them?"

I said, "Honey, that's the problem, I love them so much that I don't trust myself." She asked if I really liked them that much and I said, "I love them because they are yours and I love you for what you are."

She said, "You make me so happy. Thank you for thinking about me. You must know now that I really love you and always will." We were quiet for a while and then she said, "Do you think we will be together forever?" I said that I hoped so. Then she asked, "Do you think we will ever get married?" I said "I hoped so". She followed with "Do you think that we will ever have children". I said "I hope so". Then, without me paying attention, she said, "Do you think we could start now?"

I said, "I hope so."

"What did you say?"

I said, "I want at least twelve children," and she said, "You're gonna need more than one wife," and I said, "I think I could arrange that."

She slapped my face easy and said, "I know who you have in mind." I pulled her back and said that "if I ever had two wives, they had better make another one of you", but I thought I would have my hands full with just you. We just hugged each other and were very happy together. On the way home she said, "I loved it when you did that with me," and I said I loved it also, but we must be sensible and careful.

Being with her I completely forgot about Dorothy until I was alone again. I knew I must get her from my mind, but the phone was ringing when I walked in, so I ran to get it and it was my dad. He wanted me to help him stake off the avenues and asked when I could. I told him I would try to get out of work early tomorrow. He did all the planning himself to save money and I thought he did an excellent job. I did not mind helping him all that I could, because he was my dad and everyone else was gone now. John was in the United States Marines and Mike was in the Army. We placed stakes on all of the avenues, and then I went home and fell asleep without calling anyone. When I arrived at work, I was called to the office and was told that the J Box that I installed suddenly shut down. They called Joe to see if he could help and he was there when I arrived so we both examined it. Before I could work on it, the machine had to be cleaned and flushed with a neutralizer, because it operated on concentrated peroxide. This could remove your skin and flesh in seconds and I must emphasize the safety concerns. I was told that shortly after I installed it someone threw a live cat into the bin. It jumped out, but was dead before it hit the floor and all its hair fell off. Everyone that operated the machine was well aware of the danger. When I returned the bins were pumped down and were flushed with a neutralizer. I examined all of the circuits which operated in millivolts and found them to be constant. But after several tests, I discovered that a very small amount of peroxide leaked in to the safety circuit due to a defective gasket and I was able to repair it. The peroxide acted as a conductor and shorted the circuit.

I went back to the frame and examined our work schedule. We did not have much work scheduled and were really slowing down now. I said, "It is too late to start the frame now, because we'll complete all this tomorrow." I went home and took a shower, because I could feel that strange feeling after working with concentrated peroxide. I did not have any plans for today, so I thought I would just rest, then go to the diner for dinner and then go shopping for the Christmas gifts. I still hadn't heard from Dorothy since last Friday, but I felt I should get her a present. While I was eating I started to think about Jeanne, so I went to the phone and called her. She answered the phone, and I said, "How's my sweetheart?"

She said, "I'm fine, but I miss you so much."

I said, "Come on, it's only been two days."

She said, "I know, but I miss you even if it is one day." I said "Don't be silly and asked her what she was doing". She said, "Why, do you want to come to get me?"

I said, "I would love to, but I can't make a pest of myself."

She said, "Oh, please come."

I said, "I will tomorrow. Oh, by the way, Sparky called me." Jeanne asked "what did she want". I said, "I thought you guys were friends?"

She said, "We are, but I don't want you to go out with her." I said I didn't mean on a date. She said, "But she lied about you."

I said, "She didn't lie, she just left it up to you."

She spoke louder and said, "Are you defending her?"

I said, "No! There is nothing to defend because we both know her and don't have to say anymore."

She said, "Yes, I guess you're right." Then I asked why in the hell we were talking about her, and Jeanne said, "You started it."

I laughed and said, "I'm sorry, but she did ask me to her up sometime." She asked "what did you tell her". "I said I would call her to let her know, because I just can't shun her and she really didn't do anything to hurt me." Jeanne said I still didn't want you to. "Honey, I never want to hurt you and I thought that you and I could pick her up and you could sit next to me."

She said, "Only, only if we have to."

I replied, "I just don't like hurting feelings. Let's talk about it when we are together." She said okay, then we went on talking about us and what we planned.

I said I had to go, she whispered, "I love you," and I whispered back, "I love you, too." She laughed and asked why I was whispering. I said, "Because you did." Then I hung up and I was thinking about Dorothy, as usual, but was just giving up on her.

The last four days at work were the same and nothing new and the J Box was working fine. I was going to a store to get a gift for Jeanne and Dorothy, so I did go and I picked out two necklaces. They were the same because I did not have time to order anything different. They were eighteen karat gold and there was an angel holding a heart. I had the words inscribed on both, "Love is Forever" in small letters, but you could read it and I was picking them up to deliver them tomorrow night. It was nine thirty now and I just got home. I took off my jacket and headed for the shower. The phone rang and I ran to answer it. It was Dorothy, but she was frantic and incoherent. I had trouble understanding her, but I did understand her say, "Could you please pick me up?" I said, "Where are you?"

She said, "I'm in front of the theater and need to see you now." I asked her which one and she said, "In town." It was hard to understand her, but I knew that she was in town about one half mile from her home. I did go there as fast as I could and pulled towards the theater. She was standing near the road and she jumped into my car. She looked like she had been crying for a long time.

I asked, "What's wrong?"

She said, "We have to talk." For the first time I could see that I loved Jeanne more. There was nothing easy about Dorothy and I was always hurt with her.

I said, "Where do you want to go?" She said somewhere, where we could be alone. I went to the plant parking lot and pulled up the back road. She had been sitting close to me since she got it, but came closer. Then she put both arms around me and squeezed me very tightly. She was crying very hard and I could feel she was short on breath and trembling. I did not know what to say or do, so I just held her and let her cry. I knew at this moment that I did not want to be with her and it seemed that every time I was with her we had problems. I would normally cry myself if I saw her this way, but this time I just didn't. She kept her head on my shoulder and kept wiping her tears on my jacket. She did not talk and I was getting nervous, because I still didn't know what was wrong or why she did not call me all week. She picked up her head and looked at me.

What I saw had hurt me so much (I am so sad that I am having trouble writing this book and I have tears running down my face and must take a break. Sorry, I am back.) Her hair was not combed, and she was pure white and there was no life showing as I knew it. Her eyes were filled with fear and the only way I knew she was alive was through her trembling and trying to talk. I didn't know what was wrong, but I did know she needed help. I knew now that whatever her problems were, they were killing her and I didn't know how I could help. I was falling apart myself and didn't think I could deal with it any longer, because the memory of this night would be stuck in my mind forever. I looked at her and said, "Honey, what is wrong? Please! You must tell me." She couldn't talk and she just looked at me and held me tighter. I couldn't help it but I just fell apart. Then tears rushed from my eyes and I couldn't see. I just knew that this was the saddest time in my life. I knew that she had problems that she could not deal with alone, but not as serious as this and I was afraid for her. I had never seen anyone fall apart like this and we held each other for a very long time without talking, because right now neither one of us could. I picked up her head and kissed her without looking up again. Our tears were running down our cheeks and around our lips, then dripping onto my chest. I could taste it in my mouth and around our lips. We did not stop kissing and the only time she would stop was to breathe. Her nose was stuffed up from crying so hard and she had trouble breathing. We stayed that way for a long time before we let go or tried to talk. I finally picked up her face after she calmed down and said, "You must tell me now."

She looked at me without speaking and started to sob again. She was very incoherent and tried to say, "The person that I love the most, I know I am going to lose," and started crying very hard again.

I knew she meant me, so I said, "Honey, you are not going to lose me."

She again tried to say, "Yes I am, I know I am." I just held her and was afraid for her, but I didn't know how to handle this and I still didn't know what was wrong.

I said, "Would you like me to take you home so you can go to bed? I'll stay with you."

She screamed out, "No! I never want to go home. I hate that bitch." I stopped crying and wondered what to do. I let my seat go back all the way, then put my head by the door so I could lay back and rest, then pulled her on top of me. It was still not comfortable, but better than the way we were. We had been here almost two hours now and I still didn't know what was wrong, but she finally turned a little and got up to a sitting position. She said, "You don't know how much I love you and how hard it has been this week.

I said, "Please tell me what's wrong and why you didn't call."

She said, "It will be hard for you to understand, but I will try to explain." She was speaking a little clearer so I could understand her better and she said, "My mother told me that she told you what happened to me more than a year ago. I don't know how much she told you, but my life ended then and I knew I could never be myself again." I explained what her mother had said to me and she started crying again. She could still talk and repeated what was still in her mind. She said, "Al, that's not half of what happened. There were four guys and three girls, and maybe more. When they got me to their house the guys and girls held me down in a recliner chair. Someone had their thing out and was trying to stick it in my mouth while the others were trying to stick their fingers between my legs and into me. They dragged me onto the floor and tried to take my underpants off, but I held onto them. I was very dizzy and was getting sick, but I knew that someone put something in my drink. I was glad that I didn't drink very much and I never do. Cat grabbed my feet and pulled them up around him while others held me down. He did get my jeans off and the other boys and girls had their hands under my blouse and on my breast. They were squeezing them very hard and hurting me with their fingernails on my nipples while they were all laughing. Cat had his hand between my legs and tried to push his finger into me. I could feel his fingernails cutting me and hurting me, but I could not scream. I kept trying to scream and nothing came out. I tried to keep my legs together but the guys pulled them apart."

She completely fell apart and just held me very tightly. I knew she would need time to try and explain this, so I just held her and kept quiet. I wanted to stop here and go to Watertown and hurt them all and did think that I would someday. She finally started talking again and forgot how much she told me and I tried to remind her. She then said, "Cat got on top of me and just then I could scream. I screamed as loud as I could and freed one of my hands and I quickly tried to gouge his eyes out. He slapped me very hard, but I kept screaming. One of the guys said, 'Cat, stop. Someone will hear her,' and everyone let me go. I was able to escape his grip and then run outside. While I was screaming for help, I ran outside with just my ripped blouse and underpants and I was still screaming."

She was still trembling, but I believe that she felt better. Then her trembling had stopped and she just laid her head on my shoulder with her face against mine. I thought I was having a nightmare, which I have very often about my childhood. There is one nightmare that is repeated a lot in my life since I was very small. I don't know how to explain it, but it has something to do with mathematics. You may laugh, but this was the worst one that I had and it scared me nearly to death. The best that I could explain this is, there are many large wheels on top of a big hill and I am trapped at the bottom. These wheels have numbers on them, which you could see while they were rolling towards you. It is some kind of puzzle and if you didn't figure it out the wheel would crush and kill you, but I always woke up before they crushed me. Dorothy was now wiping her face and looking at me and said, "My mother did not tell you all that because I did not tell her everything that happened. My vagina hurt very badly for a long time and I may have caught an infection from their dirty hands. My breasts were all bruised and bleeding around my nipples from their fingernails, and I had a large bruise on the side of my neck from him hitting me. I don't think I could tell you anymore."

I said, "Is there more?" and she there is with me. I held her in my arms and looked in to her eyes. I felt so hurt and there was not much that I could do except to try and understand what this young girl, sixteen at the time was put through. I knew I had to do something and said, "Why didn't you go to the police?"

She said, "My mom called a lady she knew that worked for a law office. Then we all talked and she advised us not to. She said that there were six or more of them. I was at a bar drinking and everyone there saw me with them, then leave with them. In court they would make me out to be a whore and I would be in a worse position than if I did nothing."

I said, "You are lucky he did not enter you," and we just dropped it.

Dorothy then said, "I decided to handle it on my own," so I asked her what she did. She answered, "I can't tell you, please don't ask me to."

I said, "Well, you do know that I will have to kill him. I do have a twelve gauge shot gun home and you will have to show me where he lives."

She quickly said, "No, you won't."

I said, "Well, I won't kill him, I'll just blow his legs off."

She said, "No, you won't. Please let me handle it my way." I asked her what she meant. She said, "I can't tell you."

I said, "But you must, how can I help you if you don't tell me?"

She said, "I don't want you involved. Please don't ask me about it." She tried to get off that subject and said, "You don't know what I have been going through since then."

131

I said, "Well, what happened this past week that made it any different?"

She said, "Well, I just can't take it anymore." I said I had noticed that last Friday night. She spoke louder, "Al, that nothing. You don't know what she says to me. After you left we had a big fight. She even said that I was looking for sex and it was my fault that I was raped. She tried to hurt me by telling me that you said you have another girlfriend and she would be better for you. She almost told me that I was not good enough for you and I was just a whore. She really made me hate you at times and she was never this bad until I met you. Sometimes I think that I'm not good enough for you." I tried to interrupt her but she would not stop. She said, "I had to prove to my mother that I don't need you and I could make it on my own. This is why I did not call you and I was glad that you did not stop in or call. She told me tonight before I left home, 'Good, you lost him and he will never come back.' I got very upset and wanted to hit her with something. I just ran out the door, but I didn't know what to do and all I could think about was you. I wanted you here now and took a chance, then called you because you were always there when I needed you."

I said, "I am happy that you did call me." I didn't want to talk anymore and I think she felt the same. It was four a m and my eyes burned. I was very tired and wanted to get some sleep. I went to my house, but I never wanted to bring her there because it wasn't very much to look at. I had two small rooms, one was my bedroom. The other had a stove, sink and counter. I did not have a refrigerator and only had a small bathroom with a shower, but it was good that I had a regular size bed. We took off our jackets and I unplugged the phone, because I did not want to take any phone calls, then took off my shoes and laid on my bed with her.

She looked at me and said, "Thank you very much for caring about me and being there when I needed you." She kissed me, then fell asleep and I think she passed out, but I knew what she had been through that night and the past week. I could only feel very sorry for her and knew I was very much involved in this situation and could not refuse her plea for help now. I laid alongside her while looking at her and noticed that her skirt was way up and I could see her complete legs and butt. She really was a beautiful girl from head to toe and I held her, then I fell asleep. I awoke at eleven o'clock and did not move very much to avoid waking her. Today was Saturday and I had made plans to pick up the gifts. I tried to sneak out of bed and she put her arms around me and said, "Do you have to leave now?" I just looked at her and started thinking that I'd never seen anyone like her. At one moment she's a wild animal full of terror and hate and the next she's a meek, mellow, beautiful lamb full of love and passion.

I answered her, "Yes, I have to leave. I have to go to the bathroom."

She laughed and said, "Okay, but come right back." While I was in the bathroom my mind was going in circles and I thought about Jeanne. I must do something soon, but did not know what. I felt that I would have to wait to see what happened next, then walked back to my bed. Dorothy reached up and pulled me back into bed with her.

I said, "You're a crazy little shit," and she asked why, but I just shut up and went closer. She was all over the pain that she had been in just hours ago and you would never know that there was anything wrong. She pulled me close to her and while kissing me, she forced one of her legs under me, and then wrapped both legs around me. She put her feet behind me and forced me close to her, but I could not believe that this was Dorothy. I thought about the last Friday night when I was in bed and knew that I started this then. I started kissing her all over her lips, face and neck. I could still taste the tears and sweat from the night before. I was lying on my side and one of her legs was under me. She squeezed me tighter with her legs and arms, and then pulled me on top of her. I was lying between her legs while her legs were still squeezing me. I was paralyzed and could not move, because I was not prepared for this. I said to myself, *whatever she does next, I cannot stop her and I'm not sure if I want to.* Something told me that I should, but I didn't think I had the power to stop what I had been waiting so long for. I mean, just being in bed with her was enough for me.

She stopped to look at me and said, "I want you to make love to me."

Stupid me, I said, "Now?" but I don't think I knew what I was saying.

She said, "Yes, now! Please go easy because I'm scared, but I do want to." I couldn't move and just laid there, then finally put my hand between her legs and just held it there. She loosened her grip with her legs and gave me room to move my hand. She was able to unbutton the top of my jeans easily because they were loose from me losing weight, and she put her hand inside of them and held me. I then had the nerve to put my hand under her undies to feel her and at this time I did not have any guilt, but thought that she would be my wife. It was not sexual desire that took control, but it was love and sex together. We got undressed and I went to the shower. I was standing by the shower and Dorothy came over. She was totally naked also and I felt better. I had never seen a totally nude girl until now and she was more beautiful than I imagined. Her breasts were so firm and I thought were a perfect shape. I turned on the shower and we both went in. I washed her body and she washed mine. It was so beautiful and this was when you knew that you were deeply in love and never wanted it to end. I was so happy to have this beautiful girl that I loved for so long here with me.

We hopped in bed again and she pulled the covers over us and held each other. She pulled me on top of her again, but I was afraid to hurt her so I stopped and just rubbed it up and down. I was very excited and had never been this far before, but I was afraid to go any further. She pulled on me, then put her legs behind me and helped me push. I could feel her complete body tighten and I wanted to stop, because I was afraid I was hurting her, but then it became soft. I stopped and just rolled over then just held her, but I could feel her trembling and was happy that I did stop. We just lay there, holding each other and she said, "Thank you. I could see that you would never hurt me." It was three p m now and we were both hungry after what we had been though. I took her to her home and I told her that I would speak with her mother. When we got there, she went to her bedroom and changed her clothes. I did talk with Beatrice and explained that we did have to talk in private.

I explained, "Dorothy feels that you are trying to run her life too much and that you are forcing her on me, which is not helping us at all." She was a little upset, but I think she did understand. Dorothy was ready and we went to Al Pat's. I was very uneasy and hoped that Jeanne would not come in. We both had some food and left, because I did not want to stay there long. I told Dorothy that I wanted to take her home and we must have a talk now. We went to her house and went to her bedroom.

She laid on her bed and I sat alongside of her. I knew that I had to say this, because I would not know how to act or what to do next. I did not hesitate because I might have chickened out and I said, "Honey, your mother was right, I do have a girlfriend. I didn't know what was going on with you. I did start dating her when you said you couldn't love anyone and we could just be friends." I knew that this would hurt, but I knew no other way to remedy the situation. She looked at me with no expression and turned pale and did not speak to me for a while. She turned away from me and just laid there looking at the wall. I knew that this was kind of a shock to her and she must have believed it might be true after her mother made that statement. I waited and felt that I would have to hear her next statement before I could continue.

It may have been only a few minutes and she turned to face me and said, "Does that mean we're though?"

I said, "By no means. I have loved you for nearly two years and I will probably always love you".

But you must realize that I had trouble getting a kiss or hug from you back when you knew how much I loved you. You had told me not to love you, that you could never love anyone, that I was only a friend and that was all. A lot of times I believed that you were just using me to take you to the Bog just to see Cat. I tried to believe that we would get together and in every instance you deterred my chances. When you left for Canada you made a statement that I felt was directed to me, 'I will never get married.' What were you telling me?" I knew that I had tears in my eyes, but I was not crying. She was lifeless when she looked at me, but she knew that I spoke the truth. She did not cry and her eyes were not focused, but I knew that she could not hold this against me. I took off my jacket, laid by her side and held her, then put my lips on hers. They were cold with no response, so I pulled back and just held her. She laid there, still lifeless and I had some time to think. For the first time I thought that I had a clear mind and I did love her, but I Also knew that I loved Jeanne also. I felt that I loved them both equally, but not in the same way and I knew now That I wanted to keep them both. I mean, I did give them all the love I had at all times and I was more worried about their feelings then my own. Not realizing that I was hurting them more than anything that they could have done on their own. I now had to face it and realized that I couldn't live this double life any longer.

I laid by her side and felt sorry, but I did believe that I did help her with her problem. I think I showed her that men are not all alike and she could trust some. You just have to find the right one and not look in all the wrong places. I didn't think you would find anything different than what she found in a bar. She still hadn't said anything and I felt like leaving. I thought that might hurt her and put her back where she was the night before, so I pulled her over. She was still lifeless and her eyes were very sad. I gently kissed her, and then held her very tightly and this must have given her the feeling that she did have a chance. She held me very tightly and started to kiss me harder. She had big tears in her eyes and said to me, "My God, I'm so sorry that I was so involved with myself and my problems that I never thought about what I was putting you through, but what can I do now?"

I said, "No matter what happens, you should always be yourself and never put the past in front of you. I'm not saying to forget it, but don't make it your priority goal and always put it in the proper perspective.

She said, "Do I still have a chance?" I told her there was always a chance, that's what life is all about. She said, "Could you please give me another chance?" I told her that the most love and happiness I found in my whole life was with her. I also told her that the most hurt in my life was also with her. She said, "What does that mean?"

I said, "I don't know, I'm only making a statement of how I feel." I then said, "Dorothy, I love you with every inch of my body, but I need time to handle this problem I have now with Jeanne." I went on to tell her how much Jeanne loved me and she did not want to live without me. "I enforced my feelings that I would not hurt her and felt the same about you. I do hope that I find a way to solve this and I will need time to think."

She said several times, "Why was I so stupid?"

I said, "Life has a lot of downfalls and we seem to bring them upon ourselves."

She said, "I don't blame her for loving you and I do know what she means." I then said "I need time to talk with Jeanne and I assure that I have never done what we did yesterday and today with Jeanne and had no intentions to do so now. I continued, "It might be good if we didn't see each other every day for a while and we would just go out casually. I promised that I would do the same with Jeanne because I did have to find myself." Then I hugged and kissed her for a long time. She did say, "I do understand and I know it was my own fault, but I do know that I will wait for you forever."

I said, "I must leave now, but don't worry I will be back. You may call me as often as you like," and I went home.

When I got home I knew that Jeanne tried to call. She knew that I was not working and that my plant was closed for Christmas. I called her and said, "Hi, honey. What are you doing?"

She said, "I'm fine, but where were you? I tried to call you all day."

I said, "I'm calling you now, ain't I?" She said yes, she guessed so. I said, "I'm sorry, but I can't see you today, but I do want to pick you up tomorrow early and spend some time with you."

She said, "I would love that, but why can't you come tonight?"

I said, "I'll pack my clothes while you ask your father if I can move in."

She said, "Why are you being so smart, don't you want to see me?"

I said, "Don't you think that would be a good idea?" She said "I would love it, but I still think that you are being sarcastic". I said, "I'm sorry, honey. I thought it was cute." I then said, "I had a lot of problems and I have to go to Danbury now." She asked why she couldn't go with me and I said, "It's personal." She asked if I was going alone and I told her that I was. I said, "I will stop by your house on the way and you can see for yourself."

She said, "Good, I'll get to see you."

I said, "I'll be there in twenty minutes." I drove into her driveway and she came running out and hopped into my car, then slid over to me. She put her arms around me and kissed me in her special way. She pleaded with me that I should take her with me, but I reiterated the importance that I must go alone and I was only going to pick up the presents, but I did not want her to know. I said, "I will see you all day tomorrow."

She said, "If you don't take me with you I'll tell my father you want to move in with me." She started to laugh and then let me go and I told her that I would call her when I got home.

I finished with my shopping and had just gotten home, but I promised I would call Jen and I'm waiting for her to answer. She answered, then I told her, "I'm home now and I did tell you I would call."

She said, "That was fast," and I said, "Did you miss me?"

She said, "Of course." We talked for a while and I told her I would see her tomorrow. I also told her that I had a lot of work with helping my dad and would be very busy during my Christmas break at the plant. I hung up and then called Dorothy. I did not want her to get too worried or do something wrong. She answered and said, "I hoped it was you."

I said, "I was thinking about you and didn't want you to worry." She thanked me and I said, "I will always think about you because today you made me feel more like a man."

She said, "I'm glad you said that, because today you made me feel the same way."

I said, "Like a man?"

She said, "Don't be funny, you know what I meant." We talked for a while, then I hung up and went to sleep.

I just woke up and really slept well, although I knew I had a lot of things to straighten out, but I felt that I would manage. I would call Dorothy first, because I would not see her today and I did want her to know that I was going to talk with Jeanne. The truth must come out now and I explained to Dorothy what I had on my mind, then I told her that I would call her tonight. In our conversation she said that there was something that she should tell me and said it was something I had asked her about Friday night. I asked her to tell me that night, but she got off the subject and I forgot. She did say that there was something else that she wanted to handle by herself. I did remember that and wondered why I did not ask her then. I asked her what it was. She said, "I can't discuss this on the phone. When can I see you? I will tell you then." I did feel proud of her because I felt that now she would get everything out and feel better. I was looking forward to this conversation and told her that I loved her and what we did then was still on my mind.

She said, "It's up to you the next time could be better." I wanted to go there right now, but I knew this would only put me back and made it harder to remedy the problem, so I said, "Maybe soon," and hung up.

Because I didn't want her to feel bad when I was with Jeanne. I took a shower, called Jeanne and told her that I would pick her up in a half hour. Then went to her house and walked in. Her parents greeted me and asked if I would have dinner with them.

I said "I would love to, as long as I could finish that talk with Betty". Betty laughed and said, "I'm looking forward to it."

Jeanne said, "Al, aren't we going out?"

I said, "Come on, it's only going to be a little while and we do have all day."

I sat with Jeanne while dinner was being prepared and she said, "I could slap you sometimes." I asked her why and she said, "You know I want to be alone with you."

I said, "You will," and Betty called us to the table. It was in a separate dining room and it was very beautiful. Jeanne sat me at the table and sat with me, right next to me. I had never seen this much food at a table in my life and it all looked so good. They had Virginia Ham, Turkey with stuffing and all the works.

I did not want to be a pig, but Jeanne noticed what I liked the most. She kept filling my plate and I had to tell her it was enough. I did not have room for dessert and Betty said it was apple crisp. I had never had that, but it looked so good and I could smell it when she opened the oven. Betty did offer it to me and I said, "I am stuffed."

She then said, "Would you two like some when you get back?" Jeanne said, "Yes, you'd better save us some." I just loved this family and again thought about my childhood. I thought why did I not have a mother and father like this? I thought and said to myself, *I think my mother would have been this way if she had the chance.* Jeanne said, "Al, did you hear me?"

I said, "I guess not. I was in thought," and she asked what I was thinking about. I said in a low voice, "My childhood." I dropped it and said, "What did you say?"

She said, "Are you ready to leave?" the replied sarcastically, "I have to keep you away from my mother," then laughed. We got up and I thanked Betty for the best dinner that I ever had. They both said, "You're welcome," and we left.

Jeanne and I went to the car and she said, "Don't you want to be with me?"

I said, "Yes, of course, but I do know that you got me out of the house before I could finish that talk with Betty."

She said, "I did plan that and just want to be alone with you." I asked her where she wanted to go. She said, ":I don't know, anywhere, it really doesn't matter."

I said, "I want to go somewhere that's quiet, but first I want to go to the store. I want to get your Mom and Dad something for Christmas."

Jeanne said, "That would be nice and I want to get something also."

We went to the store then we picked out some things and I bought a nice plant for Bob and Betty. I had seen that they like plants and Jeanne said they would like this one. I then went to the Lark Drive in, the music was playing and Jeanne was just being herself. We had a soda pop and I said I wanted to go somewhere else. I was more quiet than usual and wanted to think of how to talk about the problem. She did ask, "Why are you being so quiet?"

I said, "I have problems, and that's what I want to talk about." We left and I drove up to my father's farm, because he had called me. The bulldozer had arrived and he needed help operating it. I showed her the farm and my shop then went to my Dad. I told him I would come here tomorrow, because I still had Monday through Wednesday off from work. I knew that I must have this talk with Jeanne and have been avoiding it. We were all alone here and I said, "Jeanne, I told you that I was with Dorothy last night, and I want to talk about it. You know that I went with her for nearly two years and she needs help."

I then told her about Dorothy calling me at eleven o'clock Friday night and the condition she was in. Jeanne did not interrupt at all. I said, "There are some things that should never be said, but I do love you and I feel that I must tell you the truth." I was thinking about everything and wanted this to come out right. I love your family and I was always happy when I was with them. Choosing you would have been simple and is what I really want, but if anything happened to Dorothy it would hurt me and could affect my relation with anyone in the future. I had not put this in words, but in the conversations that I had with Dorothy, I believed that she was suicidal and needed help. I said, "I told you about the rape and how it occurred and the state of mind that Dorothy is in. Dorothy needs my help, and as a friend I cannot refuse her." I followed with, I would do the same thing for you or Sparky if this should occur. I said, "Will you please try and understand?" She looked at me and I could see the absence of thought and wanted to ask many questions.

She said, "Does this mean you won't see me anymore?"

I replied, "Honey, this has nothing to do with you and me. I told Dorothy that I do love you and that you were the girl that talked to me at Al Pats. So she knows who you are."

She said in a soft voice, "I do trust you, but I don't want to lose you." She said, "Al, I don't think you know how much I love you and I have built my world around you. You are in all my plans, dreams and thoughts, but what would I ever do if you left me?"

I said, "You won't have to worry about that." I now found that I was telling both girls the same thing. I thought that I could find a solution, but in reality things were getting worse. I tried to push this from my mind and pulled Jeanne closer. I told her ten times or more that I loved her while holding and kissing her. I thought that if I brought her into the equation it may help and said, "Jeanne, maybe you could help me. You're a girl and probably know more than I.

I thought maybe this would help but she answered, "No, I don't want to see her."

I said, "Come on, cheer up. If I didn't love you, I would have not told you anything."

She said, "I guess." I started the car, but I felt that things were not as before and drove towards town.

I could see that she was not herself and said, "Do you want me to leave?"

She said, "Nooo! I'm just confused." I was out of words and searched my mind for a way to ratify this nightmare.

I said, "If you ever had this problem, would you want me to listen to you?"

She said, "Yes, but I said before she does not deserve you." I said that not the point because if I couldn't help a friend with a problem, then what does that make me?

I followed with, "Could we get off this subject? I just want to be with you." Jeanne stayed very quiet and I did not know what to say any more. She sat close and just had her arm loose around me. While I was thinking I believed that my problem was not with Jeanne. I loved her lifestyle, her family and her pureness. I thought that maybe my feelings were more to help Dorothy, and I was involved with my past where these problems were prevalent. I never knew what a normal lifestyle was, and I did fit into this situation. I could not get Jeanne into her good mood, nor could I. I became very depressed and didn't know how to act or what to do next. I tried to pull Jeanne closer and make her laugh with no prevail. My problems were prevalent and I could not find a solution that I felt was feasible. I pulled into a parking lot and just sat, then waited for something to happen. I knew that I hurt Jeanne and this was not my intention with this conversation. I said, "Why can't I do anything right?"

I put both hands on my face and she looked up at me, and then said, "I'm sorry."

I said, "I have no intentions of hurting you, but just being honest and I want to go home now."

She said, "Please don't go." I said that I was very hurt and needed time to be alone. She said, "Not because of me, I hope."

I said, "No, it's me. I always relive my childhood over and over. I guess I need to be beat down and hurt all the time."

"I don't ever want to hurt anyone, and I always end up hurting myself".

She said, "You never told me much about your past. What was it like?" I told her just a little about the bad times, the torturous life of all us kids, the hurt that I had for so many years and that this was why I couldn't hurt anyone else. I only wanted to help, because I knew what it was like not to have anyone. She said, "I'm sorry, I didn't know and I didn't mean to hurt you".

She came closer and I said, "It's not you. I just don't know how to treat people or explain things. I always get in trouble and everything is so hard to understand. Things appear to get harder all the time, but I did tell you that I love you and I was hoping that you did believe me".

She said, "Oh, I do believe you. I'm just so afraid that I will lose you and would not know what to do or if I could ever love again.

I said, "I'm only going to say this once. When this is all over and my mind is clear what I want to become a reality, and what I believe would be the best for me is, you and I get married and that we could be a family like yours. This could only be a promise or a wish, because it is not I that has the control of the future or anyone's destiny. I would love to think that you were the mother of my children.

She said, "That was beautiful and I will pray for the same thing". We then held, kissed each other and everything became much better. I thought that Jeanne's problems were satisfied but mine became worse. We stayed together and loved each other, but I could not pull myself to reality. I must awaken from this dream and have some kind of life where I don't have to worry all the time. I knew that I do love them both and couldn't hurt either one. I just didn't have the intelligence to ratify this and had no one to ask for help. I did know that they were not the problem, but it was I that created this love triangle.

I went home and sat in my only chair and held my hands over my face, while searching for answers. I knew that I could not call Dorothy and tried to believe that this problem was not all my fault. Dorothy had nearly two years to do what we did and tell me the truth. I could only believe that she led me on and kept me on a string while controlling my mind, which affected my ability to be rational or comprehensive. I also knew that what I started last Friday night and continued yesterday was my biggest mistake of all. I could not blame these girls for my mistakes and unpredictable ventures, because I wasn't looking for these problems without knowing it.

It was early enough to go to the Bog and maybe I would see Cat and work him over, because he did deserve it, but after driving for a while I changed my mind. I said to myself, *you're asking for more problems than you already have.* I then headed to another town in New York and went to a bar there. It was called Jossey's Bar and Grill. I walked in then sat at the bar and ordered a drink. A young man came up to me and said, "You're the guy that played at the Bog, right?"

I said, "Yes. Why?"

He said, "I was there and you were great."

I said, "Fair," then thanked him while he called Jossey over. Jossey is the bartender and owner.

Then he said, "Your name is Al, right?" and I said yes. He said, "Jossey, this is Al, the guy that played at the Bog Hollow."

She said, "Pleased to meet you. I heard that you put on a good show and all by yourself."

I said, "Thank you. I always give it my best."

She then asked, "How would like to play here on Saturday nights or even Friday? I would pay you very well, because we don't have a band and just the juke box. I would love for you to try at least one night. I said that I wasn't planning on playing anywhere, but I would consider it.

I sat with Roy, He was the kid that recognized me and he had another friend with him. They were very nice and so was Jossey. I had several drinks and knew that I should stop, but my problems didn't appear as bad now. I kept drinking and thought that I should stop at Dorothy's, maybe I should have sex now, because I thought I should get something for what I was going through, but my mind told me then that this was my only and biggest problem. I thought about it for a while, but I guess I had too much to drink and felt sick.

I left and started to go home, but half way home I became very sick. I stopped my car, because I had to vomit and continued home then went to my bed room and fell asleep. I just woke up and knew now what a hangover was. I didn't feel well and I had to meet my father now. It was cold out and that may help my head ache. I had not had a headache for the past eight years, but I knew how it felt again.

My Near-Fatal Accident

That was when I was twelve years old and I almost died. I found a pair of ice skates on the dump and learned to skate very well. These skates had jagged points on the front and I was told that they were figure skates. It didn't matter what they were it was a lot of fun to ice skate and I skated a lot for two years. This was mostly after dark and we only had light when the moon was out, so my time was limited. The night that I had my accident, I had my youngest sister Arlean was with me. She was just eight years old when this happened and I had just learned to jump. I learned that I could jump very high turn and was very proud. This night the moon was bright when I went skating and I attempted to jump over a barrel. We had a lot of barrels on the farm and somehow one was near the ice so I rolled it onto the pond. I made one practice run along side of it and I thought that I could do it. I got a long start but I miscalculated the distance then landed backwards. My skates dug into the ice and I went down very hard and hit my head. I laid there and Arlean came to me and asked if I was hurt. I did not answer and was in so much pain that I could not talk. Arlean said when I put my hand behind my head it was all bloody, but somehow I managed to make it to my house. We had a back stairway to the bedroom floor and I went that way to my room. I did not want to be beaten again, because I had all the pain that I could handle right now.

Lucky my sister had the brains to tell Florence that I was hurt and was bleeding. She told her that I went up stairs, so she came to my bed and found me unconscious then called my father. He put me into his truck and rushed me to the Hospital. I became conscious a few times and felt that I did not have any legs. When I tried to move I just slid to the floor, so my dad would have to stop and put me back up on the seat. When we got to the hospital the doctor took me to the emergency room and said I was hemorrhaging inside my brain and could fall in to a coma. He quickly placed a spinal tap into my spine and I became conscious. I did not know where I was or how I got there and was told about the above. I then was told that I would remain several days in the hospital and would received more spinal taps. The doctor told me that when he inserted the first spinal tap, the hose exploded from the pressure and sprayed him. I was still bleeding inside my brain and the blood would have to be drained. The doctor told my dad that if the bleeding didn't stop they would have to remove part of my skull, but after several more spinal taps the bleeding did stop. The doctor told dad and me, that I may have severe headaches for the rest of my life. The X rays revealed that my skull was fractured like an X, four inches one way and three the other. He said that I was lucky that I lived through this, because I could have fallen in to a coma. He also explained that the pressure inside my skull caused me to lose my motor ability. I am not sure that I was lucky, but what kind of a life did I survive to?

Back at the Development

I was going to see dad now to see what he had in mind. I did not call anyone today and felt that I shouldn't. He had all the permits and regulations and showed me that we have more than two miles of roadway to rough in. He was leasing a bulldozer and wanted me to operate it. His spinal surgery limits him from doing this very long. I said, "All right, when do I start?" He said right now so I told him I would work until dark and run it until Wednesday, because I had to go back to work on Wednesday, then he asked me if I could come right after work during the week. There were lights on the dozer and I could work after dark.

I wanted to call Jeanne, but I thought it would be better if I didn't call either one today. I thought about Dorothy, she hadn't had a life either and I could see she really did trust me now. I was probably the only one that could solve her problems and she had come a long way just in the last few days. I felt that if I did leave her she will go back to where she was. But I thought about Jeanne, how happy and peaceful it was with her. Her family was the image that I would want mine to be, if I ever have one. I just wanted to find happiness without hurting anyone. I knew that there was no easy solution and I must prepare myself for the worst. I do blame myself, but in reality I knew both of these girls preyed on my weakness, they knew I did not want to hurt anyone and the battle should be between them. I knew I would do anything for both of them no matter how much I hurt myself. I was losing control and maybe my mind, but I was trying my best to do what's right. I would just love both of them and don't say anymore, but I promised to help dad today. He was waiting for me and was explaining that some of the trees would have to be removed. I said I would try and do as much as I could today then started. I was able to go faster than expected and I did reach the first big tree. I just made a path around it and this will help the tree crew. From the main highway there was a steep grade so I must go around the hill to limit the incline. I did not encounter any ledge so that did speed up the process. My dad came and was surprised at how much was completed and was happy because we had such good weather. I told him I would work on this every night and next weekend. He said we should be through with the rough grade by then, and he would have his friend from Sega contractors complete the final grade with a larger bulldozer. He was happy and I saw a smile that I had not seen for a long time. I knew that he was not happy for the way his life was so far, but things were looking up now.

I was going home now, and then I would deliver the Christmas presents to Dorothy's and Jeanne's house. I would go to Dorothy's first because it was on the way. I walked in and Dorothy was in the living room and Beatrice was in the kitchen. I said, "Merry Christmas." I am going to call Dorothy Dot from now on, and Jeanne, Jen.

Dot came running up to me and gave me a hug and said, "I tried calling you all day." I explained what I was doing and would take her for a ride to see it soon. I was still holding the presents and Dot helped me with them. I gave the presents to her mother and gave Dot the necklace first and she opened it. She really loved it and put it on, but she did complain, because I did not put my name on it. I told her there wasn't enough room and gave her some other things she wanted. I stayed and had coffee then said that I had to go to Jen's house. I don't think Dot liked that but what could I do. I gave her a big kiss and told her that I would call her before I went to sleep.

I was walking into Jen's house, but she was still sitting on the couch and her Dad let me in. I said, "Merry Christmas," as I walked in and noticed that Jen was still on the couch. I gave the gift to Bob and Betty first, then I went to the living room to sit with Jen. I said, "Hi, honey," and gave her the gift, but I already felt strange because she did not meet me at the door.

She said, "Hi," then took the gift. I asked her what was wrong. She said in a low voice so no one could hear her, "Where were you all day?"

I said, "Why are you mad at me?" She said "No, I was just annoyed and I tried calling you all day". I didn't answer right away and I was a little upset myself. I said, "And where did I tell you I was going on Monday?"

She answered, "You said you were going to talk to your Dad."

I said, "And help him run the Dozer, right?" She said "I guess so". I was not too happy and this was not my Jeanne, but I may have been a little snappy.

I didn't say any more, then she said, "I tried to call you all day and I was worried."

I said, "I guess you thought I was with Dot." She said "I didn't know" and right now I felt that I wanted to scream, *why am I always on the spot?* I held my tongue and said "I ran a bulldozer all day until a short while ago. I am very tired and did not take a break at all. I don't want to make anyone upset so I want to go home.

147

Jeannie Quickly came close to me and said, "I'm Sorry, Please, I am Sorry". "I just thought something may have happened because you always call me". She had tears in her eyes and said "do you really want to leave".

"Honey I said once before, "Love is never having to say you're sorry". Then I reached over and gave her a kiss. She said "Could we please go somewhere, I really need to be with you alone".

I said "let's spend a little time with your Mom and Dad first". We then went to the car and she asked "were you really mad at me". I answered "I only get upset when someone challenges my integrity and you didn't do that"

She said "Why? Are you so different from everyone else". I said, "I'm not, I just like to see everyone happy". She grabbed me and had both arms around me before we left the yard and I felt so much better. We did not go very far just to the parking place next to the textile Plant.

Jen was tearing me apart with love, although I loved every minute of it I had to keep control of myself without hurting her feelings. We hugged and kissed as we did the time in the parking lot. I didn't know why but it just felt so wonderful, so I kept hugging and kissing her. I felt so content and I said to myself, every time I try and be good I make things worse, so why don't I just shut up and enjoy life as it happens? I was so at ease, happy and we loved each other like never before. I knew I love it and wanted never to stop seeing her. I became very excited and knew I should take her home now, because she was doing nothing to dampen my feelings and I said, "We must go home now."

She said, "No! No! Please, I want to stay here with you." I knew she was very excited also, but I did believe she could control herself.

It got to the point where I thought she couldn't and I said, "Well, let's go home." She loosened her grip a little and I said, "I do love you so very much, but what we are doing is dangerous." It came to my mind then that she would have done anything to try to satisfy me so I wouldn't want Dot, and would have given me all she had to fortify my love for her. I believe that if it was just her and I, she would have waited. I said, "Honey, I love you just the way you are and you don't have to prove your love for me." We held each other and she looked at me, her eyes were going back and forth from one eye to the other. I realize that she was the only one that had done that and it was exciting and different.

She then asked me, "Honey, if you ever think that we may break up would you please make love to me first? I do want you very much and my life would not be complete without that. Would you please because I really want you to be my first?"

I almost swallowed my tongue, but that did make me very happy and I said, "Honey, do you know what you just said?"

She said, "Yes, and I've been thinking about this ever since the last time we were alone like this."

I said, "I really want you to think about it very close and that was the nicest thing that was ever said to me. For you to offer your innocent body to me just to prove your love, means that you have more love than that pure and beautiful body can handle." I said, "I'm not planning to ever leave you but let time decide what is right." I said, "Since we are talking about that, I want you right now more than life itself, but that would only weaken your love for me and I could not let that ever happen. I love you because you are what you are and not just for a good time. A time will come when we could prove our love and I am really looking forward to that moment." We then went to her house and I walked in to thank her parents. They did buy me a gift and it was very nice of them. I did not stay long because I was tired and wanted to call Dot. I was home now, but I was late in calling her. I didn't want her to think that I was with Jen this long and I was trying to think of what to say, but I had to face it and called her.

She answered and said, "I am glad you called. I have been very lonely."

I said, "I'm sorry I'm late, but they asked me to stay for dinner and I did," I then let it go at that.

We talked for a while and she pleaded for me to come to her house. I tried to say that I was too tired but she said, "It's Christmas. Please?" I said, "Okay." I showered very fast and put lotion on my face, because I did not want her to know I did go out. I went to her house and she was waiting for me. We had coffee and some cake, then Dot sat with me and when I finished she pulled me into her bedroom. I said to myself, *Oh, not again*, because I was still suffering from Jen. I knew that I could not stay long and it would not be right to do anything that I did already. I could not let her take control of me and make me feel guilty later.

She hopped in bed and said, "Come lay down with me."

I said, "Just for a little while," and she did not make any sexual passes but did say that she really enjoyed what we did.

She said, "I think it helped me get into the real life." I said I was very happy about that, then I told her I was very tired and needed some sleep, because I had to get up early to help my Dad. She said, "You could sleep here," and I said

I would love to but I needed my work clothes and it was very late now. I kissed her, then got up and told her that I did have to go. She thanked me for coming to her house and walked me to the door, then kissed me good night. I told her I would be helping my father every night this week but I would call her.

My mind went back again and I thought about my older sister. She told me what she learned in church and catechism. I was not seven years old yet and my little sister and I went to the fields to pick blackberries. There was a little stream that ran through there and that was where the berries were. After picking the berries we both went to the stream and took our clothes off and were checking why we were different. We were looking at and touching each other. She was only three and didn't know, but we compared this with the farm animals. We seen the bulls jump on the cows and stuck this thing into the cows. We knew that they were different and figured out that was why we were different. My older sister caught us and yelled at us. She said, "Didn't you learn in church that what you are doing is a sin?" I asked her please explain what a sin is? I heard it mentioned a lot of times but no one explained it. She answered, "There are ten commandments set by God of things that are sins."

I said, "I remember this, but what are sins?"

She said, "These are things that you can't do and that they are very bad." I asked her to explain them to me and she said most of the commandments to me. I didn't think she knew them all and I asked which one did we do wrong. I did not understand the meaning of them and asked again. She was trying to explain adultery to me and I said all we were doing was looking and noticed that we are different. She explained to me how babies are made. She said, "That's when you are married and if you do this with someone else, this is adultery."

I said, "We're not married. This is my sister."

She yelled at me and said, "That is much worst and is the biggest sin of all and you will burn in hell if you touch her." I had heard about hell and thought that was where I lived. She told me that we should never look at other people that are naked. Only after you are married and this was only to have children. I did listen to all she had to say, because my sisters do love me and I knew that they were only helping me. But I did not understand all the other commandants. I thought that I may have been bad because of what Dot and I did and now Jen asked me to do the same thing. I could not understand why they did not know the Ten Commandments. I had been in church many times in the past three years and did hear the Ten Commandments mentioned many times and was given a book about them. Trying to understand this, I thought about all the times that my real mother came to see me in school and she always spoke about God, that I should obey him. Then said God loves and would help us. I always believed my mother and wondered if I was doing something wrong. Sometimes I did think it was wrong, but why didn't these girls know it's wrong. I did know that Jen and her family went to church much more that I did. I knew she was very smart and would not ask me to do it if it was wrong.

It was Wednesday morning and I was back at work. We were very slow and most of the work was finished, so I decided to leave at two o'clock. I did leave at two all this week and we had most of the trees cut. Dad had two other people cutting the trees and taking them away. Two more weeks had gone by now, I have worked every day for the past three weeks and have only seen Dot and Jen a few times. We did not have any problems, but they said please finish that job. I had stayed away from Dot several times in our past and sometimes for a week or two, so she did understand. I had been with Jen at least twice a week since I met her and it was harder for her. I promised her that this Saturday I would take her somewhere and we could be together all day. This made her happy and she said she was really looking forward to it. Friday night came and I took Dot to a nice restaurant, then we went to a movie. Then we went to her house and laid in her bed. We talked for a while and she told me that ever since that time she stayed with me over night she has thought about it and wished she never stopped me, but would not stop me the next time. I told her that I did respect her more for what she did and that I would love to continue, but wanted to wait until the time was right. I knew that if I started to make love to either one I would want to do it all the time and when would it stop? I want to make love to her right now and I became very excited because I knew I could at any time that I wanted. I felt very proud that she offered me her body after all she went through and I did not want to abuse her trust. I did not want to become another Cat in her life. Leaving that night without having sex with her was very hard, but I was proud that I did have the control to do what I thought was right.

It was Saturday morning and I was going to pick up Jen. I knew that we should not be alone somewhere too long. It was getting to the point where I would lose my common sense and would do something we shouldn't and just make things worse. I feared the ramifications this could present to future endeavors in my own plans and I decided that I would have to wait. I picked her up and we went to breakfast at a Diner in Danbury. We hadn't been here before and I did want to stay out of town. I had not mentioned Dot while I was with Jen or the other way around and when I was asked I said, "I'm with you, ain't I?" I then would drop the subject and things were going much better this way. It gave me more time to do what I thought was right. While having breakfast with her, I asked if she wanted to go to New York City. We had never been there and we both agreed that it should be fun. I also wanted to show her that I did not only want to go parking with her but to do exciting things also

We are in New York now and I have never seen so much traffic. We are both getting a stiff neck from looking up at the tall buildings. This was very exciting and I was happy we went. We drove for a while and found a parking place. We had to pay for the parking, but my car was in a fenced in place and was safe. We walked to the Forty Second street and never seen so much stuff in our life. We then found out about the subway and took rides on them. We got off at I think it was thirty forth street and walked to the Empire State Building. We had to wait a long time, but we were able to get tickets to go to the top. We got to the top and the wind was blowing and it seemed much colder here than on the ground. We did stay and could barely see the ground. The cars were smaller than the matchboxes and we could see way into New Jersey and all over. We were cold so we went down and went back on the subway to forty second street. We did mostly window shopping and did plan to come again. Jen and I could not believe that while walking on Forty Second Street we walked past several movie theaters and almost all of them were xxx rated. They were all about sex but we did not know that sex was so prevalent here and in the open because we both thought it was sacred. Jen said, "Could we go and see a movie?" and I said, "It's all about sex."

She said, "I know and I would like to see one." I said, "We don't have time and must get back to our car because it's a one hour drive to get back home." I promised her we would come back and I would take her to one, but I really didn't want other guys to see my girl watching this stuff.

We got back at eight o'clock and I stopped at a parking lot. We hugged, kissed each other then I stopped and said, "Honey, we really must be careful," because I believe she was losing control again and I believe I must be the stronger gender.

She said, "Come on, we could just play," she paused then said; "Don't you want me?"

I said, "Ever since you told me that you wanted sex with me it has been on my mind and I do think about it. But I don't think we are ready for this and I think we should wait."

She did agree and said, "But I do want you to be my first so you will know that you were." I did understand her logic and if I was her first then I would feel indebted to her. I promised that she would be the first girl that I would go all the way with. But I could see now that her and Dot are playing the same game and it is just making things worse. I am caught in this triangle of love and sex and where will it end. I wanted to go to Jossey's again and get out of this situation. I asked her if she wanted to go and she said I've never been in a bar. I told her that I wanted to see Jossey because she wanted me to play my guitar there and I would get paid for it. I did need the experience and said you could come with me when I play.

She said, "Yes, I would like to," and we went to Jossey's. I met with Jossey's then introduced Jen as my girl friend and discussed my obligations. I tried to think of a date that I would start. School vacation was coming up this coming week and I thought that would be a good time. That way I could bring Jen on a school night. I asked about this Wednesday and she replied that was a bad night. She would rather it be Friday or Saturday and I agreed for Friday. We both had one drink I ordered Jen vodka with Orange Juice (Screwdriver). She liked it and said, "I want more when we come again." We were on our way home and she said, "I feel funny and lightheaded."

I said, "It's probably the drink because you never drank before." She was kissing me all the way and laughing at me, but by the time we arrived at her house she was fine. I kissed her good night then went home. I called Dorothy and told her that I went to New York and I might play my guitar for a Night club. She said could I go, I said "I will be with other people and I don't think it would be appropriate, but I will take you some time after I get to know the people." We talked for a while and I fell asleep. It is school vacation and I have been very busy with Dad. The main road is finished and I am now finishing the avenues. There will be four avenues and forty building lots finished. Dad has sold several lots all ready and some workers are starting foundations for a few houses.

We were well into February now and we had an Indian summer. It had been warm all week and this also made my Dad very happy. It was tough to pour concrete when it is below freezing, but we did add calcium just in case it did freeze. I had been trying to practice for Friday night and had not been out with the girls very much. My Dad was trying to force the town to take over the roads and this way they would have to pave them. There is a requirement of how many homes are being built before they will accept this. If they do, then I will be through with the roads and I will be able to go back to my normal life. I called Jen and she was very happy to hear this and said, "It is very lonely not being with you very much."

I said, "It will do us both good and we will know for sure if we love each other."

She said, "You don't know for sure? I do."

I said, "That's not it and you know what I mean." I asked her if she was ready to go with me to Jossey's. I told her, "You do know that I'm going to ask you to come on the stage and sing."

She said, "Oh, no you're not, because you know I can't sing."

I said, "I did hear you sing at the lark with the music and you do have a beautiful voice." I then said, "I won't ask you to sing, but I would like you to try with me when we are alone," and she said, "I might if we're alone."

I picked her up and we went to Jossey's. I told Jossey that I was very nervous, but I would do my best. Jossey said, "Al, don't be nervous with this crowd, because most of them are just a bunch of drunks and would probably kiss your ass to be able to do this."

I said, "That does make sense," and it was time for me to set up stage. I only had my own amplifier and not the system that I had at the Bog. This place was much smaller and it probably wouldn't matter, so I set up and ran a few chords. It sounded very good and every one turned around to look, then I went to sit with Jen. I finished my drink and went to the stage. Jen walked me to the stage and gave me a good luck kiss. I played the same way that I did at the Bog with my own Duane Eddy style instrumental and the crowd went wild. I knew that they liked me and that made it easier. I then played some waltzes and jitterbugs. Almost everyone was dancing, and I noticed that someone asked Jen to dance but she refused and just kept watching me.

I finished and asked the crowd if they wanted me to come back. They all screamed, "Yeah!

Jossey came to my table and said, "My God, you surprised me. Boy, you were great!" She sat with us for a while and I did schedule another recital for next Friday night. Just then a gentleman came to me and looked at me. He did not interrupt us, but put something into my jacket pocket and just said, "Call me." It was almost eleven o'clock and Jen was to be home at eleven. I drove straight to her home, but on the way Jen told me that she had a great time and that I should be in the movies.

She said "You were better than anyone that I have ever seen."

I said, "You're only saying that because you like me," and she said, "No, really." It was a twenty-five minute drive to her house and she asked, "Could we go to your house one night instead of going out?"

I said, "I'm too embarrassed to take you there," and she said, "I want to go anyway." I then said okay. We got to her house, I walked in with her and I apologized for being late. Bob and Betty were still up and in the living room. I said that I had to play my guitar at a place in New York and just finished.

He said, "You play guitar?" I said yes and he asked me where I played.

I said, "At Jossey's," and Bob said, "That's a bar, isn't it?"

I said, "It's really a night club." He asked me if that was a nice place to go. I answered, "It's up to the individual, but I do like it."

He said, "I guess you're right," and asked Jen, "Did you have a good time?"

She answered, "The best time of my life, but you should hear Al play. I told him that he should be in the movies."

They both said, "We would love to hear you." They asked, "Do you sing too?"

I said, "Sometimes but I'm too bashful, but I heard Jen sing to herself and she has a very good voice, so I asked her to sing with me some time."

He asked Jen out of the blue sky, "Did you drink any liqueur?"

She said, "Dad, I'm a big girl now. Don't you trust me?"

He said, "Yes, honey, but I do worry about you. She said nothing would ever happen to me as long as I am with Al and he said, "I'm counting on that."

I said, "You have my word, but why don't you two come with us one night and see?"

He said, "But that's a bar and we have never been to one over there." He looked at Betty and said, "You know, maybe we need a little spark in our lives. Why don't we go?"

Betty said, "It sounds like fun to me."

Jen and I both jumped and said, "We're so happy!" I thanked them and went home.

In conversations with both Dorothy and Jeanne, I had asked them not to question me about the other or why I didn't call. I said, "If I don't call or come at a certain time, there must be a reason and I would appreciate if you didn't question me about it." This had worked very well but I knew it was only a temporary solution.

It is Saturday morning and I did not have to help my Dad, so I'm going to pick up Dorothy. Sometimes I almost forget about her and I told her I would show her what I was doing at the development. She was all ready when I got there and I did walk in to say hello to her mother. I drove up to the development and just drove by because I am very hungry and wanted something to eat. I drove to a different town that I have never taken the girls before. It was only a fifteen mile ride and it is a nice little place. We had a very nice breakfast, then we just relaxed and talked about my recital last night. I wore the same jacket as I did last night and looking through my pockets I found a business card. It was from the gentleman that came to me while I was talking to Jossey and told me to call him. He then stuck this in my jacket pocket and I forgot about it. It said, "Vinnie Lee record studio," address and phone number. I couldn't wait to call him and could only think that he liked my performance last night. I showed it to Dot, she said, "You're gonna be a star and I'll never see you again."

I said, "You're not getting rid of me that easy." We then went to the development and I drove on the roads that I built.

She said, "You did all this?" I said my Dad helped me some. I asked, "Where do you want to go?" and she answered, "To your house." I was a little afraid of what she may want to do because now I felt that I may have a chance to do something with music, and did not want anything to interfere, but we did go to my house. I only had one chair and a bed of course we ended up on the bed. She was not as excited as Jen was and she did give me some breathing room. We were just lying on the bed and loving normally, which I needed. I was very tired and I was trying to rest a little so I let her do all the hugging and kissing. I think that I could have fallen asleep because I was thinking about this Vinnie and what it would mean. Dot said, "You look very tired and I think you need a good massage." She started rubbing me all over and it made me feel very comfortable. I was very relaxed and she was behaving and had her jeans on. She ran her hand under my belt and jeans a few times then back up to my stomach and chest. She played with my titties and I thought, Why not let her? This went on for a while and I told her that I was falling asleep.

She said, "You probably need the rest," and I was dosing off from the nice feeling of her hands all over me. I came very close to falling asleep and I think she thought I was. She very gently put her hand under my jeans and was holding me. I tried to make believe that I was asleep but the softness and the movement of her hand made me very excited while she kept squeezing and moving her hand.

It got to the point that I could not make believe any longer and said, "What are you doing to me?" I did feel that she was trying to make me love her, only her and would have done anything to win me over.

She said, "Just go to sleep and I just want to play for a while." I thought that I could go along with that, besides I did like it, so I laid back and relaxed.

She unzipped my jeans and took it out where she could get a good hold on it. I stopped her and asked again what are you doing. She said, "Please, I have never seen one and I want to look. I said, "What do you mean? You saw me naked in the shower." She said, "Not like this," and I did know what she meant. She said, "I love doing this and could I just play?" I said to myself, how could I stop her now? So I just laid there and let her play.

She moved it slow and said it's getting wet and I said, "Would you just let me go to sleep because I'm embarrassed." She said all right and just played with it very gentle. I was so very relaxed and I never said another word but I did fall asleep. I slept for about an hour then she woke me up and said you're not going to sleep all day are you. I said I'm sorry and she said, "That's all I really needed." I'm so very happy that Jen didn't try to call, but I would have not answered the phone anyway. We went to a Restaurant and had dinner. I thanked her for letting me be her teacher and said I would hold classes on weekends. She laughed and said she would be there. I told her I wanted to call Vinnie and maybe I could go see him so I took her home. I tried to call Vinnie last night and did not get an answer.

I just woke up it is seven thirty I will wait until nine before I try and call him. I cleaned the house, have all my laundry ready and I must go to the laundry today. I tried calling Vinnie again, he just answered and I told him who I was. He said, "I wanted to talk to you at Jossey's but you had company," then he asked me, "Where did you learn to play?" I said I picked it up on my own. He said, "I like your style, it's different and it caught my attention." He said "I'm going to Allegro Studios in New York Thursday afternoon and would you like to go?"

I said, "I would love to, but what time are you going?" He said around two o'clock and I said, "Yes that's good because I get out of work at two." I told him where I worked and asked if he could stop there.

He said, "I will be there," and I asked, "Will I need my gear?" He said, "No I just want you to watch and talk with me." I was very excited and called Jen. I told her what happened and I was going to New York where they cut the records and I want to do mine.

She said, "If you get famous you won't want me anymore, will you?" I said, "I love the way you trust me and I am not going to be famous." She said, "I do trust you and I know you will do well."

I said, "I told you that I'm only going to watch and I don't know when I'm going again." She said, "Are you coming to get me?"

"Am I supposed to?"

"You said you would take me to your house."

I said next week and she said, "I was just hoping." I said I would come up later and I would like to show you the work I did at the development. She said, "I would like to see it," so I picked her up, then went to the laundry mat to finish my clothes first. I drove her through the roads, and then showed her the new foundations being built and the bulldozer. She said, "You drove that big thing?"

I said, "It's only a D 8 medium size one." We just rode around and I told her I would be very busy this week. I will call you when I could, but we won't be able to go out much this week."

She said, "Is there something wrong?"

I said, "No, why?"

"Because you sound like you're changing."

I said, "What makes you say that?"

She said, "You're not happy are you?"

I said, "I'm sorry," and she said, "That's all I really needed." Without her knowing it she put her future in my trust. She really is a very good person and will do anything for me. Jeanne is the most wonderful and care free girl that I have ever met. I could see that she is honest and has built her life around me. Her father and mother have welcomed me into their lives and I love them both. I believe now that if I did have a chance for any career it may be with Jen, because her college would give us several years to mature and increase our chances. With Dorothy I would probably have a chance because she is not demanding and has never tried to hold me back. I find that my love trapped in this prism is divided equal and I'm finding that there is no easy solution. I must go back to my common denominator. I am the link or hypotenuse that binds this triangle and I alone must decide.

Before I discuss this any further I must reiterate the subject of the conference I just had with Dorothy. This started after the rape episode and continued until the time that we became understanding of each other and now everything does fit in place. I told Dot that I would have that talk with her mother because I believed that she was hurting her own daughter without realizing it. During our conversation I found the missing part of the puzzle and did not decipher it until now. Dot and Beatrice did not tell me that the night of the Mickey; Dot did get very sick and started vomiting then developed the dry heaves. Beatrice said it was greenish and she had to shake and walk her, because she was passing out. Dot did drink most of the ginger ale and I believed this was what induced the vomiting. I had asked several people and a doctor about the effects of a Mickey. None of the symptoms applied with having part of a cocktail. I ran this through my mind several times and there was always something missing. My only knowledge of Dot going to the Bog on Saturday night was that there was a good chance she would find him there. I was told several times that she had to get even with him and hurt him.

I did not think by her going there and dancing close to me could hurt him, because if he treated her as he did he could not have liked her that much in the first place. I was lost for an explanation and did believe that somehow she still loved him. Beatrice finally noticed that there was something wrong and was afraid she may have tried to take her own life. I could not believe that at least not the night we were out. Because she appeared to be very happy with me at my recital and had something to look forward to. The night that I picked her up at the theater was the only time that I seen any contemplation, but I still didn't believe that she would. This past conversation did reveal the premeditation and desire of revenge. Dorothy bought some rat poison and placed small amounts in to small plastic pill casings, which she acquired from emptying headache pills and planned to empty this into the drink that Cat was drinking. She said she had performed this a few times before and had not seen any results, so this time she added much more. I could only believe that Cat must have caught on to something or just by accident the drink was switched with hers and she drank her own potion. She was very lucky that she did not drink it all because the bottom may have been concentrated. I asked her how she got them that night and she showed me she always has them in her purse. The rest is self explanatory and I promised this I would never reveal.

It is Thursday, March 7, 1958; I am just leaving work and hope to be meeting Vinnie. I have not seen the girls this week, but I did tell them that I would call them tonight if I was to return early or I would call tomorrow. I am walking to my car and notice a station wagon. A gentleman came to me and introduced himself as Vinnie. I said I do recognize you from José's. We shook hands and he asked if I wanted to ride with him. I said that would be fine, because this would give us a chance to talk. He said that he was a retired recording artist and people would hire him to get them started in the recording of music. He asked me what my intentions were and said, I would like to get to know more about you and I replied, "The same here". We drove to N Y and went to Allegro Recording Studio and I have never seen so much equipment in my life. There were several tape recorders that took up a complete room. There were all kinds of amplifiers, large and small speakers dubbing equipment and I don't know what else. I did not play this time so I just watched and asked questions.

Three other people came in and he had to be with them, because he did play lead guitar with them. I was amazed when they finished a song they could play it back and add more to it and as much as they wanted. This would go on different recorders and would play back together. If you thought one part needed a little more you could play it right in. I watched the others play and they were very good and probably better than me, but I still liked my style better and I do think mine would be liked by many more. I didn't know this but you lease this studio by the hour and ours was up so we had to leave, because there were more people waiting to go in. We then went to the Columbia Studios and had the tapes cut into dumps, whatever that meant. I think this is when it is transferred to LPs. We then went to the Fascination Restaurant and we had a bite to eat. There were many stars there and I was surprised that I was in the same place with them. After I watched them I thought that I could be a star if I tried. We then went home and stopped at Al Pats for coffee, because it was a two hour drive from New York City and traffic was very heavy most of the way so we had a chance to talk a lot. We found we were the same nationality and spoke a little in our language. We became friends then I went to his house and practiced with him. We did well together and I did not get home until two a.m. Friday morning. I fell asleep right away and just woke up, but I have to go to work and can't call the girls until I get home tonight. Fred and Charley were both there and after work I went to the office to speak with them.

Closing Shop

I already knew we were closing soon but did not know what day. They confirmed that Friday the fifteenth was the last day and I was glad in a way because my life needed a change. I went home and called Jeanne first. It was only three thirty and I knew she was home from school. She answered as usual and I said, "Hi, my love." She said "I knew it was you and how did you make out?" I explained the whole thing, and then said, "I know I could make it and I really think that I'm better than anyone that I have seen and especially with that equipment." I know that many people would like my style better. She said she was very happy and asked if I was coming to her house. I told her that I did not get to bed until three a.m. and was dead tired but I assured her that I would call later.

She said, "Are we going to your house tomorrow or Sunday?"

I said, "Maybe tomorrow and we could figure it out when I call." I said, "I love and miss you but I have to go."

I called Dot and told her the same thing as I told Jen. She said, "I knew you had it in you to do it and I thought that you should the day you played at the Bog. And if you keep playing like that in different places then someone would spot you and take you away." I said, "What do you mean take me away?" She said, "Take you in the movie business, or something like that and I would never see you again."

I said, "I'm glad you think that highly of me, but you're dreaming more than I am." I went on to say that Vinnie asked me to practice with him and he is going to call me at anytime. "Dot, you're not coming tonight," I said, "I will call you later after he calls but I do want to get a little sleep because I'm really dead," and explained.

She said, "Okay, but I would like to see you tonight if I could." I said I would try then I laid down, set my clock for one hour and fell asleep. When I awoke I took a hot shower and this woke me up. I felt pretty good but I knew I was losing the battle with the girls and decided to just give in to their wants. I thought about what to do this weekend and tried to plan an agenda. I thought it would be better to see Dot tonight because I could see Jen Saturday night

161

and Sunday. I could spend some time with Dot Sunday night. I planned this agenda in hopes that I could pacify them for now because I don't think that I could run away from it until I find a solution.

I just called Jen and I know I will have to lie to both of them but this is not new. It was now "do, die, or lie". I had never lied before this and this had become my biggest problem, because small lies leads to bigger ones and continues. Jen answered the phone and I explained that I could not see her tonight but would see her tomorrow night and Sunday. It was only seven o'clock, I told her I would stop on my way and see her in her driveway for just a few minutes. She said I'll watch for you and I drove right there. I believe Jen is becoming more important in my life right now, but I cannot forget the love I have and had for Dot. I knew that if she was this way before I would have married her and I would not have met Jen. I drove to Jen's; and she ran out threw her arms around me and said, "I missed you so much." It was dark and no one could see us from her house. She put her lips on mine and really kissed me as if there was no tomorrow. I held her equally and let her enter my heart alone. I said, "You don't know how much I love you and what it means to see you run into my arms because I know it's the best feeling I've ever had."

She looked at me with the warmest of looks and I just felt completely relaxed. I wanted so much to take her to my house and just hold her for hours. I thought it would be soon and it was hard to wait any longer. I explained that I did have to go and would call her tomorrow. I was here for thirty minutes and it seemed like only five. I left a little heartbroken to do this to her while knowing where I was going. I drove into Dot's driveway and she came running out to me. She was wearing a cute skirt and a real white blouse, I think it was silk or Dacron. It had a v-neck with exposed part of her breast. I opened my door to get out and she grabbed my hand to assist me, then threw her arms around me and squeezed me until I grunted. I said, "Let's go in the house, you could catch cold," and what in the hell am I going to do? She looked so beautiful and I don't think there is a guy that wouldn't do anything to go out with her. For the first time she looked radiant. I could see she did have a better out look towards life and showed more self-respect. This made me feel good that the sexual encounters that we experienced were medicine for her heart and mind. It did remove any guilt that I may have had about this episode. She just about pulled me into her house and asked if I wanted something to eat. She said they just finished and everything was still hot. I was hungry and we wouldn't have to go to a diner. We sat at the table then her mother sat with us, but we just talked about my music and Dots job. She received a raise in pay and was missed very much by her customers. This was very good for her and I knew that the job at the Bog was out of her mind now. I do credit this change in her life was greatly from the love and trust that I placed in her to help her find a place on this road to life.

I became confused again because I always said she had the power to polarize my mind and I was weak in defending myself. Somehow she removed all thoughts of Jen from my mind when I'm with her. It was getting late and her mother went to bed. Dot grabbed my hand and pulled me into her bedroom but I did not show any resistance. I followed her and she pushed me on to the bed then climbed on top of me. She felt so soft and warm so I just put my arms around her and held her. I rolled over on my side and we laid there just holding each other. The way I feel right now I know she wouldn't have to fight me to make love with her. I did expect her to fondle me and was looking forward to it but she just held and kissed me. We just said sweet nothings and laid there. I knew that no matter how much I wanted to have sex with her it would not be productive and could only fuel the fire in this love triangle. I was happy that she did behave and was not progressive. I finally got up and she knew that I had to leave. She walked me to the door kissed me, said, "I love you very much and I am yours to take any time you want."

I said, "I love you to," and I said to myself, "You'd better be ready soon because I know I can't hold out much longer."

She said, "I think about the time we were at your house and I'm sorry but I'm ready whenever you want me. I got home and I'm mad at myself because I have wanted this for so long and I'm refusing to feed my desires. I said to myself that the next time I will obey my needs and her desires. I know I was looking for an excuse to make it seem right, but I could not find a way to make it seem wrong either. I was really hurting, I just walked around and looked at my watch and didn't think she went to sleep yet so I picked up the phone to call her. I thought about the promise I made to Jen and hung up before it rang. My body was trembling and I was getting addicted to the feeling of wanting sex. I knew it was just a matter of time that these girls would win their battle. I wouldn't be able to resist the influence they now have on me. I felt that we want each other very much and who's to say that we can't share our love. I have never been progressive and I have denied them what they expected of me to fulfill their desires. I will not change my behavior but I feel I must yield to them. I called Dot again and she said, "I'm surprised you called, what's wrong?"

I said, "Could I come and sleep with you tonight?"

She replied, "Oh My God, yes." I drove there as quickly as I could, she met me in the drive way again and we went into her bed room. We were holding each other and she asked what happened. I said, "I just needed you, I had trouble going home and I was happy you were still awake." I said, "Is there anything wrong with us doing what we both want?"

She said, "Why don't we try and see?" At this time we were all alone in this world and I was very content. She just had her nighties on so I stripped to my undies and hopped in bed with her. She pulled the blankets over us and we clenched together. I thought, *boy this is so much better then sleeping alone.* We are excited and just fondled each other while learning about the true facts of life. We both fell asleep and I didn't awake until late morning. I still had my arms around her but felt very strange. I knew I was developing a mental problem and was becoming paranormal. I believe what is happening is that I am combining Dot and Jen into one love and cannot separate them, but most of all I don't think I want to. I may becoming addicted to sex and planned this weekend to have sex with both of them. I don't know how it started but this is what happens when we are together alone. I must admit that I don't feel any guilt and feel that somehow it may be right, since we all agree. It is almost nine o'clock and I must have passed out last night. I am really mentally exhausted and wanted to sleep all day but I knew I couldn't. I had to go see dad then pick up Jen. I promised I would pick her up today and would take her to my house on Sunday. She wanted to see how I live and I told her that it wasn't very nice. I called Dot and told her I had to leave now but I would call her tonight, then I got dressed and decided to go see her before I picked up Jen and called her to let her know.

Again she met me in the driveway and was dressed to kill. I said, "You look beautiful, where are you going?" and she said, "Nowhere. I just did it for you because I want to look nice when you come to see me."

I said, "Honey, you don't have to look that nice for me but you do look beautiful." I said, "You are radiant, you glow and you are the one who should be a star."

She said, "Don't be funny." She took my hand and led me into the house. She did not ask me but she made breakfast and served it on the table in front of me. We both ate together then we just talked about last night and when we could be together again. I did not know what to say and again had to lie. I told her that I would be with Vinnie this weekend and maybe she could come to my house and stay overnight. She looked up, and then said, "I will love that and will be waiting for you."

While I was talking with her she cleaned the table and washed the dishes then folded the laundry that she had washed earlier. She was like a mother already, she was very clean and I like that in a girl. I had to leave then, so she walked me to the door and kissed me. I told her that I would call her and left. I went to Jen's house and Bob and Betty were there so I explained my day in New York at the studios. They were impressed and said, "We both hope you make it with your music career," then Jen grabbed my hand and said, "Let' go." I said all right then we said, "See you later," and left.

I did not go through town and took the lake road. I had to pass Sparky's house and just remembered that I never called her back. I hope see does not see me and asked Jen if she had seen her lately. She said, "No, why?" and I reminded her of the time that I promised to take her somewhere or I would call. She said don't worry about it she'll forget. I did not ask her where she wanted to go I was just going to the Lark. She asked, "Why are we going this way?" and I said we were going to the Lark. She said, "I thought that we were going to see your house." I said we could do that tomorrow and she said, "But we already ate, why are we going to the Lark?" She kept talking and in her conversation she told me her plan. "We could go to your house today and have lunch at the lark tomorrow, doesn't that make more sense?" I couldn't argue the point but I was afraid to go to my house alone with her today, because someone could see us walk in and I was worried but I turned my car around and headed there. When we got there I parked behind the house so no one would know that I was home. I walked her into the house and showed it to her. I did make the bed and the house was very clean, but I really don't have time to dirty it. She said it was cute and I said, "It's okay for now." She hopped on the bed and said, "Come here with me." I laid alongside of her and we started kissing and hugging. I looked at her and I could see equal beauty but incorporated with innocence, "Beauty in the bloom". Her look was very soft and innocent and I felt totally different when I was with her. I knew that right now she was mine and only mine.

Is Intimate Sex Inevitable

I was lying on my back while she was kissing me and placing her tongue in my mouth, licking my lips on the inside. I pulled her tongue in to my mouth and sucked on it gently. I then put my tongue into her mouth and she would suck on it as I did to her. She stopped then started kissing my neck, chest and titties while sliding her hand under my jeans. I held her very tight. I said, "We must limit what we do and shouldn't get carried away." I knew this will be tough but we must and she said, "Please, I'm not going to do anything wrong I just want to experiment and I let you feel my breast. You know I have never seen or felt a man before."

I said, "I know, but . . ." and the way she looked at me I could see she is interested in learning more about me and men in general. I said, "I'm just going to lay here and you do what you want, but just be careful. She said, "Oh, thank you," and I just laid there. I was a little embarrassed because I knew that she has never seen or done this before, and I did not know how far she would go. She kept kissing me and kissed my titties while watching while she undid my belt and loosened my jeans. She reached down and found what she was searching for. She squeezed it while it grew in her hand and I could see she became very excited. I pushed my jeans down to give her more room and she was glad that I did that and thanked me. I did not want her to be any more embarrassed then she already was. She was moving it while she was studying it and felt it grow even more. I knew she was surprised but never said a word. She held it and started kissing my titties while looking at it. She pulled down on it to explore and I could see the interest she had, but did not stop her because I was getting very aroused. I put my hand between her legs and she was very warm and her panties were wet. I then moved my hand under her panties and placed my hand over her private. This felt good knowing that I was the first ever to do this. I moved my finger inside her just a little and it felt very silky and soft. She let go of me and took her clothes off. I looked at her complete body and she is so beautiful. I couldn't believe that I had this girl here with me and said I must be the luckiest person in the world. I was satisfied because right now I believed that she would be mine forever and I never want to see anyone else. She pulled off my jeans then helped me with my shirt and played with me for a while. I pulled her up where we could just kiss each other because I was getting scared that I could not stop with just playing.

We were lying on our sides holding, kissing and I was holding her to tight at times and she said I can't breathe. I loosened my arms and she put one leg over me and rubbed my private on hers. It was so soft, hot and silky. She just had the head in and was rubbing it up and down on her. She said in a trembling voice "this feels so good". I told her that she had to stop and we can't go any further because I would ejaculate and get semen all over her. She said oh please I want to watch and I was now in a spot where I could not stop. I did not tell her no, so she got on top of me and put it back where it was. She was rubbing as she was before but started pressing down to make it go into her. She was still holding it and I put my hand over hers to limit how far she could go. I felt her pushing harder and tried to push it in more but it would not go without hurting her. She still had her hand on me, I couldn't hold it any longer and ejaculated. She was rubbing it on my belly saying, "It is so slippery." She was still holding it in her other hand and said, "What happened to it?" She started to play with it and said it's not big any more. She looked surprised and asked, "Will it get big again?"

I said, "Yes, but it takes time and I really don't know how long." She got up to get a wash cloth and towel so we could clean up. While she was washing me she put her hand on my testicles and asked, "What are these?" I explained, "This is where the sperm is stored."

She asked, "Are these what they call your balls?" then asked me all kinds of questions. I said yes and explained everything the best I could. We laid here for awhile and then took a shower. I looked at her and told her that she is picture perfect. "I cannot find a thing I would ever want to change on you," I said. "I feel very bad and guilty for doing this and think it is wrong."

She yelled at me and said, "I offer you my body, my love and it is wrong? Please tell me why and I think I have something to say about this." This was the first time I ever seen her speak with authority and I do believe now that it shouldn't be just I that decides. I didn't know what to say then said, "I love you and you were pure before you met me."

She answered, "Would it have been all right if I did it with someone else first?" I said I was very sorry and never thought about it like that. I said, "I do believe you are right and it should be just between us." I do feel much better now and she pulled me back to the bed. I could see she was still excited while lying alongside her and I had less fear now than I did before. I thought about when she tried to push it in but she was to small and I knew that she was telling the truth. She put her hand on me again and got up to watch it then lifted my balls. She was interested in learning all about sex and what happens while she was playing she said it's getting hard again. She said, "I'm so excited and I love doing this." I was still holding my hand on her and knew I never wanted anything more than her. I pushed my finger into her, she was wet and I had no trouble. It was warm and smooth and I knew I really wanted to go all the way. She asked me how I felt and I said I was still very nervous. She was holding it and said, "This thing makes babies, huh?" I said yes and she still had it in her hand. She laid next to me and put her legs around me again. She started to rub it in her again and pulled me over on top of her. She still had a hold of it and was keeping it there. She had her legs and arm behind me while she was pulling me in. I did not want to penetrate her and tried to stop. She pleaded with me to push it in but I became scared.

I was still laying on top of her and she was pleading, "Please you promised you would be my first." I pushed a little and it did not go so I pushed a little harder. I did not want to hurt her and thought about what happened to Dot. She still had her legs around me then she put her arms on my back and pulled me very hard. I felt it go in past a tight spot and it was only halfway in because I had my hand there. I removed my hand and it went all the way in. Our bodies were together and this was our first time to have real sex. I just laid there and held her, but I did not move. I just knew it was all the way in and for some reason I was very happy. I looked at her, she was looking at me with eyes wide open and said, "Thank you, I love you so very much." We laid there for a long time without moving and looked at each other. We were both very happy that we did this and I said, "I love you so very much also." I put my hand on her and when I looked at it I noticed that it had blood on it. I still was inside of her and I showed her my hand. She said she was told that she would bleed the first time. She explained that I broke her hymen and this is supposed to happen. I was afraid that I hurt her but she insisted that I did not. She said, "Please don't take it out, I want you to finish." She was holding me tight and was moving her body with mine. I knew that she didn't want me to stop and I felt better. I think that the scare slowed me down and I was not close as I was. I did it for a while longer while kissing her and I could feel that we belonged this way, because it was natural.

I did not feel bad at this time and we were just enjoying each other. I was waiting to see if she would reach a climax and didn't know if girls did. I asked her and she didn't know but said what we were doing was good enough. I was happy because I felt so good and kept kissing her. I just rolled over lifeless and she got up and cleaned herself then came back to wash me. She said that there was not a lot of blood and she would make a pad out of toilet paper and put it in her panties. We changed the sheet and got back in bed. I asked her if she was mad at me and she said she has never been this happy. We just laid there holding each other and she said, "Do you believe me now?"

I said, "I always did believe you and knew you were innocent." I said, "I want to tell you this is the first time I ever went this far with anyone. I knew I loved her enough to do anything to prove my love for her also. We laid there for about an hour just talking about what we did and asked each other what was the best part. She said when you went all the way because I waited so long for you to do this. I want to thank you for my wishes and you made me a woman today. I said I did not think of that but you made me a real man and she did convince me that we did the right thing today. We were lucky that we took all our clothes off and we could put them back on and go. We both got into the shower and we washed each other again. She still was bleeding a little and asked her if it hurt. She said it was a little sore and I said I was sorry. She said, "Please, I asked for it, I'm very happy," and I said, "You always know how to make me feel good and make things right." I am washing her titties and telling her that I never knew she was so beautiful. I told her, "I love your titties," and kissed them. They were so firm and had a perfect shape. Not like the ones that I seen in books. I had to kiss the other one also so it wouldn't get jealous. I was getting to love sex so much and didn't think about anything else. I was happy that Jen and I both thought we did the right thing. We finished in the shower after washing and fondling each other. She washed me very good while studying it and asking questions about it again. I did not touch her because it was bleeding but I did ask her to explain it to me. She did explain and I asked her what part the pee came from and she showed me. She also showed me the spot that made her feel the best. I did not know the names and she told me. I do know now what the vagina, the clitoris and where she pees from. I did look inside when she pulled it open and explained the hymen and where it was ripped.

That was a great grand tour and now we both knew all that we had to know. I did explain the part of my penis that was most sensitive. We got dressed and had time to get something to eat. I was starved after this very hard day's work so we went to a nice diner and talked about today. When we finished dinner and I gave Jen a ride home. I told her that it would be good if she went home early and I should go in for a while. We discussed what we would say if we

169

were asked where we went today. We got to her house and we both walked in. We started to talk about me practicing with my guitar today and that got us on to the subject and we talked about the play that was scheduled for next Saturday night. We all had a good time and I had to go. Jen walked to my car with me and said, "I love you, and thank you. Will I see you tomorrow?"

I said, "You bet." I kissed her, went to my house and laid on the bed. All I could think about was our day here. I was so relaxed and believe happy that I did not call Dot because I needed to think about today and I fell asleep early.

Today is Sunday, I over slept and it is almost eight o'clock. I am going to Al Pats to have breakfast then try and plan my day. I told Jen that I would pick her up before noon and I promised Dot I would see her tonight. I walked into Al Pats and had to sit at the counter because the place was packed. I ordered my breakfast and got up to leave, but I would have stayed longer if I had a booth. I walked to my car and Vinnie was just pulling in. He parked his car and said, come on in and have a coffee. I said I just did but I will have another and said there are no booth. We will have to sit at the counter. He said that's o k then ordered a coffee and soon after we did get a booth. Vinnie said we would have to practice and get together on what we were going to play. He said we could go to his house later, "I have all my gear there but bring your guitar," and I said, "What time?"

He said, "Anytime, I'll be there the rest of the day," and I said, "I'll be there." It was ten o'clock and I thought that I would call Jen from here. I went to the pay phone and called her. I told her that I had to go to Vinnie's house but could come there now. She said come on so I went to her house and went in. Every one was there and I told them that I would have to leave before one o'clock to go to practice with Vinnie. Bob asked if I wanted to stay for lunch and Jen yelled, "Yes," so I smiled and said I would.

Bob asked, "Where is your guitar, at your home?" and Jen said, "No, he keeps it in his car." He said, "Could you bring it in and show us something?" Jen said, "I'll help you get it," I looked at Bob, and then smiled and said, "I don't have too much to say about it." He yelled, "Jen!" I said, "I'm only kidding." We both went to the car and brought it in. Bob and Betty sat on the couch then just watched. I was more shy here than at the clubs and I told them, "You guys make me nervous."

He said, "Come on, we're almost family."

I said, "That's why," then I set up the amplifier and played a few instrumentals. I played "Turkey in the Straw" first, then some of Duane Eddy's and finished with my own instrumentals. He asked if I could play any of Hank

William's songs and I said I could play them all. He asked me to play "Your Cheating Heart" or the Tennessee Waltz". They were swaying and singing with the sound of music, but I looked at Jeanne while I was playing it. They both said, "We haven't heard music like that in a long time," and Jen said, "I told you he was good." They replied that I was very good and were looking forward to going with us next Saturday night. Lunch was ready so I put my gear into my car and went in to have lunch with them. Soon after I had to leave and told Jen I would either stop in or call. I did not know how long I would be there and I left to go to Vinnie's.

We practiced a long time and we did a lot that we could play together with no problem. We tried to do the Orange Blossom Special with just two guitars. I had played it before, but with my friend with a Violin. His name was Carl Swanson and we did it perfect together. He was the one who taught me that and that's how the original artist played it. Vinnie and I practiced it and it came out very good. I then played my special and he liked it very much. I played lead and he did the rhythm to fill in. It came out very well and we were pleased. California Be Bop and the Grind were just starting to be popular and this style was just right for that but we would play a few waltzes and some jitterbugs. It was six-thirty now and we decided to call it a day. I told him that we could practice any night of the week, "Just call me."

I went home and called Jen. I told her I would be another hour or so and I would not stop tonight. I told her we were doing very well and have our act together for the play. I may have to practice one night during the week but I would call her after school and stop in after work. I did not call Dot and just drove to her house. She seen me drive in and came running out to my car. I said to myself, *why wasn't she like this four months ago, and I wouldn't be in the situation that I am now?* I got out and she hugged me and told me how much she missed me. I could have started to cry looking at her because of what Jeanne and I did. I went into her house and sat at the table with her but I felt very guilty. I told her that I practiced a lot and my fingers were sore. I showed her my fingers and she said, "Do you want to put ice on them?"

I said, "They will be okay," and she asked where we were going. I said, "I don't know do you have any ideas?"

She said, "There's a good movie playing at the theater." I said that was a good idea, and I could rest a little. We went to the movie and we both watched it but I could see she had changed a lot in the last few weeks, she had really grown up and is a young lady now but all I could think of was, "Why couldn't she be this way before I met Jeanne?" She did not get sexy with me at all but she was very lovable and we had a very nice time then stopped for a snack. We went back to her house then and talked for a while then went to her bed room. We just laid in her bed and talked. She did hug and kiss me but not as much as usual and she really behaved. It was time for me to go and she asked, "Aren't we going to your house tonight?"

I said, "Honey, I would love to, but I have to get up at six a.m. and it is almost twelve o'clock now." She said she understood and held me very tightly while asking, "When could we go to your house again?" I said, "Maybe next Saturday or Sunday, or I might have a night off this week. She walked me to my car and I went home. Rejecting her made me feel guiltier and I felt very bad. I had been so involved with both of them but I knew now that this must end somehow because I was afraid something bad will happen. Because we all live in this small town and we have been lucky not to cross paths.

The Final Hours at Work

It is Monday and I'm in the office with Charley, Fred and someone that I have not met until now. We were discussing this week and the closing. All the printing equipment was already moved to Derby and we only had about two days work for the frame. Most of the workers were to be laid off today. I volunteered to hand out the pink slips, not because I like to do it but I could get back at some of the workers that tried to form the union because I do believe that this is what helped close this place. I passed them around and told them all that we would not open again. They could collect unemployment compensation and explained where the office was then kept some of the workers to stay the rest of the week. We had to complete the orders that we started and pack all of the overage. Almost every lot that we process has an overage. This is from our equipment stretching the material and we could get as much as a hundred yards per one thousand. We would pack this in lots for a company that would buy it and we are assorting this now. We find a lot of small pieces, anywhere from five yards to twenty yards.

Most of this will not be sold but will be discarded so I am offering this to the folders and other workers that I kept to help of course this was with the approval of Fred. I kept several bundles of odds and ends for myself and took it home. Everyone was happy to get this and some of it was very expensive synthetics. Such as Dacron a new synthetic and Zelon which is water proof that just came out and was new to the market. We had a lot of chemicals left that were opened and had to dispose of. I had the charts of the active ingredients and an explanation of what these were, including their molecular and atomic structure. I found while playing with them we had all of the ingredients to make nitroglycerin. I did formulate some and let it set for a while then forgot that I made it. I found it at a later date but really didn't believe it would work until I threw this small amount at the concrete wall. It was about fifty feet away and it blew a hole in the cement block wall and shook the complete building. The blast actually forced me back and scared me. The shock waves loosened the lint all over the upstairs equipment and I was called in to the office. I learned not to experiment with chemicals but I did make a hair gel that I used for years.

It would keep your hair in place in a hurricane, yet wash out easily and would keep your hair from getting gray. When I found time I reviewed the mixture that I used to make the bomb, although I didn't know it would explode when I made it. It was like a soft plastic and my studies showed that it was C 4, which is an unstable substance. I was surprised because the inner ingredients were readily available. I know I will never forget how to produce it, if I need to. I found that mixing magnesium and carbon in the ingredients would increase the detonation time and become much hotter. I will not elaborate on the complete formula it could be dangerous in the wrong hands.

Today is Wednesday and we are ahead of schedule and this is the last day for all the employees. I feel it's a sad day for many workers that have spent so many years here and have no other profession. I did wonder what they would do now. I called Dot and explained to her what I was doing but would call her when I got home. I would be there to disconnect the power to all the equipment and terminate the water supply then make sure that all of the chemicals were gone or contained.

I am going to see Bob or Al at the Redi-Mix plant to see when they are going to open. They were both there and told me that it would me the first week in April but they wanted me to start early. I would have to get my truck ready and make sure the hopper was set. I would also need some assistance in moving the Train Box Cars on to the conveyor that unloads the box cars in to the storage hopper since I have never done this so I will start on the first. It is Friday noon and I am finished here at the textile plant. I have Fred and Charles's addresses, phone numbers then we had our last talk and I am leaving for good. I was sad but happy because I knew that my life had to move on. I felt that I have been spinning my wheels and not going anywhere. I have two weeks off and must decide what to do. I have no work scheduled in my shop so I bought a 1940 Mercury convertible and a 1936 Buick convertible. I want to restore the Buick and customize the Mercury. I stored the Buick and started to work on the Mercury. I removed all the lights and molding, stripped most of the paint then gave it a light coat of primer. This was to retard any rusting and gave me something to do.

I went to Al-Pats to have lunch and I'm on my way home to call Vinnie. He said that he would meet me at the club at six-thirty. This was early and gave us enough time to have a drink and get set up. Jen and her family was going with me tomorrow night and I figured I should see Dot tonight but I promised Jen that I would see her right after school at her house. I went there and she invited me in. We were all alone, I sat on the couch and she sat with me. I have only talked to her once all week but she was still sore and asked me again if I really liked it. I said, "Don't say that, my God, that's all I thought about"

She laughed at me and said, "That also occupied my mind all week." Thinking about that made me sexy and I knew that sex was getting the best of me. I wanted to make love to her again but told her that we can't let this get out of control. She said, "What's wrong with it?" and I said, "I don't think that's all we should think about."

She said, "You don't want me anymore," and I said, "Damn you, that's all I want every day now. When I'm in my bed I think about what we did there and I suffer trying to go to sleep." She said, "Why suffer? I'm willing." I thought, every time I try to make it feel wrong, she assures me that it's all right. I told her we could go somewhere this weekend.

She said, "I'm sorry, I'm just excited and love to think about making love with you. It makes me happy and I can't get it off my mind."

I said, "I know, but we have the rest of our lives and can't let this ruin what we have." I said, "I don't have to tell you how much I love you but I know I must find a way to control myself." I said to myself, *this is not right to do with two girls but I don't know how to get out of it. I wish they could become friends so I could marry both of them and that would solve all my problems.*

I knew that I would be with Jen tomorrow and would not see Dot so I decided to call her. She answered and said, "Are you coming to see me?" I could not say no and I said, "Yes, I'll be there in a few minutes, but I can't stay long because my recital is tomorrow night and we have to practice." She was waiting for me then walked out to my car and was very polite and courteous. Again she is dressed nice and wore a skirt again. She always wore jeans before and now skirts but I don't blame her for showing her legs because they are beautiful. She walked in with me then stopped in the doorway and turned to look at me. Her eyes were wide open and I think she was searching for answers. She said sadly, "We haven't seen each other very much lately. Do you still love me?" I looked at her eyes but the sadness that I could see made me sad. I wondered, *what am I going to do"!* Because I knew I was favoring Jen. I thought that a few months ago you couldn't keep me away from her and I would have walked through a storm to see her. I could see why she felt this way and I started to hurt inside because I knew it was mostly my fault.

I said I really must find the answer. I just held, kissed, squeezed her and said, "Honey, you know my life is all screwed up right now. I don't know what direction to take, I don't have a job right now and I have a lot of work in my shop that I'm not doing. I'm working on a career in music and want to cut some records while my Dad is trying to build a development. I went to the Redi-Mix plant to see if I had that job, and it goes on."

She said, "I'm sorry and I see that you have so much on your mind but I miss you. I wish I could help you. I want you to bring your laundry here. I will do it for you and I will clean your house. I will help you all that I can, Al. I want to help you and be with you."

I said, "Honey, I appreciate this and love you for it but could we go sit and talk about it, just you and I?" I seen how much she had changed and had grown up now. I wished that I could promise her more right now but when I'm with Jen I believe that Dot and I wouldn't make it because of all the hurt she put me through before. She has changed her mind in the past and I'm afraid she may again. I felt that Jen was more mine and I have never shared her with anyone. She had always loved and never hurt me once. There has never been anyone like Cat in her life and I know there have never been harsh words between us. Her family is normal and I believe they love me, and I have never had a family. This has educated me to the fact that I could have this kind of relation in my life. This has been on my mind while Dot has all her problems but with the change in Dot I could see a young woman that really loves me, has been through the ropes, has been hurt almost beyond recovery and has made herself to what she is now. I could see a good mother and a faithful wife with her. Jen is a year younger and will be away for college and may find someone else there.

Dot said, "Wake up. What were you thinking about?" I said, "My life, you and me," and she said, "Is that good or bad?"

I said, "When I do stop and think, I try not to most of the time, but when I do I know how much I loved you and I feel that we would be good for each other." She said, "You really mean that?" and I said, "I do right now."

She said, "You don't always think that way?" and I said, "Sometimes I do have my doubts." She asked why, and I said, "From the way you were before, and the things you said to me, I was hurt for more than a year and I was at your beck and call all the time." She said, "I'm sorry. I had problems, but I did tell you the truth."

I said, "I don't want to talk about it now."

She said, "Why are you mad at me?" and I said, I'm not mad I just feel the hurt when I look back. She got up from her chair; tears were starting to come to her eyes. She held onto me and both her hands were around me squeezing me very tight. She was crying and trying to say, "I'm sorry, so very sorry, but please don't hate me for what I did. You know now why I was that way and I did tell you the truth because I never meant to hurt you." She started to cry and said, "Please tell me what I could do now because I will do anything for you." She loosened her grip and said, "I know I should try to forget you and let you leave because I know you will never forgive me." She started to cry harder and ran into her bedroom. I was lost for words and I said to myself, *how much more do you want to hurt her, hasn't she been hurt enough?* I had tears in my eyes and I went into her bedroom.

I laid on the bed, held her and said, "I have loved you for nearly two years now. You told me we could only be friends and that's when I started to go with Jeanne." I felt I must bring this out now.

She got up then sat on the edge of her bed and said, "From the first time I ever seen you I had feelings for you and after I did get to know you I felt that there was always something there. You were always there when I needed you and I guess I thought you would always be there." She sighed and said, "I'm sorry. I didn't think I was hurting you and I really didn't think you loved me. I know now that I was thinking so much about my problems that I could not see yours. If anyone had asked in the past year I would have said I wouldn't want to live without you and you were the only one that ever cared about me, and if they ask me now I will say I don't want to live without you now either." She followed with, "I'm sorry but that's how I feel."

I could not continue or defend my relation with Jen and I was sitting on her bed and did not know if I should leave or face a problem that I involved myself so much with. She just waited while I sat on her bed. She was looking at me without blinking and her eyes were glazed. I said to myself, *My God, look at this little girl. She never hurt anyone except herself. Now she is losing the only one she loved, the only one that ever cared for her and needed to continue into society.* I pushed her onto her bed, laid alongside her and felt her start crying and trembling. Her arms were around me and her face alongside mine. We did not say a word because I don't think she could talk and I did not know what to say. I was afraid she would go back to where she couldn't handle it again. I pushed her face back then looked at her and put my lips on hers then just held her. I could taste the tears as before and thought of the times she has been like this since the rape but how much more crying will she have to do in her life? I just laid here and could not think about her or Jen. I knew that if there was an easy way to die I would want to now because I am saying the same thing to both girls. I am having problems facing tomorrow's and how many more will I have to. I have had fear that I would hurt one of them or maybe both of them and now I know that I will be the one to get hurt. All I have ever had in my life was these girls. They were my happiness, my reasons to live and I believed my future. They taught me how to love, live and not be shy. They gave me reasons to want to wake up in the morning and get on stage. They are the ones that made me who I really am now. I asked myself what I did wrong. Should I have known and when should I have stopped? I started to think the worst because I knew that I would lose them both and thought what should I do for now? I do not have the answers or knowledge to remedy this and have no one to ask for help. I will start to go back to church and pray for the answers.

Dorothy tried to interrupt me but I guess I did not hear her. I picked up my head and said what? She looked at me again and said, "I'm sorry I did this to you." She stopped talking, I just looked at her and seen how sad she was. My mind went back and I thought that her life does harmonize with mine, when sadness possesses your biggest memories and you know that you will never escape the pain and sadness that you are destined. It seems that for every bit of happiness I receive I will be forced to pay tri-fold in hurt and sadness and Dot must have the same destiny. Dot yelled at me, "What's wrong? Your eyes are all glassy and you're not blinking."

I said, "I'm sorry, I was just thinking about my childhood and the grip it has on me." She said, "Could you explain and tell me about it?" I said, "Sometime, but not now," and tried to get out of this mood but it just hung on.

When I was six years old my real mother came to our school a few times to see me and I remember her saying something about destiny and said that her destiny was not to be happy but just to help people that were not happy. I asked her if that was why she came to see me and if she knew that I was not happy. She said, "My child, I know you are not happy and I know a lot about you." I thought, my aunt lived close to where she is now and must have told her that I said I missed her and wanted her to come back. My aunt (Ninny) would come to see us at times. It came to my mind what she said and I wondered if that was my destiny. I finally broke away from my thoughts and looked at Dorothy and said, "I will help you." She said "What do you mean", and I said that my mother would want me to.

She said, "How do you know?" I don't know why but I told her that I just spoke with her. I was very tired, mentally exhausted and I feel as if I am a little kid that doesn't know what to do. I laid my head on the pillow next to hers and wanted to go to sleep. My brain hurt and I could not think any more because my mind is far from being nimble. She came over then kissed me but I could see I was lost for words and wanted me to explain what I meant. I started to hold her tight and felt clumsy and didn't know what to say. She got up and put her face over mine and started kissing me and ran her fingers through my hair. She put her hand under my shirt and rubbed my chest and sides. It did seem to relax me and she got up further and massaged my shoulders and arms. She kissed me harder then kissed my neck while her fingers went back to my hair and she ran her fingers through again. This time she was scratching my scalp lightly, this did make me sleepy and was relaxing. She continued to do this and once when her hands were on my sides she started to tickle me because I am very ticklish and she knew it. I started laughing and could not stop because I did not have the power to stop her because my complete body was nearly drained of life.

This did help me get from my mood. I looked at her then said, "You're a sweet heart and you really do care about me, don't you?"

She said, "I love you more than life itself." She then said, "You are my life and have been since I met you but without me realizing it until now and without you I have nothing and nothing to live for." I had to get my mind off of things because that statement was putting me back into my mood but I took it at face value and started loving her. We kissed and loved very hard and tried to be happy. I found that sex is very close to sadness because for some reason when your very sad and you want to become happy then sex seems to be the answer. She started kissing me again, it felt good and I started to relax. I don't think either one of us thought about sex all the time we were here and I don't know what happened. She put her hand under my Jeans and I put my hand under her blouse and was feeling her. I knew then that I did want her; I unbuttoned her blouse and reached to undo her bra while she helped me. I then started kissing her and felt much better. I know that this girl lived in pain and I hurt her very much tonight. I wanted her to feel the best that she ever had in her life and I was here for her tonight. *I must forget who I am, what I am but just what I want for her this night, then I could be myself again tomorrow.* Her skirt was loose and I put my hand under her skirt, then between her legs. I pulled my hand up to get them under her panties, I pushed her skirt and panties down then she was able to push them off with her feet. I got up, locked her door then went back to the bed and looked at her. There is a street light just outside her house and it lit the room just right so I could see her. I could see all this beauty and I would be stupid not to accept what she is pleading to me for. She got on top of me and held it between her legs and pushed down and it went all the way in. I just laid there and was happy just as we are so we stayed this way and just kissed.

I then rolled us over and got on top then moved until I found what she liked the most and just went gentle. She thrust her hips up to resonate with my movements and screamed, "Don't stop, please don't stop." She kept thrusting her body up and down and then stopped moving. She lifted my face up and started laughing. She said, "Oh my God, I don't know what happened and never felt this way before."

I asked, "Are you happy?" and she said again, "Oh my God, yes. It was so, oh, I can't explain." I was so happy and I know now that girls do have an orgasm. I was still hard and wanted to finish so I started again and knowing how happy she was made me very happy. I didn't go long and she started to scream again. I was close and wanted to pull out but she begged, "Please don't stop." She said it twice, then it was too late. I finished inside her and I know what she meant when she said it was exciting. There are no words to explain how it felt. She reached down between us and held it while it was still in her and said, "I love this thing." We laid there and I started to think that what I just did could make her pregnant. I did think about what the doctor told me but still knew that it was possible. I did not blame her for what happened but I did talk to her about that.

She told me she would love to be pregnant with my child and that would make her life complete even if I did not marry her. She told me that she didn't think anything would happen because her period should start in the next two days, she probably ovulated and her eggs were already out of cycle. I did not understand anything she said but hoped she was right. We both fell asleep although I did not plan on this because I have to help dad today then play at the club tonight. I went straight home, took a shower then had a very strange feeling and thought it was just a short while ago I told Jen the very same thing and at that time I did mean what I said but somehow I meant it with Dot also. I became worried and felt I was becoming paranormal and was entering a pandemonium state. I could see that this love triangle was becoming more concentrated and if I don't find the answers soon I will be forced to face and seek the inevitable. *I know it would kill me to hurt either one of these girls and I believe it will be me that get hurt in the end.*

I finished work then went to Al Pats but I just had a coffee and sat there thinking. I went back home and just laid around for a while, then called Jen and told her I went to see my father and he needed me to help him because I did not want to see anyone right now. She knew that I was out of work now and believed that we should be together much more so I told her that I would be helping dad a lot and will start my new job soon. She did understand but said, "Please come all that you can."

I said, "I will pick you up today." I went to see dad and told him I was out of work for a few weeks and about my new job.

He said, "I know Bob and Chape very well and we go fishing together and that should be a good job." My dad was very busy and did need my help because he took a contract with the state to build a road around the back side of Lake Waramaug in New Preston. I would operate the dozer and deliver gravel from our farm to the road. I picked up Jen and we went to the Restaurant out of town, and explained the work I had to do for my Dad.

She said, "Why do you have to work all the time and you will be working weekends too." I said "once I got on my feet we could go out more" and she said, "I am going with you tomorrow, right?"

I said, "I couldn't make the day without you." She asked if I was being smart. I waited to answer her, then said, "You must realize that I must work and I am also trying to do something good for our future." We went to my house because I had to change and get ready for the play.

Thinking about a Career in Music

When I got home I took my clothes in to the bathroom, showered and started to dress. Jen walked in while I had nothing on and put her arms around me and kissed me. She then reached down and grabbed me. I said, "Come on we have to leave."

She let go and said, "Can't we just play for a minute?"

I said, "Honey, I want to get there early and look at the clock now." She was still holding it and said, "Well, could I have this for my birthday?" I said, "You could have anything you want but not today." I didn't mention her birthday but it was next Thursday and she would be eighteen. I finished dressing and took her home so she could get dressed. She looked very nice. She wore a long black dress with a low neckline and a white blouse. Her hair was pulled back in a ponytail and she was so cute. We told Bob and Betty we would see them there then we drove in and Vinnie was already there. He already had the stage set up and all I had to do was hook up my amplifier. It was easier to play because the people here knew him and he was the head poncho but they appeared to be excited to see me. We had a few drinks then I gave Jen her vodka and orange juice before her father came in. The jukebox was playing so Jen and I did dance a little. She danced better than I did and asked her where she learned. She said that Sparky, her and some other girls always danced at her house.

Jen, Vin and I sat and talked until Bob and Betty came in. They sat with us and I asked if they wanted a drink. Bob asked, "What are you having?"

I said, "Vodka and tonic, because it is not so sweet." He asked Betty what she wanted. She looked at Jen and said, "I'll have a orange juice."

Jen said, "Mom this has some Vodka in it." Betty was going to say something and Jen said, "I'm only having one and it is not as strong as your punch you make." She said, "I'll have one of those," and Bob said, "I'll have that vodka tonic." I went to get their drinks for them, and then it was time to go on stage. Vinnie was already up there and we started playing. Vinnie led off with his waltzes then people started dancing and we played another for Bob and Betty as they danced. We played a lot of fast ones and I played mine. Bob grabbed Betty and started to do the jitterbug they were so good that they had the floor and every one watched. I was so happy and I did notice that some guys kept asking Jen to dance but she refused. She did do a fast dance with someone later. I guess she did not want him to hold her close as a waltz. We finished, and then went to sit with Bob, Betty and Jen.

Bob and Betty were laughing and I said, "Boy you guys were great, I loved watching you." He said Jen was right because you were better that we thought. I think Bob must have had four or five drinks and they were very happy that they came. They left then Jen and I left shortly after.

We stopped along the way to talk and she said, "I want to tell you what I want for my birthday."

I said, "You already told me and seen it already."

She said, "No, please listen. I want you to pick me up early Sunday morning have breakfast and go to your house for the day. You promise?" I said I'd think about it then kissed her and took her home. It was late so I went home without stopping. I am working with Dad and have to bring some gravel to fill the low spots. There is a small valley at the beginning and will need a lot of fill. My Dad would get paid for the gravel also. We also had to remove some large trees which we kept and sold to a saw mill. This would keep me busy both weeks and I was happy. We ran into a lot of ledge and we would have to do some demolition to blast the ledge. I was already familiar with dynamite and blasting materials. When I was eleven and twelve years old we used a great deal of dynamite.

Playing With Dynamite

Once we had a four acre swamp that we had to irrigate that was to swampy for any equipment so we would blast it. My brothers and I would set the blasting material. We would cut the sticks of dynamite in three pieces and push them into the ground about three feet. We would install a blasting cap in every other one and wire them in a parallel series. This means we would attach ten in series then parallel in conjunction with the rest. We would slice the dynamite with our jack knife and force the cap into the center then loop the wire around the stick of dynamite. We would make a slip knot with the wire and pull it tight. We placed these two feet apart and then would bring the line to where it was safe and out of the way. We had a magneto pump generator that created a currant to detonate the charge we placed. Before we connected the wires to the generator we checked the continuity with an ohm meter. This was to make sure that all blasting caps were connected. We made four ditches three hundred feet long one at a time and it was fun to watch. When we set it off you could see the ground open. Dirt, mud and water blew way up into the air and when it cleared the ditch was done. We would run close to the ditch to see the water running. My Dad would yell at us because the fumes from the dynamite would give you a headache and he was right.

When we built our first pond and removing tree stumps we also did a lot of blasting so I knew what I was doing now. At times we would have twenty cases of dynamite in our special shed and it always had to be locked. After the last project we had four cases of dynamite left over. It stayed in our shed that fall and winter. During our Indian summer when it got warm in February my father said that we must detonate the left over dynamite. He explained that once dynamite freezes and thaws out it becomes unstable. We looked at it and he said a jelly would ooze out. He was right so my brother Mike and I carried this to the far side of the pond and stacked it on top of each other on the ice. This was far away from anything then we used a Rifle (250-3000) Hi Velocity and very accurate. Mike was a better shot so he fired into the dynamite. We were way up on the hill but we could see it very well. When the projectile stuck the dynamite it looked like a bomb went off and the noise traveled through the valley. It did not make a very big hole because the water caused a reverse resonate action that forced the blast upwards. This caused a vacuum under it that caused the water to be sucked out and covered the pond with a lot of mud, dead fish and turtles.

When dad came home he yelled at us and said we should have waited for him. He looked at the pond and said, "Do you see the power that dynamite has?" Well here I am blasting again and I did surprise the people that were working here because they were not sure about me handling this. We rented an air compressor, jackhammer and I just showed them where I wanted the holes. They would drill them while I was operating the dozer then I would set the charges. I knew it was gray shale and should blast easily so I cut the sticks in three and capped them all. I would only place four or five charges at a time and it was adequate to break and loosened the ledge. The weather became colder than expected and we postponed the opening at the Redi—Mix plant. I was not finished with Dad and this gave me time to finish. My work will be finished before the Redi-Mix plant opens and I should have a few days off. I want to work on my Mercury but I know I have to keep this Sunday open to keep a promise. I operated the Dozer when I could then cut and hauled trees from the site. When I came to the end of the first avenue, I just loved that building lot. It was on the end and overlooked the mountains around it. I asked if I could buy this one from him but he said he would not sell it and keep it for me. He also said I want to keep one for each of my kids. I was so very happy not so much for me but my sisters and brothers and knew that our father did love us in his own way.

Dad appeared to be much more happy now but I think it was guilt about what we went through as kids and he was never there to protect us. I left work early because it was Jeanne's birthday and I want to see her. I went home to shower and get dressed then stopped to get her a birthday card. I picked out a smile face and wrote just "Me" on the center, then drove to her house. She came running to the car and said, "Oh, I didn't expect you this early."

I said, "Happy Birthday, my love," and handed her the card. She opened it and said, "What is this smile face?" and I said "What does it say?"

She replied, "All it says is 'Me'." I said, "Well," She paused and said, "You mean, you mean, I could have you and do anything I want?" I said that's what it says. She said Oh, I love but I can't wait, then through her arms around me and kissed me. We then entered her house and her mother teased her about the screwdrivers she had at the club but we all had fun and were laughing about what we did there. Jen was teasing her Mom and Dad about their dancing and Jen said to her mother, you talk about me having one drink; you were drinking like a fish and you to Dad. We all laughed and agreed we did have a lot of fun.

They said they would like to go again and this made me feel as if I was part of their family. They were always good to me and I stayed until almost nine and Jen walked me to my car. She hopped in with me then held and kissed me and said I love my card it's the best one I ever got. I said I must leave now because I to go back to work. This job is very hard and I have been working twelve or more hours a day. She said, "You are taking me to your house on Sunday aren't you?"

I said, "It's this Sunday?" She said, "You forgot!" I just laughed and she said, "Darn you why do you always have to tease me?" I said I will call you tomorrow when I get out of work. I know I promised to call Dot so I will go home then call her from there. She answered and I said, "Hi honey, did you miss me?" She was smart and said, does the sun come up every day and I said not this weekend.

She laughed and said, "When are you going to finish that job?" I said in two weeks, but my new job will be a lot of hours also but I only work there eight months of the year and I will have four months off. She said, "I can't wait and could we spend the four months together?" I said, "You don't look ahead, do you?"

She said, "Why don't you just come here now?" I said I do have to work all day tomorrow. She said, "Just for a little while," and I said I know what our little while is. I said I promise I will come see you tomorrow. I went to bed and was happy that I ate something at Jen's or I would have to go out to eat.

I'm back at work and I told Dad not to get the compressor or the jack hammer because we could get it on Monday. I don't know how much snow we're getting but I want to level the fill because I think I could break the ledge at the other end with the bulldozer and he agreed. I leveled all that I could, then went to break that ledge and was able to break it to below grade. It is five o'clock and it is starting to snow. I will finish and cover the dozer then put our tools away.

I'm on my way home and I want to lay down for a while. I'm just thinking how to plan this weekend but I must leave Sunday open for Jen. I have tonight and tomorrow then Sunday is Jen's birthday. It's snowing so I don't want to go anywhere because of the storm and was going to sleep. Dot only lives three miles away and it is all highways with no big hills. I just twisted my arm and decided to surprise Dot. I drove to her house and she must have been in the kitchen because she did not see me drive in. I knocked on the door and she answered.

She opened the door and said, "Oh My God! You're here," she threw her arms around me and just held me. I tried to push her into the house because it was cold out here. I did manage and closed the door. She dragged me to the kitchen, sat me at the table then made me a cup of coffee and said, "What are you going to do?"

I said, "I just came to see you now because I'm going to be so busy tomorrow." She said, "It's snowing how can you work?" I said, "I know, I want to get there before the ground freezes to much but the snow will help keep it from freezing," but she did not know that. I sat with her and had coffee then she told me that I had to stay overnight with her because the roads were too bad for me to go home. I said, "I just drove on them, they're fine," and she said, "Well I tried."

I said, "You know I can't stay much longer." She said just come to my bed room for a minute. She grabbed my hand then led me to her room and I laid along side of her. She asked were you happy that I got my friend. I said what friend and she said you know my period. I said Oh why do you call that your friend. She said all girls refer it to that and I said that's not my friend. She quickly said it was this time then I said I guess your right and that's probably why it got that name. She said were you really happy because I wasn't and I really felt bad. I said it's not being happy or sad it being realistic. She said some day and I said I never did tell you this but I should tell you now. I explained about the mumps and what the doctor said. She was sad and said maybe he was wrong and you do have that ten percent chance.

She waited for a while and said, "Then why were you worried?" I didn't answer I was tired and just wanted to go to sleep, but she asked me if I would make love to her and just hearing that did something to me. I said I would love to but I must go home because I'm very tired. She was rubbing me all over and grabbed my penis. She said it's hard and I said, "Honey I have to go home." She slid her hand under my jeans and held it. I just laid there for a minute and she said it's not that late it's only ten thirty. I laid there while she unzipped my jeans, and then undid my belt. She started stroking it and I guess you know who won. I said we shouldn't and she said why are you scared. My sister has two kids you know and she hasn't had any more in seven years. I said, "Why?" Dot told me that her sister said that the safest time is the first week after your period and said it is not one hundred percent but almost. I was losing the battle and was getting very hot. She was holding it and went closer then kissed it and said this is mine.

187

I did not answer and pulled her up along side of me. She started loving, kissing and massaging me all over while she was playing with it. She got up, locked her door and took all of her clothes off then pulled off my jeans and undies. I helped her take off my shirt and climbed back into bed. She managed to get both her legs around me while we were laying on our sides. Then was able to pull me on top and I guess you know what happened. We finished together then just laid there and were very comfortable but I finally got up because I was falling asleep. I had all I could do to stay awake but I did not ask her why she held me so tight and thought that she didn't know it at the time. She said I'm sorry that you are so tired and kept you here. I said I loved it but I must get home. The roads weren't too bad when I looked outside so I kissed her and went to my car. I told her while I was walking out, "I'll call you tomorrow."

I went home slowly then tried to sleep but I may be over tired and for some reason I am not comfortable now. I don't know what it is but I feel like I'm being trapped into something. I don't know why I think this tonight but maybe I think she's trying to get pregnant because what other reason would she have to do that every time and she always wants sex without any precautions. I wasn't prepared for this tonight but don't get me wrong I did like it. I hope it's because I'm so tired and not getting much sleep. I did fall asleep and maybe slept to hard because I am still tired.

The alarm did not go off yet and I was just laying here. The phone rang, It was Dad and he was upset and told me that his brother, my favorite uncle Jack had an accident and was in the hospital. He had to have one leg amputated just above the knee. He was using a grinding wheel that he made and put the grinding stone on a very high speed motor. It could not sustain that speed and came apart at a speed of twenty thousand revolutions per minute. A large piece struck him in the upper leg and almost severed it. Another piece went through the ceiling and dining room floor then through the roof. This piece traveled between the legs of his daughter in law just missing her within inches. Dad had to go see him but I'm very sad and hope that he is all right. Dad told me that I did not have to go to the job and he did call the other workers. I went back to bed because if I did go with my Dad I would not see Uncle Jack anyway. I fell asleep while still thinking about that.

I did notice that the storm subsided during the night and we did not get very much snow but I slept until noon then thought about Dot. I wondered why she always wants to make love and is it just immaturity or part of a plan. I would marry her if she became pregnant but felt that I was not ready at this time. I did think about a career but have not increased my goal in the past few months and felt that I was slipping back. I spent a lot of money buying tools and equipment for my shop and was not saving much cash. I thought leaving here and go to California. I knew that I needed a break from the status quo because I have been indecisive with my problem. I know I'll never get out of this love triangle and thought that maybe I should find a new girlfriend, and leave this area.

My Dad called me and said Jack was in surgery today because all they could do yesterday was control the bleeding and give him blood. He said that he went to the house an found that the grind stone broke in many pieces and Jack was lucky he was not killed. I said I'll go see him next week then called Jen and Dot to tell them what happened. I said I was very upset and would not see them today. They understood and said they were sorry to hear that. Jen did not mention my promise to her for tomorrow and I did not think about it. Before I heard this news I was already confused and uncomfortable. I can't justify the criterion of this triangle love dilemma. The roads were not to bad but I decided not to see anyone today. I went to José's for lunch and I wanted to schedule another recital. I told her Friday night was good then had lunch and talked with Jossey. She was very understanding and I felt that I could confide in her. I asked her if I could ask her a question. I explained the dilemma and how I became involved in it. I stayed there a long time and she did talk with me when she could.

After hearing what I was able to tell her she looked at me and said, "When in the hell are you going to think about yourself? You have a talent that I have not seen around here and you are so good in what you do. Why aren't you playing every weekend because word is already out that you are the best and your playing alone has more controversy than any band that we had here. All my customers want you to come back here now and you could make real good money. I could have you here two nights a week and do much more business if you want to play here. I am not asking you to only play here and think you should go to some better places because you just don't know your potential." She emphasized, "I would not let these two country chicks interfere or slow you down and ruin your chances of a career that could make you someone. Al, can't you see that they are using you, they could see where you are going and want to be involved with you. Why do you think that they are throwing themselves at you with their sex and tears?"

I already had a few drinks and stayed there a few more hours. I loved these girls and did not want to believe that they were using me because I always thought that I was using them. She came to me again and said, "Al you're drinking too much. I am going to give you just ginger ale and when you get home drink a lot of water." I said I hate water and she said, "Then drink soda."

I took her advice and drank two glasses of ginger ale, went to the bathroom and then home. My vision was blurry but I drove careful and I did make it home safe. I laid down and the phone rang twice but I did not answer it. I did not want to talk to anyone but I'm very happy that I had that talk with her and she shined a new light on my life. I did drink too much and knew that was just a cop out. The ginger ale did help and I did not get sick like the last time. It was only six thirty and I did sober up. I was not drunk and I think the pressure was too much to let anything else effect my mind. I went back to Jossey's and felt much better. She made me a cream drink that taste very good and it did not contain any alcohol. She said it would settle my stomach and we sat there just talking then a few other people sat to talk with me. They were here when I played and they did mention it. They were nice and were not heavy drinkers but just came to dance and have fun. While we were talking and I don't know how we got on this conversation but I did tell someone that I had my guitar in the car. They told José and she came to me to tell me that some people asked if I would play for them.

I said, "I can't now because I'm not in the mood." She said, "Al, they pleaded with me." I said no I can't but they did talk me into it. It was getting late and I would not have to play very long. Several people came to my car and carried in my equipment. I set up and asked, "What do you want, fast or slow?" They said, "Fast, fast and loud." I played all my favorites and some special new things I learned. Almost everyone was dancing and many of them singing. I played a lot of fast and just mixed it to what they wanted. I seen that some were tired so I spun with out stopping into waltzes. Most of them just started waltzing and more came up. It was very nice and I could really see they did like my style. I finished with a number they could Jitterbug or Be Bop to which is also popular here, then mixed a few of my own.

I thanked the crowd for their applause and went to sit down. The same kids that helped me before also took my gear to my car. Everyone here said they would be here next Friday night and I was not shy in front of this crowd. I knew that I could make mistakes and they would still like me. I then went home and was happy that I did go back. I felt better and I knew that I must ratify my life style. I cannot allow my feelings to apprehend my better judgment and deter my future.

I awoke at six a.m. and went to the seven o'clock mass at the Saint Francis Church that I used to go to. I seen many people that I knew from my employment. I don't know why, but just being here made me feel better. I did upon leaving go to the alter and prayed to God to yield me the power to make the right decisions, pave me a path to righteousness and away from where I was placed in this road of life. I got back home at eight fifteen and laid on my bed then thought about my Mother. I was trying to comprehend the statement she recited to me, "She was put here, not to fulfill her desires but to help those in need." She also said that was the word of God. I said how would I know and would I get a sign. I thought am I worthy of this and did I get the sign last night.

I called Jen and said I would pick her up and we could have breakfast. I took a shower dressed and went to pick her up. I notice that every time I do pick up one of these girls I must think of an excuse for the other. This is becoming problematic and I am not comfortable with it. I went to Jen's house; she was ready to go and met me at my car. I said, "Why didn't you wait for me to come in?" and she said, "I want you to be with me, not them," meaning her parents.

I then said, "Well, how are you?" She said, "I'm fine, but I tried to call you last night because I knew you were upset about your uncle and I wanted to see how you were." I said I spent the day at José's. She said why I said, "I got drunk then went home took a nap and went right back. I did not drink anymore and played for them until late."

She said, "Why didn't you pick me up I would have loved to have gone with you." I said I was very depressed and didn't want to ruin your night. She said something and I said, "I really don't want to talk about it."

She said, "Are you mad at me?" and I said, "Why should I be mad at you?" She said she didn't know. I said, "Do we have to talk about this I'm hungry and want some breakfast."

She said okay and came closer to me. I did put my arm around her and kissed her then went to a different diner where I don't go often and it is more for the grownups. I said, "I'm sorry that I'm down and would rather talk about us because I don't want to be in this mood."

She said, "Are we going to your house?" I said I've never broken a promise yet and we left the Diner and I went towards my house. I did not stop at my house but went to the lake because I wanted to show her what I was doing. I had to cover my tracks and I knew the reason why she wanted to go to my house but I also knew that I couldn't break this promise. She asked, "Why are you going here I want to go to your house?" The way she was holding me I could see sex all over her and I answered.

I said, "When we get to your house tonight and your Dad ask us what were you doing all day are you going to say we stayed in bed all day and made love at Al's house?" She said I never thought of that and I said, "I want to show you this so it will be on your mind." I did drive on my new road as far as I dared because I did not want to get stuck. I did take her to Kent Falls and showed her that a few weeks ago and if I'm asked I will say we went there to. She said, "Now I get it, you are pretty smart, aren't you?"

I said, "Jen, I love your family and hate to lie to them but I do realize that I would have to if I was asked about our intimate relations." I then went to my house parked in the back and we went in. Walking in I did not have that very exciting feeling as before but I did make this promise and believe that I owe her this day. She has never really made love and the last time she was hurting, scared and it could not be sex as she expected. I shall yield to her desires today but consider my priorities here after. I unplugged the phone and laid on the bed. She laid along side of me and said, "Honey you're not happy! I waited for this a long time and I want it to be beautiful." I had no worries of hurting her and knew it is what she wants. At this time I thought no more harm could be done and I was holding her with one arm and pulled myself on top of her, her legs parted and allowed me to lay between them. I pushed my groin against hers with force and she put her legs around me and squeezed me tight. I felt how much she wanted what I was doing and how much she longed for what was in store for her. Her skirt was up and I felt myself get hard. I moved so she could feel it against her while we laid there and I knew that I would yield to her desires.

Right or Wrong and Will I Ever Know

I explored every part of her lips and mouth with my tongue and I felt that I must give her all I have to offer. I believed that further sex with her would be limited and I treated this as our last. She was beautiful and I considered this to be a privilege to make love to a girl with this character and beauty. We were still fully dressed and only had our shoes off. I got up and said lets shower then we could really make love. We got in to the shower and I could see she was in a hurry to get back into bed. She laid on the bed with her legs apart and I looked at her and said I'm a very lucky guy to have her here with me. Her complete body was beautiful and her breast stood up like heavy artillery and I was holding a Titan Rocket. I knew she did not have the fear and was ready for anything I could give her. I got back on top of her and rubbed it between her legs. We were both very wet and I pushed it in. It was much easier this time but I went very slow so I wouldn't hurt her then just laid there and asked how she felt. She said while trembling "It's very nice, Oh I love it, but I love it only because it's you." I took it out and just laid there. I didn't want this to end because we have all day.

She took it in her hand and just held it. We kissed for a long time and I put it back in then went nice and slow. I pushed a little harder each time and it was not long after that when she was squeezing me very tight and I knew she was close, she then stopped moaning and released her grip. Then said, "Oh my God," and just laid there and stared at me. We just laid there together and she was still breathing hard then squeezed me hard again and said why did you stop. I said I wanted to give her a break, I She said, "But I want you to be happy." I rolled over to take a break but she started playing with it, then I never felt anything this good and she stayed there until it got soft then ran into the bathroom. She came back and held me very tight and asked me if I liked what she did. I said it's the best I ever had I couldn't dream it could be that nice. I asked her, why did you do that and she said I did it for you because I wanted to give you all I had and make you feel real good. I said boy you really did that but how did you know I would like it. She said do I have to tell you. I said I would like you to and she said Sparky told me a long time ago that was what guys like the best, I never thought I would do that but I did want to give you the very best I could. I said Honey you did that just to please me. This really told me how much she loved me and would do anything for me. How could I not love her, and it seems her complete life is me.

We went back in the shower and I washed her and she washed me very well and said I want this thing to give me a baby some day. We crawled back into bed, pulled the blanket over us and laid holding each other. I know I left my brain turned off today and must say it was the most exciting day of my life but it was her birthday not mine so I started kissing her belle then made her feel as I did. I hoped I gave her a good eighteenth birthday present. I don't think she or I will forget this day but I fell asleep and guess she didn't. It was only two thirty and we had the rest of the day. I know these are the most exciting moments of my life and I knew it could never be better. She said, "Do you know how much I love you now and how much I loved this day?"

I said, "Happy birthday my love," and she said, "I know I will never forget my eighteenth birthday." We laid in bed for about an hour and decided to get some food. I could not stop holding her and knew she thought so much about me today and it was so important for her to please me. I took her to the nicest restaurant in Danbury because it was still early and she didn't have to be home until nine o'clock. We both had steaks and the works because we were both very hungry. We went back to the car and held each other and talked about our day. I took her home early to make a better impression. I walked in to the house with her then told Bob and Betty that my favorite uncle had a bad accident and I was going to the hospital to see him. I left without question because I did have a quilt complex and did not want to stay. I stopped to see Dot, She was worried about me and my uncle but she also said that we are not seeing each other as much and asked if there was anything wrong. I said, "No, but I do want to talk about things while we're alone at the table." I told her that I have not made any improvements in my life and thought that I was falling back. I told her about José's and I would start playing a lot. I will play every Friday night there and I am looking for an answer from the Berkshire Lodge Night club. I said that she might be able to go with me some times. I said, "I don't want you to be alarmed I just need some time to find myself and start a future."

She said, "Do you want to stop seeing me?"

I said, "You really have to listen to what I am saying. I don't have a good job now and I do not want to drive a cement trailer forever because I have

194

nothing to offer you. What if we did get married and had children would you want to live in some cheap apartment while I drove a truck? Would you want to dress our kids nice, and I could go on. I don't want to live as I did as a child when I know that I could be someone. I need this chance but I still want to see you."

She just looked at me and said, "I'll do anything that you want from me and you know I will wait for you." I stood up then held her hand and she stood in front of me. I held her in my arms and could see the maturity and the makings of a good mother and told her I felt that if I were to get married I would choose her. Jen is a bundle of love but was much less mature. She acted much younger and always wanted fun but after this weekend, I do believe that our romance was sex oriented and not lasting love. What bothers me the most was that she wanted to learn so much about sex before she met me and tried to learn so much from Sparky, then remembered everything she told her? I do feel that while Jen is in college we would part and she would have these same feelings for someone else. I have never seen a more beautiful, sexy and a perfect body as hers, but I could see that everywhere we went she attracted many guys. The only thing that I had was a very nice car, a convertible and was shy. I believe that I was a challenge because of Sparky and Dot and my weakness made me available.

I also impressed her parents to allow her to go out more even to a bar. I know I was exciting for her and she knew she took me from Sparky and maybe Dot but I feel that I must think this way. We were only out a few times when she asked me to make love to her. I told her then that I believed it is just an infatuation and mostly sexual. This may very well be on my part also and I know that every time we go out sex is involved. I believe that I love her for more than sex because I love her looks, her family life; she's very intelligent, very sweet and kind. We have never been upset with one another. I say and I feel that I am in love but I said I love you to Sparky when I spent the night with her. I ask what is love and if I date another girl tomorrow will I love her also. I believe if I did posses love it would have to be with Dot. I loved her for a very long time before I got a kiss. I was never promised sex and I did not need that to love her. I loved her because she was her and I was happy just to see her walk by. It took me a very long time to show her my trust and I do believe I earned it. I must put this out of my mind for now and follow my common denominator.

I was still holding Dot and she felt better in my arms now that I did try and analyze the complete scenario. She looked up at me and started to say something but I interrupted her and said, "I know what am I thinking about. I said you and me, every time I think about my life, I think about the last two years and how much I wanted to be with you. Not for sex or promises but just to be with you. I have never lost that feeling but did come to the conclusion that I may not win your love and I would have to go on with life. I have always wanted you to love me and in the back of my mind I relive these thoughts."

She interrupted me, "My God Al you know you have me now and I love you with all my heart." She held me very tight and said, "I loved you for the last two years also. I just didn't stop to think and said no one ever knows for sure but I don't think that sex is the answer either and I'm afraid that it will interfere with love." She said, "We don't have to do that anymore and I will love you if we never did it again. I only did that for you because I knew you had to know the truth."

I stopped her and said, "I don't mean it that way, I mean I want to be loved for me because every time I think about life you become involved in my thoughts and I'm not blaming you for what happened. I will always believe that our sex relations were the best thing that could happen to us. I am very proud of what happened between us," and we just held each other. I did not want to talk about this anymore because I knew that Jen was very much involved in my thoughts. I could never hurt her or a family that I admire and have welcomed me into their family until I know the truth and hear it from her. This is a problem and if I wait I believe that Jen will make the first move while in college. I am going to play my guitar everywhere that I'm wanted and try not see either girl as much. Dot was sad and I did not want to leave her this way. To reinforce my love I told her that I wanted her to come to my house one night this week.

She said, "Really? You mean it?" and I said, "Yes honey," and said to myself who ever waits for me as long as she has must love me. Thursday night has come so I called Dot and told her that I would pick her up in a half hour. She was ready when I arrived and I could see that she is very mature about life in general and discussed all aspects. We did make safe love and she stayed the night. I took her home in the morning and went to work with my Dad. I would finish this job on Thursday of next week and have not heard when we are opening the Redi-Mix plant.

My Dad said he took another contract with the town of New Milford to remove some large trees in the middle of town and hired a tree climber and if I could work with him. I told him to call me when he is ready. I played at the Berkshire and it turned out very well but after this performance I knew I was good and maybe the best around. I did make one mistake and announced that

I would be at José's. The management did not like that and told me that I could not advertise a competitor. I apologized before I went home and remembered I was supposed to call Jen but I will call her tomorrow. I went home then went to sleep but Vinnie awoke me before I could call Jeanne. I called Her to tell her that I had to practice with Vinnie and were discussing me cutting a record with him and planning to go to New York again next Thursday.

I called Dot and told her the same but I told Jen I would pick her up and go to lunch tomorrow. Jen did go to lunch with me and I had to leave to meet Vinnie. She was not happy but said she understood. I took her home and went back to help Dad. The trees were very big one measured five feet at the bottom and were in-between two houses. We had to top them branch by branch and I had to learn to use climbing spurs but I did climb the tree with no problems. We always had a saddle and safety rope attached to us but it was very hard work and I was tired. The past week went by and I was offered to play at a private party at the Lake Waramaug Casino. I did accept it and it is scheduled for next Thursday night. I will take Dot with me since I always take Jeanne. Besides, it was a school night and Jen couldn't go anyway.

This was the best recital of all and everyone seemed to be very happy with me. During the break I danced with Dot because someone would play the juke. I noticed that very few danced then but when I played my style and my specials every one danced and screamed. Then the following Friday I was invited to play at a school dance so I went as scheduled and found these kids do love loud and fast music so I gave them everything they wanted but they will not let me stop. I loved the recognition and did keep playing for them. I would play a very fast tune to get all of the Be Boppers then the jitterbug and the ones that didn't know how to dance but they moved to the sound. While playing this I would spin in to a very slow waltz then watch them try to chance and most of them did. I played until Eleven o'clock and was only supposed to play until ten. I turned the jukebox back on, then sat with Dot. While I sat a very well dressed blond asked me to dance, but I have not danced with anyone other than Dot and Jen.

I was shy and really didn't know how to dance well so I didn't answer but she reached for my hand and pulled me to the floor. She said as we walked to the center of the dance floor, "Al my name is Judy. I really love the way you play that guitar and I want to ask you a question. I have a brother that likes your style and ask me to ask if you would teach him how to play."

I said, "Why didn't he ask me?"

She said, "He's very shy, and I told him I would." I said, "okay, but I'm too busy to teach anyone now." We danced the whole dance then at the end she said, "You could come to my house to teach him and I'll be there." That statement made me believe that it wasn't her brother that was interested. I looked into her eyes then found that they were beautiful and I never seen eyes so soft in my life. I said, "I'll let you know," and she had a piece of paper with her brother's name and phone number and she handed it to me.

She said, "Please try to come," then I went to the table then sat with Dot but Judy walked me back to the table and said, "Thanks for the dance." Dot did not look too happy and said, "And who in the hell is that?" I gave her the note and said read it. Judy was behind Dot and I noticed she was watching us. I explained our conversation and said, "Honey, you're jealous."

She said, "You're dammed right I am, look at her. She's beautiful." I said, "She's a blond," and Dot said, "What does that mean?" I said, "I don't like blondes and let's not talk about it. I am sure there will be a lot more like her and she's just a kid looking for a good time." This was a very nice party because there was no liquor here. We started to leave and two young men approached me and asked if they put on a show for the kids, would I volunteer to play for a few hours. I like doing things for kids and said as long as it doesn't interfere with my schedule. I gave them my phone number and asked them to call me ahead of time. We then left I dropped Dot off and had to go home myself. She was funny and said, "Stay away from them blondes."

I said, "I'm going there now," then laughed and went home. She shouldn't have said that because this got me thinking about Judy. My mind goes back to when I was dancing with her and I never held a girl with such blue eyes. They were not like anything I have ever seen or was close enough to study. They were not like marbles but big pieces of different shapes of blue. They were not piercing but very soft but had a magnetic power to compel you to look in to then and it made me not feel shy.

Another Mistake or
Did I Get the Sign

I don't know why because I always liked dark eyes and dark hair. I was happy that I attracted her but I don't have any intentions of going out with her and will try not to. I know that I have her phone number and I thought about her but I felt she left her mark because she really had the looks to make you wonder. I would not mind if we were friends but I have enough problems now then went home. I had to play the next two nights and knew that I would be very tired. I will start my job on Monday and I heard it was very hard work. I fell asleep and woke up a little late but I met Dad on the job and started work. Tree climbing and topping is also very tiring. I just got home and I'm beat so I am going to lay down for a while. I got right back up because I promised to call Jen so I did and she asked me to take her to Al Pats. She asked, "Is there any way I could see you more because I miss not seeing you." I assured her that it would only be for a few more weeks and I would have more time. We did talk about things and I did feel hurt when she talked about the love she had for me that we shared together.

Driving Tractor Trailer

It's the second week in April and I have been on my new job for two weeks but I do not like it. It is very hard work and I'm not making any more money than I was at the Textile Plant. I don't only drive a bulk cement trailer but I have to move the box cars (Train) with a special bar. I put this under the wheel and force the wheel to move. I have to move these up to two hundred feet and it is very hard at first but once you get them rolling then it goes easy. There is a hand brake to stop the train and the box cars have shoots on the bottom which I must align and attach to an underground conveyor. Then it goes to a large hopper where I load the cement. The box cars are equipped with vibrators because the powered cement will stick to the sides. I then drive my truck under the storage hopper to load my truck and I'm breathing cement powder all day. I then drive the trailer to the plant and transfer the cement to the hopper. I must make sure that this hopper is filled at all times. The plant closes at noon on Saturday but I must stay until the hopper is filled for Monday. I have canceled a few recitals because my muscles hurt and made it hard to play the guitar. I know that I will not stay here very long and will tell Bob and Chape to find someone to replace me. I did very little for the past two weeks with my personal life and only played at Jossey's both Saturday nights.

I have been sleeping late on Sunday and only see Jen and Dot once a week but last Wednesday Dot spent the night at my house. I have not taken Jen out and promised to tomorrow afternoon. I am going to José's to play and will ask her if she could find someone else to take my place for a few weeks because it was to muck for me right now. I decided that I will put in my notice this Monday at my job. I went straight home after I left José's and unplugged my phone. I did not set the alarm clock and I awoke at eleven o'clock. I hopped in to the shower then turned the water much hotter than usual and it did make me feel better. I called Jen and asked her if she wanted to go out, she said Yes Please come and get me. I pulled into her driveway; she was ready and met me outside. She hopped in and slid over to me and when we were out of sight she put her arms around me and started kissing me all over then said, "I miss being with you."

I said, "I miss you too," and told her I was quitting my job. I did not like what I was doing and thought that it should be a two man job. She said I'm happy but what are you going to do for work and I said I want to play music. We just talked and I took her to the lark. I was hungry and needed some coffee to awake me because I was dragging and just couldn't get with it. Jen tried to comfort me by massaging my arms and neck it did feel good. I asked her what we were doing today and she said, "What is there to do?"

I said, "Not much and why don't we go to New York and get drunk like everyone else in this town." I said I think that the drinking age is too young and should be twenty or over. She said I do agree and said that two of her schoolmates were killed driving back from there. I also heard one of my coworker's sons was killed. He was only eighteen, it was a black family which I liked very much but I also lost a few of my friends and school mates. We couldn't think of any place to go so we ended up at my house. I do not have anything here and there was not much to do. I laid on the bed and she laid alongside me but it was nice to just lay here. I was very sore from the road work, topping the trees and the trucking. I did not have a break in five weeks so I just laid here with my arms around her. She started to massage me then pulled my shirt off and did my arms, neck, sides and would scratch my stomach and chest. That was so relaxing that I was falling asleep. I was just about asleep when she pulled of my trousers.

I did not feel her unbutton them but she had them off while I was falling asleep. I have to admit that this was the best massage that I ever had. She massaged me from my toes to my ears and did not miss a spot in between. I lost all my stiffness except in one place and she found a way to remedy that. I just laid on my back and let her take charge because I did not have the power or desire to stop her. She said, "What am I here for if I can't make you relax and feel better? I do love you and will always be here for you." I held her and thanked her for the best massage I have ever had. She kissed me and said, "I better be getting home," so I took her home then went back home myself.

I felt bad because I said that I didn't think she loved me and it was just an infatuation. I am very confused about love and really love both Her and Dot. I wish this could go on forever because I am very satisfied to have both of them. I hung up after talking to Dot and wanted to go to sleep but the phone rang. It was the kid that asked me to play for a school benefit dance. He said it was scheduled for next Friday night at seven thirty. I was not playing at José's now so I said yes I would be happy to. This time it would be in the town of Washington Depot. They have a lot more programs there and the kids are involved in many activities. They have different ball teams, all kind of sports and the States best varsity with Cheerleaders.

I called Dot back and told her about it and said I would like to take her. She was happy and thanked me then I fell asleep. I went to work today and told Bob that I wanted to put in my two weeks notice. He tried to do everything to keep me and even offered me a raise. They did know how hard the work was and should have not waited for me to quit to offer me what the job was worth. I said I'm sorry but I'm leaving for California soon and will have to leave anyway. I worked very hard and knew I was not happy here but I won't have to do this very much longer. I worked until six and went to Dot's. She seen how hard I have to work and I was covered with dry cement powder. My face was gray and she said this is going to ruin your skin. My fingers were all wrinkled and not nice as when I worked at the textile. This also hurt my fingers and made it harder to play my guitar.

I spent some time with her and told her I must go home but I would pick her up after work on Friday then she could come with me to change at my house. I left it at that and went home. The week was as usual and I worked very hard but wished that I could just quit. I only weighed one hundred seventy pounds that was all muscle but I needed to put some fat on these bones. Someone much bigger than me should have this job but I worked harder and faster than usual to fill the Hopper. I left work at five then picked up Dot and I have to play for the school tonight. She had her clothes with her, we went to my house and I just laid on my bed. She yelled at me and said, "You're getting your bed all dirty." She reached for my hand and helped me up. I stood there while she pulled my shirt and socks off. Then undid my belt and helped me with my jeans and underwear. She walked me to the shower and I said that's enough I don't want you to get all dirty. I reached in to the shower to let the water get warm then asked her to get me a towel and get my clothes ready. I only had one closet and one small dresser.

I said, "Pick out what you want me to wear." I was finished with my shower and she brought me the towel. She said I had to get dressed in my bedroom and had all my clothes ready. She pushed me on to my bed and put my socks on, then put on my underwear when she got close to me she kissed my joy stick then stopped before I could say anything and helped me get dressed. It is six thirty and I want to get there early. I had the directions but was not sure where it was. I did want to get some rest before I went there because it was a hard job standing on stage for three hours after a day like I had. I did lay on my bed for fifteen minutes and Dot just laid alongside me.

We left and I found the school without problems and Tom showed me around. It had a very large stage and a sound system was the best arrangement since the Columbia and allegro studios. I used their speaker system and Tom helped me set up. He knew a lot about music and I was all set up before anyone showed up. I ran a few chords and adjusted the amplifiers and was ready so I sat with Dot. They had a soda machine and Tom gave us two cokes. I opened my coke and before I could take a drink, I could not believe who walked in but Judy. Dot did not notice her and she was with some kid but I did not know if this was her brother or her boy friend. She spoke with him momentarily and walked straight to our table and said thank you for coming. I did not know why she was thanking me then she said I'm the one who scheduled the dance and asked Tom to call you. I said come sit with us and why did you want me. She said, "You're the best and everyone that heard you the last time wanted you to play for them."

I said, "Thank you," then introduced her to Dot as my girlfriend. Judy said, "Hi I'm pleased to meet you and do you ever play with Al?" Dot said, "No, but I always go with him to help." She then said, "Well, excuse me, but I have to get things ready." She walked away but I could see that she was dressed to kill, she had a short skirt on and her eyes were trying to tell me something. I could see Dot getting very jealous so I said, "I'm surprised and I didn't know she was involved." I didn't think Dot believed me and said, "You were with me when Tom asked me." She said, "I didn't say anything," but I said, I see the way you're looking at me.

She said, "I'm jealous because she's much better looking than me, look how she's dressed, and I heard her say, 'You're the best, Al.'" I said, "Come on, Honey I don't like blondes." A lot of kids were coming in now, some came to me to thank me for coming and I told them it was my pleasure. It was time for me to go stage so I kissed Dot and went up. I was a little shy and nervous because Judy is here and I knew she was watching my every move. I opened with my special and used my Trembar and Reverberation. They all loved it and everyone was dancing but Dot did not dance. I think these are just school kids and they stick together. I noticed that Judy danced very well but I also noticed her watching me as I thought she would. I felt that she really wanted to know me better and I tried not to think about it. I did not want Dot to catch me looking at her so I played for my first hour just looking at all the kids and played all fast music.

I danced with Dot while they played the jukebox so Judy would not ask me to dance again. Tom came over and sat with us. He said, "Where did you ever learn to play and get that style." I said I started with Duane Eddy and added what I thought made it better then I redesigned my guitar to add sound refraction's and second harmonics. He said, "I do play guitar but nothing like that and I would love to play with you some time but not on stage because I'm not that good." I said never to say that, always tell yourself you're the best and work for your own style.

I asked, "Are you Judy's brother?" He said, "No, why do you ask?" I told him that Judy asked me to teach her brother and just assumed. He said, "She's the best girl we have here, she is our head cheerleader and in charge of entertainment." I said, "She seems very nice," and it was time to get up again. I did a lot of combos and somehow Judy ended up dancing close to the stage and winked at me. I did not see her dance with that kid she was with so I figured it was her brother.

I also notice she did not dance with the same person twice and assumed that her boyfriend was not here. I would like to see what kind of guy she would go out with. I finished my second part and sat with Dot again. I told Dot that I had to go to the men's room and she wanted to go to the ladies room. I walked her there and went to ask Tom to do me a favor. I said, "I notice you dance very well and I would like you to ask Dot to dance."

He said, "I would have loved to, but didn't because she's your girlfriend." I went to the men's room and met Dot on the way to our table. We got right up to dance while I held her very close and knew she liked that. I kissed her before we sat down and she said thank you for that. I had to assure her that I was with her. This was my final time to play tonight so I got up there, I was very loose and I had to give it all I had because these kids were great and I want to be remembered by them. They were a very nice crowd and I also did it for Judy. I started to play loud and I gave them fast, slow and spinouts then I played a long waltz so Tom could ask Dot to dance. She did dance with him and they danced very well together but I could see that he could dance much better than me. It looked like she was having fun and when she looked at me I would wink. I wanted her to know that I didn't mind and played this longer than normal to give her a chance to really dance and have fun. I was almost finished so I paused playing and asked, "Does anyone want more?" They all screamed, "Morel More!" I played my special and added more, then used my reverb and Trembar like never before. I could hear the echoes bouncing off the walls. I then stopped but before I could get off the stage dozens of kids came to thank me and said this was the best time they ever had. I felt like King Tut and smiled and said I also had a very good time.

I went back on stage and got all their attention then told them, "You guys were really great, I enjoyed playing for you and you're the best crowd I ever played for." I sat while they played the jukebox, Tom brought us another Coke and was thanking us when Judy asked me to dance I looked at Dot and she nodded yes. We went to the middle of the floor where there were other kids dancing. She thanked me and said, "You were better than the last time." I don't know why I said this but I did say it, "I did it for you" She said thank you and then asked me why I didn't call. I said, "Honey, I mean Judy," then she interrupted me and said she didn't mind me calling her that. I said, "I was trying to tell you that I have a girlfriend but I didn't want to end this dance."

I knew that Dot would be jealous so I told her that I had to get back to my table. She said, "Please call me." I said I just might and sat with Dot. I asked Dot if we could leave because I could not look into those blue eyes anymore because they were so inviting and I could feel there is more to it then music. In the car Dot said, "That girl just won't leave you alone will she?" I said she knew someone that wanted me to play at a private party and they would pay me very well but I would let her know and Dot said, "I'm sorry I'm jealous, but I don't want anyone taking you from me."

I said, "Honey, you must have some trust in me and if I was interested would I take you with me every time." She said, "I know." I took her to her house, walked in with her to her bedroom. I laid with her for a while because I did not want her to feel bad and she may have seen the sparkles in my eyes when I looked at Judy. The way I feel right now is, I just want Judy for a friend and not allow myself to get involved with anyone else right now. I told Dot I would call her after work tomorrow but I had so many things on my mind. I started to think about what José said about these girls and I could still see those big blue eyes in my mind again. I know there is something about Judy that is persuading me into a new realm of life and I want to find out more about her. I know I could really like her because she is so different but I know I will just get deeper into this triangle of love. I know I never want to hurt Dot or Jen and have no intentions to. They were always my very best friends and were always with me. I have no other real friends and would be very lost without them. But the more I think about this only reinforces my desire to leave here. I was told that The M.G.M. Studios in Los Angeles has tryouts for new talent and that may be the place to go. I think for the next few weeks I will advocate my desires to leave. I just finished work but I am very tired. I feel so weak lately and feel that there may be something wrong but I know I am just tired from doing to much. I need to take a shower but I will stop at Dots first so I don't have to make another trip. I pulled in to her driveway and she came running out. She said My God look at you, I wish you would quit that job, you look as if your almost dead. I said I know and I can't keep up with the amount of sleep I'm getting. She said come in and I said, "Look at me, I'm covered with cement."

She replied, "Well, take me to your house and I'll help you clean up." I said thanks but I will be too tired to bring you home. She said you could bring me home in the morning on your way to work. I was too tired to argue so I told her to get in then we drove to my house. I stood by the shower while she undressed me, then undressed herself.

She adjusted the water temperature and we hopped in then she washed me all over. She walked to the bed with me and laid along side of me while I fell asleep. I didn't awake until morning and asked how her night was. She said, "I just love being with you," then I took her home and went to work. I never have time for breakfast and always go to work without any. I could see I'm losing weight again and thought I had to do something because I'm falling apart. When I had a break I called Dot and Jen and said I want to go home early every night this week because I am always tired. I said I'm getting run down and don't want to get sick. I also told them my doctor told me never to get this weak because of the trouble I had with my heart as a kid. They both did agree I should take better care of myself. Dot offered to come to my house every night and Jen offer to come every weekend. I said thank you but I don't think I would get any rest.

I went to work today thinking about Judy and thought that I should not get involved with her but I believe she may be able to help me in music. I do plan to call her but I believe I must make her wait. Today work was very hard and I'm getting to hate this job but I must finish my two weeks. I went straight home and took a shower because I was covered with cement. I finished with the shower and just laid down when the phone rang. I wished that I unplugged it because I was to tired to talk. I knew it had to be Jen or Dot so I let it ring for a while but I did answer it. Because my dad has it but he wouldn't call me at this time unless it's very important. I answered it and a girl said, "Hi Al, do you know who this is?"

I said, "Yes, it's that cute blond I danced with and was asked to call."

She said, "How did you know?" and I said, "Who else would call me?" She said, "I would but you don't want to call me," and I said, "I would have but I have been very busy."

I said, "By the way, how did you get my phone number?" and she said, "You gave it to us." I said, "Who is us?"

She said, "Tom and I when you were at the school but I thought you're not going to call me so I called you."

I said, "Well, you got me," and she said, "I do?" I said, "Yeah, on the phone," and she said, "How would you like to play tomorrow night?"

I asked her where and she said, "Here at my house, and you could play with me." I said, "What do you mean, play with you?" She hesitated and said, "I mean, bring your guitar and play for me." I said I would love to but I already made plans. She said, "Don't you like me?" and I said, "Yes but I'm afraid of you."

She laughed and said, "What do you mean, you're afraid of me?

I said, "You're beautiful and I don't know if my heart can handle it." She said we could go very easy and she would take care of me. I said, "That's what I was afraid of, and let me think about it but I am going to dinner now, would you like to join me?"

She said, "I would love to and when are you leaving?"

I said, "I'm all ready and was walking out the door when you called." She said, "Do I have time to get ready?" and I said, "Don't get too fancy because I just have my work clothes on." I asked her where she lived and she gave me directions. It was not far from the school, so I told her I would have no trouble finding it and I would be there in twenty minutes. I can't believe it because I am not tired now but I was almost dead before she called. She was at the door so I got out and went to walk her to the car then asked, "Should I meet your parents?"

She said, "You don't have to they were at the show and know who you are." I walked her to the car then opened the door and seated her. I got in, then said, "You look very nice and I like your hair down." She asked where we were going and I said to the Bantam Steakhouse. She said, "Oh! I love that place." We drove towards the steakhouse and she came and sat close to me. I really was scared and didn't know what I would do because no girl had ever sat this close the first time they were with me. When we got there she took my hand and we walked in together. We both had a steak dinner and I treated her. She asked about Dot and I said we have been going together for a long time. I did not want to talk about Dot so I told her I play a lot in New York and have been very busy. I wanted to get off this subject and talk about her. I wanted to know more about her and why she is interested in me. She explained that she was the head cheerleader and in charge of the entertainment committee. We left the Steakhouse and I started to take her home then asked her, "What do you do in music?"

She said, "I help arrange the schedules and look for talent." I said you search for talent then why are looking at me. She laughed and asked me to pull in to the school yard.

I did and she said stop the car right here. She turned and put her arms around me and our lips went together. She kissed me very sexually for a long time and I did not try to stop her. I looked into those very blue eyes and her long blond hair was all over my face. I could not think because I never expected this to happen. She finally stopped and said I'm sorry but I wanted to do that ever since the first time I met you. I said thank you, I think I liked it but it was quite a surprise. She interrupted then said there's a lot more where that came from and all you have to do is ask. I said I don't know how to answer that and I'm, I mean I wasn't prepared for that. She said "You didn't like it" I said yes I loved it but I see you have a way to polarize my mind and could we do that again to see if I like it. We did and this time I knew what I was doing. I told her Yes, I do like it but I really didn't know what to say because my life is already confusing. I took her home then walked her to her door and said I will call you. I said good night honey and she said I like that name. I went home to get some sleep but I could still see those eyes inviting me in and felt that long hair on my face. It was so soft, she had that certain smell and the feel of her body against mine that could persuade you from past thoughts into a new realm of excitement. But I also knew that if this went anywhere I would be forced to eradicate the present situation with Dot and Jen. Besides even now my performances and answers must be equivocal to avoid interrupting the present situation. I did not plan this but it appears to be prevalent in my lifestyle. I went to work and was glad I only had one more week here. I thought about Judy all day and didn't know what to make of it because I know there is no way I could fit her into my life right now. I would love to keep her as a friend because we have a lot in common and she is very interested in music. I do believe she could expand my opportunity and find me a lot of places where I could play to be more popular. One good thing is that she lives in a different town and does not come here very much. I know I'm thinking about her to much and this could spell trouble. I went home and took a shower then tried to get my head together because I must plan what I'm doing tonight. I was just getting out of the shower and the phone rang. I answered it and it was my younger sister Arlean. She also plays the guitar and asked me if I could play with her at a private party tomorrow night. I told her I would love to but I have to play at José's and I told her to please try and let me know ahead of time.

She is just sixteen but she plays very well and has the best voice I ever heard. Her boy friend bought her a hollow body Martin guitar. I have a Fender Jazz Master, a Magnatone Typhoon and a Magnatone Amplifier that I customized and this is what I use the most. I designed the electronics to what I wanted. I designed an inductance system that has its own pick up mounted inside to the back of the body along with the triple pick-ups under the strings. This allows secondary harmonics to enter the amplifier and makes it sound as if I was playing two guitars. These are secondary sound waves or refraction's of the initial sound because the carbon crystal microphone has a slight delay. I did tell Arlean I was planning to go to California then told her I did not tell this to anyone except where I worked. It was very nice talking to her and I don't know why but all of us kids (brothers and sisters) did separate and hardly ever see each other. I believe we all have a mental block from our childhood and just can't break away from it. I tried to plan my week end and thought I would take Dot out tonight and Jen to José's tomorrow night. I called Dot, it is after seven and I told her I would pick her up at eight. I told Jen I would pick her up after work tomorrow at noon. She asked me to please come there now but I explained I'm too tired but we did talk on the phone for a while. I picked up Dot and went to a restaurant in Danbury. I was getting very confused to where I would take these girls so they wouldn't cross path. I don't like doing this but right now I have no other choice and although I love both of these girls it is not an easy life. After dinner we went to a movie and we had a lot of fun. I did talk about my future in music and she did agree I should not quit. I told her that every since she came back from Canada all we did was have sex and no other fun but we must start thinking about our future. I said I don't know why I was so immature and careless. I thought to myself about having sex with Jen also and we are all lucky nothing has happened yet. I think about this now but when they are all over me with their hands in those spots I know I can't control myself. We did have a very good time tonight and we didn't have to have sex as always. On the way to her house she asked me if I would be mad if she did get pregnant and I asked her why.

She reiterated, I want a baby even if we don't get married because this would give me a reason to live. I wish she hadn't said that because it will make it all the harder to control myself but I did go home and fell asleep. I called Jen and told her I could not pick her up at noon but I will pick her up tomorrow at six o'clock to go to José's with me. She wanted me to come there now but I told her I'm tired and wanted to stay home. Dot did call and I knew I could not see her this weekend so I took her to dinner then to my house for a while. I thought that I would have to unplug my phone because Judy might call and what would I say. I am a little afraid after what Dot told me about her wanting to get pregnant. I do believe it would be good for her because if we never get together she would at least have a baby to love and raise because I don't think she will ever love again. This may be all I could ever offer her and she may feel this also. After I took Dot home I called Jen and I told her I would pick her up and she could go with me to change. When I got there she was alone so she left a note for her mom and dad that she was with me. She got into my car and went to my house. I asked her to get my clothes ready while I was into the shower. She came back to the shower naked and hopped in with me I did not say anything but I didn't expect this. She just said I want to help you wash. We finished in the shower then I laid on my bed and told her I really needed some sleep. She started to massage me, I fell asleep and when I awoke she had my clothes ready. I said what else could I hope for then we went to José's. We had some food and a drink before I had to play then I went on stage and played until eleven o'clock. I felt very tired and knew I needed rest so I told Jen I think I'm getting sick because I'm tired and weak all the time. I took Jen home and I went home to sleep. When I was with Judy I had a very sharp pain in my chest and thought it was indigestion so I didn't think about it anymore. On my way home I just felt it again but I ate at José's and I thought it was when I eat a lot. I went to sleep and woke up fine but I was a little weak at first and thought I just needed more rest. I called Dot to tell her that I may have a problem and about the heart problem I had as a child. I think that every time I get a pain there it's my heart. She said I want to come and stay with you to make sure you're all right so I went to get her then she came with me. I laid in bed, she massaged me and I told her it is probably nothing to worry about but I must be careful.

She was worried about me and was very nice to have here. She was very careful and massaged me until I fell asleep. When I woke up I was very hungry and I took her home then went to Al pats for breakfast then went to see my dad. I was very tired and lost my energy about noon so I told Dad I didn't feel well then went home. I fell asleep until eight o'clock then called the girls and told them I was not feeling well. I told them I wanted to stay home all weekend, they were sad but what could I do. I did call them both on Sunday and told them I felt much better. We talked for a long time and they were happy that I called them. I awoke early Monday morning and went to work but when I bent down to unhook my connector to the hopper I nearly passed out. I got a very bad head ache which I never have and a sharp pain in my chest again. I tried to attach the hopper and my chest tightened up and I felt a lot of pressure and pain down both my arms then up into my neck. I stood up and both my arms locked up. Both of my biceps felt very hard and hurt. I just sat for a moment and went to the office. I knew I had to quit this job because it was killing me. I told Bob I was having trouble and asked to go home after explaining what happened. My Heart Attack

He asked me if I needed a ride home then said I think you should go to the emergency room. I said I just need rest, I left to go home but on the way home everything happened again and my vision went blurry and I had a fire in my chest. I had to pull over and stop because I felt that I couldn't drive this way. I sat in my car until I felt better and well enough to drive. When I got home I called both girls and said I was going to sleep but would call them tomorrow. I did explain why and they both said I should go straight to the hospital. Jeanne started crying and wanted to come stay with me because she said I should not be alone. Dot also wanted to come to stay but I said it would be better if I stayed alone but I would call a Doctor. I awoke early in the morning and I called my cardiologist which I have not seen in nearly four years. He said I should have gone to the emergency room but I said I just want to come to your office. He said it sounds like an emergency and gave me an appointment for that afternoon. I did call the girls and told them I was going to the doctors today but I would call you when I get back. I went there on time and the nurse took me into his room after taking my blood pressure she drew blood and a urine test. The Doctor examined my test and asked about how long have you been having this problem.

I said I felt weak for a few weeks then had a few chest pains that I thought was indigestion and just tried to rest but the last one scared me because I had a lot of chest pain, both my arms locked up and I almost passed out. He said I may admit you to the hospital the enzymes show you had a heart attack but I have to take more test. He said you have a bad heart murmur that could lead to a severe heart attack or stroke. He checked my health history and was upset that I have not seen a doctor in so long. When he was through scolding me I asked what is a murmur. He said that you have a double murmur. He explained that two of my heart valves were not closing properly and the blood was bypassing in my heart and I was not getting enough blood to my brain and this is serious. He took me in a different room and took chest X-rays and brought me back to his office. He then told his nurse to give me a shot of antibiotics and he was going to review the other test. He came back and said I am admitting you to the hospital. I need an Echo gram and a Cardiogram and I have ordered it to be taken today. He would not let me drive so he called an ambulance to take me and I left my car in his parking lot. When I got there they put me in a plastic tent and were giving me oxygen. I waited for about an hour and they took the Cardiogram first then the Echo gram which took much longer and I watched hundreds of pages being printed. I was then sent back to a room and stayed in the tent. Doctor Coleman who is my Doctor came in later and said he seen the test reports and said I want to keep you here overnight because you have a reoccurrence of Rheumatic Fever and you must take heavy doses of antibiotics which I want injected intravenous. I pleaded with him to give me a shot now and I will come to his office every day. He said that's what I mean, you don't know how serious this is and you could die. I want you in bed twenty four hours a day for at least two weeks and I may keep you here. I said I had this before and I stayed in bed for six months that time. I know I could do it but he said I may let you go home in a few days after I check your blood again. I must have been tired but I found that you can't sleep in a hospital because as soon as you are asleep someone comes and ask you if your asleep then gives you a shot or ask if everything is all right. In the morning when the Doctor came in I asked to go home but he said it was against his better judgment and wanted to keep me longer.

After the second day I pleaded to him to let me go home and I promised that I will stay in bed. I told him I have my dad, my sister and my girlfriends. I will have someone there all the time and I promise I will only get up to use the lavatory which is close to my bed. After a long battle with him he told me that the hospital would not release me and I would have to sign an affidavit to leave them harmless in case you have another heart attack and something bad happens to you. I promised that I would stay in bed so after I signed the affidavit he drove me to my car and yelled at me all the way but I knew it was for my own good. I went home, got right in bed and laid there for a while because I was a little weak. I called Dot first and told her I was admitted to the hospital and how I fought to be released on my promise. She said I wondered why you didn't call and why! What happened. I said I had a heart attack and I promised my doctor that I would stay in bed for the two weeks because I'm not allowed to do anything but go to the bathroom. He told me I came very close to having a stroke and wanted to keep me in the hospital much longer. She said how are you going to eat alone. I said I'll have Arlean stay with me or I will go to her house. She said oh! please let me come stay with you and you know that no one cares as I do about you. She said I'll come stay with you please let me. I said thank you and I will let you know because if Jen ever found that Dot stayed with me even for a few days it would kill her. I told her I want to be alone tonight because I just want to go to sleep and I don't want to get excited. She said I understand but please call me when you wake up. I said I will but I will call Arlean just in case I need her and I want to tell her what happened. I called my dad next, I told him what happened and he said I will see you in the morning. I called Jen, she said I can't believe it, I'm sad to hear this and asked how she could help me. I said a few months ago I needed more rest and everyone thought I was avoiding them. I said something was wrong but I did not adhere to the warning and here I am. She said Me! did I do that" I said no it wasn't that but no one listened to me then. She said I'm sorry and I will skip school to come stay with you. I said Honey! I appreciate that and I love you for it but I will be all right because the pills they gave me make me drowsy then I hung up and went to sleep.

My dad did come this morning and noticed that I didn't have a refrigerator so he said he would bring me one latter today along with some food and drinks. He did come back and brought me all healthy foods. He also brought me the refrigerator and set it up for me. I called Dot and Jen, I told them that my dad was here and will come every day and he put the refrigerator next to my bed. I could get food and drinks without getting out of bed. They were both happy but upset because I wouldn't let them stay with me. I made it through the first week and I feel like new. Today is Monday and Dad stopped in to bring me my last paycheck from the Redi Mix plant. He said that Bob said he lost a very good man. My dad did understand why I quit and even more now after what happened. He checked my supply then replaced what I needed and my sister brought me some homemade food. I think I'm getting spoiled from all this attention and everything was fine until Thursday after noon. The phone rang and it was Judy, she said I'm glad I caught you at home. I said why and she said I tried calling you several times in the past couple of weeks. I said I was home I just unplugged the phone. She said why? I said I had a heart attack, she said stop kidding me. I said really and I told you that looking at you would do that. She said now I know your joking and I said really. I explained what happened but I have to go back to my doctor this Monday and he may order me to stay in bed much longer. She said I will come and stay with you and I said my heart definitely couldn't take it. She said I was calling for a date but I guess I will have to wait and asked me what caused it because your awful young for that. I said you don't know my two girl friends. Between them, my job and me playing late at night I wasn't getting any sleep. She said "You have two girl friends" I said yes and you don't want to hear about it. She said yes I really do and I said please, some other time. I said I will call you after I see my doctor maybe Tuesday night. She said I'll be home, if you need anything just call me and don't be afraid to ask if you need money because I will take it from my college funds to help you. I said you don't even know me and she said but I really hope to have that opportunity. I said you will and thank you very much. I thought that was very nice of her and I am happy she called. I started thinking about her again and how could I refuse such a beautiful, considerate, thoughtful and compassionate girl. I could see she is so much different than the other girls and appeared to be very sensible. I really did not know what she seen in me or why the first time we were alone she kissed me. I guess when she wants something she really goes after it.

I called Jen and told her I may pick her up Saturday and bring her here to my house. This made her happy because she said I'm dying to see you and I miss you so much but I laid here and couldn't stop thinking about Judy. I'm really thinking about going to California and I don't think I will start another job before I leave. I fell asleep and had a bad dream about Dot. She was crying and begging me to help her but for some reason I couldn't get to her. She was being hurt by someone while screaming my name and that's when I awoke but I had trouble getting back to sleep. I was thinking about her and awoke up at seven but didn't want to call her that early. I made oatmeal for breakfast and it was good with milk and sugar. This made me think of my childhood when I had to eat it plain. It was almost eight o'clock so I called Dot and told her I was coming to get her now. I showered then went to pick her up and drove into her driveway. She came running out, I got out of the car and she threw both arms around me. She walked with me into her house and made me some coffee. We were just talking when the phone rang. I did not mention this but the Restaurant where she worked before was closed for two weeks for remodeling. This is her boss calling her back because she did not want the late shift. He just now offered her the hours she wanted. Her hours would be from eleven am to seven p m. She thought this is very good and told him she will start on Monday. At this time very few girls owned or had a car to drive and I told her she should save for a car. She said I don't want to drive and I tried to explain how important it is to be independent. She said but I never drove before and I said I could teach you. I was getting tired and said I wanted to go home but she insisted I stay here and lay in her bed. I finally did because it is very lonely home all alone. She came in the bedroom with me, tucked me in then went to do the dishes from breakfast and cleaned the house.

I just laid there but did not get to sleep because she would come in and kiss me then leave. This was very hard to do and she did it a few times but this time I grabbed her then pulled her in bed with me. I held her tight, Kissed her and had my hands all over her. She yelled at me and said you know you can't do that yet. That just makes you heart work harder. I said it is all right and my heart needed the exercise. She said maybe after your doctor's visit. I said that's two weeks away and she said I'm sorry. I knew she wanted me as much as I wanted her but I just laid there and heard someone drive in the yard. Her mother was at her other daughter's and just came home. She does not drive either and her daughter dropped her off so I got up and had a coffee with her. I did talk about my music and I want to try to make that my career but I have not been doing anything about it. I'm not working now and after I pay the hospital and doctor I won't have very much money saved. I said I want to talk with Vinnie and ask him how to get started. I went back home and I feel very good again but I will have to take it easy. I am at my doctors now and he drew blood again but I have to take more test now. When I finish here I must take a stress test and a cardiogram. My doctor said I will most likely always have a heart murmur and will always have to take antibiotics for a prophylactic. He said I could go home but I must limit my walking for two more weeks and no lifting of any kind. I have to come back in one month for a follow up. I went home and looked to see if I needed anything because Dot wanted to go shopping with me. After shopping I took her home because she had to go to work but I told her I would pick her up and she could stay overnight again this weekend. I just laid down and heard a car drive in. It was dad. He told me that my uncle Jack is out of the hospital and thought it would be good for both of us if I would go stay with him. I agreed and he asked me if I wanted for him to take me there. I said no because I would need my car to get things for him. I said I will go there tomorrow because I have only seen him once when he was in the hospital. I called Dot and Jen and explained but I will try and get here this weekend and spend some time here. They said they did not like me leaving but did understand, saying it may be good for me. Jen told me her mother called her and told her she did get the job at the phone company. She will just work weekends from seven am until three p m and full time this summer. I was happy because everything was making it easier for me to go to California.

I don't know why I want to go there but I just have it in my mind that's the place to go. I went to my uncles and he was very happy to see me. He still can't believe that he lost his leg and talked about it a lot. He said the hardest part is that he could still feel his toes and they are always itching. He had a new television and watched it most of the time but it was nice to watch because I never had one. I stayed until Wednesday morning and drove home. I arrived at my house at noon and did not call anyone. I wanted to see Judy without anyone knowing I was back. I took a shower and got dressed. I was getting excited and maybe a little shy but I am happy it is warm today. It is in the sixty's and the nicest day we had this year. I drove to the school and went to the hall where Judy told me to meet her. I was a few minutes early but she was there and walking towards me. She took me to the auditorium and gave me a coke then we sat together. She told me she had to leave me for a minute while she changed her clothes. She was joking and asked if I wanted to help her change. I said Honey I already had a heart attack and she smiled then walked away. I waited a while and I heard someone walking. It was the Cheer Leaders coming from their dressing room. I just looked because they were so beautiful and I never seen cheer leaders this close before. I was surprised, then Judy walked up to me, I felt my chest tighten because all I could do is hold my breath and look at her. She wore something like a two piece bathing suit with pompoms and cotton balls all around. I could see her complete legs and stomach and could only think why does she wants to be with me. This put me on top of the world and my ego shot sky high. She walked right up to me and put her arms around me then kissed me in front of all the other girls. She backed up and said "How do I look. I said breath taking, you all look so nice and I have never seen so much beauty. They all thanked me then Judy introduced me to them, She told them that I was the guy that rocked the floor here and I said stop bragging. I wanted to hold her again right now and I still can't believe she wants anything to do with me. I'm just a poor farmer, I have no money or education and I don't even know where I am going. Before the game started they all paraded around the hall. They yelled letter by letter "Washington High Varsity" They did cart wheels, hand stands and they all looked so beautiful. I loved watching them and I am proud to sit with them. They repeated this at breaks and at the end. I was very happy I could see this and so very happy I did come. It was a show of a lifetime; I was watching Judy and I can't explain the beauty. I would place her looks and body above anyone I have ever seen. She could be my sunshine while I'm just a flower in bloom. When it was all over, Judy talked to the girls then took my hand and we went to my car. I opened the door for her and helped her get seated. She moved over close to me and I could see how much she liked me. I was choked up just looking at her and asked "how come you didn't change your clothes.

She said you're taking me home and I could change there. I walked with her into her house and she sat me on the couch. She asked me if I wanted something to drink and I said no thanks. She went to get changed and I looked at the house. I did not wander but I just looked from where I was and this is the nicest house I have ever been in. I could hear the water in the shower and knew she is taking one. While I was waiting I thought about when I went to Church and asked God to place me in the right road to life. I was wondering if this is it then she came out. She walked up to me and put her hands on my shoulders and kissed me. Without stopping she put both her arms around me and kissed me even harder. I was sweating while melting in her arms and I knew she knew it. She stopped and asked me where do you want to go or do. I said anywhere with you and we left to go to the Steak House. We just had a soda then I started to go to her house. She said I don't have to go home yet and I asked what else did you want to do. She said we could just ride around and talk about your plans because I want to know more about your music. I said I want to cut some records and I'm going to Columbia Studies with Vinnie my friend. He has something to do with Records and is interested in my style. She said I could see why because you really are good, I mean the best that I have ever heard. I said that's because you like me.

She asked are you leaving and I said to go to New York and she said no, I mean are you leaving Connecticut. I said no not right away, why and she said I don't want you to leave. I laughed a little while I turned the car around and went toward Bantam Lake. I went to Beverly's and parked behind there near the beach. It is just getting dark and the moon is shinning across the water. It is so pretty but while I was looking she pulled me over, started kissing me again and without stopping she got up on the seat. She pulled me over while spreading her knees and I was laying between her legs. I kissed her and really enjoyed every minute then remembered what Jossey told me. I stayed that way for a while and I could feel her sweating. I parted from her lips and looked at her in the moonlight. I said to myself I wish she was the only girl in the world because I became afraid that I may fall in love with her. I don't know how or why because my life is already so confused. She looked at me and asked me "what's wrong" I said nothing but I think I should take you home now. I said it's seven o'clock now and I asked if her parents would be mad. She said they trust me and told them if I was not home I would be with you.

I said you had a lot of trust that I would come today and why don't they care if your with me. She answered I believe that you think as I do and want to get to know me also. I said yes I do then she said my father and mother do like

217

and respect you. I said they don't even know me. Well they watched you at the play and said you are well mannered but most of all they noticed that you love kids. Dad told me that is a very good sign. She continued but it's not only that he does trust my judgment. She pulled me back down, kissed me then helped push me back up and we went to her house. She sat me on the couch and asked if I wanted a drink now. She walked over to me and I was happy that she put on her Jeans. I know I would have had Roman hands and Russian fingers but I can't get over her eyes and the power she has on me. I think that right now she could put a collar around my neck, tie a leash to it and I would follow her anywhere. She is very demanding and seems to take control. I said I want to look at your eyes and see what compels me to want to be here. She said we have a lot in common and maybe the same ideas. I did love being with you at the beach and want to thank you for your decency of being a gentleman. I like being treated as a lady and you really are everything I thought you were. I said what is that and she said someone you could love and respect. As we were talking she asked me how I liked the Cheer Leaders and I said the girl sitting across from me was beautiful but before I finished the last word she said sarcastically "she has a boy friend" I then said "don't worry honey she's no match for you" and that made her happy. She's a very smart girl and I could see she lives on principles. I thought at the time when she had her legs around me that I was being tested and I believe now that I was right. I also know I can't be to free with myself and believe that Judy needs this challenge also. I could see by her home that she has never wanted for anything and could probably have most anything she wants. This makes me believe that I must be a challenge and try to be the stronger gender. I know because I did the same thing to Jen. I don't want to reject her and have no intentions of interrupting her plan. I want to follow this through but I know I can't make any first moves.

I am home now and I don't want to talk with anyone so I pulled my car behind my house. I thought about my past life with Dorothy when I offered her everything I had and it wasn't wanted until I rejected her. I thought about Jen and Sparky and when I was a challenge they wanted me so I think I am learning. I hope I am right because I would love to spend some time with her and really get to know her better. I laid down on my bed and finally fell asleep. When I awoke I thought Judy was just a dream and when I realized it wasn't I still can't believe she likes me this much. I believe that this episode in my life may lead me away from the road to life where I was placed and when I left her I told her I would call her at three o'clock. I laid in bed all day watching the clock but did not want to call her right at three because I wanted her to wait for a while. I suffered and waited until three thirty then called her. She answered on the second ring which was good and I knew she was waiting for my call. She said Hello, I was waiting for your call and I said that makes me happy because you are a beautiful girl. She said thank you then I said I also love your long hair, it is so soft and you keep it so nice. She said you don't know how much work it is and I said I'll come comb it for you. She said I just washed it and you could brush it for me. I said I would love to but I must go out of town. She asked "where are you going" I said to Bridgeport. She said when are you coming back, "I answered next week end" well could I see you before you leave. I said why and what do you have in mind. She said I was hoping we could go somewhere this Friday night. I said I can't but how about next Friday night. She said well if it has to be but when are you leaving and I said tonight. She asked could you come here first and I asked "what time" and she said now! I said I will find out and call you back in five minutes then hung up and went to get a glass of soda.

I waited by the phone for ten minutes and called her back. I said I could come just for a few minutes and she asked are you coming right now. I said I have to get dressed because I just got out of the shower and I'm standing here naked with just a towel around me. She didn't answer right away and I knew or hoped she could visualize me with just a towel around me but I really didn't take a shower. She said I'll be waiting, I thought boy is this exciting and I took my time getting there. I drove into her yard and she came running to my car. Her hair was like gold strands of silk blowing in the wind. She hopped in and held me then put her moist lips against mine. She lifted her head and said you really know how to hurt a girl.

I said what did I do I'm here. She said I find someone I really like and now your leaving. I said I'm only going to be gone a week or two and she said what do you mean "or two" I said I will be coming home in between and I started my car. I asked where are we going and she said it doesn't matter. She sat close to me and I just drove north on Route Twenty Five. I didn't care where we were going as long as I have her with me. She held me very tight for a while and I knew she is also very happy to be here with me. We stopped at a stop sign and I could see the look in her eyes that first attracted me then drove a short way and pulled off the road. I just held her and loved holding her with the same in return. She asked me what time I had to leave and I said I should leave at six but I will stretch it a little. She said Oh good and I said where do you want to go now because I can't park along side of the road. She said I don't know "pause" oh yea I know a place. There is a horse corral that no one uses and we could go there. I turned around and went back towards the school because she said it is just past there along the river. When we got there I spotted an access road for the Utility Company and I drove up it. I drove over the hill and found it very secluded. I turned off the engine and it is just getting dark because we had a lot of big trees all around us. We are totally alone at last and in our own little world. We looked at each other and our lips went together. I think we did talk but I don't remember about what. I held her close and kept kissing and at one time my tongue went into her mouth. I didn't know if she liked that but shortly after she put hers in mine. I sucked it gently and put mine in hers while exploring every part of her mouth. I could see that she loved it and we took turns experimenting. She pushed me back and put her legs around me as before. This time she was losing a little control and was moving her groin up and down while tightening her grip with her legs. It took all my power and I thought, I don't want her to think that this is all I want so I pushed her up and said I'm sorry but I must leave now because they will be waiting for me.

She said I'm sorry, I became so excited but I want you to stay with me. Do you really have to leave now because this is the most exciting moment in my life? I replied, mine also and you are a wonderful person to be with but I do have to leave now. She said I could see that you have so much control with yourself and over others. Do you wonder why I love you and I said "what did you say" She said I mean I like you more than anyone else ever. I paused and said I must say the same then started the car and drove her home. I walked her to her door and asked, when do you want to go out again. She answered promptly tomorrow night. I said come on and she interrupted me well you asked me. I said all right, I will make a special trip but when should I call you. She said call me at three and I'll be waiting. I really didn't have to leave but this will let me know how she really feels about me. I have learned that absence makes the heart grow fonder and the thought of absence is worst then the absence itself. I do know that it would be better for me to spend more time at my uncles because I'm worried about what I'm getting myself into. I know I can't face Dot or Jen now and I don't know how to act around them. I could feel myself changing and I really didn't want to but I did warn myself that I was treading in troubled waters. I seem to get into these problems without trying but I love being with Judy and it is a new high for me. I left to go to my uncles and I got here at nine thirty. I drove into the drive way then went in and he seemed very happy that I came back. He started crying and I did not question him. I was just watching television and thought that someone could have the best day in their life yet someone could have their worst. Life does have many questions and I'm starting to think you should live your life for the moment because tomorrow's are only promises. I asked Jack who was going to stay with him and help. He said I don't know, maybe my daughter in law Ruthy and I said I could stay for a while. He said thank you and you are a good boy. I do worry about him because he can't drive, go shopping or get to his doctor. I do hope that Ruthy does come to live with him because he does need someone here with him. I waited for school to get out then called Jen and this made me very sad. I explained it to her and told her I would see her on Sunday when she gets out of work. I finished talking with Jen at three fifteen and called Judy. She answered and said hello Honey, I said but this is Al and she said I know and do you think I would say that to anyone else. I said but what if it wasn't me, she said I would say excuse me but I thought it was Al, o k. I said you are a real clown then told her I had more problems with my uncle and I have to stay with him longer now. I told her that his wife just left him and wants a divorce. This means he has no one to help him.

She said "Oh No" My mom and dad are leaving for a week and we have the house to our selves. I am not going with them because I can't miss a week of school. My brother is staying with me but he never gets home until after eleven o'clock. I said well when do you want me to come and she named of the days one by one Monday through Saturday. I said you would get sick of me after all that. She laughed and said Tuesday would be the best and you could come here at three. I said would it be better if I pick you up at school and she said "Yea" pick me up at two thirty and I said all right but I will call you Monday at three, I hung up then went back to Jack's. I wanted to call Dot and pick her up but I have a guilty conscience and wonder if I should but I do remember she did this to me for nearly a year. Should I not venture into a better future or must I accept the status quo. I don't know the answer and feel I must follow my heart. I know I will do all I could for her and Jen to find their way in this road to life but I know I must end the present life style with them. I really love them both but continuing could only aggravate the situation more and deter and future in music that I may have. It is only ten o'clock and I know Dot doesn't expect me this early but she looked out and seen me drive in. She came running out to meet me as I got out of my car. She hung on to me and kept kissing me so I just picked her up and carried her towards her front door. I let her down and we went in to the kitchen where Beatrice had coffee ready. After we had our coffee and talked I asked Dot if she wanted to help me at my house today because I would have to go back tonight. She grabbed my hand and pulled me toward the door and said lets go. I went in to lay on my bed and she laid alongside me. I still didn't know what I was going to do yet and said I must take a shower. I did not take one last night or this morning and she said good I'll take one with you. I liked that because I have not been with her like this in a long time and after what Judy put me through.

I turned the shower on and we hopped in. We helped wash each other and this is when I realized I did miss her very much. She washed me all over then squeezed me and kissed me so hard I had trouble breathing. Spending this time with her really has me confused and I really don't know who I love the most. I appears that I love the one I'm with at the time. I think a lot about what José has told me and I can't believe that Dot is using me now. She may have in the past only because she was not in the right state of mind to think about herself or anyone else and she really has been a young lady since our talk.

I could see where Judy's coming from with all her wealth and she could have almost anything she wants. I am the new Kid on the block and this to her is exciting. She really doesn't know me and every one does think I will make it big in music so I'm sure she would like to be with me then. I know I must be careful but I won't quit until I understand her desires and the way I really feel. It always appears that when all fails I fall back to Dot.

Dot and I stayed in bed all night then I had to take her home because I wanted to cleaned up the house and go to Bridgeport before I picked up Jen. I made sure Jack had everything he needed and had everything ready for him before I left. I arrived at Jen's house just after three and she was waiting for me. We went for lunch then to my house. I again parked behind my house and we went in. We laid on the bed and she said she really was missing me much more then ever. She was almost crying at times and would not let go of me. I felt very bad and didn't realize I was hurting these girls this much. We laid hear for hours and never thought about sex but just being together but we both ended up in the shower and the rest is self explanatory. I took her home but I did not go to Jack's house, I just stayed here thinking about what I must do. I had no answers and know now that I have no other recourse but to eradicate my relations with all of them. I will try to limit our relations gradually until I find a solution. I just laid in bed but not without worrying because Judy has opened a new chapter in my life that may have fortified my desires and reasons to leave. I don't have the mental ability to comprehend the situation but I know now I must expedite a plan to gradually rationalize the situation. I will presently endure the status Quo and play this to the end. While laying here I know I loved Dot and Jen very much and never wanted to lose either one but I believe now I may be falling in love with Judy. Because my total outlook on life has changed, because when I am alone I know I feel that Dot and Jen are just my friends now and I wish I didn't feel this way. I am afraid for both of them but mostly Jeanne because she was the innocent one. I know I lured her in to my life to suppress my feelings with Dot. Dot gave me many reasons but not since our first encounter of real love together but I believe now it may be to late. I fell asleep and was very uneasy but knew I must make the right decision.

I think about Judy now and why we became so close so fast. I don't think it is her looks alone but compatibility. We did not talk about sex and love alone although it was the most important to me at the time, but in many conversations we spoke so much about music. She offered to help me in every aspect including the lyric's and melody. I know or at least believe she could help me the most. I fell asleep but not without worrying, I was very uneasy and knew that I must make the proper decisions. It is morning and I am on my way to Bridgeport to help my uncle. He just awoke and I made him coffee and sat to talk with him. He was still very sad that he lost his wife and I thought that I may being sharing these same feelings very shortly. I tried to take his mind off of her and talked about his accident but that only exasperated the situation. He started screaming about his failure not to notice the speed of the motor he used and especially since he is a Mechanical Engineer but I told him we all make mistakes. I helped him with his choirs then told him I will be back tomorrow. I thought about the triangle of love and now with the new factor, Judy. Is this the sign that I have been waiting for or just an addition to this intricate and complex situation. I know I have always tried to be conscientious but know now that I must restrain from offering any further concessions. I don't know how this relation with Judy could help me but I wasn't offered any other choice.

Real Love or Sexual Infatuations

I could break out in tears when thinking about hurting anyone. I know that they followed their beliefs and did trust that I would use proper judgment. Where did I go wrong and why couldn't I see the intensity of what was happening or see this coming. Who should I hurt and was it up to me to hurt anyone that I cared so much about. I'm becoming more confused and scared that I am disregarding my obligations but I can't make the proper decisions on my own so I will try to find them in this venture with Judy. I hope that I will receive a sign because I am not in the road of life now but the road of confusion. It is almost three o'clock, I must call Judy but I will not make her wait and called right at three. Her phone is ringing and she answered on the second ring again. She said Hi Al. I said Hi love and what's wrong with Hi Honey. She said are you coming now, I said I'm all ready and I will be leaving soon. She said yes I'll be waiting for you. "This is what I mean, when I am talking or with Judy there is no one else on my mind". I drove to her house and she met me by my car again.

I watched her run towards me, she had a short white skirt with a pink and white blouse that had a low cut neck line and if the sun stopped shining I would still see her glow. She grabbed my hand and walked me in to her house. She brought me a soda and sat on the couch with me. I said where are you taking me and she said we have the whole house to ourselves. We could stay here for a while and I said could you show me some of the house. She said sure then we took a grand tour through most of the house, it was beautiful and I told her that. She went to her bedroom last and laid on her bed. It was the nicest bed I've ever seen and her bed room proved that she wanted for nothing in her life. I stood there while looking at her, I started from her feet and could see her skirt was high enough so I could see her panties then some of her stomach. I went up to her eyes and the golden blond hair, some was over her face and her arms were reaching out for me. She said come here and lay with me so I put my hand out and froze there. She grabbed my hand then pulled me towards her and at the same time spread her legs. I laid there between her legs while she put her warm and wet lips against mine. She searched my lips and mouth with her tongue while her hands were on my back digging her fingers into me. She put her legs around me and pulled me in tight. I laid there but did not feel my heart beet fasted but harder and I could only hear it echo in my mind. I must have fallen into a trance or something because I could not move. I laid here for a long time and did not put my hands in any forbidden places because I could not handle any more than what I had. She then rolled me over and got on top of me. Her silk like hair was all over my face and she had her knees tight against my sides. Our lips stayed together and her hair crawled over my face with her movements. I knew now that I did have sex before but this is the first time it was different and wanted very much to make love to her. I just laid here and felt that she knew more about how to make me want her than I did. I did not expect this today but I knew it was inevitable in the near future. I also know that I must find myself because she has full control of my heart and mind which makes me more confused but also excited.

I really thought that she was of a much higher caliber and had a different outlook on life. I did not believe when I first met her that sex and love was her main goal but apparently it appears that way. We knew each other for to short of a time to be intimate and I didn't know where this would lead me but only increase the pandemonium that exist in the present love triangle. I feel now if I continue I will only appear to be impertinent, not only to myself but all that is involved. I picked up her face to see if this was real, then looked into her eyes and said "what are you" I have never felt this way before and have no control of what I'm doing. She said I'm only showing you how much I love you and I do love you. You are all I can think about now and think about you all day. I did not answer, she got off and I was still thinking about this sudden outburst of love and sex. I stopped her and said, Judy! I do love you and your all that I think about now but I cannot respect myself or show any respect for you if I continue. I am involved with Dorothy and Jeanne, and I have promised them my love and until I ratify my relations with them, I am not free to proceed. I want you very much but I will have to wait until I can fortify my true feelings and this is only fair to you. She spoke up and said Al! how can you say you love them when you're here with me like this. You just said you love me and how could you mean it. I said You don't understand and I'm not sure I do now but I don't want to hurt them. I said you wanted me to tell you about these girls and I told you some other time well I guess this is it. I explained my complete involvement and how it got to where it is now. I started to feel bad and she just held me and said You know there is no easy way out but You said Dorothy didn't deserve you in the beginning and Jeanne knew you had a girlfriend when she first met you. No matter which one you may ever end up with you may always believe it should have been the other. But if you want my opinion you will most likely lose both of them anyway. I am sure they will find out some way about your double romance and could you live with that. She looked at me and said I know I love you and it can't be anything else but love because I have never felt this way in my life. I will never offer my body to anyone else and I really admire your respect but what you just told me could only make me love you more. I do know enough about sex to know how much you want it with me but I am proud that you have the power and control, that is greater than this moment of uncertainty. I said, I know I really do love you because I don't feel any hurt when I am with you and I don't have to lie to you. We stopped talking, held each other, kissed and talked about us. I said you have a very good chance that I will find that I do want you and only you because I do believe that I do love you more than anyone in my life. She said before we leave I want to tell you this! Throughout high school and with the dates I have had, I came to believe that when I didn't give them my sex they didn't want me. I do want to keep you and never let you go. I have lost two boyfriends because I wouldn't let them have sex with me and I was afraid I would lose you also. I did have a bad experience once and I do want to tell you about it some time.

I said you don't have to but it is a shame that a girl has to feel that way but believe me they didn't love you in the first place and it was just a sexual desire. I said this makes me want to be with you more and not have sex until we are sure of the consequences. We then got dressed and went to the Steak house. Throughout our conversation we both could not emphasize enough how much we wanted each other and we learned a lot today. She tried to tell me things that have happened in her last relations and I told her she did not have to explain but she said it would make her feel better. She said I want to tell you that I am not a virgin and want to explain this to you. I interrupted her and asked her how old are you. She said I will be eighteen this summer and I said you look older. She said I always did and it has something to do with what I want to tell you. When I was sixteen I had a boy friend, we went to school together and we were with each other all the time. I really did like him and we were friends for a long time before this but after several dates with him this one time I went with him alone and he had his hands all over me. He grabbed my tits and put his hand under my dress. He said he wanted to fuck me and I said I have heard that word only with filth and he should have never used that with me. He apologized then took me home but I accepted it and we went out again. He said he only wanted to feel my breast. He handled them, sucked on them and I did not stop him because I was only sixteen and foolish. He then put his hand between my legs and was rubbing me. I tried to stop him but he continued. He is two years older than me and stronger. He pulled my panties hard and I told him to stop but he kept pleading with me to let him. He kept begging and said I won't do much I just want to rub it on you. I said no please no but he pushed me over and said if you don't let me I never want to see you again because it means that you don't love me. I didn't want to do that but I didn't want to lose him because I thought I did love him. He pulled my panties over, rubbed in on me then pushed very hard and forced it in to me. That hurt very much so I cried, I felt that I was bleeding and had to go home. He started to cry and apologized then said I don't know what got into me and took me home.

I seen him in school and he said he was sorry. I believed him and was his friend again. Two weeks went by and he did it again but this time I let him then in a very short time he ejaculated inside me and just took me home. He did not even kiss me or ask about me. I was afraid I may get pregnant and seen him in school. I asked him "why did you do that and why did you lie to me" He tried to blame it on me and he told some of his friends what he did but he said I begged him for it. Another girl said he did the same to her and I cried for being so stupid. I stopped her because she was crying and said you don't have to explain any more. I know what you are and I love you for just that. Don't let the past get in your way and never put it in front of you. She said I haven't and I think it made me a better person but I did want to tell you that I did get my period then. I was afraid to go out alone with boys until I met you. I said I have experienced this with my girl friend and she was raped when she was sixteen. I mean a brutal rape with five or six people holding her down. I said we should be fortunate that we could look back and know it was a mistake just to better ourselves but not forget what the real world is all about. We arrived at the Steak House then had a steak dinner and just talked. I asked her if there is any where you want to go or do. She said we could go to my house and watch television. We did that and did not watch very much but spent the night talking about ourselves. She did say that she wanted to go out with me all she could and maybe we could get married when she finishes college. I said it does have a good chance and agreed I will try to keep in touch while she is in college. I said joking do you still want to go out again. She said every day we could and Al, I love you, what do you mean. I want to see you all that I can and if you make it big in music I would buy all your records and tell everyone that I made love to you. I said maybe I will write a song," I made love to Judy" she said you probably would do that and it will be the first one I buy. We were hugging and kissing and after I heard her story I wanted to make love to her but her brother should be home at any time. She wanted me to wait for him to come home and I did. He came in and was surprised that I was there. He said Hi my name's Mat, I'm happy that your here and I wanted to meet you. I did remember him being at the parties and he said I would love to have you teach me some guitar. I did not have a chance to say a word.

He kept talking but stopped to ask are you and Judy going together because Judy said you two may get married. He said I hope so you could live here because we do have a big house. I said thank you very much but Judy must finish college first and I have to cut some records. Judy and I are talking about it but it will be in the future. It was getting late and Judy needed her sleep especially after today. I told Mat that I would try to come and show him some of my style. He thanked me and Judy walked me to my car. We hugged, kissed each other and said we loved each other then I asked if I could come here on Friday. She said yes I would love you to; she held me tighter and said I love you so very much. I left then went to my house and laid down but my mind was spinning. I knew Judy was special and felt that I did want to marry her. I felt my life with her would be fulfilled with all my wishes. I believe that our desires are in harmony with our abilities and we will both work together to achieve our goals. I laid in bed and broke into a cold sweat because I know how much I loved her now. I did not want to share my love with anyone else and didn't know what I would say to Jen or Dot. I felt that this would have to come to an end now and I should not prolong it. I must tell them personally but I don't think I could hurt them that much and I need some time to think this out. I thought about leaving and maybe this is the best time. I could not sleep; I just walked the floor and just made up my mind that I will leave soon to go to California. I can't take any more and I know I will go crazy so I will leave on Saturday, June 7th. I will have a small going away party at the Lynn Deming Park in New Milford on the eve of the 6th. I fell asleep then I woke up early and went to Bridgeport. I told my uncle that I was leaving and asked when Ruth would be here. He said Saturday morning and I said I'm very happy for you. 1 just laid around and knew that this was the only way out.

The hardest Thing I ever did

I'm afraid to go anywhere or answer the phone because someone is always demanding something from me. I called Dorothy and told her I would come see her on Thursday. I could not go to sleep so I drove around but my mind kept spinning. I wanted to leave tonight and not talk to anyone so I didn't go back to Jack's but just drove around and decided to go home. It was too late to call anyone so I laid down and I may have slept for an hour but I could not sleep any more. I did not know how I would tell Dot and Jen so I tried to rehearse what I wanted to say. I don't want to hurt them and know I am hurting for them now. I am happy that they both have jobs and will have their own money. I left my house at six a m and went to Al Pats. I had a few coffees and sat there until seven thirty. I then drove around until eight o'clock then went to the pay phone and called Dot. Beatrice answered and said she was sleeping. I told her I was on my way home and please have Dot call me when she awakes. She called right away and said she was happy to hear from me today. I went to her house, went in and she gave me a hug when I walked in then walked me to the table. She poured me a coffee and sat by me. I said I have to leave, I'm going away. She looked up and said what do you mean. I said I'm going to California because I must do something with my life. She said "For how long" I said I don't know it could be a month or two. She said will you still want me. I said it's not that and will you want me. She said when are you leaving, I said Saturday the Seventh and she said that's not far away, Why! why all of a sudden. I said I have no job, no money, no career, I'm doing nothing for myself and I have to find myself. I said I will call you and give you my address when I get one then we could write. She said I can't take you leaving me. What will I do without you; she started crying and held me tighter. She was sobbing and I said I'm very sorry but it has to be this way. I said if you want I will pick you up Sunday and we could spend the day together. I will also stop in tomorrow to see you. She stopped crying and said could you pick me up tonight after work because I get out at seven. I said yes I will and that made her feel a little better. I wanted to bust out crying but I knew I couldn't. By not having much sleep made me numb anyway but I looked at her and seen the hurt in those eyes. Her eyes were red and cloudy with tears, her face was wet and she kept wiping them. I could not hold back any longer, I busted out crying, my eyes filled with tears and I could not see so I said excuse me then left. I went to my car and had problems seeing to drive. I just wished that I was dead and I tried to sleep but the pain grew even stronger inside of me. My whole body hurt and I said what in the hell did I do.

I started crying again and knew that I had Jeanne to cope with. I really don't want to go through this and wanted to go somewhere and get drunk. I knew that Jen gets out of school at two and I decided to go to her house to get this over. I got there at two thirty and she was just getting off the bus. She ran to my car and hopped in then seen my eyes and asked what's wrong. I looked at her and the tears filled my eyes again. I said I'm leaving and I don't know how to tell you. She said what do you mean you're leaving, and I said I'm going to California. She said When, Why, Did I do something wrong. I said No I just have to get my life together and I can't do it here. I pulled her over then held her and didn't want to talk because it hurt too much. She asked are we through and I said that's up to you. I will give you my address when I get there and call you, I will also write to you all the time. She said how long are you going for and could I go with you. I said I must go alone and don't know how long a month maybe two or more. She said I'll wait for you, I'll be in college anyway and we could write to each other. I said what do I have to offer you, I don't even have a job, I have no money and no place to live. She said I do understand and don't blame you but I will wait for you forever. She did not cry but did have some tears in her eyes. I said I will still be here for another ten days, I want to see you and could I pick you up from work on Saturday. She said Yes Please I will be waiting. I said I have a lot of things to do but I will try to stop and see you tomorrow. We sat in the car, held each other and I felt better with her because she did understand as always. I did not want to go in the house because I didn't want anyone to come home and see me this way. We held each other for a long time; she kissed me and kept telling me not to worry that she would wait for me. She was silent for a while then asked, is there a chance that you will never come back. I said how could I guarantee that I won't get killed on my way out there. She said I don't mean that I mean could you fall in love with someone else and not want me. I said that is hard to answer but I will promise that I will not fall in love with anyone for a long time because I still love you very much and I really don't want to get close to anyone out there. I just want to find myself and try to start a career. I hope you understand that I want to be somebody. She said I know and I'm sure you will. Her Dad drove in and I had to get out of the drive way. She kissed me and I said I will call you. I waved to Bob and went home but I don't know how I am going to keep all these promises.

I still have go to Bridgeport to help Jack, its six o'clock and I will pick up Dot at seven. I went there at seven and she came right out then hopped into my car. She put her arms around me and squeezed me very tight and said I can't let you go. I want to get married first then go with you and I don't care how bad things get as long as I'm with you. I did not wait and I said I must go alone because that's the only way I could ever be anything. I have nothing and can't live with myself right now so please try and understand. I thought about this while you were in Canada and I know I have to do this now. I will write and call you every chance I could. I then asked her, where do you want to go now. She said I want to spend the night with you. I told her please I don't want to talk about it anymore because I hurt enough now and can't take any more. She looked at me and said I'm very sorry but I just don't want to lose you and would rather die. I said Honey! You are such a beautiful girl and look at it hypothetically, what if I died or didn't come back, could you find someone so much better than me. Every place I took you I seen so many guy's looking at you, you could be a model and you have more potential than I do. She said thank you for your compliments but your wrong and I don't have these things. I said ask someone else and I bet that they agree with me then I pulled her over and held her close. I said Look here! I'm not going for ever and I am coming back. She stopped and kissed me very hard then said I just love you so much. I held her tighter and said I don't want you to worry because I do love you. I kissed her and started to caress her. She started to relax and picked up her head and said I want you to make love to me every day that you're here because I want to have your baby. We began to kiss in a way to get sexy but I'm not sure if I could. I was very tired and really did not want sex but it was the least I could do for her. I knew I had to lie and would probably never come back because I do not know at this time what will happen. I had to show her that I did have a lot of feelings for her and I did not want her to fall back to where she was. I still love her very much in many ways and I do want to make this a time she will always remember. I took off her blouse while she kicked her panties off. I was kissing and fondling her breast and there were no holds barred. We got up and took all of our clothes off and went into the shower. We did not stay there long and wanted to get back in bed. I did love her but also knew she was the one at fault. I knew that I could no longer just blame myself but make it as easy as I could for her.

We made love and she said I will pray to get pregnant because this will give me a reason to live. We left in time for her to go home to change her clothes and dropped her off at work. She kissed me and said I will wait for your call. When I got home I made some coffee then thought about life and why are there so many problems. I knew that when I left I would be giving up all the happiness I ever had and hurting people by doing so but I could not think of any other way. I thought that maybe after a few months I could return and one of them would be waiting for me then I could start over. I was too tired and dried out to think properly but I did fall asleep. I awoke at one o'clock and made more coffee and knew that I had to go to Bridgeport but I thought I would stop to see Jeanne on the way. She seemed to be the most understanding, always easy to talk to and never gets mad. I remember the first time Jeanne and I were fully undressed together because I told her that I knew nothing about a girl. I don't know what they like or want and she was a virgin but she did explain all about a girl to me. She showed me all her parts while being very shy but she did it for me. She also explained what they did and the names. She showed me her hymen and explained why she had it. She also showed me where she peed from and the parts that were sensitive and where it felt the best. She explained about her period, how much she would bleed and most girls will have this every twenty eight days. Then she continued all about ovulation and their movement through the fallopian tubes to her ovaries. I did not know that a girl could get pregnant any month of the year and she did explain everything in detail. This was the only sex education I ever had then I also showed her my parts and explained the names and what they did. I also told her that a man ejaculates seamen with sperm when they climax. I showed her where the sperm was stored and that they were made in my testicles. We both learned a lot and I will always remember this. She was the one to make me understand women and how to make love. I know these thoughts will always resonate in my mind and I know now that our love affair was not meaningless.

I went to her house and she just got there. She was in the house and seen me drive in. She was like a little kid and I knew that I would miss her the most. She had a special look that I have never seen in anyone else but that is probably what attracted me to her in the first place. I believe now that if I met her first I would ask to marry her before she went to college and I think I would have waited for her. I look at this innocent girl and I feel real dirty about what I have done with her. I know now that I had no right to use her as I did because she has always been honest, truthful and pure. I know she has never cheated on me and I must live with it on my conscience the rest of my life. If we never get together I wish that she finds someone better than me. I know that she did plead with me to have sex but I believe she thought that I was the only one in her life. She hopped into my car and asked what's wrong. I said I'm going to miss you so much. She said don't worry I will be making money and I will call you. I don't care how much it cost and I also get a good discount because I am an operator. I will write to you from college and if you're not back yet I will wait for you, because we're both young and have a life time to plan. She always makes me feel better and has the right things to say. I just held her and she asked me again are you picking me up Saturday. I said you could count on it and I had to go to Jacks so I left after a little while. I told her that I really loved her and I knew that I did more now than before. As I drove to my uncle's house my mind went back to my child hood and how much I have been hurt. I have always said I could never hurt anyone because I knew what it was to be hurt all the time. I was never allowed to have anything but now I wanted to own everything and everyone. I did not know how to let go of something I wanted and most of all not hurt someone. I know that you cannot follow your heart or in my case or your mind either but what should I have followed or known. I had very little education and was not allowed to do home work for school. I was forced to quit school with only two years of high school. I had no place to live and had to leave home at a early age. I know that I will be punished for what I have done and if not by the Lord then by my own conscience and will have to face what's coming to me. I know I promised Judy that I would be at her house at three o'clock but I have time to visit Dot, she did not know I was coming and was very happy. She was in a better mood than I expected and she told me that she slept with her legs up on pillows. I can't believe how excited she was then she told me this coming week was her most fertile time. I told her I will give her all that I could but I do have a lot to do before I leave and we talked for a while before I took her to work.

She asked me if I could pick her up at seven, I said I don't think so but I will be back before midnight and she said could you stop then. I said yes and if I get back sooner I will go to your house. I went back home and didn't know how I could handle all this and would increase my chance of another heart attack but I knew that I must take it easy. It was eleven o'clock and I went home and fell asleep. I awoke at two fifty and knew I over slept. I called Judy and she was home and answered so I told her I just woke up and would be late. I said I had to shower and change but she convinced me that I should go there to shower. She said this will save time so I grabbed some clothes, left to go there and she was waiting in the yard for me. She came running and did a car wheel. Her hair was all over her face and she did not pull it back. She came to me and I had to peak to find her eyes. That blue shinned through her hair and she looked so nice. I knew she was the prettiest girl I've seen, she was truly radiant and not a blemish that I could find. She is a perfect model of life itself and she was running towards me. I believe now that I did get the sign that I was waiting for but I also believe it came too late. I knew that this girl could be mine but I also knew that I could not be hers at least not now. I knew I have all ready promised myself to someone else and I was venturing into unchartered territory. I knew that I did not have the right to offer myself to her and if I can't respect myself the least I could do is show the respect that is well deserved to Dorothy and specially Jeanne. She noticed the chill that came over me and asked if there was anything wrong. I said I am very tired and had a few bad days. She took my hand and led me into the house. I grabbed the clothes that I had brought with me and went in with her. She said she had to practice for her cheerleader event and had to change to her uniform she stripped of her clothes and put on her uniform. I asked, why are you changing in front of me, she said I want you to see all of me and it may help you decide. I cannot explain how she looked and what it was doing to me. It would have been better for me to never witness her performance. I wished that someone could have removed my brain and let me go forwards from here. She put on a beautiful show, I said you were very good and I never seen a wrong move. She took off her uniform and was standing there naked. She walked up to me then stood there and said I think after our talk we do understand each other better.

I was still sitting so I put both hands on her buttocks, pulled her close and kissed her belle. She led me into her bedroom and then to her shower. She undressed me then got into the shower with me and I knew that I had to put my past behind me for this moment because I believe that this is the girl I want to spend the rest of my life with. Right now only the future holds the answers and I cannot find a reason why we can't venture in something that we both want very much. She washed me all over and I did the same for her. We spent some time exploring each other and she went to her bed. She laid on the bed and held her hands out to invite me to come in bed with her. I held her hands and she pulled me to her while spreading her legs. We worked ourselves to the center and fondled for a long time while our lips stayed together. I lifted my head then looked into her eyes and knew she had full control but I was satisfied with that. I kissed her breast then her belly and wanted to satisfy her so I kissed her where she loved it the most. I did not plan this but I knew

I couldn't stop now because I have never seen anyone so excited in my life. She was trusting her hips up and down and grabbed me by the hair then pulled me in closer and started to scream. She then stopped and pushed me away. She was breathing very hard and just held me close to her. When she caught her breath she pushed me over and did the same for me. We then went to the shower and laid down again. She asked me why I did that and I said the same reason you did it to me. I have never felt this way before and I felt she was very important in my life now besides I wanted her to wait for me while I was gone. I felt together we could reach most any goal because we shared the same ideas. We were both relaxing and just laid there for a while. We still had a lot of time before I had to leave and she asked do we have enough time to get something to eat. I said for you I will make the time and we went to the small Diner that I took Dot to once. It was closer from here than our house then we both had a Hamburg, French fries and a coke. We arrived at her house and started to hug and kiss then ended up back in bed. We stripped of clothes and she lay on the bed waiting for what I was to give her. She had her legs apart and I laid between them while she reached down and put it where she wanted it. Our bodies just clenched together and I never felt this way before. She was quivering and I couldn't believe how I felt. I could see we were a perfect match and I picked up my face to see if this is real.

She had the same look on her face and our lips went together again. I can't believe how long this lasted but we both wanted it to last forever. We did not rush it and I knew I never felt quite like this before but I believe I did discover true love and sex together. It was time for me to leave and I asked her for her exact address in case I want to send her something. She said why I said there's a good chance that I may have to leave for a while and if I do I want to send you my address. I want to call and write to you while you are in college. I'm going to try to cut a record and don't know how long I will be. She said I don't want you to leave and I said don't worry it won't be long. She gave me her school card with her name on it and wrote her home address on the back. I loved her so much and told her that I was hurting inside. I wanted to change my mind about leaving but knew it was to late. I kissed her and told her I loved her then went home but I did not tell her that I was leaving for California because I thought it would be better if she didn't know. I just wish that in the future we could meet again and continue with our love affair. I do plan to come back to be with her and maybe after college we could start where we are leaving off. I feel very sad because she became the love of my life and I wished it didn't come so late. I went home and tried to put my head together because I didn't want to leave and became afraid. I just wished I knew how to handle my problems here but knew I could not turn back. I had such a head ache and couldn't stand the pain. It came on very fast so I just laid down and tried not to think. I knew that every move I was making was wrong but I could not find any other answer. I knew that California was far away and I have never been past New York City. I really was scared but I knew I would not change my mind. I laid here for more than an hour and knew what I had to do with Dot but didn't know if I was up to it. My biggest and strongest thoughts were about the trust that Jeanne had and still has in me. I went to Dot's house and I still had all those pains in my head and she was waiting for me as I thought. She came to the car while I was still sitting. She opened my door and said are you coming in. I said what do you want to do and she said I want to go to your house. I said I need some aspirin so she ran in then grabbed some and we went to my house.

She could see I was not feeling well and got me a glass of water for the aspirin. She cuddled up to me and just laid there with her arms around me. She looked at me sadly and said you don't have to do this for me. I said I will but I just want this head ache to go away. While I was laying here I thought about Judy and felt that she could get over it fast but I thought about how long it will take me to get over her. I knew that the first time I slept with Dot that she was my life's dream. I think about the time Jossey told me to dump them and worry about myself. I said these girls are not just my lovers they are best friends, my only real friends and how could I just dump them. I was losing it and did not want to be here I just wanted to be alone. I wanted to scream;" I need a break" I got up and took all my clothes off. I then started to undress Dot. She helped me finish undressing her and we laid together. She was very beautiful but in her own way with her big dark eyes and long ebony black hair. I knew she attracted me at first sight and looking at her now, how could I hurt her more after what she's been through already. I put my face near her ear and said I love you so very much. After this we managed to satisfy our moment of desire. We were in a much better mood and laughing about what we did but agreed that we must love each other. I took her home at midnight and said I will see you on Sunday but I will call you tomorrow. I went to the farm at ten o'clock and talked with Dad and Florence. I told them I want to put my cars in the barn and keep them until I get back. I also unhooked all my power tools and covered everything. I then locked the door and left the keys with them. My Dad said he would help me move the cars tomorrow. I went back home and laid down for an hour. I had to pick Jen up at three and I drove to the phone company where she was waiting. She hopped into my car then slid right over next to me, held me and gave me a kiss. She said did you miss me and I said "Of course I missed you" I really did because she is always so understanding. She smiled and said I'm hungry, I said how hungry and she said I'm starved. I said how about a nice steak and she agreed and said that's sounds good and I took her to the Bantam Steak House and we had a nice steak dinner. I wasn't afraid that I may see Judy there because she said the only time she's been there lately is with me.

We went to my house and on the way I asked are you sure you want to go to my house. She said Yes I'm sure I'm not going to see you for a long time do you think I would miss this. I said I'm only kidding, I just want to know how much you want me and she said I'll show you. This girl is the sweetest girl in the world and always makes me feel better when I'm sad. She always seems to have the right words. She was dancing on her way in and I said you really are something. She smiled and jumped up on me she had her arms around my neck with her legs around me. I just walked over and threw her on the bed but I think the only time I laugh is when I'm with her. It does hurt that she has so much trust in me and believes that I won't let her down. I got on the bed with her and held her tight. She hopped on top of me and started tickling me and it made me laugh so hard. She then got off and rolled me off the bed then jumped up and said off to the shower. I was still on the floor laughing and she pulled my Jean's off. I could not stop laughing because she was so funny. She then pulled off my undies then I sat up and took off my shirt then reached under her skirt and pulled off her panties while we were both laughing. I got up off the floor, undid her bra and we were totally naked. I held and kissed her and she felt so comfortable in my arms, almost as if she belonged there. We hopped into the shower and washed each other. We played in the shower for a while then hopped in bed. We then did our kind of love but Jen and I have our own style but it took a long time and we agreed not to share our secrets. I was time to tickle again, I haven't had this much fun in months and I think it was with her then. We played for hours and never laughed so much then I took her home and said I would call her on Monday. I explained I had to move my cars and get things ready tomorrow. I arrived home at nine thirty and decided to call Dot and we talked a lot about what I would do in California and where I would go. I told her I want to go to Los Angles and have an address of a place to do tryouts. This could take weeks before you could get in for someone to hear you but I think that I am good enough so I won't have to wait too long. She said she was worried that I was going alone and was afraid something may happen. I then went to the farm and moved my cars under cover and did all that I had to do there. All I have to do is pack my things that I am taking with me. This only took me until eleven o'clock and I went back home. I waited until three and went to pick up Jen.

If I was there after three she had a ride home but I did get there in time and she watched me drive in and came to the car. She slid over to me and kissed me as usual. I told her I was almost ready and my Dad helped me. She said I'm so sad your leaving but I'm also happy for you. I said did you have lunch yet. She said a little and I said do you want t go to the Lark. She said that would be great and we went there, the music was playing loud and she was singing with the music. I said you really do have a very nice voice but she just kept singing as if she didn't hear me. She was always easy going, easy to understand; she let everything out and had no skeletons in her closet. We both ate and moved to another spot where we could be alone. We talked about the future which I did not want to talk about. We did hold each other almost all of the time. She looked at me and said could we make love again. I knew that I had nothing to offer her and I just couldn't refuse this last request. I know that I am going to miss you very much and I would love to. She said I want to give you something to remember me by. I said Honey I will be thinking about you every day. She was holding my hand and started to suck my finger. I stopped her and said if you keep doing that you will not be home on time tonight. She laughed and said do you know what I have in mind. I said I will pick you up at the school at two tomorrow. She said in her cute voice, I will be waiting and I said you really know how to make me suffer as I drove her home. I stopped on my way and picked up Dot and went to my house. We talked a long time and did understand things better and reinforced my feelings in wanting to get pregnant. She said that she believed that she would never get married if I didn't come back. So I did know that it was very important to her and if something did happen to me at least I would have barred a child that would be loved more than I was. She said I did not have to do this again tonight and I said I will. She woke up in time for her to go to work and I drove her there and went home and back to sleep again. I was getting worn out and did not get up until noon. I had to do laundry because I only had six towels and they were all used. I went out and checked my car and made sure It was safe to go and seen that I would need tires. I went to the Circle Texaco garage, where I knew them and made an appointment for tires and a oil change. I did my laundry and went to the school. I felt now that I should have made this another day but time is running out. She came running and said I am so excited I thought about this all day. She slid over close and kissed me while putting her hand on my lap while searching for what she wanted. When she found it I started thinking if I had enough energy to do this anymore.

Right now I know I will be with Jen next and will love her the most. I need help! I keep having these night mares, I just want to be alone and believe that I'm becoming monomania. I parked in the back of my house again then we laid on the bed for a while and I believe we were both lost for words. She didn't want me to leave and I could see it in our conversations but she understood. I felt bad for her and wondered if I was doing the right thing now. I started loving her to make her feel better and went to start the shower. We hopped in and washed each other then went back to my bed. She was very loving and repeated "I will wait for you forever" I know I could never forget her and hope that we could be together again in this so uncertain road of life. But I find saying this with all three of them. She said I wish I was in college now because I would be busy and don't want to think about not having you with me. I know I will be very lost but if we can write and talk on the phone it will be all right. I said I will also be alone while driving thirty six hundred miles and I know you will be in my heart every day. She said I know you and won't try to stop you but I am very afraid of you going that far alone. I would love to go with you but I do understand it would be hard for you to take me. She always made me feel better and understood me more than anyone else. I knew I am leaving someone I love very much and she will always be a great part of my life. I then took her home and walked with her to her door then said I will pick you up after school on Thursday because this will be the last time we will be together for a while. I didn't say any more because we both started crying. I left her house and went straight home because I did not want to see anyone right now. I lay in bed and wanted to change my mind about leaving but how in the hell could I stay now. I said why things can't be different because I want to marry all three of them. I know I do love them all and don't want to leave any one of them. I promised to pick up Dot so I laid her until almost eight o'clock then went to her house. When I arrived there she was standing by the road and ran to my. I said what's wrong, she was shaking and incoherent and just said I'm going to kill that bitch some day. She was crying and I didn't say any more. I just drove to my house and knew this was a bad time for this to happen.

I drove around back then went to open her door and helped her into the house. I was finally able to ask her what happened and she said her mother is always on her ass. She said her mother blamed her for me leaving and I was never coming back. The bitch said I was using you too much and that's why you are leaving. I said Honey we both know the truth and don't have to listen to any one. She then pleaded with me to take her with me but I replied I told you I don't have enough money to take care of myself and I Know I will never get a chance to what I must do now. I just held her and she finally stopped crying. I said let's get something to eat and you will feel better. When you go home just tell her you spoke with me and we both know better. Then tell her it's your life and none of her business what happens between us. What could she say then and she said I have already tried all those things. She started crying again and said that's what she wants is to see me cry. I walked her to the car and we drove around before we went to dinner. We ordered some food and she appeared to feel better but she was very quiet. We left there and I drove around the back sand held her in my arms and kissed her then whispered in her ear. I love you and things will work out because I should be back soon. She looked at me with those big sad eyes and said "will I ever be happy" I said happiness is not a gift to all of us and some of us must work for it. She said I know but the only real happiness I had been with you. I wanted to get off this subject so I asked how is our baby, she smiled and I said you could tell your mother that we are trying to have a baby, You know mothers always love to hear that. She said yes I will tell her that because she thinks I will never have sex with anyone. I could see she was not happy because she was just staring at the ceiling. I started to rub her stomach and said did you forget our baby. As tired as I was I still made love with her then we fell asleep. I wasn't really sure if she was really having these problems with her mother but maybe trying to make me take her with me. I took her home in time to change and get to work on time. I had to got to my uncles so I asked Jen if she could go with me. She was very happy to and I introduced her as my fiancée to him and Ruthy. They both told me she was a wonderful girl and I should hang on to her. Jen told them that she is an operator and will be in college until I get back. I took her home but I told her I would pick her up tomorrow after school. I drove to the school and she was waiting for me but she did not come running to the car as usual.

The day of Reckoning

She sat in my car without closing the door and said what's going on. I said what do you mean and I could see she was very hurt and angry. She looked right at me and said what is Dorothy to you. I said why? She said an operator that I work with stopped at the restaurant where she works and told my mom and I, that you two are getting married. Now my dad and mom don't want me to see you anymore and I don't know what to say to them. I didn't know what to say but I knew I was in trouble. I said she was my girlfriend before I met you and since then I have only been trying to help her. I said Jen I love you and you must believe me because I have no reason to lie now. I spoke a little harsh and said I'm leaving tomorrow night and if you want to see me I will be there. She said please don't get mad at me, I do love you and I don't care what other people say. Al you know how much I love you and started crying. She closed the door so I took her home. We waited in the car and talked until it was time for her father was to be home. When I left, I told her I love you very much and please try to come to the park tomorrow night. She stopped crying and had a little smile then kissed me without ever wanting to stop then said I'll be there. I went home and packed all my things I was taking and put them my car, I then called Dot and told her I was not coming tonight and if she wanted to see me, I will be at the town park tomorrow night, then hung up the phone. I had trouble trying to sleep but I knew this was inevitable and I stayed a few days to long. I awoke early then packed some tools, extra gas and water then went to see dad. I made sure everything was set for me to leave and kissed dad and told him to be careful. I knew we needed some beer for tonight so I went to José's. I bought two cases and went to the park. When I passed Jen's house I could see her father's car was there so I just blew my horn. I wasn't at the park long when I noticed Jen walking down the hill so I went to meet her. She seen me drive by and walked all the way here. Her eyes were glassy but she was not crying, I just held her and started crying myself. I felt so bad because I have lied to both these girls for a long time. But I told her I will love her until the day I die.

She said she feels much better because we could talk on the phone and she will write every day until I return. I drove back to the driveway before hers and went back to the park. Most of the people I invited were there and we started drinking beer. I have not seen Dot and its eight thirty now. I just kept drinking with my friends. It was nine thirty when I seen Dorothy drive in with someone I never seen. She was sitting on the passenger's side. I was about half drunk and I did not like the way she was yelling at me. I did not understand her and she did not get out of the car. I finally heard her say I hope you never come back. She really hurt my feelings so I yelled "Your not my girl friend" Jeanne is and I love her. I don't think she heard me because the window was closed before I said that. I started to walk back to the beach and I heard Jeanne yelling Al, Al I heard you tell her "You Love, Me. I said how did you get here and she said she ran most of the way. I said boy am I happy you found the truth before I left and I do love you. She said Oh I love you so very much and just hugged me to no end. I now that I do love this girl and I will miss her very much. I told her that if I had any brains I would stay here and marry her. I was walking her home but when we got to the end of the park her father was driving towards us. She told me she had to sneak out but I walked her to the car and said Jen I love only you. She closed the door and I could see her looking out the window waving to me. I threw her a kiss then left to go home. I locked up the house, turned the power and water off. I grabbed my thermos bottle and made sandwiches with all the food I had left. I stopped at Al Pats and filled my thermos. I was very scared but knew it was to late to change my mind now. I left Al Pats and the girls that I loved so much on June 6th 1958 just before Midnight. I did have a map sketched out and a plan on how I would go.

Driving Across Country Alone

I headed for the George Washington Bridge then onto the New Jersey Turnpike and on to Highway Forty. After paying all my bills I had very little money left so I just filled up with gas and ate very sparingly. I drove all night and stopped at a truck stop and filled with gas then asked the attendant if I could stay in the parking lot for a while. I explained that I drove all night and just wanted to rest for a little while. He was very nice and said as long as you want then pointed where I should park. I said thank you and drove there. I slept until Nine o'clock then headed west again. I drove all day and stopped in Ohio at a rest area. I used the rest room then slept in my car for about four hours. I continued to drive until daylight then stopped at a Cafe in Indiana. I had some breakfast and filled my thermos then continued only stopping for gas but it was early evening and I was hungry and discouraged. I already ate the sandwiches and couldn't spent much money for food but I stopped at this place that looked like a Cafe and went in. I ordered a coffee and a sandwich but everyone appeared to be very friendly. One guy sat by me and started talking as if he knew me.

I thought it was nice to have a friend or at least someone to talk to. We talked a little then he asked me if I wanted to go upstairs because it's a nice place to rest so I said why not. I said why not followed him. When we got there I had to pay ten dollars. I didn't want to spend that much money but thought it was to late to back out because he was so nice. I went into this room and found a lot of people there. I did not understand what was going on so I just sat on the bench with my new friend. I sat near the door but I noticed that the room was full of smoke and this was burning my eyes. People here were all very strange; because some were dancing and lying on the floor laughing. I could see something that appeared to be a stove in the middle of the floor but it was strange because it didn't have a stove pipe for the smoke to go out. I thought that was unusual and became afraid. I wanted to leave but there was always someone standing at the door and I didn't know if I could just leave. I asked my friend if there was a bathroom here and said it loud enough for the door man to hear me. The door man did hear me and looked at me then said Yes it's down stairs. I walked to the door and he took my hand then stamped something on it. He said I would need this to get back in without paying again. I went downstairs then quickly to the door and left. I was very scared because I never seen anything like this and I was getting a headache I didn't know what it was but I associated it with some kind of drugs or dope. I stopped at the next rest area and felt as if I wanted to vomit but I bought a coffee from the canteen then felt better. I got back into my car and just wanted to get out of Indiana. I did not like this state because I don't think they have any laws here. There were no speed limit signs, "it just read Drive Safely" I did not speed here and just followed the traffic but drove nonstop until I noticed a sigh "Welcome to Illinois. I was happy to be here and stopped at a cafe that had a lot of trucks there so I thought it would be a safe place.

It was nice and all the people were normal so I ordered the days special. It was priced reasonable and I was glad I ordered it because it was big chunks of meat over egg noodles. It was very good and I was served all that I could eat. I was really full and comfortable then looked for another rest area. I became concerned about how far I was driving every day and didn't think it was this far. I know now that if I knew this I would never would have left home. I became very lonely but I slept until daylight. I could see the sun coming up behind me but could still see the moon. All I knew was that I was driving west from the sun and east towards the moon. I was very scared and felt very strange. I drove on to Cedar Rapids Iowa and stopped for food again but just had a coffee and snack but I did feel a little better. As I drove on I found it is cheaper to have one good meal instead of junk food. It is midnight again and I noticed another rest area. I drove in and discovered they have a shower here. I was happy because I needed one. There was no one around so I stripped off my clothes and then took a real long shower. I felt much better then fell asleep for a little while. I needed to make better time so I drove nonstop to Cheyenne Wyoming. It was in the afternoon when I arrived here and had to stop for the Cowboys riding their horses. They were doing everything from shooting at each other to lasso. I didn't know what they were doing but found that they were filming a movie. I never seen anything like this and it was very interesting. This went on all the way to Laramie, I really enjoyed the ride and I had something more to write about to Dot and Jeanne. I continued on and went to Salt Lake City, Utah. I was very tired and had to sleep so I parked near a big lake. I tried to get some sleep but a Police Officer awoke me and told me I could not park here. I did not ask why but asked him where I could stay. I told him I just wanted to get a little rest then spend a little time at the lake. He noticed that I had Connecticut Registration Plates and was very nice. Then told me about a parking lot near the lake where I could park and I could stay as long as I wanted. I thanked him very much and went there. I was about ten o'clock now and I have not had any sleep in a long time. I did fall asleep but the voices of people awoke me. I found a lot of people had swim suits and were swimming. I did have a pair of shorts that would work so I went into the dressing room there and changed then walked into the water. It was cloudy and when some splashed into my eyes it burned very bad. I could taste the salt but I did go in and swim. I noticed I could float very easy here and asked a lady why. She explained that the salt content here is the highest in the world and a potato would float on the water. I was so amassed and found this was so exciting. I have not seen any pretty girls since I left home and it was nice to see girls faces, legs and tummies.

There were many very good looking girls here and more blondes than brunettes. I noticed a hot dog stand and went to get a hot dog with a soda. I stood there for a while but my skin started to burn and turned all white, then I knew why they had so many showers around. I noticed that more than three quarters of the people here were female and I thought this would be a good place to live because this would meet my quota. I could see it was a very big city and wanted to walk around a little. I thought it would be good for my legs and dry my shorts. It was a very nice place because I never seen so much flat land and the highways were straight for miles. I was still hungry and got another hot dog with different toppings. I sat in my car and watched all the pretty girls but this made me miss my girls. I thought that I better get back on the road again and drove on to Sparks Nevada. I stopped at Little America; it was very big and had many gas pumps with food places. I went to a restaurant and could over look the valley. I gassed up and ate there then went to Reno. I drove through Reno and stopped only for a look. I noticed that every place I went there were slot machines even in the rest rooms, groceries stores and gas stations. I then continued towards the mountain. I saw a parking place near a stream and I was very hot. I still had my shorts on so I jumped in to it but I jumped back out and nearly froze to death. The water was ice cold and I could not understand it. It was over ninety ° out and the water was so cold so I just washed a little then went on. I found out later that this was melting snow and ice from the Sierra Madras Mountains. I was now on highway fifty which changed from forty and I drove on through the mountains. I have never seen anything like this, you could look out your window and see thousands of feet down. It had a lot of curves and kept going up, I kept going and stopped almost in Sacramento, California. I finally made it and I stopped here to rest. It was a few hours from morning and I wanted to get some sleep but the traffic was so noisy I awoke at seven o'clock. I studied my map and had to go south on highway ninety nine, then I started to go until I found it. I could not believe the traffic, it was bumper to bumper at times but once I got away from the city it got much better. I started to make good time now because the speed limit was seventy miles per hour and everyone was doing eighty.

I drove all the way to Fresno without stopping and needed some gas and food. The traffic was very heavy and I took a side road. I was on South Chance Avenue but I became lost and stopped at a house where a man was mowing his lawn. Since he was pushing the mower and wouldn't be able to hear me, I left the car and walked towards him. He shut the mower off and came to me, I told him I was lost and where I planned to go. He said did you just get here to California, I mean from Connecticut. I said yes I drove here without stopping only for sleep and some food. He was looking at my Connecticut Registration Plate and asked if I knew where Danbury was. I said Yes I live in New Milford the next town and he said you must know about the Lee and Mc'Lochlin Hat Factory's. I said my oldest Brother works there. He told me that he was in personal and lived there for about ten years. Then asked, would you like a beer and I said yes I would love one. He took me to a bench on the shade side of his house and said we have things to talk about. He said are you in a hurry and I said I don't know what I'm doing or going. I told Him I want to get involved in music and he said I don't think you'll get to much here maybe Los Angeles. He knew where the studios were and said it was M.G.M. Then he said he would explain how to get there. As we were talking he said Boy you have bigger balls than I do and aren't you scared. I said I'm scared to death now that I'm here. He asked me what I played. I said guitar and I have my own style that everyone seems to love. He said come in to the house I want to introduce you to my family and tell them where you're from. I said I would love to then we went in and she was a lovely lady. They have two children a girl three and a boy five. I sat in the kitchen while he told his wife what I was doing and that 1 drove all the way from Danbury. She said Connecticut, he said yes I told him that we did live there once and she said you must be tired. I said yes I am but I'm also disillusioned and scared because I thought it would be easier. Henry jumped in the conversation, he said why don't you stay for dinner and you could shower. I said I really don't want to impose on you, you have been so nice already and they both said no we would love to have you. We got talking and he remembered that I said I lived in New Milford. He asked if I knew any of the White family. I said I know Dick and Charley. He said Oh my god Charley's my cousin. I said I know him very well and I was his boss at the textile plant. He said he is much older than you, you're just a kid and how could you be his boss. I explained everything that happened up to the time they voted in the union and we closed shortly after.

I explained that I was a Foreman, Supervisor and the Chief Technician. They could not believe it but did believe me. I said if you like I will play my guitar for you. They said we would love you to, Henry and I went back outside and sat on the bench. I told him that I may need a job and I did not bring a lot of money. I told him that last job I had was driving tractor trailer. He told me that his uncle Jim drove for P. I. E. Pacific Inter Mountain Express and would ask if they need any help. I thanked him and we kept talking then he asked why I came way out here and thought I would have a better chance in New York. I said, I really wanted to get away from New Milford. He said could I ask why, I said I would have to explain the whole thing and it would take some time. I gave him a brief idea of what was going on between the two girls and I could not hurt either one. I just wanted to get away as far as I could he laughed and said the only way to go further is to get a boat. I laughed and said well I must start a new life. Dinner was ready and we were called in to eat. I found out that Californians drink a lot of beer and wine but I never had wine before so I asked for that. We had a very nice meal and I could feel the wine creeping up on me. Ann,

Henry's Wife) said why don't you bring in your guitar while I clean up the kitchen. I asked Henry to help me because I had a lot of things in my trunk. He came out with me and we started to move things then I remembered the material I brought from the textile plant. I showed him what it was and he said yes he could use it for sheets and curtains. I was very happy to give this to them, then we took the guitar and amplifier out. We brought it into the house and I explained to him what I did to my amplifier. He said boy how did you learn all this. I said I read a lot and I love to learn but most of it I remember from my last life, then laughed. He said maybe I could ask you a question. I am designing an air cooler for my house that will use just the domestic water from our supply. He already had most of it built and it was out in his garage. He took me to see it then explained his idea to me and it was almost ready to install. It was a radiator which matched the width and the height of the opening. He would run the water through the radiator and the water enters at an average of sixty degrees.

He would run the water slow and when it left it would go into his pool which needed water all the time anyway. He had a galvanized shield with fans directing the air flow from behind the shield through the radiator. It was a fabulous idea and I said if you want I will help you install it then I studied his plan and found some flaws. I said would you mind if I pick out a few problems. He said No! That's why I asked you to look at it. I asked do you have a condensing pan. He said what's that, I said the difference in potential between the ambient temperature and the cold element temperature will cause a lot of condensation and on a humid day you could produce ten gallons of water. You will need a pan to catch this and drain it out side. I noticed that you made the hole in the wall in the center. It would operate more efficient closer to the ceiling where the warmest air is and would have a better circulation, because in the center it will cause refractions in the air and it will not circulate as well, also you are directing the water from the bottom up. He answered that will keep the radiator filled. I said yes but you want the coldest water on top but the way to do that is run your return water through a loop higher than the radiator and this will keep it full and also prevent a vapor lock.

He said I can't believe it and I think I'm talking to an export. I said I do a lot of this kind of work and have had experience with air handling. I said I will stay and help you get it installed then Ann called us in to the house. He started to tell her what I told him and I was an export but I said he's exaggerating. I knew they were waiting for me to play so I plugged in my amplifier. Then asked if I could have a little more wine, I have to build up my nerve. They laughed and said you don't around us we're just hillbillies our selves then she brought me a glass of wine. I had to tune my guitar from the different climate and I always loosen the strings when I don't use it much, this is to prevent the neck from warping but I drank the wine while I was talking and tuning. I asked if they liked loud and fast music. They said yes so I played a few rhythms without my reverb and asked how that was. They said it was good. I than told Henry to notice the difference with my reverb, I did my special with the reverb and the trembar. Their eyes opened and they said Wow! the kids were dancing to the sound. Henry said you built this, I said not all just the deep base sounds. They both said they never heard anything like it and boy you are good. I said that's why I want to go to try outs. I did a few songs and they sang them with me then said that this was the most fun they had in a long time.

I said I will look for a night club to play for and you could come. They said that would be great. They showed me the room and said I could leave my stuff there for now. I thanked them very much and was thinking about getting lost in Fresno California, thirty six hundred miles away from home and to find a family like this on my first stop. I thought about Jen's family and Jen and I will go to the phone booth tomorrow to call her. I fell asleep and did not awake until I heard voices. I got dressed and went out, they offered me breakfast and I told them that I never eat breakfast but I would like some coffee. We talked about Connecticut and all the changes they made. I told them about the flood, how I helped the rescue teams and they did hear about it. Henry did not mention about him not going to work and I did not ask him but hoped he was on vacation. I took a ride to town with Henry to pick up a few things because I wanted to write to the three girls that I miss so much. He took me to the store, showed me how to get on the highway then said he called Jim and he may stop in tonight. We went back to his house and dinner was ready. We had our dinner and junior kept saying more music. I took my guitar outside on the back porch and played some soft music for the kids. In a short while they were all out there so I kept playing. I was just putting my gear away when a car drove in. Henry said It was Jim and asked if I could play for him later. I said sure and went in and sat in the living room and was introduced to him. He was very nice but was heavy and had a beer belie. His complexion was red and I thought he was a boozier. He said that he had not been to the terminal but would ask on Monday and I thanked him very much. He said I hear you play the guitar and said I did as a kid but never stayed with it. I said I have it hooked up on the porch so he grabbed a beer and came with me. I played a few of my specials and he said I wish I could have played like that. I thanked him and asked if I was taking his room. He said hell no I only come here on vacations and when I want to get out of Riverside. I told Jim I was going to the M G M in Los Angles on Monday or Tuesday and hoped I could get in to tryouts.

I had another beer with Jim and I told him I have been driving trucks since I was old enough to reach the peddles. He said I would have to take a driving test and I said I don't mind. Jim left so I went to sleep and I was awaken by voices again. I know I'm getting much more sleep than I have in a long time and it feels good to sleep in a good bed. I said to Henry maybe we could finish this today. We had it all attached and it worked very well. It did remove a lot of humidity from the air then he said you were right the radiator began to sweat and water was condensing into the pan. We went in then had dinner and we all just sat around. It was only seven o'clock and I am going to go call Jen. I went to the pay phone and called but Bob answered, I said hello could I talk to Jen and he just hung up. I knew that he was still mad at me and I hoped that he told her it was me on the phone. I thought I will call her next Saturday when she is working but I will try her home at three before anyone else gets there. When I finished helping Henry then went into my room and wrote to all the girls. I'll take them to the mail box later. I gave them this address because even if I'm not here I could stop and pick up any mail. They were not long letters but I just told them that I did love and missed them because I was hoping I could talk with Jen on the phone. I woke up early and laid in bed until I heard someone talking again then went out and had coffee but I was sad and wanted to be home. But even if I wanted to go back I didn't have the money and would have to get a job. Henry and Ann did not mind me staying here but I felt that I was imposing on them. I went to a few places and asked them if they needed help. One place I just called was a textile place and when I called they said they were closing the plant. The other was a garage that repaired auto's and no one needed help. My only hope was Jim so I came back to the house and sat on the bench. Henry came out to ask if everything was o k and I told him I need a job because if Jim couldn't get me in with him I would need money because I can't sponge off you forever. He said I was thinking, my mom lives in Modesto which is just north of here. She lives alone and asked me a lot of times if I could do a few things around the house for her. He asked if I would help him and I said if it is something I could I will do it myself. He thanked me and said he would take me there after lunch. It was almost time for lunch now but I told him I wasn't hungry so we left shortly after that and drove to her house.

She was an elderly lady but was very sweet and reminded me of my aunt. We sat outside and had a beer but she had to tell me that she does not drink beer but keeps it there for Henry and some friends. I told her I hardly ever drink much. I could see her picket fence was bad and needed some work then painting. I stayed here for a week and repaired all that she needed. She was very happy and I refused to take any payment but she stuck something in my shirt pocket. It was getting late and I wanted to call Jen. I went to the phone booth I seen before then called. I was so happy to hear her voice I said Hi this, she interrupted me and screamed Al oh my god. She was excited and said where are you. I said in Fresno, California then said I don't have much change and could not talk long. I told her about the family I met and gave her the address. She said she already wrote me a letter and would send it tomorrow. I told her I loved her and that I really missed her but I was sorry that I left. I told her I am very lonely and want to go back home. She said she loved me, missed me so very much and please come home soon. I started crying because I knew how much I missed her and wanted to be with her right now. She knew I was crying so she started to cry, the operator cut in and I had to hang up.

I sat in my car and could see her the last night I was there. I watched her looking from the car window and wondering what was in store for her. I remembered the times we were together and the fun we had so I just screamed,

Why did I leave her and I should have brought her with me. She is eighteen and no one could stop her. I wanted to go to Los Angeles and find that place. I went back to Henry's place and asked if Jim called and he said not yet. I told him that I was leaving for my try outs tomorrow because I must find out what I'm going to do. He did understand and said I could leave the things that I didn't need here while I was gone. I did leave a lot of things there and that way I knew I would have to come back. I was time for dinner so we sat and ate. I did not eat very much again because I was sad, I was thinking about my life and how much I missed the girls. I also felt very sorry and hurt about Dot. I decided to write her another letter and give her my address again and ask her if she would write to me. I had to be careful of what I wrote and I did not know how far she would go to hurt Jen because she told me she hated her just before I left. I thought she may show Jen the letter so I decided to write her a note.

I wrote I don't know why you are mad at me. I gave you all that I could and helped you every time you called. I tried everything I could to make you happy even when you told me to find someone else because you could not love anyone. Please don't blame this on anyone but yourself, you could write to me if you care and I will response to your letter because I did love you very much, Love Al. I also wrote to Judy and explained that I was in California and would like her to write to me. I said I missed you very much and wished I was there now. I am very lonely and I am sorry I had to leave when I did but hope you will understand. You were the love of my life and I know I will never forget how you made me feel "I love you" Al, and my address. I had breakfast with Henry and Ann then left for the big times. I made it to Los Angles and had trouble finding a parking place. I had to park a long ways from where I was going and I walked down Hollywood Boulevard between Fifth Avenue and California Street but I have never seen so many strange people. This was hell in disguise and I became more scared than ever. I went back to my car then put my guitar in the trunk and walked back without it. I seen people that couldn't walk and had trouble talking. Someone would stager over to you and grab you and ask. Do yah got ah smoke and I just kept walking. I seen people with hypodermic needles and was afraid I would get stuck with something and I hated L A already. But after getting the run around I did find the place and went in. There were hundreds of people there for the same reason that I was. Some were not shy at all and were playing in the hall. They were very good and I asked a kid that was sitting on the bench what he was here for. He said he wanted to play some things he wrote to get him into music then said he loved music and had a good group. I asked him how long he has been here, he said this was his third week waiting and was here every day. I left there and was very upset that I was so stupid to even come this far without knowing anything about it. I went back to my car and left. There was so much traffic I missed the turns and drove all the way up to the top of Hollywood Boulevard to the cul-de-sac and back down. I drove until I got to Santa Monica Beach and found a parking place. I got out and walked around the beach for a while. I seen bathing suits that I could not believe were legal and you could make these with a few pieces of tape. I do have to admit that some of the girls had very nice bodies and were very sexy.

I stayed there for a while and started to drive again. I saw a sign that said Long Beach and my oldest brother John was in the US Marines and I know he was stationed at Camp Pendleton in Long Beach. I wanted to go there and I found the sign that said Camp Pendleton. I did not go in because it said private property. I drove all night and got back to L A late in the morning and ended up in Echo Valley. I found a parking place and went into a small cafe. The place was crowded and I sat by a short bald man. I did not have much money left so I ordered a Hamburg and coffee. The bald headed man started to talk with me and said he noticed my Connecticut Registration Plates. He said you are far away from home. I told him that I haven't ʰad any sleep in two days and was very tired. He knew a lot about Connecticut and New York and he seemed very nice. We talked for a while and he told me that he owned a home on top of the mountain a short ways from here. He invited me to come to clean up, get some rest and I could give him a ride there. He said he always walks and didn't own a car. I thought that he was very nice and I didn't mind giving him a ride home. We finished eating and went to my car. I drove to this mountain and pulled into what looked like a drive way. It was actually an elevator that takes you and the car to the same level as the house. I thought that if he did own this he was a multi millionaire. I got out of my car and he walked me into his house. The elevator led into an inside enclosure that was as large as my house. There was marble everywhere and a large marble step to a large crystal like door and matching side panels. We entered into an all marble area that was at a lower level than the next level and I believe this was the main living area. The floors were all carpet about one inch thick and it felt as if you're walking on a cloud. Of course there was a place to take your shoes off before you went to that level. I could see a one step higher level that was surrounded with etched glass. I was standing in the middle of all this trying to pull my thoughts together. I could not believe my eyes and had to believe it was not real. I walked straight to the windows where I could see the whole city and one street that was all lit up. He walked over to me and said that was Sunset Boulevard. I turned to my right and seen there were circular stair cases on both sides of the area with no glass but did not go there. He took my hand while I looked at him then said I'm lost for words and I know why it is on top of a mountain. We must be what my Mother called heaven.

He led me to a bath room where the bath tub was bigger than most bath rooms and I never seen anything like this. There were several handles recessed in to the wall and several shower heads all controlled separately. The water temperature was preset automatically but there is a control where you could change the temperature if you chose to. He handed me a robe that was heavy and yet very soft. I put on the robe and he took my clothes to wash then dry them. After my shower he walked me to a reclining chair that felt like angora and it had a vibrator built in with different settings. He turned on a sound system that was second to none and I laid back while still in a trance. I never once wondered why he asked me to come to see this or did not think how long I would stay here but it was the nicest place I have ever seen. I did not have the intelligence to comprehend life itself and wondered why I was being pushed to the top and then dropped to the bottom without warning. I thought that if he lived alone and was lonely I could stay here then he could help me it to the music business and I could keep him company for a while. I fell asleep and must have been sleeping very sound but I was awakened by some one that had my penis in there mouth. I did not open my eyes and thought I was dreaming but when I did open my eyes it was that bald headed guy. I froze not knowing what to do. I became very afraid and thought he may want to hurt me if I tried to leave because I have never heard of a man doing this. I moved then sat up and he stopped without saying anything. He didn't seem to be bothered by me knowing what he was doing but I just knew that I had to get to my car and get out of here. I did not dare act mad and I just asked him what time it was and said I had an appointment at the studio. To make it look better I quickly asked if I could come back here. I think he did believe me and gave me his private phone number then told me to call and he would let me in. He had my clothes all ready so I got dressed and walked me to the elevator. I went down and the door opened without me doing anything. I then got in my car and left to go straight to Henry's house. I know I slept for a long time and I do believe that I awoke when he first started that but I don't know for sure how long he was there. I found my way back to the golden state highway and headed north.

I was happy to see the sign Fresno and arrived at Henry's after dark. He heard me drive in and met me there. He asked how I made out, I shook my head and said I just want to go back home. I told him and Ann about the try outs then about that street I was on. Henry said they call that Skid Row and it's the worst place for any normal person to be. I said I could believe that and something else happened but I don't know how to handle it. I am very bothered about it and I got up and walked to the outside bench. I still couldn't imagine what happened. Henry came out and said what's wrong, I said I just couldn't repeat it in front of your wife and he said what? I explained how I met him, the entry to his house and what it was like. I told about the shower all about the robe and the chair then I then fell asleep. I then told him what awoke me then I explained the rest. He laughed a little and said I have to tell Ann. I sat outside while he told her because I was very embarrassed about it. He then called me in and said I have heard of him then mentioned his name. He was one of the richest persons in Hollywood and owned most of the music industries. He said it's too bad that happened because he could have made you the biggest star in Hollywood. I finally laughed and said maybe I should go back because I do have his number. I then said I could never do that and I am afraid of him now. They laughed very hard then told me I have to call Jim. He called for you just before you came in so Henry called him and gave the phone to me. Jim asked me if I was sure that I wanted to drive. He told me he accepted a new run that requires two drivers it would be from Los Angles to Seattle. I said I would love that then he said I will schedule you a driving test for Friday and let you know what time. I told them what you told me but it won't start for two weeks. They need help as a yard jockey would you want to do that and I said I will do anything. The cement trailer was one of the hardest things to back up. The Tractor had a long wheel base and the trailer was short. I had to back this within an inch to align it to the screw escalator that was on a side bank. I told Henry and Ann about the news and that I was happy. I went to sleep and had a night mare about skid row and all the drug addicts that Henry told me about. I woke up early and asked Henry if there was anything I could do around here to help. He said you could take a ride with me I have to go see my boss today. I said sure and we drove to the other side of Fresno then Henry went in to this big building. I never asked him what he did and I found out that he worked for the city in the office.

They are allowed four weeks' vacation but Henry takes three in June and July and one at Christmas. I was very lucky I came when I did or I would never have met this wonderful family. On the way back we stopped at a little bar where Hank would stop for lunch. It was a nice place and was not rowdy and we both had a cold draft beer then left. He told me people never go east from her and that's why they say I'm going out west and back east. He laughed about the size of Connecticut and said you could put two of them in the San Joaquin Valley. I said yes but almost everything is made in Connecticut then said all the Ball Bearings, Machine parts, Aircraft, Rifles and Pistols and I went on. We got home and just talked but they asked me more about my girl friends. I told them a little more about what happened to Dot and why I wanted to help her. They agreed that I did the right thing but I did not like talking about them because I became lonely and missed them both. I felt sorry for Dot and hope she does write to me. I thought I would get mail today but I didn't and don't know how long it takes to get cross country. Jim called to tell me he would pick me up tomorrow afternoon and take me for my test. I went to bed early and was a little nervous because I did not know how bad the test would be. He picked me up at twelve and went to his house in Riverside. He said I shouldn't do this but these are the answers to the written test you will get. I am glad he did give me this and I think I may have gotten a few wrong because I never took a test before. I read them over and over not to forget them. We stopped for a beer and I had a coffee and Hamburg. My stomach was nervous and I thought that it would help to eat a little. I went for the written test first and passed it very well then I had to go for my driving test. The instructor's name was Joe, he took to me to the Tractor (truck) then told me to get in and he would go with me. I walked around the truck and checked everything. He said you don't have to do this you all ready passed the safety test inside. I got in and I drove around the block to where the trailers were parked. When I got to the yard he pointed toward a trailer that was parked inside at the loading docks. He told me to back up to that box and hook up. I backed up close to it and got out then walked to the rear of the truck. I looked at the spot in front of the fifth wheel pin and I noticed there was a swale there, so when I got back into the truck Joe asked why I did that. I told him that this spot was new to me and I did notice the Swale.

He said I have never seen anyone do that. I replied you probably seen a few hit the pin pretty hard then. He said your right then I backed up to the swale and I knew that the trailer was the right height so I could back under it safely. I backed up slow and went into the pin gently. I locked the parking brake (the Johnson bar) on the trailer. I then attached the clad hands and the electrical connector. I went to the trailer and jacked the dolly wheels and walked around the trailer to make sure it was clear. I got into the truck and locked the trolley brake and tried to move my truck forward then knew that I was connected properly. Joe said you're doing good so I drove out and we took a ride to where he normally goes for test then I drove into the yard. Joe showed me where to back the trailer so I swung in so my truck would be on the left of the trailer. This way I could see where I was backing easily. He then made me drive out and come in the other way so I had to back in blind. (We call this the blind side) I had only on my mirrors to count on. I did this every day at the cement plant; so I backed in first shot then got out to unhook the trailer. Joe said not so fast I have to dock you one point. I said why then he walked me to the back of the trailer and he asked how could they going to open these doors. I said I thought they were overhead doors. I know that I should have checked them and I am sorry. I hopped back into the truck and pulled ahead. I opened the doors and backed back in. I then cranked the dolly's down and took the weight of the truck. I unhooked the glad hands, electric plug and released the fifth wheel then drove the truck out. I waited for a response from Joe and I apologized again. He said you don't have to apologies and I wish half of our drivers were as good. I said I passed and he said you have a job my son. I thanked him and jumped with joy. While we were walking he told me that I am the youngest guy driving for them and he asked if I wanted to jockey. I said sure he said do you know what that is. I said move the trailers to the loading docks and separate the doubles. He said you got it and I was to start on Monday. I went in to meet the dispatcher, his name is Joe also and I told him I would be here on Monday. He seemed very nice and I think I will like him. He told me to start on Monday so I am here. I am working as a jockey and have been here three days now. I know that Joe likes me because he could see that I am a hard worker. He said that I have moved more trailers in a short time than most of the drivers. It is hard work and I am cranking dolly's all day. I don't mind doing this for a while and it is building up my muscles.

I will be going on the road with Jim in less than a week and I will like that much better. I have been staying at Jim's for the past two days because it is much closer and I'm happy to make some money. I will make much more than I did at the Redi Mix plant and I the most I have ever earned. I want to go to Henry's tonight to see if I have any mail. I called them to let them know that I'm coming and he said I did have some mail. I was very excited and went right there, I got my mail and there were two from Jeanne. I looked at the postal marks and noticed that they were sent on the same day but I opened the smallest one first. I thought that would be the one she wrote before I called her. I opened the first letter and it started off, Dear Al I love you so very much and I am sorry I could not stay with you any longer the last night you were here. My Dad is very mad at you and me and I am not allowed to talk to you. It is very hard living at home now because he doesn't believe anything I say.

He was very mad when I snuck out to meet you at the park, but I don't care. I will just wait until you come home and maybe we could get our own apartment. I couldn't read the second letter and was crying. I really missed her so very much. I fell asleep and dreamt that I was home with her. the rest of the day was very tough and I wanted to go home to be with her.

My first run would be driving doubles to Seattle Washington but we could not take doubles through Oregon. I t was over the state's overall length limit. We would be bringing steel to the world's fair that was under construction then. During the time I was jockey I had to apply for a California Class "A" Chauffeur's license. I did pass the test and I applied for the Has Mat position with P I E and they said I was put on the list. I drove for two weeks with Jim but he did not like this long haul and wanted to get back to his regular location. He did get his old job back and I would drive alone until they found a replacement for him. I knew we were running behind so I talked to the dispatcher and asked if I could drive more hours than what was mandatory. I told him I could carry two logs, he said be careful and just don't get caught. I said we were never checked in Washington or Oregon yet and I'm a good talker but I was stopped for a safety check in California. This was before going down the steep hill into the San Joaquin Valley. I ended up keeping a log for each state and was making two runs a week. We were not being paid by the hour but by the mile. I was being paid for the full trip and this was by far the most money I ever made. I was always tired and did not have time to write. My mail address was still with Henry and I was never in the same place very long. In my second week I did get a speeding ticket and went to see Joe. It was for seventy five in a sixty five limit. Joe said the company would handle it but do drive careful.

One of the reasons that I was driving so fast was this was the hottest summers in history and it did not go below one hundred degrees for one hundred days. Everyone I worked with chewed tobacco and said it was to keep their lips and mouth wet. I had very dry lips; the skin was peeling off and hurt. I tried an apple plug and it made me sick so I finally tried to dip snuff. It took a little while but I did which stopped my chapped lips. While waiting for a load today I did write a letter to Jen and Dot. I told them both what I was doing and I knew Jeanne was working full time as an operator now. I did call her when I was on the road. I talked to her at the Phone Company and it did not cost anything. I told her I would come back home this fall some time before the snow and she was very happy. I am in my sixth week on the road, I'm doing very well and have developed a system that is working. When I got back to the home terminal Joe asked to see me. I went to his office and told me that the Teamsters Union was asking for more benefits and a pay raise and were threatening a strike. I knew what that was because I had all the paper work because the Union Steward told me I had to join.

I did not submit the application because I was on the road so much. I timed my trip so I would be in Los Angles between midnight and five in the morning. I told this to Joe and he said that technically I was not union and I could still drive. I was happy at this time; I had finished the run to Seattle and was hauling Produce which is popular this time of the year. Since I had to go through Fresno I stopped to see Henry and family. When I got there the kids were happy to see me and I told them I would play them music. It was Friday night and I did not have to report to work until Monday morning. I had a hand full of letters from Jen and two from Dot. I was staying there that weekend and I would read the letters in the bed room later but was happy when I got them. I was after dinner when I got here but Ann fixed me a plate and said you lost weight. While I was eating, Jim walked in and asked how I was doing. He sat with me and Ann also fixed him a plate. He asked did you hear about the strike. I said yes Joe called me in and told me that I was not a member of the union yet so I could still drive. He quickly said Don't try that, these union guys will try and kill you. They will get on the over passes and throw stones threw your windshield or shove crow bars through your radiator. I told him thanks for the advice and I would tell Joe.

I finally went to my bedroom then started to read the letters and I read them all. I followed the dates on the post stamp and read them order. I read the letters and the four of Jen's were all alike and told me how much she missed me and wanted me to come home. I read one of Dots letters and she said she received my letter and said she was very sorry and stupid. She did not blame anything on me and knew it was all her fault. She begged me to come back and marry her then said I cannot live without you. She said I'm telling everyone that we are getting married. I was a pretty long letter explaining everything that happened to us and why. I read the second one which was dated seven days later. The letter only had a few lines and started with I have changed my mind. I don't want to marry you and I never want to see you again. She skipped a few lines and said I hope you never come back here and I hate you. The words were not legible and the letter was written with big and small words. The ink was all running and water spots that dried then left wrinkles on the paper. I knew that she was crying out of control and worried about her intentions. I will write to her tonight and tell her that I will always be her friend and will help her all that I can.

I knew she must have had a fight with her mother because this was the only thing that has caused Dot to get this way in the past. I did not read the rest of Jen's letters. I was so hurt about Dot and did not want her to kill herself because I did fear that. Jim told me that when they go on strike we could go to the State of Washington for the summer and work with the potato packers. He explained what it was and I said I would go. I went back into my bed room then put Jen's letters in the drawer and fell to sleep. I'm at the terminal and getting ready to go to Moses Lake Washington. I made one more trip with P.I.E. then was told that I was to return my truck and trailer to the main terminal. I said how much bad news do I have to get and when is it all going to stop. When I got back to L A, Jim was there. He said he was out of work to. He said he will be getting part of his pay from the union dues but I won't get anything and I went in to see Joe. He said that the strike affected the whole west coast and thirteen States. He told me that they needed a driver in Has Mat to drive to Spokane Washington then to northern Idaho. I accepted the opportunity considering I would be hauling concentrated Nitric Acid and I love doing dangerous things.

Nitric Acid is the most toxic and corrosive chemical we have. If one drop gets on your skin it will eat to the bone and then the bone. I took the load to Spokane and arrived there at five thirty a m. I rested then continued on to Idaho. I don't know what they did at the terminal but the load felt much heavier. I drove over a hill and never seen hills this high before. I was over the clouds at times. I became tired and stopped at a rest area and walked around the tanker. I had this weird feeling and I could feel my skin itching. The smell was burning my throat and I did not like what I was doing on such steep hills. If I ever had an accident I believe they wouldn't find my body. I finished my run and told Joe I was afraid to drive this during the strike any more. He said he didn't blame me then went back to Henry's and Jim said we could leave this weekend to start the Job in Moses Lake. This is just for the summer and just until the strike is over. We stayed at Henry's that weekend then left Sunday evening but before we left I read the other letters from Jen. The rhetoric was not what I wanted to hear in her last letter. The first one was that she was fighting with her father and was thinking about moving out. The last one she sent read said she did move out and was living with a friend. I could only assume her friend is a male because there was no love mentioned of us. She ended it with I am not going to college. I became very sad and could see I'm falling to the bottom again. Jim and I drove all night and arrived there early Monday morning. We needed to find an apartment and after reading the adds we found a basement apartment next to the lake. It was a two bedroom, kitchen, bath room and living room. We both liked it so we rented it. We then went to this large agricultural building that harvest potatoes. I was told I would drive a V Bed truck in the field alongside a harvester then found Jim would do the same. I drove one for three days and did not like this at all because it was one hundred degrees out and the dust was unbelievable. Jim also said he didn't like it and may leave to go back home.

Someone told me that they needed baggers in the grading room so I went to see the Foreman. I told him I would rather be a bagger then drive the V bed truck. He said he would rather have me in bagging and I could start right away. Jim told me he didn't like it here and asked if I would take him back to Fresno this next weekend. He already quit the job and would wait.

I went in to the grading and just watched for a while because I have never been in a place like this and I wanted to learn about it before I started. It was interesting to watch. The trucks would dump the potatoes into a hopper then the potatoes would go up a conveyor with metal rods that vibrate. This was to shake all the dirt and small stones off. Then there was one wide conveyor belt that eight girls on each side. Most of these girls worked for a Work Force and were mostly Latino's and are called graders. The conveyor then divides into three smaller ones and all the very small potatoes and stones go to the far left one. The other two divide the grade A potatoes and the rest is sent to different baggers. There is a shelf over the conveyor for the baggers to store the bags and on my side I control the gate that goes across the conveyor to control the direction for the potatoes. There are two bag holders and when one is full the gate will direct the potatoes to the other bag. You then remove the full bag, set it on the scale then tie it and grab the next bag that is filled. T his goes on continuous and as many bags as twenty per minute. I did not like this because my fingers all swelled and hurt but I only had two days before the weekend and this gave my hands time to heal. I took Jim back to Fresno but found that I did not have any mail. I did stay for dinner then went back to Washington. The several girls that operate the conveyors are ages from sixteen to their early twenties. When we waited for the next truck to bring more spuds, I would go and talk with the girls. I was the only male here and I liked that. I did not know any Spanish and they knew very little English but I spent all the time I had teaching them English. It was a lot of fun but they always teased me. They would ask me questions in Spanish and I would say Si or yes then muy bueno without knowing what they asked. They would laugh their ass off but just having fun. I became very friendly with most of them but liked Beletta the best. I let her and her girl friend stay at my place one weekend because I need someone to share the expenses with me. I still had Jim's room furnished and I didn't mind. Beletta always teased me the most but I liked that because she was the prettiest. One afternoon they were all teasing me and Beletta came over to me, put her arms around me and kissed me then went back laughing. I knew they had a bet or something but I liked that because I haven't had a kiss since Jen. I walked back where they were and did the same to Beletta. I believe I shocked her but they were all laughing. After that she appeared to watch me much more and always smiled.

My First Spanish Girlfriend

That night I picked up a translation book and learned some Spanish that I wanted to know and was ready for them. I said to Beletta that when you kiss me you should mean it (si usted me besa usted debe signifircarlo.) Then one girl said usted habla Espanoles and I replied Poco. I may have not said it right but they knew what I was telling them. I studied this all the time I could and remembered some from driving truck. I asked Beletta if she wanted to stay at my house again and she said Muy Buenos but I know she was copying me. She couldn't explain much but I could see she was excited. I don't think she has ever been anywhere but just to work and was also destined to an uncertain future. I had nothing to do over the weekend so I took her to the A & W Root beer stand and she was able to order what she wanted because someone spoke Spanish there. I asked her if she wanted to take a ride but she didn't understand but I pointed to my car and the road and she said Si. I drove to the Grand Coulee Dam because I always wanted to take a tour through it. I tried to explain what I was doing but I just held her hand and she followed me. We bought our tickets then got in line and went for the tour and it was very exciting. We went hundreds of feet down the elevator and seen the generators and how they make electricity. I could not believe the size of the generators or all the equipment and all the different clocks. It was very educating and I enjoyed it but I could she was excited also. I don't think she has had much in her life either and was destined to a future such as mine. I was becoming attached to her and wanted her to be with me a lot. I just needed a female friend and the other girls knew it to. I knew that I had to be careful I only had about three or four weeks left to work here. What would I do with her then and knew I couldn't lead her on. I have been seeing her a lot for the past few weeks and she stayed with me this past weekend. Last night she came and got into bed with me. I held her and she looked at me a lot. It was very hard not speaking the same language but she said something in Spanish that I think I did understand. I don't know how to spell it in Spanish but it was something like "To quetto Chocha" I heard that word at work and I knew it meant her private part and I said no hourda. I asked one of the girls that was my friend and she spoke English the most what that meant and she said I was right. I told her not to say anything to Beletta and she promised me she wouldn't.

I tried to tell her that I am leaving here in a little while and what would I do. She said it doesn't matter if I leave and she may only want to do it once or twice. She understands that you will go soon and that's why she wants to do it now. I was shocked and said I am so old fashion it stinks. I thought sex was sacred and not just for fun. I guess if I don't do it then I am not with the times and stupid. I was surprised how she answered me. I said she wants to make love to me and she don't care if I leave right and it'd no problem. She said you do her tonight and me tomorrow night this Mucho Buenos and we like to do this. I said to myself I have about sixteen days left here and why don't I do them all I guess there's nothing wrong with that. I know that I'm living in a different world then I was raised in and it reminds me of a joke I heard when I lived on the farm. It was about Papa Bull and Baby bull I quote (Papa and Baby bull was walking over a mountain and baby bull spotted a herd of cows down it the pasture. Baby bull aid Papa, papa, look at all the cows, lets run down and f—k one of them but papa bulls said, no my son lets walk down and f—k them all) and I feel like Papa bull right now. I worked all this week and it was very busy. Beletta spent a lot of time trying to learn more English and I was really getting to like her. I believe I was trying to forget my past and forced my feelings on her. She wanted to stay with me again this weekend and I did not have to ask her any more she just got into my car as if she was supposed to. I was hungry and didn't buy any food to cook. There is a A&W Root Beer food stand and I took her there and we listened to the outside music and had a Hamburg, Root Beer float and had a lot of fun and I would take her to a movie but she wouldn't understand it. We went back and walked to the lake. It was dark and the moon was bright with a street light in back of us. She put her arms around me again and kissed me softly and looked at me again. At that moment I could see Jeanne with that long black hair and very dark eyes. I couldn't understand her language well but I did understand her eyes and what they were telling me and I do believe that she wanted more than sex and was looking for a future which I can't blame her. If my life was different and I had a place to go I wouldn't mind taking her with me because she was very nice and I was lonely. She was still staring at me then said, Deseo Casarle. I nodded and tried to tell her I don't understand. She held me and kissed me as if I said yes then said Volunted usted me casa, She waited so I took her hand and led her to my room.

When we were there she said Por favor, Yo le ama' I still didn't understand but I could see why she wanted to be with me. I have always treated her as a lady. I then laid on my bed and she laid alongside me. I held her for a while and tried to say I don't understand. She looked confused and said Deseo el ti hago amante. I got up and grabbed a towel to take a shower and started to undress. She started to rub my face and chest and said me, me. I think I found she was trying to tell me she wanted to take a shower. I looked at her and said "no problem" and I thought she knew I didn't mind if she took a shower. I don't know why she asked because she has taken showers here before. She had a big smile on her face and I went to the shower and turned to water on to get it warm and I turned around and she was naked. I started to take off my shirt but she started to take my jeans down. I knew I was losing the battle so I let her continue and see how far she would go. She really had a beautiful body and reminded me of Jen, he same dark eyes and long dark hair. She washed my complete body then I did the same for her but I did not touch her private part. She took the soap and made lather and took my hand and put it between her legs then put her hand on mine. I could see she was getting very excited so we rinsed and she took my hand and pulled me to the bed. I was not sure what she wanted next so I just laid there and left it up to her. She put one leg over me and started kissing me very sexually, her lips were soft and warm and very inviting. She then got on top of me and guided it in to her and moved in various ways. It was very nice but I rolled over on top and we finished together. It was still early and I wanted to get out of the house for a while and we went back to the A&W and had a float.

We rode around then we went home and she slept with me in my bed. When we got in bed she grabbed it again and I tried to tell her no and she did understand and we fell asleep. I said My God she must have waited a long time for this and thought it would be her last. I became very sad and just wanted to go to sleep because I did not want to think about her now. We both fell asleep and went to work and had to work just a part day today. I don't know why but I was very tired. Work was normal and I was told that we would finish here in two weeks. I did offer to drive some of the equipment back to Wasco California because I was one of the few that had a Class A license and a ride back here to get my car was prearranged. I would return with someone driving produce or milk that was not affected by the strike. Beletta stayed with me every night during that time and had to leave after the two weeks. I did not want her to leave but she was with the work force and could do no different. I was not there when she left and she did not know she was leaving that Friday afternoon. I thought that she would stay with me that weekend and never had the chance to find where she was going and they did not know until their boss took them there. I was very sad that I could not see her off and asked the Forman if I could reach her in any way. He told me that he could give me the address in Los-Angeles of the work force and I did take that address with me. I stayed for another week loading the box cars and loading equipment onto the trailer I was driving back. The day before I left the Foreman approached me and asked if I would give someone a ride back to Wasco. He said he missed his ride with the work force and he would appreciate it. I said sure. His name is Bilco and he helped us load the trailer. This was Friday, and we finished with everything at three o'clock and I took the kid with me. Bilco was my age and seemed to be a good kid. We went to the A&W and ate then went to my place. I was prepaid up to date and told the owner I would be leaving tomorrow morning. He told me to leave the key on the dresser and thanked me for staying there. I told him it was a very nice place and I enjoyed staying there. I talked a lot with Bilco and we got to know each other better. I let him use my shower and packed everything into my car. I took a few things for the trip in the truck and I left my car in the warehouse. We left at four thirty in the morning and only stopped once for food and the rest room. Bilco told me he was living in Lamont which was only a short ways south east of Fresno. He gave me his address and told me to come over and stay there a few days. He also said he knew a few nice girls and I could meet them. I arrived at the ware house and parked the trailed and left the keys where I was told to. I asked Bilco how he was getting home and he told me someone was picking him up here. He did make a phone call when I called for my ride and the truck driver that was giving me a ride back to Moses Lake said he would meet me here.

He did come and picked me up in a car. There was no one else here and Bilco said his ride should be soon and he wanted to wait here and would lock the gate. I went to the terminal and we left for the trip back. I arrived in Fresno at three p m and parked at the park until four because I wanted Henry to be home when I got there. It was so very hot every place I went. I went to Henry's and wanted to see if I had any mail from Dot or Jen and I thought I may leave to go back home. There was nothing to keep me here now.

I went in the house and had a cold beer with him and it was much cooler in here and the radiator idea was working well. We talked about my job in Moses Lake and I told him about my tour through the Grand Coulee Dam. He said he would love to go there. I told him that I would like to take them there one weekend if they liked. He said he would let me know. I told him I may have a substitute job and I asked if I had any mail and he said no. I was hurt that the girls did not write. I wondered about Jen and what she was doing and it was only a few months since I left. How much could she love me if she couldn't wait that long and moved in with someone else? I know that sex was the most important part of her life and she might not want to be without it. Well I can't do anything about it and will just go on with my life. I did not hear from Judy at all and I did send her my address.

I thought about my childhood and what I have been through. When I was just sixteen through eighteen, I tried so hard do everything right and yet in less than a year, I have become indecent, immoral and disrespectful. I ask how did it happen and where did I go wrong. I stayed at Henry's last night and I'm driving to Wasco. I went to the address Bilco gave me and stopped. I went to the door and knocked and a young girl came to the door. She had long blond hair and very blue eyes and for some reason I fell some kind of attraction. I was trying to ask her where Bilco was and had trouble talking. This girl was a combination of Jen and Judy and was extremely beautiful. I asked her if Bilco was here. She answered no he's not. He is over to my cousin's house and it is only a few miles from here and I could tell you how to get there. I said o k. and she said it was easy to find and had only a few turns to remember. This was in Arvin California it was like part of Lamont. I really wanted to get to know her and told her I get lost very easily. I was hoping that she would say she would take me there. I just waited and she said would you like me to show you. I was very happy and I smiled and said I would love that very much.

She had a pair of tight shorts on that were cut from a pair of jeans and a loose tee shirt on. She was bare foot and started to go towards my car and I went and opened the door for her. I watched her get into the car and I could see enough of her to see she did remind me of Jeanne. She got into the car and I said my name is Al, She answered my name is Bonnie. She had a real southern Drawl and it was cute. She asked me how I knew Bilco and I said I gave him a ride here from Washington. She said yah he told me you might come here. We went there and he was just going to catch some soft shell crabs. The Irrigation ditches were full of them and I did go with him. When we got to where the crabs were I found a lot of people there, most of them teenagers. Some boys and girls that had jeans on and they shredded the legs. Then they would walk through the ditch and the crabs would grab the strands and not let go. They would come out and pull them off and put them in pails of water. They had a lot more nerve than I did. Together they would catch hundreds of them. I walked to their car when they loaded it and Bilco told me to follow him. We walked about five hundred from we were and he lifted a stone and a snake came out and it coiled up and was getting to strike. I went way back and Bilco had a stick and was teasing it. It finally went away and was going sideways and I knew it was a Side Winder Rattle Snake. He told me to be careful where I walked and I did not like that and I knew I'll never go first. He said he and some of his friends had motor cycles and they would go down further and chase them and it was a lot of fun.

They then went to their house and I just followed them. Bilco offered me a beer and I sat outside with him. This was a wooded and hilly area and the mountains that are near us are called Bear Mountains. I asked him if this was his family and he said no I'm from West Monroe Louisiana and I met this girl about three months ago and I stay here whenever I am around. He said Bonnie, the girl that brought you here is her sister and said, Nice Huh. I said very nice and she is very good looking. He asked do you want to go out with her. I said I would like to get to know her but I do think she's beautiful. I followed Bilco back to Lamont and went into the house. Bonnie was alone and we went in. It was a small barn type house and not very well managed. You could see that these people just lived for the day. I was talking to Bonnie she said I like your car and would like you to take me to the store if you could because I always have to walk.

We talked about everything we could think of but I had trouble adjusting to their accent. They all had a southern accent but Bonnie and her sister had a southern drawl and talked very slowly and I think their complete vocabulary consisted of one hundred words or less and they shortened their words. Bonnie was very interesting and was different in so many ways. She had a very nice shape and her breast seemed a little larger than other girls I have dated. She was very friendly and not a bit shy. She wore a large tee shirt and when she bent down you could see her complete breast. She didn't seem to mind but I tried to avoid looking at them but she did know I was. Throughout our conversations I found out that her Father had left when they were young and their mother was raising them alone. She worked at some kind of night club as a bartender. Sometimes she would bring different men home with her and they would spend the night. Bonnie did not mind telling me these things and she said her mother was at work now and wouldn't come until after one a m. I was a little hungry and asked her if there was a small place to eat around here. She said yes, there's a Café on Panama road, come on I'll show you and we walked out to the car and let her in. I had the top down and she said she never rode in a convertible and was excited about that. I could see this was a poor family and it reminded me of my own childhood. She was also a natural clown and very funny and a personality so much as Jeanne's. She took me to a small café and it did match the neighborhood. It was old and run down but it did look as if they did keep it clean. They cooked their own food and had several pies. I had a cold sandwich and a beer and she also had a beer and a Hamburg. We both had a piece of apple pie. I must say the food was plentiful and very good. We then went back to her house.

She acted very nice and was a sweet girl but she did ask me a lot of questions about myself. When we got back to her house I went in with her. I told her that I was going back to Fresno to look for work. Bilco said there's not much work around there now. I said what could I do for now because I will be working for P.I.E. very soon I hope. Bonnie said you could go to work with me tomorrow. I said why would you want me to work with you and she said, I like you and you're very nice. I was happy that she said that because I did like her. I said you are a very sweet girl and I like you also, then asked her what kind of work she did.

She said pick cotton and I thought that was funny but I did not laugh because I would like to know more about her and have a good friend. She said you don't make too much money but it's better than nothing and said I'll try it. She worked for a work force and they would pick her up when they needed her and she would be working for the next three days. She said they pick her up at five thirty a. m. because it is too hot to work after two p. m. I told her I would drive her there and she told me that I should wear a long sleeve shirt and my genes because I would get sun burned. My arms were tanned but not my body and I told her my arms would be o k and I could were a tee shirt. They did not have any spare rooms but she told me to stay overnight. I did have my pillow and blankets that I brought from home and went to get them from my trunk. I did not have a mattress so I just left them folded and slept on them on the floor. Bonnie slept on the couch near me and I left my shorts and tee shirt on. She wore her long tee shirt and just her undies.

I fell asleep and she woke me early but I don't know how I awoke. I did not hear any alarm and she was already dressed. She wore the large tee shirt and a pair of shorts that were cut from a pair of jeans again. She had not combed her hair yet and it was all over her face. She had a lot of hair and was very heavy and was a strawberry blonde. I looked at her fixing her hair and did realize she is very good looking but was just a bouncy kid and didn't seem to have a worry in the world. The work force drove in and she ran and told them I was helping them today and we would follow them. They left so I followed and asked Bonnie if we were going past a place I could get coffee. She said yes but we can't stop because I don't know what field their going to and we must follow them. We were almost to the café that we were last night and he did pull in. He came over and said you could get a drink then he went in so I followed him. We got a coffee to go and I followed him to a cotton field.

When we got there the Foreman explained that I would get paid $2.50 for every bag I filled and the bags were weighed. Bonnie told him that she would show me how to do it and at the beginning of the rows you take a white bag it is about eight feet long and one strap goes around your waist and the other over your shoulder. This leaves a loop on your side to put the cotton in and you would go down the rows and pick the cotton balls. The cotton starts growing in a green pod that opens when the cotton is ripe. Then the cotton puffs out. If the pod is too tight you can't pull the cotton out until it is really ready. Then the pods dry out, they are very sharp and if you push too fast it pricks your fingers and hurts.

I noticed that there were several work forces there and about fifty young girls. They aged from thirteen to nineteen years old and most of them wore large tee shirts with no bras. Some did not have any boobs yet, and some were large and there was no way they could hide them with a tee shirt. I have never realized that this existed and I was not raised this way but I did get my education on boobs. Although I was the only guy working with them they did not bother me and they just went on with their work. Bonnie worked the other side of the row with me and was on her second bag. I don't think mine was half full yet. I did not get a good look at the girls when I was in my row and wanted to fill my bag fast so I could turn it in and get where most of the girls were. It was ten o'clock and we took a short break. They checked my bag and it was not full yet. Bonnie already turned two in and had her third one nearly filled. I knew I could never be a cotton picker but it was worth it for the education I was getting. We did not bring lunch because it is too hot to eat but we went to the truck and they had soda that you could buy or cold water. Bonnie told me to drink just water. The soda would make you feel hotter. I finished work and they weighed my bags and only filled one and part of another. My name was attached to the part-filled one and I would start with that one tomorrow. I only made $2.50 that day. I would have never gone back but I did like being with Bonnie and did not want to miss the scenery. It was very exciting for me to see so many boobs. I knew I would probably never get the chance again. We finished for the day and I took Bonnie home.

We both took a shower, but not together and just sat around. Bonnie asked how I liked the day and I said I didn't like the work but I like the scenery.

She said I did notice you looking at the boobs and at mine too. I said I'm sorry I never seen many before. She picked up her shirt and said here do you like them. I was shocked but I did take a good look at them and said they are beautiful and they look so firm. She said thank you and I said thank you! I talked about back home and how the girls dress and you would never see this. I also told her that everyone there was so modest. I changed into my shorts and put on a clean tee shirt and Bonnie also put on different shorts. I think they called them hot pants and I could see why. Bilco drove in and we talked.

I found while we were talking that Bonnie was only sixteen years old but she looks like she's eighteen or more and I was so surprised. In a short time I would be twenty one and it scared me to know she was only sixteen. I have seen twenty five year olds that would love to have her body. Later that evening I did take Bonnie to the same Café and we had dinner then went home. There was nothing to do and I was afraid to be with her alone and I felt many things could happen so I asked her if she wanted to take a ride with me. We drove around for about two hours while she showed me where everything was, plus the post office and a phone booth. It was a very nice night to just drive around in a convertible. I looked at her a lot and wished she was older. Her age did bother me and she was so beautiful, I really wanted to hold her and kiss her. It would have been different if she did not show me her body and acted her age but she wanted to be a grown up and tried to make people think she was. We got home after midnight and had to get up early to go to work. I did promise that I would go today and I did.

The day is just like yesterday and I spent more time looking at boobs then I did picking cotton but it did not matter because I knew that I would never do it again. We went home and changed and did nothing the rest of the day. Bonnie did change her tee shirt in front of me and I did see her boobs again. I wish she wouldn't do that because I am having trouble keeping from holding her and kissing her. I would love to go and hold them in my hands but I knew better. Bilco came in and asked me if I wanted to go out to a bar to have some fun. I told him I promised Bonnie I would take her to dinner. He asked if he could go with us, I said sure and we went to the same café because I did like the food there. We all ate and Bilco had two beers. I do not drink much and did not want to go to any bar then stay all night. I told him I would go later but I didn't want to stay long. We went just before midnight and every one there was just about drunk and the girls there only wanted to make money. One lady about twenty five or older offered me sex anyway I wanted it for money. I asked Bilco about that and he said you didn't know, she's a prostitute I said no and told Bilco I wanted to leave. He said go ahead, I have a ride home and he was spending a lot of time with a girl much older than him. I went back to Bonnie's house and she was awake and glad to see me. She asked me why I came back so early, I said because you were alone and I worried about you. She said I am always alone but thank you for thinking about me. I took my blankets and pillows then I laid on the floor.

Bonnie came to lay down with me and said, "You don't mind if I just lay here, do you?" I was lying on my back and she laid alongside me. She did put her arm around me and when I turned to look at her she kissed me. Her lips were as soft as they looked. I put my arm around her and we both fell asleep. I must have slept very sound. I did not hear anything until Bonnie woke me. She knew I was not going with her today but I told her I would see her tonight. I gave her a note for her boss to give her any money I made, and she could have it. I went Back to see Henry that afternoon because I wanted to see if I had any mail and I wanted to talk to Jim about my job back at P. I. E.

I got there before Henry and Ann gave me a beer. She told me that Henry would be a little late. I told her I wanted to run to the store and I would be right back. I asked if she needed anything. She said no. I went and bought two cases of beer and brought them back to them. Henry was there then and said I didn't have to do that. I said I wanted to show some appreciation. He thanked me and I did have a letter from Jen. I did not open it and drove to the park then pulled off the road because I had to read the letter. She said that she hoped I was doing fine and she did miss me but she was living with another guy who treated her very good and they had their own apartment. The next paragraph ruined my life. She wrote it as if I already knew. She mentioned when Dorothy killed her mother with multiple blows to the head with a hammer. I could not read any more and I burst out crying and could not see to drive. I pulled my car further in to the park and sat there in a trance and felt as if I killed her myself. I sat here for about an hour I know I lost it and was having a problem with dealing with it. I didn't know where to go or do. When I could see I drove to the phone booth and tried to call Dorothy's house. There was no answer so I called my Dad and he was home. I asked what happened. He told me the same thing and everyone in town is in shock. He was still talking when I hung up and I knew what happened. Dot did say once that she wanted to kill her some day and I felt that was why I got that bad letter from her and I did not get any more. I found that this happened a while ago and wondered if Dot wrote the last letter right after this happened. I know this is my fault and I was the reason why and if I was there this would never have happened because she did warn me that she might do this. The night that I picked her up at the theater I knew she lost it and did not know what she was doing that night.

I knew while sitting there that I had no place to go now. I could never go home again and what would I find there but heartbreaking memories. I know that Dot's father will blame me for what happened and Bob and Betty must blame me for Jen not going to college and shacking up with some guy. I said too many times life is too hard to live and I really don't care anymore and I do wish I get killed or die somehow. I know that I have always been a loser and just don't know how to go on. I left the phone booth and headed back towards Bonnie's house but had trouble seeing. I was still trembling and I think in a trance because I cannot believe this. When I got near I knew I did not want to see her either. I keep thinking what I did to Dorothy and how I ruined her life. The only life she ever had was with me and I worried about her and what's going to happen now. What can I do and is there any way I could help. I should have dropped Jen and married Dot. Then this would never have happened.

I did not go to Bonnie's house I just rode around and had to stop because the tears were blocking my vision. I was searching my mind for answers and wondered what I did to deserve the life I had and what could I do to change it. I have given all that I have to give. I got back on the road and knew I had to go somewhere because I did not want to be alone any longer. I thought I would like to call Jen but I did not have her number and didn't know if she still worked at the phone company. I went to another pay phone and asked the operator if she could place a phone call to that phone company and I needed to speak to that operator. I gave Jen's full name and she said she would try. She did make contact with that location and was told that they could not accept it. I said thank you, and hung up and knew Jen must have ordered not to accept any calls to her. I started shaking again and just screamed, "Why Dorothy, Why her, hasn't she been through enough already?" I started to cry harder and did not know what to do. I had problems seeing and had to keep wiping my eyes but I think I may have lost it. I floored the gas and was flying down the back roads. I did not see the stop sign and flew through it. I didn't get far before a State Police Officer pulled me over. He came to my door but I did not look at him and I just stared forward. He asked me for my license and registration but I was still trembling when I reached for the glove box. He noticed something was wrong and ordered me out of the car. I opened the door and almost fell out so he grabbed me and helped me up. I looked at him and he could see my face then knew I had problems.

He said, "What's wrong?" I tried to answer but I was incoherent. I was still holding the letter and handed it to him. He was very nice and took the time to read it then I explained the rest. He placed both hands on my shoulders and said, "You must get a hold of yourself." I stopped crying and nodded yes. He said, "Come on son, I don't have to read anymore to see something is very wrong and know you have problems." I looked at him and said I was sorry but I would be all right. Then he said, "But if you don't straighten out I will have to take your keys because I can't let you kill someone else with this kind of attitude." I said I'm sorry again and said I promise, I also thank you for being so understanding. He did not give me a Citation but just a verbal warning. Then I said I am lost and want to get to Panama Road. He said just follow me, which I did. Then he pointed when we were there. I sounded the horn and continued.

I didn't know where else to go so I went back to Bonnie's. She saw that something was wrong and asked. I said there was a death in the family and didn't care to elaborate any further. It was almost midnight, and I told her not to worry about me, and she could go to sleep. She put my blankets and pillow on the floor then fixed it for me. I laid down and she did lay with me but I had my back to her so she would not see me cry. She just held me and said she would help me in any way she could and I did miss you tonight. I knew she was a good kid and meant well. I think we both fell asleep and I was awakened by her mother coming home. She had some guy with her and I could see that they were both drinking. Bonnie also woke up. Her Mom asked me are you messing with my girl! You better be careful. Bonnie spoke up and said Mother please leave him alone, he has problems. She took the guy into her bedroom and closed the door. I said to myself, my God you only read this in books. I looked at Bonnie and felt sorry for her. Now I know why she has no scruples and I knew what was coming up next.

On My New Road to Life

I laid down again and Bonnie looked at me and said see! My mom doesn't care what I do and does trust us. I woke up before she did and I was turned towards her. I looked at her for the first time and studied her for a different reason. I did not look at her age but the actual beauty and I was happy that she liked me because she is all that I have now. Her eyes were closed and I looked at her hair it was spread out over my pillow and her lips were larger than the other girls and a perfect shape. I wanted to kiss her then but knew I couldn't so I just wanted to look at her some more because she did take my mind off the problems. She did wake up and I was still looking at her but she did not know I was. She put her hands up to push her hair back and put her hands behind her head and stretched. While stretching she lifted her chest and I could see that she was not that sixteen year old I was so afraid of, but a young beautiful lady. I did not say anything.

She turned towards me and said what are we going to do. I put my hand behind her head and pulled her over and kissed her because I could not resist it any longer but with this kiss I realize that I really did like her. I backed off and she asked me why did you do that. I said I didn't she said what do you mean. I said my whole body did it and I couldn't stop it. She knew then that I did like her more than I showed before. I started to get up and she pulled me back and kissed me and said I couldn't help it. I did feel better and she did give me some reason to want to live. I said let's go to the beach and she said it's a long way. I said it won't be if you come with me. I could see that made her happy and she gave me a kiss then got ready to leave. It was early and I stopped at a clothing store and told her I would buy her a bathing suit so I asked her to pick one out. I also went to find one for me and went to the counter to pay for them. When we got to the car she showed it to me. It was cute, it was a two piece like I seen at the Santa Monica Beach. We drove to the lower part of the beach where there was no one. She put her top piece on under her shirt and then took her shirt off. She then undressed her bottom and put on her suit. She looked very nice in that suit and it reminded me of Judy. I looked around and there was no one in sight. I then slid off my shorts and underwear and put on my bathing suit. We locked the car and went for a walk along the beach. I thought that I should take a picture of her now and send it to Jen and show her who I'm living with. I decided against it because I have no reason to and I still love her for some reason. Bonnie is not prettier than the other girls but is cuter and more down to earth. For the first time I was very happy to have her for my friend. I do not know if I could call her my girl friend yet but we had so much fun and we played in the water and looked for shells. She kept a bucket of them as we found some. We played in the sand and she would write Al & Bonnie in a heart shape and she said I have never been this happy before.

Looking back I think this was the most fun that I had since Jen. We stayed here all day. There is a hot dog stand at the other end and we went for lunch there. It was late in the day and we decided to take a ride before we went home. I put the convertible top down on the car and left. She did sit close to me, and I did not mind but was happy to have her there. We stopped for an ice cream soda and then went home. It was just before ten p m. and there was no one there. We were both tired from all the things we did today. I laid on the floor and she laid along side of me. This was the first time that we really did kiss and I found more love for her. Her lips were the softest of any the other girls and it was a new exciting thing all over again. We still had our bathing suits on and she got on top of me to tickled me. She found I was ticklish under my arms and sides. We both laughed and she took her top off and said it hurt her. I could see the marks on her and they were all red. She was still on top of me and I could see her beautiful titties and when she bent down to kiss me again I could feel the softness of them on my body. I was worried that she did not have her top on but she said it's Saturday night and you won't see anyone until sometime in the morning. She then laid along side of me and pulled me close then started kissing me. She got up and put on her tee shirt and said I did that because you said you liked my boobs. I said I loved the feel of them also and I said you're lucky I didn't try and rape you.

I don't know what I said wrong but she jumped up and screamed "don't say that" and walked away and started crying. I jumped up and said Honey what did I say wrong but when I turned her around and kissed her, I could feel she was trembling. I said Oh No not another Dorothy. She started to kiss me harder and said I'm sorry I didn't mean to do that. I did not ask her to explain but I took her hand and went back to lay with me again. She laid there for a while just holding me and said, "I'm sorry". I just held her for a while and when she stopped trembling she said I'm sorry but please don't say that. I said honey please that's why I asked you about having your top off. I would never try that with you and I know you're too young. She said I don't know what happened to me, I am very sorry and always want you here with me but don't say I'm too young because I'm not. I said honey I really love to be here with you, and will never do anything to ruin that. I told you when you took your top off I did not expect that but I do understand now. I really didn't understand but I knew she did have a problem with something happening to her and it is trapped inside of her as it was in Dorothy.

I will not question her and if she wants to tell me I will let her on her terms. I don't know how and I really tried not to because of her age but I am falling in love with her and I want to be with her all the time. I know I could be with her every night and did not have to worry about the other girl finding out and I did not have to lie any more. I was all right then but when it all sank in I started to worry about the problems with Dot and I couldn't live that life again. Bonnie fell asleep but I am having problems trying to figure things out. I broke out in a cold sweat and thought that maybe I should leave. Bonnie acted almost the same as Dot and I know I jumped into this affair totally blind but I don't think I could handle this now. I seem to be falling back to when I left home and I don't like this feeling again. I know that I was really lost in life and refused to think or better it but just bury it in the back of my mind. For some reason I feel that I will not be alive much longer and I don't know why I think this but I do.

For the next few days all I did was ride around with Bonnie and when she worked, I would just ride to different places. Some part of me wanted to go home and the other wanted to stay here. If I try something else I know it would go bad. I am happy that I saved all my money and I don't spend much to live. Gas is twenty nine cents a gallon and I only tank up once a week. The rest is on food for me and Bonnie. I don't mind spending money on Bonnie because she has no one else to help her. She has to work some days this week and I am going to take a ride past Camp Pendleton. I went south on highway ninety nine and seen a sign about the nuclear power plant and wanted to see it but when I drove in the guards stopped me and said I could not go in but I did see it from outside. I then continued south and noticed a sign to a beach. It was called Black Beach so I went in but was stopped at the entry and was told that I had to be a member to get in. I told him I want to become a member and he seen my registration and said boy you're a long ways form home. I told him I live here now and was just looking for another beach. We started to talk and he asked me if I knew what this beach was. I said No and he said it's a nudist beach and you don't wear clothes here. I told him I never heard of this and asked why. He said these people believe in it. We talked for a while and became a little friendly and he said I'm not supposed to do this but I'll give you an application and if anyone asks, you want to become a member then said he will take me for a walk. We waited for a little while and when a worker walked by he called him over to manage the gate.

There was a big club house and he took me there first. Some of the older people had shorts on and the rest were totally naked. There were boys and girls of all ages and everyone walked around as if it was nothing. I looked at lots of girls and so many were good looking and had very nice bodies but I don't think I could do this. I asked Paul why everyone is not excited and he said, they are for the first few days and then it's nothing. I asked if we could walk to the beach because most of the girls were there. He said we can't be long and I was glad. I never knew there was so many nude girls all in one place. Some were so beautiful and sexy. I was getting excited and said we better leave. On the way back I asked Paul if they ever have problems with them making love. He said it's all in the rules and if you get caught you are out forever but I think some of them must find a way. I left and went back to Bonnie's. She was home and wondered where I was. She heard me drive in and came running out. It was after seven and she got home at two thirty.

I told her I went to the Nuclear plant that I wanted to see and then went to a beach. I told her what happened and she said, "Ain't I enough for you?"

I said, "Honey, I told you it was an accident. But you asked him to take you in to see. Didn't I tell you everything and not hide it from you?"

She said, "I guess." And I reinforced her feelings that no one there could come close to second place with you. I told her as long as I have you I will never want for anyone and please believe me. She hopped up on me and kissed me and I held her very tight then she said, "You don't know how I feel about you but I know you were different after the other night."

I said, "Honey I am sorry but I had a girl friend that was raped before she met me and that came back to my mind. But if you want to tell me about your problem I will listen and try to help." She started crying and said I'm sorry and I do want to tell you. I said not now because I want you to be very happy today. She said why, and I said, "Honey would like to get a surprise?"

She said, "What, what is it?" I said do you want a surprise. She said What again. I said it's a yes or no question. She said, "Yes tell me!" I then showed her the tickets for Disneyland for all day Saturday. She lives a half hour away and has never been there. She jumped up and said, "I love it, I love it." She hugged and kissed me and I was happy to see her this way. I know she has had nothing in her life either and this girl had nothing to offer me but her love.

She said, "You could have me any time forever and any time you want. She was offering me the only thing she had to give and it made me feel sad. It's sad to see that a girl has to offer that just to keep something they wanted. I told her that I would stay with her and do all I can for her even if she never let me have sex with her.

I said, "I'm with you because you're you, not just sex." She thanked me and had tears in her eyes and said no one has ever said nice things to me. Saturday morning we left early and she was so excited and she loved It' a Small World the best. I took her through the Cinderella Castle and the Safari and she hung on to me all day. She also liked the Trains going through and over the mountains and said they look so real. Seeing her this happy was worth a million words and seeing her this way I knew how much she needed me and I needed her because it was her love that allowed me to forget the past and realize that I really do love her. I know I really want to spend the rest of my life with her. She is more than I ever expected to get and I am not sure I deserve her. On our way home she explained what happened to her.

She started to work for a work force and was only thirteen. Her father left her, sister and mother without notice for another woman. They had little money saved and her mother was forced to work at a bar because that was where she could make the most money. She was still not meeting ends and Bonnie and her sister had to quit school to work to meet their obligations and have food to eat. Bonnie at her age could only find work through a work force that did hire young girls. She said that almost all the girls there were ages from thirteen through eighteen and there may be a reason for that. She was picked up by her Foreman and given a ride as most of them. Her job consisted mostly of picking cotton but at times may be picking vegetables or cleaning. There never were any male workers but just the Foreman to watch over twenty some-odd workers.

One day while picking cotton she experienced several improper remarks with vulgar language and later that day her foreman walked up behind her when she was in the isle alone. He reached around her and grabbed her breast but she pulled away and yelled, "What in the hell are you doing?" He replied that he would give her money if he could just play with them. She refused then he went to the next isle where there was just one girl. Bonnie was young but was built as if she was much older and had nice size boobs then. That afternoon he dropped all the other girls off first but instead of taking her home he took her to some shed. He said that if she didn't let him play with her she would not have a job. She did not answer but just ran outside but he ran after her and caught her. He forced her back into the shed then pulled her t-shirt off, and then while holding her he started to suck on her boobs then forced her to watch while he masturbated. She didn't know what that meant but she knew it was dirty. She started to leave and he called her back. She turned around and he handed her a dollar then said he will give her the best jobs and more hours than the other girls. She needed the money and more hours so she didn't tell anyone.

She was not scheduled to work the next day but he said, "I will pick you up the same time and will give you more hours." The next day after work he did the same thing and took her to his shed but held her and put his hand between her legs and tried to push his finger in her. She screamed and said it hurt so he stopped but kept his hand there and masturbated again. He gave her another dollar and said, "I will give you much more if you let me do that."

She said, "No I don't want to do this and I know it's not right," he then took her home but dropped her off before her house so no one would see her with him at that time. She didn't go to work the next day and told him she was sick but he did pick her up the next day because her mother said you must go to work. She still was afraid to tell her mom and went with him again. That night he did the same thing and took her to the shed. She screamed, "I'm not going in there anymore and I want you to take me home now." She wanted to run away but she did not know where she was or how to get home. But she ran away anyway but he was able to catch her. He picked her up and carried her while threatening her not to scream. Then promised her many more things then she started crying so he took a handful of money from his pocket and said this is yours but put it back in his pocket. He said, "I won't hurt you and I am sure you will like it," then pushed her on some hay that was on the floor. He held her down and moved her shorts over ant tried to stick his penis into her. She started to scream as loud as she could and was able to turn to her side to stop him. He got up and was kneeling in front of her and was masturbating again. She put her hand between her legs to protect herself and noticed it was all bloody. She yelled, "Look at what you did." He grabbed her hand then ejaculated into her palm then told her to rub it on her and it will stop the bleeding. He stood up to button his fly and gave her a chance to run out but he got into his truck and told her he would give her a ride home.

She still didn't know where she was so she got in. He told her if she tells anyone that she will never get a job again and he will tell her mother that she was grabbing him and was asking for it. She became very scared and didn't know what to do because she needed her job. She went to another work force and told another girl then the girl went to her Forman. Bonnie explained what he was doing and told him about the shed. He was fired on the spot and someone came to talk with him before he left.

I told Bonnie I wanted her to show me where he is or give me his name because I want to find him and stick a stick up his ass as far as it will go, because he should be dealt with properly. I reiterated so many times, "Young girls have no protection against these pedophiles and the law enforcement's just don't give a darn. We the people must find a way to prosecute these kinds of behavior." I am still very upset about this and three of the five girls that I have dated have been raped at a very young age. Bonnie and I are just fine now, we never have any problems with each other and I thanked her for telling me because it just reinforces my love for her. I held her in my arms and told her this will never happen to her again. We got up Sunday morning and I said lets go for a ride. She really didn't care where I took her just as long as we were together. I was getting a little more comfortable with my life but every now and then I really wanted to find out how Dorothy was. I called my dad again and he told me that her father took the rap. He confessed to killing her and they could not prove any different. He told me that Dorothy was in an institution for the mentally ill. I felt like crying and really wanted to go visit her but had too much hurt to deal with it. I hoped that someday I could help her and I don't know why but I do feel responsible. My dad told me he was hired by the town as a Special Police Officer. That made me feel good and I said I would call him next Sunday.

Bonnie and I went for breakfast then south on ninety nine and I took her to Knott's Berry Farms. They had a lot of souvenirs there and I thought she would like some. We spent a few hours there looking around and left. She did get some things and a jar of jelly. We got home early and Bilco was there. His car broke down and he asked if he could take my car to the store. I said, "No booze and no stopping at any bar," but he said trust me so I gave him the keys and he left.

He was gone less than a hour and handed me the keys. The only thing about him not having a car was he was always here and we could not be alone. I did not mind some of the time and I knew he had no money and couldn't buy another one. I hoped they could fix his. Bonnie told Bilco we were going for a ride. He asked if I would drop him off at the bar and he should find a ride home. I told him to call me if he didn't. I noticed he filled my gas tank and thanked him. It was almost on empty when we came back and he seemed to be an all right kid. I just didn't like his drinking, although I have never seen him drunk and if I don't help him then who will. I have always been a giving person and I guess it makes me feel good about myself. Bonnie and I laid on the floor again and started kissing. I knew that sex was inevitable in the near future but knew that I should wait and knew after her problem I would leave it up to her. Her lips were softer every time we kissed and I never felt better. She knew I was ticklish under my arms and she got on top of me to hold me down. We played for a while then she rolled off of me and laid on my side. She held me very close then reached and slid her hand under my bathing suit. She found what she was searching for but I pulled her hand back up. I didn't have time to say why because she had a very strange look on her face and had the look of a little child.

She said, "Why did you stop me just when it was getting interesting?" It was such a cute look and how could I stop her. I said I'm sorry and you could do anything you want. She pushed my suit down and took hold of it again. She looked so interested and was playing with it while it grew. She said, "I love it," then I said I'm afraid about what happened the last time. She said I told you I was sorry but I want to prove to you that I do love you." I said wouldn't it be better if my bathing suit was off. She smiled and quickly pulled them off, then smiled at me while she removed hers. She appeared to be a little scared but it didn't take her long to get it back to where it was. She got back on top of me and kissed me while she guided it, then started to push down. She went very easy until our bodies were as one. We just stayed there for a while without moving and I could still feel her trembling but soon after she started to move in a motion that she liked and I haven't felt this way since Judy. We rolled over then made love for a long time and took our time loving each other. She squeezed me very tight with her legs and we finished together. I was so very happy and proud of her for forgetting her past and loved me as she did. I told her this was the best time in my life and she said, "Did I really make you happy?"

My Home, My Wife and My Future

I said more than words could ever say, then she told me how she felt but at first she was afraid because she never felt this way before, then followed, "We have to do this more." Then thanked me for the best time in her life and said she will add this to her collections of her best times and they were all with me. I told her I will do the same because I know it is the truth and she is my new love, new life and everything I ever wanted. I was with her every night and I did not have to worry about the other girl finding out but most of all I did not have to lie any more. I felt I have found my life's dream and was never this happy. Bonnie awoke me early and she said, "I'm so happy I don't want to sleep. I want to be awake so I could be with you and do things that I always wanted." I asked her how she felt and she said, "The best ever because I am very happy we did that."

I said, "Let's take a ride I want to see Joe to find when I could start work." She didn't care where we went as long as she was with me. We stopped at the Café then went to L A and into the office. Joe was there as usual and I introduced him to Bonnie. He said, "You're a beautiful girl and I think you made a good choice with Al." I thanked him for both complaints then he explained that after the strike all the work was handled by the union and only union members were called back. I said, "What about a jockey?" and he said, "Yes we need one and I could start you right away but you must join the Union." I said I had all the papers filled out and I would bring them with me. I explained I was supposed to submit them before but I was never here and always on the road. He said bring them in and you could start in a week, I said please call me because we are getting married and I want to get a home. We drove around looking at the area and I wanted to get our own apartment but Bonnie said we should discuss this with her mother because she didn't want to just walk out on her. I agreed that was right and we did talk with her.

She said, "Why don't you live here because I own this property then you could fix this better and add on for now." She showed me the property deed and I did not know she owned more than two acres. I discussed this with Bonnie and we decided we would add on some more rooms. Bonnie and I were very excited and stayed home almost all the time.

I started drawing the plans for the addition and she watched. Bilco's car broke down and he has been using mine for the last few weeks. I really don't like this but he always brings it back full of gas and I told him absolutely no drinking when he has it. I finished the plans then we went outside to the rear of the house and I described it to her. She helped me measure it then I told her I would pour a cement slab and use a lot of rebar connecting the floor to the cement block walls. We do have earthquakes here and I want this to be safe for our kids. I had the experience to do all the work myself and we started right away. We measured for the footings and Bonnie held the stakes while I drove them in. I then grabbed the shovel and started to dig but she took it from me and said, "I will dig all day to help you." We stopped and just held each other and said, "We will build our home together," then we both jumped with joy and she uttered, "Till death do us part." We went back into the house and looked at the plans and Bonnie said, "What about our Baby?"

I explained it to her and showed her the plans again. "This is your mother's bedroom and we are not going to change that. This is our new bedroom and it has its own bathroom just for us." Then I asked, "What is this room?" She had a big grin and said, "Our Baby. Oh I love you so much." But she had to be smart and said, "What if we have a boy and a girl?" I said, "We will name them after us," and she said, "That's not what I mean." I said I know what you mean but we will have our new house built by then. She asked could we go outside and you show me again. I said yes but not right now. Her smiles and attitude were priceless and that made me want to just hold her forever. My life became happier every day and we both shared the same dreams. I said we finally found a place for us in this so uncertain world and I was finally building my foundation over new bridges on this new road to life. It is still early so we both went out to have dinner. While we were there we still discussed our plans and went straight home just to be together alone. We reached our house about nine thirty and Bilco asked to use my car again. I said, "Yes but it is tough on us not to have a car around in case we need to go somewhere and when are you going to fix yours?" He said soon and I really felt he is taking advantage of me now. I don't know why I started this because I would never let anyone use my car before. Bonnie fixed our blankets on the floor and we took a shower. We were both being foolish and laughing very hard but just having fun. I know this is the most exciting time of my life, we were both falling over each other and couldn't do anything right. We finished washing then she ran to lay on our blankets.

I looked at her and seen all the love I would need the rest of my life. I knew she was mine and she said before we started, "You better not forget our baby."

I kissed both of her breasts, then said, "This one is for a boy and this is for a girl." I don't think I was ever this excited and I wanted her to have everything. I did tell her about the problem I had with the mumps and I may be sterile. She said try to be optimistic and don't think about it. I thought about us, our life together and it is a pleasure that sex is not the main course but just the dessert. I was happy that we did wait for this because it seemed more decent. I do believe that I am sterile but I would love for her to have my baby. We just laid there then I said I wanted to do it again and she said, "I hope you're joking." I laughed and said I wanted to talk about our wedding because I wanted to get married right away. She said, "Oh my God I'm so happy and excited," so we just loved each other. We both said we really do belong together and talked about our kids and new home. It was after two and I worried about Bilco having my car but I heard a car drive in and it was Bilco. He came into the house and apologized for being late then left with someone else.

Bonnie did fall asleep and I awoke her and said, "I want to make love." She opened her eyes big then started to say something but I said, "I'm really hungry and want to go to the Café." She said you know it's late and why don't you just go to sleep. I tried to go to sleep and maybe I was but Bonnie got up and said, "Well lets go now that you awoke me." I said I was only kidding but we did go. We went to our favorite Café because it is open all night, she played the juke box and we had Ice Cream Sundaes. We went back home and she said let's try and go to sleep now. I kissed her and fell right to sleep and didn't even hear her mother come in. We both slept until nine o'clock and I awoke to a more trusting and comfortable life just doing things together. It was a very nice day and in the seventies so I said, "Today is Sunday, why don't we take a ride?" We put the top down then went to the beach and this girl is so full of fun and ideas I'm always happy. We left the beach and drove south when we seen a Mexican Café because we both like Mexican food. She is so easy to please and appreciates everything I do with her. We left then headed to our favorite café but not to eat but play the juke box. Then I called dad and he told me he really liked being a police officer and I congratulated him. I told him I am getting married and I found the nicest girl in the world and would let him know when we're getting married.

When I got back to the car Bonnie asked me what we talked about for so long. I said everything, "My Dad's a Cop now, and I asked about Dorothy then I told him about us. I told him I found a gorgeous girl and we are getting married." She said, "You really did?" and smiled. We went home and she fixed our bed then we fell asleep. I awoke early and hoped to start work this week and knew I just had few more days off before I would. The sun was just going down as we drove in our driveway and she grabbed my hand and pulled me to the back of the house. She said, "I want to talk about it because I could see our kids playing here as we did as kids." I asked her, "Do you want to know where our baby's room is going to be?" and she smiled and said, "I'm standing in that spot." She was leaning on the stake we drove in and said I will dig some more tomorrow. She said, "Are you sure you could build this all by yourself?" and I said, "No not without your help because together we can conquer the impossible." She then took my hand and we went into the house.

She fixed our bed and we were just getting ready to lay down when Bilco walked in. I just threw him the keys and said, "Come home early." He said thanks and I will make it up to you. He left then Bonnie and I started fooling around and we both fell asleep. I think I was just about asleep and Bonnie shook me and asked if I was awake. I said, "I am now," so I turned towards her. I seen those two beautiful big blue eyes looking at me very inquisitively and she asked, "Could we make love now?" I pulled her over because I have never seen anyone cuter in my life and the expressions were worth millions. I did not answer but I started kissing her then her neck then her titties. I was so very excited and happy she asked so I kept kissing her and I could also feel she was equally excited. She reached down and held me so I put my hand on her. I could feel that she wanted me so I pulled her panties off and then mine. She said, "You're not mad at me are you?" and I said, "Yes because you didn't ask me sooner."

She laughed and was squeezing it and said, "I love you so very much," so I asked, "Were you saying that to me or what you have a hold of?"

She said, "Both but this could give me a baby while squeezing it harder." She got up and asked if she could play with it again. I said, "It's yours to do what you like." She was really looking and pulling down on it. She kissed it then said, "I love this thing."

I said, "Honey you're making me very hot and you must stop that." She said why should I stop and I said, "Some stuff will come out." I knew I shouldn't have said that after what happened at the time of her rape so I said, "Why do you want to see that?"

She said, "I want to see what happens," and I felt much better. I just pulled her up and rolled over on top. This was so beautiful I never wanted it to end. I just moved slow and easy for a long time then we would stop to look at each other and know how happy we are together. She did remind me about our baby and she said she wants one now. I just love this girl so much and I started to move again but this time faster and she held me very tight and dug her fingers into my back, this made me very close and we finished together. I just laid there loving her then we went to take a shower. We both washed each other and talked about our baby. She wanted to talk about our home and was excited to help me. I told her that I will make the house earthquake proof and it will also withstand hurricanes to protect all that I love.

Back to the Old Road to Life

It is November now and I left Connecticut just five months ago but I seems like years have gone by. I will be twenty one this month and Bonnie will be seventeen. I am so very happy that I found her or we found each other because I do believe that I got the sign that I was waiting for because I love this girl more than anything else in this world. I don't know if this is paradise but if it's not it must be very close because I have everything I have ever wanted and never have to look anymore. We are planning to add on to this house and I will start tomorrow with the footings then the slab for the floor. I will cover this with insulation and place a wood floor above the concrete. This will keep it warm and the moisture out. I also want to make it strong to protect Bonnie and our children, because if I can't have my own then I will adopt some. It won't matter that much because I love all kids. I will start work with PIE in a few days and will have all the money that we will need. I told Joe that I will work as a jockey until he can find me a local route because I don't want to be away from Bonnie for even a day. Every place we go we are always together and I want it to stay that way. I still let Bilco take my car every night and Bonnie and I stay here alone. I told her I want to write a book about my life and she said she would help because it will be very interesting.

I would like to write a novel and name it "Bitter Sweet, The Road To Life" a story that everyone should read. Then maybe someone could learn from my mistakes and experiences and find happiness in the end. It was Wednesday morning that I was awakened by a car driving at a high rate of speed around the corner then drove into our driveway. I thought it was Bilco and I wanted to kill him. Bonnie and I were sleeping on the floor with nothing on so I quickly put on my t-shirt, my jeans then my shoes with no socks but grabbed my jacket and ran outside. I noticed my car in the drive way but Bilco was not around. The convertible top was down and I looked for him them called out loud. He did not answer so I started the engine to put up the top but as soon as I sat two police cars drove into the driveway. One parked right behind my car and the other was along side of me. One came to me and asked if I was the owner of this car and I said yes. The other went to the house and entered. I yelled to him that my girl was naked and sleeping on the floor and don't go in there. I was very worried about Bonnie but the other cop asked me for my driver's license and registration. I took my license from my wallet and got my registration and handed then to him.

Living In Jail,
Guilty Until Proven Innocent

He said in a very nasty voice, "You're going to jail for a long time." I quickly said, "Why? I didn't do anything, and I was always with Bonnie, my girl." My mind went back to when I was beaten by the cops in New York and became this would happen again.

He said, "You're in a lot of trouble," and I said, "I asked you to talk to my girl because she could verify what I'm saying." He then said shut up while he was searching my car and I noticed a lot of stuff under my rear seat. I didn't know what is was or where it came from but I said Bilco has been using my car for the past several weeks. The other cop was still in the house and I was very worried about Bonnie because I was afraid he would try and rape her. I don't trust any city cops and know they are all alike. He asked me how to open my trunk and I told him I have a switch inside the car. He ordered me to open it but when I walked back past the opening on the convertible top I noticed a long crow bar so I grabbed it while he was searching my trunk and hit him behind the head or neck. He fell into the trunk so I dragged him out and started to leave. I could not go backwards so I drove across the lawn and left. I don't know why I did this but I knew I would be blamed for whatever was wrong.

I knew all the shortcuts to highway ninety nine and head for Mexico because I didn't know where else to go. I thought about what I did and couldn't believe that I did that but I knew that I could not trust these cops with that attitude. I needed to go someplace where I could think and drove for a long time. I drove into a road block on the highway and I was going well over one hundred miles per hour. I knew I couldn't turn around so I headed for the space between the police cars. I hit them at a very high of speed because I had the gas to the floor. I could see the police cars go air-bound but I didn't get far. The impact bent my bumper into my tire and my car flipped over. I was just a few hundred yards from them and was able to crawl out and run towards the orange groves. There was a fence there so I jumped over it then heard a lot of gunfire but did not know if I was hit. I already hurt very badly from the accident and my face was bleeding into my eyes. I didn't know how bad I was hurt and

I didn't care. I ran a long way but got very tired and rested for a while then I could feel my back burning. I was very weak so I rested near a tree but it was almost day light and I heard the police dogs coming so I just held my face and waited for them.

Living in Jail, While Not Guilty

I heard the police dogs coming closer so I just waited for them. I held my face while they put me in handcuffs and a chain around my waist. I couldn't run another step and don't know why they did that. They did not help me with the pain in my face or my back and did not care that I was bleeding. But at the police station an ambulance came and took me to the hospital but two police stayed with me at all times. They asked me so many questions but all I could say was I did not do it and the only thing I did wrong was hit the cop because he shouldn't have treated me that way. They asked me so many times why did I hit the cop. I said he was very mean and told me I was going to jail for a long time. I knew I didn't do anything wrong but I knew he would pin it on me because of how he acted so I just panicked. There were police there all the time while I was in the emergency room. I knew I should have had stitches in my face but they just washed it off and put a bandage on it. My back had several lead pellets from a doubleought shot gun that just penetrated the skin so the doctor just took them out and put Band-Aids on them. They did not give me anything for the pain when they did this. I was a criminal now and treated as one and I was taken into interrogation. It was at this time that I found that you are totally guilty on all counts alleged against you even if you are innocent. Don't believe the rhetoric that you are innocent until proven guilty. I do not remember anyone giving me my rights and was treated as a criminal from the start.

I was interrogated the rest of that day and night and part of the next day. I was questioned about every criminal case that wasn't solved in the state and I do believe they tried to implicate me with everyone. It seemed that they didn't care who they put in jail as long as they could close the case. I was stripped of my belt, wallet and watch then they kept everything in a bag. I had nearly one thousand dollars in my wallet and yet all they marked down was one wallet. I was not allowed to question them and I was refused the right to make a phone call. I was taken to the jail cell and we walked past several tanks before I got to the one I was to be in. The tank consisted of nine small cells all in a row. The only door was at one end and there was a long steel table from the door to the other end and then there was one shower. All the cells had separate doors and

I found that this tank was designed to hold two people per cell which has only two bunks and there were more than double that amount locked up in here. When they took me to the tank they opened the door removed the hand cuffs and shoved me into the tank. There was a very large black man standing by the door but as I have said I do love black people and they have treated me the best. The guard just shoved me in and slammed the door shut.

There was standing room only and I have been without sleep for a long time. The big black man said I like that jacket and I think I want it. I did not think and I said, "You'll have to take it off my dead ass." I stunned him and neither one of us said a word for a second. I then said, "I just want you to kill me," and looked right at him when I said that. I don't know what words he used but it was, "I think I like you." I was ready to pass out from all the stress when he asked what happened to my face. I told him and I was also shot by the cops. He put his hand on my shoulder and I was starting to fall from being so weak. He grabbed me so I wouldn't fall and held me up. I put my arms around him and I awoke several hours later and was in his bunk. I didn't know what time I got here but I knew it was before noon. I looked up and the man who helped me and he was standing here by my bunk. He helped me sit up and said, "My name is Clayton, they call me Clay."

I said, "My name is Al and I want to thank you very much for what you did." He explained to me what to expect here and you get to eat just twice a day, once in the morning and once in the afternoon. He told me I missed the dinner but he saved it for me and I almost cried when he told me that because he was so considerate and thoughtful. The food was junk because everything was instant and the coffee was black with no cream or sugar but Clay did give me some sugar. When you are here for a while you find how to live with the system. Breakfast is either oatmeal a container of milk a piece of bread and two packets of sugar. We learn to save the sugar for our coffee from people that don't use it. I found out that Clay was the head of the tank, you get this with seniority and he has been here the longest. I finished eating the cold food and Clay invited me to come out to sit with him on the bench. I told him what happened and why I was here. He said he was here just for protecting himself from police brutality. He said that the law requires that you could make one phone call. I was never offered that and told him that I asked several times but they would not even answer me. Clayton and I became friends right away and I am so happy to have him for a friend because he is really a great guy. I found out that I do not have a bunk and have to sleep on the floor under the bunk with a small thin mattress that I will get at eight o'clock at night. I cannot lay down during the day unless someone allows me to use their bunk. I have been here for several days and was just told that I will be taken to a court for an arraignment to enter a plea. Clay told me to plead not guilty and ask for a Public Defender because this is mandated by law. He told me it would be a lawyer and could help me. I did not know that and I thanked him for the advice. I was called to the bench but did not enter a plea I just asked for a Public Defender. I was appointed one right away and his name is Brian Hislop. He took me to a room and I explained everything to him. He asked me several times why I hit the cop and I told him what happened. I also told him what happened to me in Brewster, New York. I gave him Bonnie's phone number and address so he could ask her what happened because she was awake. She ran to the door as soon as the other cop just barged in on her and was still standing there when I left. I am very sad because I am worried about her and I don't know what the cop tried to do with her. I did not have any paper or pencil and could not write any letters. I did not know about the visitors and I hoped that Bonnie could come. The last time I seen her she was standing in the doorway naked with a towel around her. She was laying on the floor with nothing on when that cop just walked in to her house and I did not know how he could do that without a warrant.

She did not come to visit and I did not see anyone. It is nine o'clock Monday morning, almost three months have gone by and they just came to take me to court. I was hand cuffed again and attached to a long chain with other prisoners then taken to the courthouse. When my name was called I stood then heard the charges against me and was in shock. There were several drug stores that were robbed and the truck I drove from Moses lake was robbed of all the tools plus the acetylene torch and welder. Now I know why Bilco wanted to wait for his ride there. He helped load the truck, knew where the key was and what was in the truck. I pleaded not guilty to all of the charges and Brian took me to a room but I don't think he believed me. He said, "Did you tell the police about this Bilco?" I said I did tell the one outside also I said they could ask Bonnie and her family about him. He said the police investigated that and could not find anything about him. I said what about Bonnie I was with her all night. He said they talked with her and said she was sleeping so they would not use her testimony because of her age and she did not sound creditable. I said they just don't want to know the truth. He asked me if I knew where Bilco lived and I told him as I told the police with Carol, Bonnie's sister at her cousin's house. This just came to my mind and I told Brian that I couldn't think of this before but I remember he said he was raised in West Monroe Louisiana. He wrote all this down and I told him to call the New Milford Police and they will tell you about me. I told him that my Dad was a cop there also.

He said, "We all ready did and we do know that you have never been arrested before." I asked him about the police officer I struck. He said I hit him on the shoulders and knocked the wind out of him. He had a real big bruise but he's all right. I said, "I am very sorry I did that and I don't know why I did." I continued by saying he should not have said I was going to jail before he searched my car or asked me any questions. Brian asked, "He did say that?"

I said, "Yes that's why I hit him and he said he didn't care about getting Bilco." I told him he was probably running to Carol's house but didn't care because he had me, my car and the evidence. Brian said it's my word against his. I said, "I don't know how long Bonnie was watching but maybe she heard it too." He told me not to talk to anyone after this and I was only to give my name.

I was taken back to the cell and Brian told me if they could convict me on all these charges, I could spend at least fifteen years in prison and this was the first time that I thought about anything. I had no money I could get and could not make any phone calls to try to get help. I could not write and I felt that they could keep me here forever. I talked with Clay and he told me I could request a meeting with my lawyer because I forgot to ask him about a phone call. I did the next day and waited for a week before I had that meeting. I met with Brian and asked if there was any way I could make a phone call to my Dad. I told him I asked the cops when I was booked but they ignored my request. He said, "They have to let you make a call."

I told him I asked them several times and they would not answer me they just threw me in the tank. He told me that he does not make a lot of money as a Public Defender and was chosen at random. But he said, "I think this is going to be a very interesting case." I used the phone to talk to my Dad and I told him to please send me a few dollars. Brian took the phone and talked with him for several minutes. He did tell my Dad that he would help me and did believe me then told Dad to send a money order made out to my full name. I would never get any cash because it always disappears. I asked Brian I had a thousand dollars in my wallet and the police did not give me a receipt. I went back to my tank and forgot to ask if he talked with Bonnie so I asked for another meeting.

Two more weeks have gone by and I have been doing a lot of exercise. I arm wrestle with Clay because I want to build up my arms as much as I can. I am not weak because I was raised lifting heavy objects doing hard work on the farm and working at the Reddy-Mix, bagging potatoes kept me real strong and Clay was surprised. We always played cards, we worked out together every day and he taught me the walking ten. You do one push up and stand and walk back and then forward and you do two pushups and repeat until you reach ten. I do this four or five times a day. Behind our bench or table (I call it a bench), there are the steel bars keeping us in. There is a plate of steel welded about eight inches above the bench. I stick my feet under this plate between the bars and sit on the bench and go down backwards until you could touch the floor with your hands over your shoulder. This is the hardest exercise and we also hold the bars on our door and push our feet as far away as we could and put our head down between our arms then pull your chest and head back up. I must do this because I would go crazy. The Western Union came and I signed the receipt and signed one for the jail because Dad sent me twenty dollars. The commissary comes to our door every day and you could buy things such as milk, candy, cigarettes, tobacco and what I want, pen, pencil, paper, envelopes and stamps. Now I can write to Bonnie, I told her to find all she can about Bilco and told her what he did to me. I told her I have a good lawyer that is helping me get out and I would write to her a lot. I also told her that they took all my money because they were holding it as evidence and I had to wait for Dad to send me money so I could get everything I needed to send letters. I was told by Brian not to write anything about any evidence concerning the case. It took almost two weeks to receive a letter and I did not know until now that when I send mail they kept it here until they could screen it and use anything they find against you. It was the same with the mail coming in. She said she was very sorry about what happened, the police had no right to do what they did and they walked in without knocking when she was naked.

She said, "I was glad I was holding a towel but I cry every night because I miss you so very much." She also tried to come in to see me and they would not let her because I was allowed to have only immediate family. She told them we were getting married and they said not for a long time. As I said before, you are guilty until you prove yourself innocent. You are totally incarcerated and all your rights are taking away from you. My birthday was two days ago and today is Thanksgiving but I did not want to think about it. We actually got a piece of turkey and some good food. I am still waiting to hear from Brian and don't know what takes so long to do anything. It seems that no one cares even when you have not done anything wrong. The weekend went by and all I did was arm wrestle with Clay but I did my exercise. Clay is my only close friend here and I would be lost without him. I started smoking again the other day and found when you buy cigarettes everyone wants to be your friend then smoke them for you. I have learned you will always have friends if you have something that they want. When you run out of what they want you will also run out of friends. I stopped buying them and I am buying a bag of Bull Durham, a can of Prince Albert tobacco and rolling papers so I could roll my own.

It is Monday again and I just went to Brian's room. He told me he talked to Bonnie and she did hear the conversation and repeated what you said. I told him I got a letter from her and she did not mention it. He said, "I know I told her not to write anything in there about Bilco or you concerning this. I also gave her my card and asked her to call me if she could think of anything else. She asked me to please get you out soon and you did not belong in here." I asked Brian how long before I get a trial. He said, "I'm not ready and I don't have the evidence to properly defend you. I need more on this Bilco and no one could find him."

I asked, "Don't they have fingerprints because they won't find mine on anything but the crowbar," then I said, "What about a polygraph test? I'm willing to take one." He said that was in the works and the prosecutor's office is asking for one so I said, "Tell them I'm ready." It took two more weeks and I was given a lie test with the polygraph. I passed it one hundred percent but the prosecutors said it may help us go after information but is not admissible in court for a defense. I said what a waste of time. Bonnie sent me another letter and a picture of her which made me so happy to have it. I started to cry and I hung it up in my cell. I was already sad because it's just a few days until Christmas and I am so very lonely. I wanted to be married by now but I don't know if I will ever get out of here.

I just received a letter from Jen, she wished me a merry Christmas because she still remembers all the good times we had and she misses me very much. She also sent me a picture of her taken by me when we were together. She said "I am sorry for what happened to you and I know you are innocent. I hope you get out soon and I am not living with that jerk any longer. I'm just living alone now but I think my mistake was being with you so much and always had you when I needed you. I just didn't think and I'm also sorry to hear about Dorothy. She is really out of it, she's in a mental place and it is sad what happens to people. I am giving you my address in hopes you will write to me because I would love to hear from you. I miss you. Love, Jeanne."

I said to myself, "Why did she write to me now? I have enough trouble dealing with life now and this does hurt to hear from her." I don't love her anymore and I do love Bonnie. She has hurt me too much to ever go back and

I know I must forget about her but I also know that I did love her very much and wanted to marry her before. I started to cry and my mind became very confused. I thought about the nightmare I had about her and know my mind is playing tricks on me and I'm thinking of all the good times we had together. She was always so understanding, lovable and right now I just wanted to hold her. My mind went numb and I punched my fist hard against the steel wall. Clayton came right in and seen me crying.

He said, "What's wrong?" I said I just can't take any more and I just want to get the hell out of here. I didn't do anything wrong and I never hurt anyone but myself. He held me like a father would and said I could use his bunk to lay down. He helped me to his cell and I took Bonnie's and Jeanne's pictures with me then fell asleep but I awoke in a cold sweat and my fist hurt. I was still holding the picture's and I smiled when I looked at Bonnie's but I had Jen's behind hers and did not want to look at it now but I said I will never do to Bonnie what I have done to her. I will always be honest and I guess you could call it cheating. I know I want to marry Bonnie and I will forget my past because it was not just I that is to blame. I did write to her, I told her that I did wait for her, I would have forever and was coming home but when I got her last letter I knew I would never go home again. "I found a girl that I want to marry and I love her as much as I did you. It was you that broke it off and I learned to accept it then I went on with my life after being very hurt and crying for a long time. It is too late for me to ever turn back the clock and I know I can't but I know I will never hurt my new love for anyone. I will always have love and memories of you in my heart but I am very sorry for what happened to us. I will write to you if you like and if I ever do come back I will always be your friend. I cannot blame you for everything that happened and I must also accept my share. I would love to hear that you do go to college because I do care about you and your future. "Your friend as always, Al." I was very sad and I wrote to my dad and asked if he would please get me Dorothy's address because I wanted to write to her. I do worry about her and that's the least I could do for her. I know I still carry some love for her and Jeanne in my heart. Six more weeks have gone by and nothing has happened. It is almost the middle of February and I'm still waiting for my trial. Brian asked to see me and they took me to his room. He said my trial was scheduled for this Tuesday and he asked for a continuance. He said he had some news that could be good. He said Bonnie found a letter to her sister and it led him to check with the Louisiana Police. The report came back that there is a warrant out for Bilco for burglary and they want to question him on another case. He said, "This could change your whole case. I would like to wait a little while and see if they pick him up."

I got another letter from Bonnie and she told me that she has her sister helping her find any information about Bilco. She said she was told that there was a warrant out for Bilco now and I hope they find him. I now have my own bunk and I put the picture of Bonnie above my head. I also put the picture that Jeanne sent me when we were together and I put that one up too. I spend a lot of time when I am locked in the cell looking at them. I did have a picture of Dot but it was in my wallet.

We were awoken early because they brought in a new prisoner and he was put in my cell then locked us in again. I did not get to go back to sleep and I talked to the new prisoner. His name is Leon Cox and he escaped from prison. He was serving a life sentence for murder because he killed his wife who was a school teacher. This was in all the news and I do remember when it happened. He is blond about thirty years old and after exchanging names we talked and he asked me why I was in. I told him and he told me after our conversation, "N matter where you go, if it's a felony you will probably go to Quentin and if it's a misdemeanor it could be a road camp or industrial camp. When you get there they will ask you to fill out a report of what you do best or the most of. Tell them you are a cook and that is all you know how to do." I asked why and he said cooks have special privileges. "You will work in a kitchen cook or prep the food and you will eat better. You will also have a bunk house that is not confined as all the rest. If you're in prison it is still better to be a cook and Industrial places at least most of them will be on chain gangs working in the hot sun all day. I thanked him very much and he asked me for a favor. I said what? He said, "I am having some hack saw blades coming this week at seven o'clock at night. I just don't want you to say a word to anyone," and I said, "You have my word," but I never noticed this until I just looked. The guards make their rounds on the hour and the same time. They just walk up to the last tank which is ours and walk back. Between our bench and the outside wall is a dead space thirty six inches wide and used for maintenance. The bars on the windows are built the same as the ones around our tank and are also welded to a steel plate. There is a small space between the plate and the window sill. As soon as the guard left that night Leon took his blanket and pushed it close to the window. A few minutes latter two blades came under the window on to the blanket. He pulled the blanket which had the hack saw blades and he had his blades then bought a lot of chewing gum from the commissary. Clay and I wanted no part of what he was doing and it was too bad he was in my cell.

I just arm-wrestled with Clay, did my exercises and stayed out of my cell as much as I could. I don't want to know anything while Leon spent all day cutting the plate that surrounds our cell. He started where the water pipe comes to our toilet because there was plenty of room to get the blade through. He kept a wet rag from the shower against the wall to silence the sound and kept patching what he cut with the chewing gum. It took over a week to cut through the plate big enough for him to get through. Behind our cells is also a dead space for maintenance. When he reached the outside of our cell there were bars there before he got to the windows. He cut through them and put them back with the gum. No one ever goes back there and there is no reason to except for repairs. He had two more blades pushed in at night and I don't know how he made contact with the outside. I know he had visitors but their conference is monitored. I didn't much care and would have not left if they left the door open. Leon did cut through those bars and started to cut the ones on the windows. He cut through as far as he could in four spots and was finished for the night.

He always explained everything he did to me because I think he just needed someone to talk to. He said that there are rollers in the outside bars and when the hack saw tries to cut them they just roll so I said, "What do you do then?" He said, "I all ready cut the outside. Now I will use a blade on both sides of the roller and cut from both sides. I pull the two hack saw blades together at the same time and the rollers won't turn." He was almost through with just one more night to go but at twelve midnight our tank was raided by several armed guards. We were all taken out and the tank was searched. My cell is where Leon was escaping from so I got the worst of it. They took Leon to a high security block and we all had to wait in line where we were hand cuffed to a chain. When the search was over I was led to a room which was downstairs and interrogated for hours by several officers. I told them all that I could tell them but they kept asking me who gave him the blades. I kept telling them I would have no way to know. I said, "I don't know him, I'm from a different state and had no way to know him or anything about him." This was not good enough for them so I was threatened me then stripped of all my clothes and led into a room that was forty degrees or colder.

I had thumb cuffs placed over my thumbs and a rope pulled me up so my feet just touched the floor. I was very cold and my thumbs started to swell then hurt. I stayed there while they enjoyed watching me and just talking to themselves. You could see the look on their faces that they were having a field day. They asked me again, I said, "I told you all that I know so why don't you just kill me and get it over?" They finally said I guess he's telling the truth, then let me down and let me get dressed. They took me to my cell but when I was let in I found my pictures and letters were all torn up in little pieces. A lot of my paper and pens were broken or in the toilet. I knew I had to swallow my tongue or go through this again. I just knew that I would hate cops the rest of my life and more than I did before. I thought about the abuse I took from them creeps in New York. They must get their rocks off when they torture innocent people. I will say that many of the people in prison or jail are innocent and no one here cares because they actually have more fun punishing the innocent. I did not sleep the rest of the night and talked with Clay. I told him what happened while I was in the cooler and he said that was because I was in the same cell with him. This gives them the right to do this.

I said, "I didn't ask them to put him with me and can't believe that our laws uphold this kind of treatment even if we were animals." Clay said there is no law when you're in jail and they will do what they want. I said, "What could I have done, I told the truth and this guy is a murderer but should I have called someone and squealed." I would probably be dead before I walked out of here and I requested a meeting with Brian but I was sitting and talking to Clay when the whole building shook and sounded like thunder. Clay pulled me under the steel table and I was glad he did because pieces of cement fell from the ceiling and hit the floor. I thought a bomb went off and things kept falling. Clay said, "It's an earthquake and just stay under here because we did get them here. After what I have been through I don't think I am afraid of anything and welcome things like this. Maybe the bullies will have more to do then pick on the handicap. It was all over and there was stuff broken all over and I could hear the ambulances coming but we were lucky because there was not too much damage to our block. I found out later that part of the far end of this jail did collapse and people did get hurt. We still could hear the many ambulances come and go.

I waited for Brian to come and waited for two days now. He normally comes the next day and I waited until Monday then made another request. I did not receive any mail last week either. Today is Tuesday almost a week since I made the request so I asked Clay what to do and said that he most likely isn't getting the request because of what they did to you. He said, "But don't worry when he wants to see you they can't stop him." I was happy to hear that but he did not come again today. I laid here and asked when is this going to be over? I have been here more than four months and I don't know any more now than when I got here. I was talking to Clay as usual when the guard came in and took Clay with him. He said he was waiting for his lawyer and might get out soon.

I said, "I hope so but I will miss you a awful lot." He came back and told me it would take less than a week to process the papers for his hearing but he will be leaving any time now and he was very happy. I bought more writing material and wrote a letter to Bonnie and Jeanne. When I finished with those letters I did write to Judy. Her memory came to me and I just want to see how she is. I still don't have Dot's address and I am waiting for a letter from my dad. I gave them the P O box number and I did not mention the jail. I told them all what happened with the earthquake. I knew if I mentioned the raid they would never get the mail because it would get lost here in the jail. I wrote Judy a nice letter saying I missed her and I was sorry I had to leave without seeing or telling her but I thought I would have been back there long before now.

At two o'clock Brian requested to see me and I asked if he got my two requests. He said he got one this morning and I told him I made two last week. I then told him about the raid, what they put me through then how they hurt and tortured me. I said, "My thumbs and shoulders still hurt." He took notes of all of this and would use it in my defense. He said, "Do not mention this anymore," and said he would check why he did not get my request. He then said, "I have good news for you." When I contacted the police in Casper, Wyoming I found he was arrested there and a warrant was issued for his extradition to California. They had to get permission from the Governors of each state they crossed. He is now in custody and has admitted to the robberies while driving your car the night that the police came. He is a heavy drug user and was found with cocaine and other paraphernalia. He will be charged with that also.

"All of these charges will be dropped but you are still charged with assault to a police officer, resisting arrest, and reckless endangerment when you went through the road block with a lot of property damage. This is still a felony, a very serious charge and the police officer that you hit wants to bury you. I will do all that I can but you could be facing five to seven years max and would be five years max if I could reduce it to a misdemeanor. I will ask for a lesser charge and you may go to an industrial rehabilitation camp. I will try and get your case to go forward in the next ten days." I told Brian that they never told me I was under arrest and I think Bonnie will verify that. If she heard what the cop said before she must have heard it all. The very first thing he said after I told him I was the owner of the car was, "You're going to jail for a long time." If Bonnie heard that she heard everything. He told me he would get a statement from her for that. He said she all ready signed the first one. He said, "After I get these and the paper work from the prosecutors at the other court I will push your case as fast as I could."

I said, "Brian, I will always be grateful for what you have done." He made a phone call before I left and told me they were holding my mail. When I returned to my cell the mail was brought to me shortly after. I had three letters from Bonnie and one from Jeanne. I told Clay the good news and he was happy for me too.

Friday morning around ten o'clock the guard came to the door and said "Clayton" then his last name, "You're going home, get your stuff together." I ran to hug him and I said, "One more thing before you leave." He said what's that and I said, "I need to arm wrestle with you." He laughed and said okay. We held each other's arm for about two minutes and neither one could put down the other.

I finally put his arm down and said, "You let me didn't you?" He said, "No, I really didn't," but I will always wonder. He left and that was the last time I ever saw him. It was a very lonely weekend without Clay but I hoped to be out of here in the next two weeks. I finally received a letter from Judy and I didn't think she would write after me not telling her I was leaving. At least something was happening and of course I read Bonnie's letters first and I just love that girl so much. I read the one from Judy. She was very upset and wrote me a letter that I probably deserved. She said, "Why? All I ask is why did you have to lie to me and did I do something wrong? I thought you were my whole world. I gave you my trust and body. I told you everything about me while you were setting me up just so you could get what you wanted. I heard the rumors about your other girlfriends, were you screwing them too? I went a long time thinking, 'Why did I trust you?' You were the second person I ever went out with and was used again. How could I ever trust any man again and how could you do this to me? Did I hurt you and did I not give you all that I had to give? It is nearly a year since I have heard from you. What is it you want now and I just wished I had your address sooner. I got your letter and you apologize for leaving without telling me. How could you say you loved me, yet it wasn't important to tell me you were leaving and I don't understand that. Would you please write to me and tell me the truth? I thought about you a lot and now it will be more." She said, "I waited by the phone every day at three o'clock and every time I called your number it just rang and the last time I called the phone was dead. It would only take a single call and I waited every day for it. Signed; A very hurt Judy."

It is eleven o'clock Monday morning and I was lying on my bunk. I am sad that Clay is gone, I don't know what to do and I have no one to talk to now. I still have Jeanne's letter and have not opened it. I do not want any more guilt trips forced on me and have enough problems. I'm sure my time in prison will heal their wounds. But I don't know how long mine will haunt me. No matter what letters or how many I do get now what could I possibly do? I know that when I was with any one of these girls I would have given my life for them. I decided not to read the letter from Jen now and will keep it to read later. I feel that I need to send Judy an explanation first. After reading her letter it appears that she did not receive the letter I sent her last year and I do feel very bad. I think she was the one that gave me the courage to leave.

I wrote, "Dear Judy; It appears obvious that you did not receive the letter I sent you last summer. I did give an explanation, my address and was hoping I would receive a letter then. I am very sorry that you feel the mistrust for me while I have always tried to be candid and forth coming with all matters and concerns of others, especially those that I did admire and have been diligent within all my decisions. I know I mentioned the girl that was raped and this is one of the rumors because I have tried to help her back on to the road of life. I knew that she was incapable of achieving that on her own and time has proved me right. Since I have abandoned her plea for help, she has killed her mother and is now in a mental institution. I was the only person she could confide in and I carefully handled the situation based on opinions of other's and not arbitrarily. I have given this matter all I could offer until it affected my own ability to fully understand the situation and then became a victim of my own destruction. Since then all my relations became naive and not analytical.

"When I met you I did feel my life was complete and there was nothing more I wanted than to be with you. It was not my decisions with love that led me away but the confusion of life itself while I was losing the ability to coordinate my priorities. If an apology is needed for being humane then I will extend it gracefully. I can't emphasize enough that I did not use you but we used each other at a time when we were both vulnerable and did jump into this blindly. Please respond to my letter. Love Always, Al."

I then read the letter from Jeanne and will only highlight the subject. I did not read but a small part of it. "Dear Al, I am very sorry I have not written to you very many times and have always hoped you would return before now and I would have wanted to marry you because my heart has always been yours. I know I have made a big mistake and should have gone to college. You would probably have been back by then and I could have continued with my dreams. After your last letter I did decide to go to college, but I did tell you in the last letter that I threw the jerk out and I knew that I was still very much in love with you. Well, the jerk is back again, because I cannot make it on my own and I cannot go back home. I have missed my last two periods, I believe I am pregnant and going to have his child, so I must try and make the best of my life now. When you come back, would you please call me at the phone company? I still work there and will for a long time." She apologized for hurting me and said it was not intentional and she was sorry, but would like to make it up to me. "I know I will always love you and really want to be your friend. I would like very much to be with you just once more and hope you can forgive me. Love forever, Jeanne."

I am just a little over twenty-one and laying here in jail. It is no big surprise to me, because I have been in jail most of my life in my own mind and I am waiting once again for the road of life and I wonder what it will bring next. I lay here thinking of the girls that I thought I loved but in reality I have destroyed each one. Did Dorothy have a chance before she met me? Would Jeanne have gone to college and become someone? Judy is all upset and can't trust men and Bonnie is waiting for someone to get out of jail. I felt hurt and started to believe that Bonnie would become my next victim.

What could I promise her and if I am in jail for three more years, would she wait? Should I expect her to waste her childhood waiting for me? I knew I would also have to give her up, and I will tell her that I don't expect her to wait for me. If she finds someone she likes I will not blame her for it. It is in the middle of March and I am still awaiting my trial, but it should be any day, but I realize why I am here now, and it was not by chance, but to pay back for all the disparities I have given to the three girls that I thought I loved so much. I am laying here, very sad, and can't think of what is right from wrong any longer. I meant to hurt anyone, but I realize now that I never had the intelligence to properly conduct a sensible solution to the never-ending triangle of love.

The guard took me to see Brian and he said our case is on the calendar for this Wednesday. He said he wanted to go over the questions I would be asked at the hearing. I would plead not guilty to resisting arrest and Nolo Contendere to the other two. He said that means we are not contesting the charges but asking for lenience. I said okay. My trial came on schedule and they took me to the court. The judge was nasty and did not want to hear any excuse nor allowed me the opportunity to rationalize what I felt was the corrupt behavior of Police Officer's that were hired to protect us. He told me I could get the mandatory sentence, seven to fifteen years but my lawyer did a good job in defending me and brought up my perfect past record then told the judge my father was a cop and I already spent six months in jail. He asked the court to release me on parole then emphasized that the policeman violated my rights and none of this would have happened if the officer conducted his job properly. The judge denied that request and gave me the five years. He then read the sentence and said he would use me for an example to avoid this kind of behavior then continued with the sentence, five years with three years suspended and the jail time as time served. If I completed this term with good behavior the felony charge would be reduced to a misdemeanor.

I didn't know if that was good but I was allowed to talk with Brian before they took me away and I asked, "Brian, where am I going?" He said, "Kern County Correctional Institution," then said we did very well and you did hear what you could have gotten. He said, "Be very good and you will have a chance to get out in less time. They put me back in cuffs and were taking me away. I rode in a bus and was taken to Bakersfield. We drove off the road a long way and drove into a fenced in area. The fence was about twelve feet high and had swirl razor wire on top. I was led in to a building and was given different clothes to change into. They were a dark faded green with black letters over the left pocket and large letters on the back. It read, "Kern County Correctional Institution". I then had to fill out a questioner, Leon was right and I became a cook. I was instructed not to try to escape and would be shot if I tried. I was also told not to fight or give the guards a rough time and if so I would be sent back to jail to be retried then serve the full sentence. I was then led to a barracks with rows of double bunks on both sides. It was about seventy feet long then I was assigned a bunk number and the head chef took me to the kitchen. He was bigger than Clayton and was also black. I was happy for that because I have always got along very well with black people I think because of my black friends when I was growing up. It was right before dinner and I had to help prepare food. His name is Sam they call him Big Sam. Sam told me to start preparing something and I asked him what he meant. He yelled at me and said, "Do you know how to cook or not?" I said I did not have a lot of experience but I will do anything you tell me the very best I could but he didn't seem happy. We had a big drum to peel the potatoes. I just poured in a fifty pound bag and turned it on. I had to cut and chop onions then peel carrots. I was cutting onions but he grabbed my hand and showed me how to hold things when I was using a knife. I did not talk much and did everything as fast as I could. I worked for about two hours without stopping and had everything ready when he expected it. He asked me if I wanted a drink and I said, "I am not finished with the beans."

He said, "Come sit down here," but sounded mad and I did. He said, "You are a good worker but I need someone who knows what they are doing."

I said, "Please show me and I'll do it." He asked, "Why did you ask for this job?" so I told him about Leon Cox and what he told me. I also told him what they did to me in the jail. He said they really did do that and I told him why I was here. He did not report me and we did become friends. By the end of one week I could do everything he wanted and he was happy that I was working with him. He said, "Boy, you're not lazy, are you?" and walked me to the barracks. I could not believe it because we could walk around without hand cuffs. Sam took me to my bunk and said wakeup call is four thirty.

I was awoken and all the lights went on and I went to the kitchen with Sam. We were serving scrambled eggs, biscuits, pancakes and sausage. We also had sausage gravy, biscuits and grits. We had to serve six hundred people at each meal. We had twelve other people in the kitchen and they all had their own job. It was a very big kitchen and had four five foot flat top grills. There was one cook that just made pancakes. He had a long cylinder with a trigger on the bottom. He would pull it and enough mix would come out to make one pancake. He would fill at least three grilles and come back to flip them then come back and take them off. When all the food was ready we put it in large casserole pans and rolled it out to the service lines. There were two service lines one an each side of the entry door and there is four cooks on each side. They would put the food on the tray and you would tell him how much you wanted of each. You could have as much of anything you wanted. The only problem was you had to eat everything on your tray. When you finished you must take your tray to the check out window and if there was any food left your number would be attached to it then you would have to eat that before you could get anything else. I did not go out to the line and Sam kept me in the kitchen.

At eight o'clock every day we had to feed about sixty state police, prison workers, and highway employees. They had better food and were all served on plates that we fixed in the kitchen. They would not come in at the same time and some could be an hour late. We also had to do the same at dinner. The kitchen work was not all that easy and did keep us busy but we could eat anything we wanted and never had to wait in any line but I do thank Leon for that. We would only get one hour off during the day and I was allowed to go and walk around. On Sunday we were allowed to have visitors and I wrote to

Bonnie and asked if she could find a way to come and see me. Saturday and Sunday the only people that worked were the farm and kitchen help. I never got a day off while the other workers would go into the fenced in area and play ball and just do what they want. We only served two meals on Sunday because many inmates would have visitors and would not eat anyway. The visitors were not allowed to come in the fenced area they could stay outside and talk through the fence so you could also kiss them through the fence. This Sunday I knew that Bonnie would not receive my letter to come so I took a walk.

I walked to the end of one of the fields and took off my shirt and wanted to get a tan. I was so nice to have this freedom and lay in the sun. I then went back to the kitchen I did not like to watch all those people kissing their girl friends or wives. It made me sad because I missed Bonnie and I'm hoping she could get a ride to see me. I miss her so very much and in her letters she said there was not much work and the work force did not have any work for them, I knew she did not have any money and I did not have any to give her. I did write to my Dad and have not heard anything. I haven't received any mail since I've been here. Some of Bonnie's may still be at the jail. They are having blood drives twice a week and you get five days off for every time you give blood. I gave blood twice a week for the first three weeks and passed out and had to go to the hospital and get blood. They would not let me give any more blood but I was still credited the thirty days.

I have been here one month and just received a letter from Bonnie. She told me that her Foreman from the work force was finding work for her and he would bring her to see me this Sunday at two o'clock. I was so very happy she was coming. I was waiting by the fence close to the entry and she came in with someone in an old truck. She spotted me and came running to me, then she held her fingers through the fence and I kissed her. She looked so beautiful and I could see why I wanted to marry her. The guy that brought her was in his thirties and sat in the truck but he did not come over. I told her I only had ten more months and I should be able to get out. She seemed more happy to see me now then when she first came. She stayed for about two hours and he came over and said he had to leave. I told her many times how much I loved her and I wanted to get married as soon as I got out. She had tears in her eyes when she left and said she had trouble getting a ride here but hated to ask her Foreman because he made her work more hours without pay. I didn't have enough money to get her a taxi but I did write to dad to ask for some. I don't know why but he never wrote back and I only received one letter from my family. It was from my sister and I wrote her back. I became very afraid because I didn't want to ever lose Bonnie.

I tried to get some money from my allowance but they told me I could only get it when I leave. I was sad because she said her mother wasn't making enough money and she would have to move out. She said I have to find some kind of work and don't know what to do. I started to cry and thought about how we were before this happened. We had everything we ever wanted and were so very happy. We were building our home and planning to get married. I am so afraid that if she moves out she may do something wrong. She sent me another letter and said she had a job working with someone cleaning industrial buildings and she is very busy now but her letter was different and not like all the rest. It was short and nothing about us but she said she would be here this Sunday. I felt there was something wrong but waited by the fence. She came over to the fence and kissed me but she was not her usual but very cold. She said she had to leave and ran back to the truck. This was not the same truck she came in before and it was a different person and maybe a little older.

I wrote her another letter and asked what was wrong and please tell me. She wrote back and said she will be here again this Sunday at three o'clock. I waited but when she came it ended my life. I want to die and cannot face what's coming. He had his arm around her when they first coming but she pulled away when she seen me. She came to the fence and said, "I am sorry but I can't wait any longer and I'm living with Joe now. I'm pregnant and I'm going to have his baby."

I said, "I wish you all the luck in the world but I am very hurt to hear this." Tears came to my eyes and I said, "I really did trust you and would have waited for you forever." I said, "Will you please tell me the truth is this the same jerk that raped you?" and she answered as she walked away, "Well he really didn't rape me." I did not want to hear any more and walked back to the barracks. I laid on my bunk and cried until there were no more tears to come out. I said to myself I only have six more months and I should be out, why couldn't she wait? I was in great shock and could not believe this was the Bonnie that I knew and loved so much. I think if it was with anyone else I could have handled it but not with a child molester that raped her when she was a child. My whole body hurt and I don't know if I could handle any more. I became sick and wanted to vomit but just laid here until Sam called me to work.

I really suffered for the next six months and was always very sad. I know I did not do my work right but didn't want to lose my good time. I thought, "What kind of a life is she going to have now because this jerk works for minimum wages and will never have anything? How could she do it when she knew what we could have together?" I tried hard to do my work and felt a little better because I forced it from my mind. I know I will go back home when I leave here and just start over again. We had a complaint from one of the local police officers about his food so I told Sam I wanted to get even. I took an old boot and cut the sole from it and shaped it as a veal cutlet then breaded it and made sure it got to the proper officer. I had made friends with a few state police officers and told them why I was in here. They said that most of the local city cops don't belong on the force and their just cowards hiding behind their shields. I told them about my plan so they expected it an applauded me for it. It was so funny to watch him try and cut it but he must have become embarrassed and picked up the whole thing and tried to bite it before he knew it was a prank. All the other officers laughed their ass off but he got mad and I was a little scared to lose my good time but the other police that I told settled it. Shortly after I had to go for my parole hearing and told them I wanted it to be transferred to Connecticut, they said it would take a several days and I would have to stay in California until then. I told them that I did not have a place to stay and wanted to leave as soon as possible. They asked there supervisor then he said he could transfer it to my state and I will have to report there. They went to a locker and handed me a bag of belongings and I opened it up then checked my wallet.

I found that there was only eleven dollars in there so I asked them why and I had a thousand dollars in there when they took it. They said, "I'm sorry but this is what they sent from the jail and could you prove you had that much?". I knew it was gone and they stole it but we get punished for what they could do when they want. We have a fair system, don't we and I just want out of this corrupt place. They gave me my allowance and it was near seven hundred dollars then provided me a ride to the bus station. I went in and bought a ticket from the money I earned then walked out on the street. It was so nice to be able to walk the streets in freedom and my ticket was good for thirty days. I don't know why but I wanted to see if Bonnie was still at her mother's house and if I could find where she was. I flagged a taxi and gave him the directions to get there then asked him to wait while I seen if there was anyone there. I knocked on the door and Bonnie answered it. I looked at her and she was just as beautiful as ever but she did have a big stomach and I knew she wasn't lying. I asked her how she was and if she got married. She was not acting right and started to tremble.

She said, "No, he left me right after the last time I seen you because we had an argument over you. I told him I loved you and I hated him for forcing me to do what I did." The taxi driver started blowing his horn so I told her I have to go and I was going back to Connecticut. I turned to leave, but she ran over and grabbed me then held me. I could see that she was gasping for air and I was worried but I don't know why I did this. I turned all the way around put both arms around her and held her tight while our lips met. She would not stop only to breathe and was still panting. I let go and said, "I'm sorry but I'm leaving and I don't think I will ever be back."

I turned then went towards the taxi and I could hear her scream, "Al, please don't leave me. Please, I beg you." I kept walking to the taxi, but she ran after me and hung on to me. I paid him, gave him a good tip and asked for the number so I could call so he could pick me up. He handed me a card and said call any time. I went back into the house but she was still holding onto me and held me tight enough to choke me. I held her until she stopped shaking, then told her, "I will stay for a while but I am leaving but I will help you as much as I can."

She said, "But I love you so very much and I am so sorry. Please believe me." I went to the couch then put my hands over my face and said to myself, *I still love her with all my heart but I know I could never love that baby.* I didn't know what to say next and I knew I had to leave because I would be in jail again or hiding from the law the rest of my life because I knew I would have to kill him if I stayed here. She came over and started to hold me again but I did not say anything because I was searching my mind and started crying. I was sorry I didn't go back with the taxi but I knew I just couldn't walk out while she was crying and begging for me to stay. I know what I am doing could only hurt us more so I got up then walked outside, she followed me and I stopped crying but my vision was blurry. I walked behind the house so no one could see me and she was still with me. I seen the stakes that her and I had placed and they were right where we drove them in to the ground. I grabbed one and pulled it from the ground then threw it and said, "This to my love and happiness and here's to our love and future." I grabbed the other one then threw it also, and busted out crying very hard and walked slowly back in the house.

I went back and sat on the couch then put my hands over my face and held my head up with them. I was far from being nimble and unable to comprehend future consequences of any decision that I make now or the detrimental outcome. I'm still searching my mind and could not conceive a solution but feel I must be complaisant with her and yet not yield to promises I cannot fulfill.

I sat here without looking and she came to sit by me. I did not talk to her while I was meditating but I knew how much I loved her and I know I would give my life for her but could I ever love her as I did before. I also know I could never love that baby but I could and would if it was anyone but him because I hated that bastard so much. First he rapes this thirteen year old girl and gets away with it. He comes back when she is delirious and in the need of money and a job. He promises her anything he could just to screw her again, knocks her up and leaves. I knew that if I did stay here I would have to kill him and I will keep saying this until I do because I could not live with her as long as he was alive.

I looked at her and she was waiting for me to say something. Her eyes were asking me a hundred questions and I did not have an answer. I kept looking at her and could not find one word to say. I don't know what she was thinking but I could see she did not know what to say or do and was waiting for me to make the next move. I couldn't and I put my hands over my face again. I thought about her life with no education, a drunk for a mother, and no father. What could she do? Without talking I pulled her over to me, kissed her a small kiss and said, "I'm sorry but I do have to leave." She started sobbing again then held me very tight and would not stop crying. She kept her head on my chest and I could feel the tears running down towards my stomach. I knew what she was going through and it killed me to see her this way but I also know that I must be analytic and make the right decision. I have no money, no job and there isn't any work here because I don't have a car now but most of all I would have no future. I would watch her bare a child that I would most likely hate and I said there is no question to what I must do. I picked up her head and wanted to die when I seen her eyes. There are no words to explain what I saw, I felt her body go limp and she had no more will to fight.

I could only think about that night with Dorothy and what happened to her when I left. I pulled her close to me and kissed her then she pulled away just a little and she looked at me. She said, "Why? Why can't you love me, you did before and I only did it because I had to." She started to cry harder and said, "I never wanted to hurt you."

I stopped her then said, "Bonnie, You just said you never wanted to hurt me yet the last time you came to the prison it didn't bother you to say 'I'm sorry I don't want you anymore.' You looked me straight in the eyes and never shed a tear. You stood there and what you said was sticking a knife through my heart. It didn't bother you then but it did leave a scar in my heart that I don't think will ever heal."

She screamed, "I didn't think you were ever coming back because he told me you would be in there for fifteen years. I had to support myself and could not find any other way but believe his lies." I said, "I'm sorry I do love you but I just can't love that baby." She started to cry again and ran to the bathroom and slammed the door. I heard her yelling and I could not imagine what she was doing. I got up and opened the door then found her beating her fist on her stomach but I did not have the chance to ask.

She just screamed out, "I'll kill it, I'll kill it for you." I said, "You're not doing it for me and it wasn't my mistake." I did not want her to put a guilt trip on me as all the other girls did. She kept pounding her stomach so I grabbed her then pulled her from the bathroom and said, "Please! How is that going to help?"

She said, "I hate it already and I will never love it either." I knew I should never have said that because I did implicate myself into the equation and I knew that I must remedy that allegation. I walked her over to the couch and pushed her onto it. Then kneeled between her legs then put my head on her chest and held her. She put her arms around me with her hands on my back and I could feel her quivering. I had a very funny feeling being between her legs because I have not been there for nearly two years and it brought back memories so I got up and sat on the couch with her. We held each other without talking, then my mind went back to my childhood and I tried to compare it with hers. I thought about Judy with all the wealth with her parents. Then I thought Jeanne with wealthy parents, a beautiful house and not wanting for much. Dorothy didn't have wealthy parents but she always had nice clothes and never went hungry.

What does Bonnie have, and you could put all of her clothes in a five pound paper bag. Not a decent pair of shoes, no jewelry or make up and never had a bathing suit until I bought her one. What does she have for parents a mother that is a drunk and I believe a whore so what is her future? Knowing this is what makes it so hard for me and if I had a gun I would probably do her a favor if I shot her but no matter how hurt I will be. I know I cannot stay here. For the first time in a long time I believe I am using my Common Denominator. I turned to face her and said, "I'll tell you what I will do. I will stay with you tonight and we will talk about it tomorrow."

She said, Thank you for caring about me because I have no one else and I must tell you the truth because I don't want to live without you." I waited everyday hoping you would come back to me, but . . ." I interrupted her because I can't take anymore and I don't want to hear her excuses. It was near six o'clock and I asked her if she was hungry because we both haven't had anything to eat. I didn't see any food in the house and I didn't know how she stayed alive. Although her stomach and breasts were larger, I could see she was losing weight and her face was thinner. I did not have a car and did not want to pay for a taxi so I asked her if she wanted to walk to the café. It was almost two miles away but she said, "Yes, I'll go anywhere with you," and we took our time.

I was not cold out but enjoyable, I did not have a jacket because I left it at the jail so we walked slowly and made it there. We both had some food and walked back. It was so nice walking with her because I have not walked much outside in a long time. When we got home she put the pillows and blankets on the floor. These were the same ones that I left from before. We both laid down and talked about the jail. She thanked me for the food she had then told me there was nothing to eat and they didn't have any money to buy anything. I turned away from her and started crying again. I have never been in a predicament like this before and I don't know how to handle it as I said before life is too hard to live. I just wished that the cops used a rifle instead of sawed-off shotguns and it could have been over then. I wouldn't have been put through all the misery in the last two years or what I'm going through now. I know I can't walk out on her, but there is no way I could stay. We laid along side of each other then I turned to kiss her and I could feel those lips that I waited so long for. I knew I was getting carried away but could not stop. They were so wet, warm and when she put her tongue in my mouth I just melted in her arms. It was a long time since we were together like this and I thought about this almost every night when I was gone.

I put my hand between her legs but up until this moment I was saying no to myself that it would not be a smart move but my better judgment was losing the battle. I knew I shouldn't have made that move so I just pulled my hand back and said, "I'm sorry I did that."

She said, "What do you mean, you're sorry? I want you to and I want you so very much." She was joking and said, "Are you afraid you'll get me pregnant?" She stopped talking because she knew she shouldn't have said that. I did not like it and it made me think of him but I think she felt the cold chill that came across me. She then started kissing me and put her hand in my jeans.

I stopped her and said, "No matter what we do I still have to leave so you could stop now if you want."

She said, "I will beg you to stay until my last breath but if you are going to leave, I still want to do this so you will remember that I never did stop loving you." She got up and walked to the door then just stood there. I walked over to her and seen that cold look again and her eyes never blinked while I was talking to her. I kissed her ear and whispered to her, "I do love you." She turned slowly and said, "How can you say that and tell me you are going to leave me? Don't you know how hurt I am now for what I have done? What did you come here for anyway?"

I said, "I loved you enough to come to tell you good-bye but I also wanted to see the girl that made my dreams come true and would have given my life for until it was brutally destroyed at the prison fence. It would have been different if you just came alone and told me but to bring that bastard whom I hated the most in the world and held him in front of me. Was I supposed to laugh and say, 'I'm happy for you?' No, but I did. You not only stuck a knife through my heart but you left it there. You ask, "Why did I come here,' only because you said you were having his baby and I thought you would be very happy. That was what I expected and not this but if I knew this I would have not come because it hurts me even more to see you this way. Every time I look at you my heart gets torn apart more and how hurt do you think it was for me then?" I stopped talking because I was a little upset and said, "Damn it, I don't want to talk about it anymore or I will leave right now." I walked back to the couch and sat down.

I watched her walk towards me and said, "I am sorry. I said, "I'll tell you what, when I get home, have a good job and a place to live, I will come to get you. I will take you and the baby back with me then I will marry you. I will love the baby as long as I will never have to see him."

She said she hoped I could do this soon because she couldn't go on alone. "I know now after what happened and your here I don't want to live one day without you." I said, "I promise you what I said," then took her hand and said, "I love you more than life itself. I have since I first met you and I know I will until the day I take my last breath."

She said, "Thank you, I needed to hear that." I pushed her onto the couch then we both held and kissed each other. After that she took me to our blankets and we loved each other as before. I do feel much better then I have in a long time and wanted her now. I knew it had to be up to me now so I said, "I want to make love to you right and I don't want to wait any longer." I pulled her t-shirt up, kissed her nipples and pulled them into my mouth. I could feel that they were bigger and softer but tried not to think why but I never want to make love to anyone but her. We talked, kissed then she put her hand on me again and played with it. It did not get hard and knew it was because I was thinking about him then wondered how she was with that old Bastard. I thought and knew that I would have given anything if that didn't happen. I also knew if I made love to her the more I would wonder. It would have been different if it happened before we met but not during the time I was planning to marry her. I said, "I don't know why this happened but if this was my baby I would be the happiest man in the world. I would love it so much and know where I was going."

I stopped her and I wished I hadn't done that because for some reason I could see him on top of her with it in her. That made me sick and I felt dirty but I did not say anything to her because I couldn't hurt her anymore. I wondered if I could ever forget that or would I wonder every time we made love. She fell asleep while still holding me and every time I moved she would jump. I was afraid for her but I did mean it when I said I would come back for her. I am looking at her now while she is sleeping next to me and can still see all that beauty. She really is everything I ever wanted and I finally fell asleep with her in my arms. I don't know how long I slept but she woke me and looked very sad and said, "I'm sorry but I can't sleep." I was exhausted and still half asleep but I found myself making love to her.

This put my mind back to where it was before and I became more confused. I must have passed out from exhaustion and Bonnie awoke me at eight thirty. Just down the road from her house is a small convenience store where they have fresh made coffee and food so I had a coffee and bought some things for her. We walked around the block and I tried to explain that I did have to go back home. I told her I have no car, no job and no money but I gave her three hundred dollars plus all my writing material. I also gave her the address to my Dad's farm and I would be living there until I get back on my feet because I would have no problem getting work there. I told her to please write to me and I would write to her then if everything goes well home, I could come and get her very soon. She was sad that I could not stay but she said she did understand. I walked her back to her house and we held each other as if it was the end of the world. I knew now that if I still had a car, some money and my job back I would stay but I was still afraid I would not like that baby. She stopped and said, "We didn't do very much last night, could we do it before you go because I want you to be very happy when you leave." I felt this is all I could offer her now and we went back into the house. We laid on the blankets and made love like we did before then I called a taxi to pick me up. My bus ticket was good for thirty days and I did not have to report for probation for two weeks. I could have stayed a few more days but it would just make it harder for both of us. I called Henry and told him I would be up there to get my belongings and we both waited for the taxi. She held me all this time and did not say much. The taxi came and she gave me a big kiss and said, "I don't want to live a day without you." then ran without looking back. I think she was trying to say, "Please don't go, I need you," but she became incoherent from crying and sobbing.

I just said, "I will be back," then got into the taxi and left without looking. The taxi took me to Henry's house and I found all my things on the lawn. I only had my guitar, amplifier and a bag of clothes. I knocked on the door and no one would answer. His car was in the driveway and I knew they were both home. I did not occur to me that the theft of the truck I drove from Moses Lake was on the news and in the local papers so they must have assumed that I was the crook.

Jim was the one that got me that job and I'm sure he must have thought the same. I walked away and put the things in the taxi. We then went to the bus depot and I had trouble shipping my things on the bus because they weren't in boxes but the bus driver was nice and we managed so I tipped him. I got in the bus and said good-bye to California. I left most of my life, my love, my car, my money but most of all, my dignity and self respect. I could see I was born a loser and nothing has changed. This has always been on my mind but I always feared to mention it.

When I turned eighteen years old I had to register for the draft for military services. I went to the city where I lived when I was first born and they did not have a record of my birth. I went to the towns that I lived since and found the same. I then went to the city of Bridgeport where my family lived before I was born but still no record. I was amazed because I and everyone I knew had never heard of anything like this. My dad had an idea and told me to go to the Saint Vincent Hospital because that is where my sisters and brother was born. He also told me that I was born at home by a midwife but he remembered that a doctor did come to our house then. He also told me that we were living in Bethel then but I was born in the house in Bridgeport. I went back to the town hall in Bethel and told them about the problems I was having. I gave them my date of birth, November twenty nine nineteen thirty six. They spent several weeks trying to find a birth certificate with no outcome but they were still searching and told me that I could have not been born on the day I was celebrating because the doctor that came there was killed in an auto accident before then so it must have been an earlier date. I went to dad again and he said it was definitely in November and close to that time. Then said it could have been the preceding week but no earlier. He gave me a statement to take to the town so I went back to Bethel. The lady that was there was also amazed but very helpful. She took the information from my dad and all she could get from me and said she would contact Bridgeport and the Saint Vincent Hospital because they will have to create a new birth certificate. I was told to wait a few weeks then come back here to get a copy. I did and it was ready when I arrived. She told me that several copies were made and had to be sent to various places because I noticed that my copy was dark and had a long wide black space down the left side with some blurry spots on the face.

She said that was normal so I thanked her for all she has done. I sent the copy I had to the registration board along with the questionnaire and found that I could never be drafted because of my heart problems. I did not keep a copy then but knew I should have one so I went back and she gave me another copy. I never studied it only to see my full name on it until I packed my belongings to leave for California. I examined it and could find so many errors, my dad's name was not spelled correct and most of all the year of my birth was missing and left blank. I had this strange feeling and felt that I was not born with the hands of the Lord but by Satin himself and have been stigmatized to the point of never ending sorrow. Once again I will block this from my mind and try to carry on but I am finding it is inevitable and will not change while on this "Road to Life". I could see the signs that we were on highway sixty six but could only believe I am still on the road to Hell. We drove through Needles Arizona then we stopped in Phoenix where some people got off and more got on. The bus was full now and had very little room. I had a hamburger and coffee there then went back on the bus. We drove on into Albuquerque New Mexico and we had a one hour wait but I stayed on the bus.

I wondered about Bonnie and what she was going to do. I knew that there was not much in Connecticut and I was looking forward to getting letters from her. I started to miss her already and knew I was never hurt by anyone in my life as much as I was over her. I know I was going home but did not think about anyone there because Bonnie was on my mind all the time. We continued in to Colorado then ran into a blizzard. It was very cold out and we had a lot of ice on the road so we had to stay here for the night but I stayed on the bus and almost every one did. I fell asleep and was woken by the guy sitting alongside me. He was very restless and had his hands on me a few times. I did not know what he was doing and don't think he knew either.

It became morning then the food places opened and I walked in to get some food and a coffee. I only had a t-shirt on and I was cold but they gave us small blankets on the bus which helped. I walked into the restaurant and reached for my wallet. It was missing so I ran back in to the bus and looked all over but could not find it. I told the bus driver and he helped me search. It was not in the bus or on the ground outside. The guy that sat next to me was not around and I asked the bus driver if I could get his name. He said when he got back on the bus he would question him.

The bus driver did know I had my wallet when I got on because I tipped him for helping me with luggage. Everyone got on and the guy said he did not have it and he didn't take it but did not sit next to me again. The bus driver said there wasn't anything I could do about it. I knew he took it and that was why he had his hands all over me while I was sleeping. We still had at least two more days before we get to Danbury, Connecticut and I just had a little change that I would have to keep for the pay phone. The bus driver did buy me a coffee then we were able to leave when the sun came up and the roads were safe. I was very hungry and tried to sleep but I said what is going to happen next?

I started thinking that I should never have left Bonnie and started missing her very much. I think right now if I had any money I would have taken a bus back to her. It took two more days to get there, I was very hungry and only had water for the last three days. It was cold out and I was at the bus station in Danbury and it was not very warm in here either. I tried to call my Dad to tell him I was here when the operator said, "Al, where are you?" I recognized it was Jeanne and told her I was in Danbury.

She said, "Oh my God, I can't believe it's you and your back." I asked how she was and she replied, "I really don't want to talk about it." I said, "Is it that good?" She laughed and said, "I wish," then she told me that she had a daughter and was expecting again. I live from day to day but what else could I do. She said, "It would be very nice if I could see you because I still think about us when we were together but I'm not asking for anything but just to see you again." I did not promise her anything and said maybe someday. I would have liked to see her but knew it was not beneficial to either of us. It took my Dad over three hours to get here and I talked to Jeanne all that time. I know she did not want to hang up and I was sad to hear some of the things she told me. I believe she was crying at times but I knew it would have to stay in the past. I did not mind talking with her and I do not think it hurt just to talk. My mind did go back to the times with her but the love I had for Bonnie was overwhelming and I knew I could never love anyone as much as her. My Dad came and I hung up saying, "I wish you the very best" I did not have any money and went to work for our family friend Terry. His real name was James Terry.

He was black but we considered him a part of our family and we all loved him. He drove the hearse when my grandfather died. He had an Auto Repair

Shop and did auto body work also. I worked for him part time and did a lot of side work. One day I mentioned Jeanne to Terry, he said he knew her family very well and did some work for Bob at his office. He also knew Jeanne very well then told me something that really hurt. Terry often drove up behind a gravel bank near her house, where he could look down into it. He told me that he had seen Jeanne in different cars with different guys in the back seat naked with them. This was in August and September after I left. This was just two months after I left so after hearing that I never tried to contact her again. I heard that Dorothy was out of rehabilitation but I have not made any attempts to contact her either and believe I must restrain from being reminiscence. I did write Bonnie a letter and told her if she needed some money I would send her some. I told her what happened on the way home and what I was doing now. I also told her that I should be able to come soon to bring her here with me.

I am at the farm walking around and I could see the race track that was almost finished but never knew why my Dad had to stop. He had never explained that to me so I feel that I must discuss this with him now and hope to get the truth because I do not need any more skeletons in my closet. I am at the lowest point of my life and need to know what direction to take. We had a long talk and he did explain what happened. When he came to this country he was just born on the ship they came over on. Somehow he was not a citizen of the United States but did not know that. He found out when he was arrested for a felony with the black market. Somehow he could not get a citizenship or not having an education to know how to do so. He told me a lot more that I don't understand but he said a close friend black mailed him to stop building or complete the race track. I don't know if the state stopped him after they had evidence of this or if it was just the black mail. A very wealthy person, Pratt, assisted that friend with help to achieve this. His friend was Lee Pasquale, the man at the Ford place that I liked so much and worked for but I wish I knew it then. Not only that but my dad gave Lee four acres of property in his development and it was Lee that didn't want to hear the noise. The Pratt party owned a lot of property in the area and was a friend of Lee and helped Lee black mail him. I was very upset and I am learning that you cannot trust too many people.

I know that this cost dad a lot of money and I could see why he has not been happy and his health is failing. I had no way to go back to any of my old jobs and I wasn't sure that I wanted to. I wanted to start a new life at a new time in the road of life. But my mind went back to my childhood and it didn't appear to be any better. I also worked for a farmer that was only one mile away where

I could walk to. He gave me a job to dismantle two large barns that were very old. They were built with chestnut lumber which was going extinct and was worth money. I pulled the barns down with the tractor and took the barns apart piece by piece then I piled the lumber in piles for him. The foundation was made of field stone and I pilled that up to with the tractor. In one corner of the foundation there was a small section that was closed in with field stone. It was about six feet by three feet and was filled with hay that was all rotten but dry. I dug out the hay and found a Flint Lock Rifle and a Sword. They were wrapped in some kind of cloth and in very good condition. There was also a box made of metal with a lid on it. I forced it open and it had some kind of powder, some small balls and some small rope. I did not tell anyone about it and took them home. I showed these to my uncle Jack and he told me they were worth a lot of money and he could get enough money so I could buy a new car.

I asked my Dad if I should return them first, he told me no they have been there for two hundred years and I was the one that found them. I asked him if should let my uncle sell them for me and he said yes. I trusted my uncle because I did a lot for him. I did not have my two old cars any more, my Buick and Mercury because my stepmother junked them while I was in California. I still had my old ford and fixed it for the road and registered it again. I drove past the Park Cadillac Oldsmobile garage and spotted a Jaguar that looked like the one I wanted. I stopped to talk with John Taylor my friend there and he told me someone left it to sell for them. I asked if it had a bad clutch and he answered, "Yes, that's why it is not in the line to sell now." I looked the car over and the name on the sales slip and it was the same one. It has been in storage all this time. I asked him to see if I could buy it as is and how much. He did come back and tell me the bottom price was $3,500.00. I only had $2,200.00 saved and I asked Dad if he would cosign a note for me.

He said no and I had to argue with him then he said it was too fast for me and he was afraid I would get hurt. I finally convinced him then I went and bought it. I drove it home and found that after adjusting the clutch it did not have to be replaced right away. I am so happy to have this car but I will have to work much harder to pay back the loan that Dad signed for me. Terry while knowing that I needed to make more money gave me some lawn maintenance jobs and this helped a lot. The concession stands were still there and I asked dad if I could open my shop again. He said yes so I started to repair some cars there. I did not have many friends now and became a loner so I didn't get very much work for my shop. I did call a friend I had before I left to go west, he said he could get me some transmission work at the drag strip. I did a few but noticed my Dad was having more health problems and was taken to the hospital. I was told that he had Tuberculosis and was sent to the Grace New Haven Hospital. I did not go to the hospital that day because he was having so much testing. I was called the next day and was told that the findings were not Tuberculosis but Lung Cancer. This is another down fall in my life because there is no cure and he would not have long to live. This on top of everything else in my life, I did not have to lose my Dad now because he is only in his fifties. This hit me very hard and I just wanted to go there to see him. I was driving the Jaguar and flew home to change because it is fifty miles to the hospital but I wanted to get there. I knew he would want to see someone so I was driving over one hundred miles per hour and about eighty when I pulled in to the driveway. There is a big stone about twenty feet from my driveway and I slid into it. I tore the door panel off the door on the passenger side but I was so upset about Dad I didn't care.

I changed then flew to the hospital but when I got there my Dad was in a lot of pain and in hysteria. He said, "If you ever get cancer do not let them do this to you because you are much better off dead." They said the cancer spread to his other lung and spleen. They did more surgery and sent him home and said there was no more they could do. I watched my Dad die a little every day. They showed Florence how to inject him with Morphine and Demerol and he was like a vegetable. They finally took him to the New Milford Hospital and I was holding his hand when he died. The last thing he said to me was, "Take good care of Mother,"

I did not know who he meant, Florence or our real mom and assumed that he meant mom because we never called Florence mom. I have not seen my Mom in many years now and did not know where she was. I was told that the divorce forced her in to an institution and she was deaf and blind but after this I had nothing all over again. Terry did drive the hearse as he did for my grandfather. The farm was sold to pay for the hospital bills and Florence kept a small part and the development which still had buildings lots for sale. I did not have a place and stayed with my sister Arlean sometimes. She was just married and I did not want to impose on them.

I had some real tough times after my Dad died because I had no one to talk to or help me with problems and cried a lot about Bonnie. She never did write to me and I keep wondering what could have happened. I did tell her I would come to get her and I hope she didn't go back with that creep foreman again. I hope she at least writes to me and tells me the truth some day. I had trouble working and was not thinking about my future but I really didn't care

321

anymore. I have not played my guitar since I left California and don't care about that either. I think I just wait every day for Bonnie to write to me so I could go and get her because I miss her so much. I remember that I did pray to the Lord not to take her from me and I can't understand why this happened. I ask *Why* did I let Bilco take my car, why were the police so rotten and not rational as we expect but most of all why couldn't Bonnie wait just a few more months for a lifetime of love and happiness? I just can't accept what happened and will I ever get a break in my life but I believe it still has something about my birth certificate and what happened when I was born. I felt so bad I just drove to the town park because I had no place to go and I thought I would sleep here in my car. I drove in and went to turn around then stopped.

I could see Jeanne running down the hill towards me but I knew my mind went back to the last time I was here. I became very sad and drove out because I don't need any more torturous memories. I drove around and wanted to drive to California but I feared that she may have moved and I wouldn't find her. Then what would I do? Besides, if she really did love me she would have written or called me. I did try and call her but just to find the phone disconnected.

The next day I went to see Terry and he asked me if I wanted to drive a lady to New York City, then wait two hours for her and drive her back here. I said who and he said a friend of Bill Styron the famous book writer and my brother Mike and my sister Arlean worked for him. I said sure and it would be just two days a week but I would be paid very well. I told him I would and drove her there three times. She was a very nice lady and also had some hard times in her life. She looked to be near seventy years young and I did listen to her tales of woe. On my fourth time driving my Ford to get her the lower ball joint broke on my car. This allowed the A frame to drop to the road without notice and the frame caught in the blacktop, then the car turned over. It was a convertible and I only hurt my elbow. I do have seat belts installed but was happy I wasn't using them because when the car started to go over I pulled myself under the dash on the passenger side.

I walked to the nearest house and met a girl I went to school with and her brother was there. He offered to bring my car to the back of his house so I didn't call the police. He had a back hoe and turned my car back on it's wheels and towed it. While we were talking he mentioned that I could get a job with Roger Straiton the well driller. I was glad that I did not work for Styron long because Arlean was a baby sitter for his daughter when she was fourteen and she said he tried to rape her when his wife was in Martha's Vineyard but he said

322

he would have her arrested for stealing money and she was making this up. I know what the cops are like and I'm sure he would win because he is popular and has a lot of money but it wasn't much after when he lost a million dollars in a law suit. His wife was backing into a parking spot when she backed into a young girl that was a model and crushed her legs. This happened while she was at her resort in Martha's Vineyard. I worked for Roger until winter and he said I was a very good worker and operated a drilling rig alone just after a few weeks. I drilled about one hundred wells with him then worked for a building contractor building new homes. His name was Lee Perkins and I helped build several new homes on Pleasant Rise in Brookfield. Before this I did not have a place to live and stayed in my car a lot or with my sister Arlean but it was a long drive to her house. I knew I needed I had to save money because I wanted to go back to California to find Bonnie. I still think about her every day and miss her very much and I am very upset that I didn't bring her with me.

I was lucky because a co-worker had a room he would rent to me and I took it. His name is Ed Shrack, his wife Margaret with two daughters Libby and Marie. After staying there I just loved that family and they reminded me of the Watkins in Fresno. While living here I noticed a pretty girl walking near her almost every day and she started to wave to me and I would wave back. I have not had a girlfriend since Bonnie and I became interested in meeting her. I asked Margaret if she knew her and she said, "Yes, that's Sherry but be careful because I hear she's a heart breaker."

I said, "What else is new?" Again I got a break because my sister Arlean moved to the apartment just above Ed but not knowing it when I went up to visit her I found Sherry was there and I was very surprised. This complete episode occurred during the transaction of me acquiring my gasoline Service Station and Auto repair while I was very busy and not heard from Bonnie since I left her more than a year ago. We talked a little and I knew I would love to go out with her. She didn't look like Bonnie but acted a lot like her. She left and said, "I'll see you around." It was on a Sunday and I would come to rest in the afternoon for a few hours then go back to work.

This one Sunday Arlean was having a clothing party but didn't tell me. I was sleeping on her couch as I do many Sunday afternoons when I was awoken by girl's voices. I did not want them to know I was awake but when I peeked through my hands a noticed a lot of girls in the next room trying on clothes. I couldn't believe it, not only was Sherry there but I watched her take off her bra and try on several different ones. Her breast looked exactly like Bonnie's and it really brought back memories. Just then Arlean showed up and shortly after the girls left. She came to me and shook me and said, "Get up, it's almost three o'clock." I sat up and noticed that Sherry was still there. I became shy because of what I seen and may have showed it.

I had a coffee then said. "I have to go to work," but I did remember that Sherry also had to go home. I said, "I will give you a ride home if you want," and she said, "I just live on the corner."

I said, "I know, but I'm going right past your house now." She said, "Yes, I would like that," but as we were in the car she asked me, "Were you sleeping all the time we were here?" I said, "No, I awoke and seen you change your bra. She didn't look surprised but said "Well what did you think?"

I said, "What do you mean?" and she replied, "Well, did you like them?" I said, "What the bra?"

She said, "No my boobs."

I said, "Why was I supposed to?"

She said, "You could at least say yes." I said I was only joking but they're probably the nicest that I have ever seen. She said, "You really did like them."

I said, "No! I loved them." We got to her house and she said, "I'll see you around," she stood with the door and said I go to Arlean's a lot so I said I may see you there. I left and said to myself this is the best thing that has happened to me. I did not see her all week but just to wave to her when I passed her walking but I did tell Arlean that I would like to go out with her. That Friday I had to go to get some auto parts so I took the back road, and stopped at Arlean's. I found Sherry there but she said she was just leaving because she had to go to work. She works for the First National Store and starts at three p.m. It was only twenty after two and I asked why she was leaving so early.

She said, "I have to walk there, so I said I'll take you if you want." She said she would like that so we had time to talk then I took her to work. She thanked me very much with a beautiful smile and that made me feel good. I went back to work thinking about her and knew she walked back home at ten p m, so I went home at ten fifteen and hoped she was walking. I did not see her so I went to Arlean's and not to Ed's. She was not there but I did stay to visit. I noticed Arlean's guitar and asked if I could play it she said yes and I started to play it. This is the first time I played it since Fresno. While I was playing it the phone rang and Sherry asked who was playing the guitar and she said Al so she asked if I would play one for her. I said I'm too tired to go there now but she said I mean over the phone. I said okay and I'll play "I'm Gonna Knock On Your Door" she told Arlean that I like it very much. I went down to my room and fell asleep. I went to work and thought about Sherry, she is a very good looking girl and acts much more mature then the others. She has long dark brown hair with brown eyes and I would really want to know her better. I stopped at Arlean's again and she told me Sherry wants to go out with me. I went to her house and knocked on her door and her mother answered. I said, "I am here to take your daughter out." Sherry yelled out, "You don't have to ask her." but I said I like to be polite. Sherry came over and held my hand so I said it was nice talking with her then left. She sat right next to me and I put my arm around her and held her close.

She told me she remembered me from when I played at José's and I was with Jeanne. I said I don't remember that was a long time ago. It was too late to go to a movie so we went to the Sycamore Drive In. They also have very good food here, loud music and car hops. We finished our food and she came over and kissed me on the lips and said that's for buying me the food. I said couldn't I get a bigger payment, she laughed and our lips went together and we stayed that way, while I was enjoying every moment of it. I said thank you and that was very nice.

We have dated several times now and were getting very friendly but I could see I liked her more every time. Sunday afternoon I picked her up to go to the Drive-in Theater because she wanted to see Love Story. We got there early and walked around the kids play ground and she said, "You really like kids don't you.?" I said I loved them and wanted my own some day. She did not answer and we got back in to the car. We talked about life and its downfalls without revealing our own past. But our conversation appeared to be congruent and much easier to conciliate then the younger girls. She is older and much more mature and shows it in every way. We watched the movie but she did notice that I was very quiet and asked, "What's wrong?" I said I'm just sad when I think about my complete life. I was really missing Bonnie and I know I was trying to replace her with Sherry. I feel like I am doing something wrong but I don't know why she never wrote to me, so what am I to do. Sherry said, "Could you explain it to me?" and I said I would, but please not now.

She came close to me and just held me tighter then made me happy because she said, "You'll never be sad with me." That was very sweet and comforting and I almost believe it, but my past experiences may prove different. We left the drive in but I didn't want to go home yet so I asked her if she wanted to go to the back to the Sycamore Drive In. She said yes and we listened to the music. She talked about her past problems but I did not indulge into mine. We did agree that we should work for a strong and secure future together. Because, I do believe that we are searching for the same goals now.

It is summer and she asked if we could go to the beach tomorrow. I said, "I would love to, and maybe I could see more of your sexy body."

She laughed and said, "Now you're dreaming," but when we got there she changed into a two piece bathing suit and I told her, "I just love this dream I'm looking at." She thanked me and took my hand and found a place where we could lay in the sand. She really is beautiful and I am very proud walking here with her. She turned a lot of heads and I never noticed her making eye contact with any of the guys there. While I was laying there with her I know I am forgetting much of my past. She asked if we could go to the other end because there are too many people here and they seem to love to kick sand in your faces.

I said, "I know a place where no one goes and we could walk there," so here we are. She put the towel down for us and we laid in the sand. The bank here was steeper so we just laid with our legs in the water. We were kissing each other and she put one leg over me and her knee was on my stomach. I reached down to hold her leg close to me then turned to face her. I was still holding her leg but she held me even tighter. I kept kissing her then her neck and ears while holding her and moving my butt up and down. She started to breathe a little faster and harder and I could feel her sweating. Not saying that I'm not. This told me that she wanted me as much as I wanted her. I heard some voices so we got up and left. I went the back roads to Danbury but had to pee very badly and I told her. She said, "Go along the road like all guys do."

I said not here and went on an old abandoned road. I stopped near a big tree with a sandy area and went there but as soon as I took it out she sneaked up behind me and held it. I said, "What are you doing?" and she said, "I just want to hold it and watch because I've never seen this." Of course I stopped peeing and she still had a hold on it so I said all right. I started to pee again and she was so curious and was trying to write my name in the sand with the stream. When I finished she kept hold of it and was squeezing it and I said, "Please." She said, "But what's happening to it?" and I said, "You know what's happening, but please," then she stuffed it back into my jeans. We then drove to the Sycamore and we had a snack then just drove around and talked. It was getting late so I drove to her house. It was dark and I shut the engine because I wanted her to stay here for a while but I didn't have to ask. She turned towards me and kissed me while putting her hand on my lap and was searching for it but did not have to search long because she could feel the bulge now. I just sat still and kept silent and let her have her way. She slid her hand under my jeans and found it, then squeezed it. She removed her hand and opened her door and started to get out. I said, "Hey, what was that all about?"

She said "I just wanted to know how much you wanted me and you just showed me". I said, "Boy, what a dirty trick," then I grabbed her and pulled her back over to me. I held and kissed her and said, "I want to make love."\

She said, "When?" and I said, "Right now." She laughed and said she still couldn't believe I made her make the first move. I said I respected her and wanted to gain her trust. She said, "My God, you know I trust you," so I started the car and drove to the vacant lot across from Ed's house. Our lips went together and our bodies united. I was in heaven again but could also respect her maturity. I was very excited, then felt her tighten her legs and she screamed, "Don't stop, please don't stop," and we finished together.

My First Really Bad Accident

Sherry and I had been going together for about four months now and were very compatible because our thoughts were congruent and we are congenial. I know that I love her very much now and I am happy to be with her all that I can. We have gone somewhere almost every weekend and to most of the amusement parks. We never have cross words and both wanted a nice home and children. One day while driving home from work, I had almost reached town when I stopped for a traffic light. I looked into my rearview mirror and could observe an auto coming towards me at a high rate of speed. There were cars right in front of me and there was nothing I could do, so he struck the back of my car. I was thrown backwards, then against the steering wheel. I felt excruciating pain in my neck and back, then just slumped down into the seat and the next thing I knew the ambulance was there. They strapped me to a board to support my neck and found myself in the emergency room. After several hours I was told that I had fractured my vertebrae. The doctor came to the room and stated that the vertebrae nearest my skull was fractured and the disc was crushed and I needed surgery, but there was a chance I could be paralyzed. I said, "But I am all right now," but he told me about the chances during surgery. At this time my life further became incredulous and I didn't want to hear anymore. I declined any surgery and he said they would have to put a cast around my neck. I allowed that but told them I did not want to stay here any longer.

I had to sign some papers then they discharged me. I called my brother and he came to get me, then we went to look at my car. The complete rear end was smashed and the gas tank was shoved under the back seat. He said I was lucky it didn't explode. I uttered, "Why was I lucky?" I went to Arlean's and then called Sherry and she came right over. It was Saturday and she wondered why she hadn't heard from me. I told her that I don't have a car now but Mike told me to call his father in law so I will later. I did call him and I was going here in the morning. I took Sherry because I wanted her to pick out the one she wanted. The first one she spotted was a white Chrysler Convertible and I couldn't change her mind. I bought it, then put my plates from my Ford on it and we drove home. I was still in more pain than I had yesterday and just wanted to lie down. The next day I did go to work but could not do much but just be there, but after a few days I was able to help. Sherry and I still dated, but it was hard getting around, but I was happy just to have her with me to help me try and understand life. Three months have gone by since my accident, they took my cast off and I feel well. Sherry and I are just fine and looking at different homes we would want. We talked about our future and hoped to have children. This took me back to Lamont when Bonnie I and were planning our home and the room for our baby. I remember driving in the stakes and how happy she was. I know these memories will never leave me and tears came to my eyes. Sherry asked what was wrong and I told her my past will always haunt me. She said, "But you're crying," and came to hold me tighter. I said, "I know, I am so afraid I will lose you also."

Leaving California

My mind goes back to when I left Bonnie and I could see her screaming for me to stay but I was too hurt for what she did, but I think now I did more wrong then she did and will suffer until I know the truth. When I first took the room with Ed and Margaret, I had a very bad nightmare about Bonnie. I dreamt that I missed the bus and was still in California so I flagged a taxi and went back to Bonnie's house. I knocked on her door but she did not answer but the door was not locked so I walked in. Bonnie was lying on the couch with her hand hanging to the floor. I ran to her and she was covered with blood, I kneeled by her and kissed her on the cheek but she was cold, her eyes were wide open but were not focused. I screamed, "Bonnie, Bonnie," while I picked up her hand I found she cut her wrist and knew she was dead. I screamed, "No! Not my Bonnie," I was still screaming that when Margaret came to my room and was shaking me.

She said, "Al, it's just a nightmare," but I kept looking around for Bonnie. I looked at Margaret and screamed, "Why her? Why her?" I was having trouble breathing and was gasping for air and it took a long time but I did realize it was just a bad dream. But I know I could never be happy until I go back to Lamont to find the truth. Ed and Margaret went back to sleep but I couldn't. I had many bad dreams but this was too real and I know I was really there. I could not sleep and the more I thought it, I knew it was some sort of transmigration of souls and she was warning me. I had no right leaving her there in that condition and I already killed Dorothy's mother for the same reason. The nightmares did not stop but I was able to control them better. But I did have another bad one. I awoke and Bonnie was standing at the foot of my bed pointing her finger at me. I just looked at her and said, "Are you ever going to forgive me?" Then she disappeared. I had many more of these then, but since I met Sherry I have had very few. It was strange because one night while parking with Sherry she said, "I have known you since you played at Jossey's and you look the same, you haven't gotten any older have you? What are you?" She looked at me very strange and I said my life stopped when I left California. I was only joking but it does seem strange because I am twenty three years old and Sherry is eighteen and when we went to a night club they carded me and not her. Everyone that doesn't know me tells me that I look like I'm no older then eighteen. I do know my age but I can't explain it.

My First Business

I bought into a partnership in a gas station, garage with Mike's brother-in-law, Fred. It was owned by Fred and his brother Vinnie so it was just Vinnie and I now. We worked together very well for a few months then I bought him out. I finally had my own auto repair business but later I made a mistake and took my uncle Jack as a partner. You remember that he was handicapped and lost one leg. While feeling sorry for him I allowed him to become my partner, then we incorporated and him being much older I made him president. He became very bitter towards life and took his mistake out on everyone. It came to the point that I wanted him to buy me out or I had to leave. After all these years working for my own business I find another snag and once again from someone I tried to help. Then after several arguments, one was that I built my own car from all pieces and parts. I used the jaguar frame and engine that I saved from my accident. When it was nearly completed everyone stopped to look at it and it had future designs. This just fueled the fire between us because he believed that I did not have any free time and should work every hour to make him money. I only worked on my car on Sundays and late after hours but he started to believe that he was the owner and I was just a mechanic.

I pacified him as much as I could because I did feel for him but we had another fight because he hated Sherry. He told me I shouldn't have a girlfriend and should be working more. I was working between seventy and eighty hours a week and that wasn't enough for him. I told him he was useless to me and should leave or I will. He knew he couldn't operate it without me so he left. It was just one week later that my uncle came back. He was driving a new Pontiac but I didn't know at the time that he sold my sword and rifle that was made in the seventeen hundreds. I found that this is how he bought his new car. He apologized for being mean then told me he was moving to Garden Grove, California. My heart went into my throat because this is just a few miles from Bonnie's house and I know I must go there. I have not heard from her since I left her but I am scared after my nightmares but I will never rest until I find the truth. He told me he was leaving in a week and was driving out. I knew I had to go there. I started to think about the way we were, why she never answered my letters and why her phone was disconnected but I knew I would have to find the truth and this will probably be my only chance. I buttered him up and told him I would drive him there. I assured him that my brother John, Jacky, and Bobby with their friends would operate the business while I was gone. He finally agreed and I am heading for California. I knew all the roads and the fastest way to get there. We drove nonstop and I drove most of the way but took a few breaks to rest my eyes. The closer we got the more afraid I became. I just wish she's not married because I know I will just grab her and hug her. Right now my complete life went back to when I was with her and I couldn't think about anything else. I spotted the sign, "Garden Grove" and I found the house with no problem.

We were at his son John's house, who is my cousin and started there for a while to visit, then went to his daughter's house where he was planning to stay until he bought his own home. On the way there I asked if I could take his car because I wanted to visit a friend but he said, "Your flight isn't for another week and you could take it anytime." We drove into their yard and they expected us and met us outside. Her name is Inza and her husband is Jack. They also have a daughter Patty, that I remember from when they lived in Connecticut but she was very little then. We went in and had lunch and talked for a while but I talked to Patty mostly. She was my age and was very nice. We got along like brother and sister and we went to the beach. I used my uncle's car and it was the Santa Monica beach where Bonnie and I always went and I started to hurt very much because I could see her writing my name in the sand.

Patty noticed that I was sad and asked, "What's wrong?" I told her a little about what happened and she interrupted and said, "You lived here?" and I said, "Yes, in Lamont." I said, "I wish I knew you lived this close because I would have come to visit." *I said to myself, I wish I did know then, because Bonnie could have lived with them while I was in prison.* Her and Patty were the same age, I know these people are kind and that way with people. We had a lot of fun, but all I could think about was seeing Bonnie. When we arrived to her home, I told my uncle I wanted to take the car tomorrow afternoon and he agreed. We had dinner and they showed me where I would be sleeping. I awoke when I heard voices but was still tired because I was so excited about seeing Bonnie but thought, what if she moved or got married? I really want to see her and her baby because it would kill me to go back and not see her. It seems very strange because now that I am back here it doesn't seem that I left and it would be normal for me to see Bonnie. I waited until after lunch then left to what I was waiting for so long. Traffic was very heavy so I took all the back

333

roads, then finally passed our favorite café. I was very nervous and I believe trembling a little but I want to appear normal when I see her. I drove slowly into her driveway and could see that no one has lived here in a long time. The grass was grown high and there was grass growing up through the driveway. I left my car and knocked on the door, but with no answer but I could still see her standing here pleading with me to stay. I tried to look in the window but it was dark and the windows were cloudy.

I walked to the back of the house and seen the ditch we dug, although it was all grown over. I became afraid because I remember what the police did to me here. I drove to the café because I wanted some information and sat in the same place we did then. I ordered a coffee and a sandwich and asked the waitress if these are the same owners that were here two years ago. She said, "They have been here a lifetime," so I asked if I could speak with one of them. She said yes and took my order. I drank some of the coffee but when I took a bite of the sandwich it would not go down and I had to take it from my mouth and wrap it in a napkin. I guess I was too nervous to eat.

The owner did come over and I said, "I need some information that is very important to me and I hope you could help me."

He said, "Yeah, sure, if I kin." I then asked if he remembered Bonnie and I when we came here a lot two years ago. He replied, "You do look familiar, but I'm not sure." Then I said she was a young blond that lived just around the corner and I explained the house to him. He said, "Yes, Yes, there was a suicide there," then called to Millie, his wife. My chest tightened and I could feel the cold sweat come over me. She came right over and after he told her what I wanted to know she said, "Yes, the girl that lived there killed herself." She said the complete neighborhood was talking about it because she was pregnant and was close to delivery. I heard talk that they tried to save the baby but they got there too late.

I was very incoherent and asked, "How long ago did this happen?" and she said, about two years ago." I could not hold up any longer and went hysterical. I tried to scream, but nothing would come out, but I was sobbing very hard. I had so much trouble breathing and did not want to do this in public. Millie left, but came right back with a wet towel. It was cold and it helped my eyes so I was able to see. 1 got up and started to walk out but my knees gave out and I fell back into the seat. Millie tried to comfort me and I could see everyone watching. I tried to get up again because I was so ashamed to be here this way but a customer came and helped Millie walk me to my car. When I was seated she asked, "Was that your wife and baby?" I said, "No, she was my fiancée and the baby was from when she was raped by an older man. She was also raped by this same person when she was thirteen but the police wouldn't do anything for her." I gave her his name so she could tell everyone.

She said, "I do remember now when you and her came here before and I am so very sorry." I said thank you very much then I noticed there were still people staring, so I drove to the nearest place I could pull off and found my life so absent. I know I could scream but who in the hell would care? I tried to tell myself that it was not my fault and that is was the fault of the rapist, but I knew that I could have kept her alive. I hate myself for not staying longer, at least until she could understand what I was telling her. But where ever she is I want her to know I never stopped loving her and never will. Tears were flowing from my eyes and I did not want to go back to Jack's house so I pulled into a parking lot and just meditated. I know now that I was here to witness her execution and it was not a dream but she did find a way to have me there through transmigration of souls. I know now that no one will ever measure up to her and she will always be my only true love. I know my love for her is imperishable as hers always was for me. I was just sitting here crying but I did remember that I begged the Lord not to take her away from me and I screamed, "Why? Why did you, and you took them all from me and where were you when I was a child? When I was being tortured every day and the worst thing you did was to take away my chances of having children. I remember going to your church when I was just a little boy and walked seven miles in the dark and cold because I believed you would come to help. I asked for nothing but just stop the beatings and mental torture. I can only believe that you were never there for me and I was born in the hands of Satan. I know now that I will have to live with it, or myself pay the ultimate price. I also know that everything I do from here will be a cover up to escape the real truth. I hurt so very much and really don't know what to do because I believe I could have avoided her death, but again this may have been predestined and is where I was placed on this "Road to Life"

I drove back to her house praying this was just another nightmare but found the same. I walked to the back of her house and could visualize her with the shovel digging the ditch which was her foundation of our love and happiness. I fell apart again and kneeled on the ground and again screamed, "God, where were you when she needed you and what did she do so wrong to be tortured as a child and had to pay the ultimate price?" I know she never hurt anyone but herself and when we were together we were congruent and always congenial with each other, more than anyone else I was ever with. I just wished there was a way to conjure the last time we were together so I could give her the gift of life which she deserved more than most. I know I could never really love again although I may believe I will at times.

I will just want a companion so I don't have to live alone and I'm not sure what my relation with Sherry could be now because I'm sure I will have trouble dealing with this for a long time and probably the rest of my life. I know I still love Bonnie and told her I will until death, so how could I ever love again? I drove to her sister's house, then went to the door and I did not know these people. They said they bought this place last year and did not know the previous owners because it was vacant then. I drove around and stopped at the park until I felt better because there were no more tears to fall. I went back to Jacks house and they noticed that I have had a bad time then asked what happened and if they could help. I just told them that a very close friend was raped when she was thirteen years old and he kept raping her. The police would not help her because of her parent's history, so she ended it the only way she knew. I just hung around Patty, but I did not want to discuss this any longer. I just told her Bonnie was my girl friend when I lived here and what Bonnie meant to me. Jack and Inza said they remember that it was on the news. I asked them please not to talk about it anymore because I was too upset and I wanted to go home.

My flight was for Wednesday with Los Angles International and Patty called the airlines to find a flight that would be sooner. She found a flight for one person out of San Francisco International for Monday morning. I called the bus lines and there was a bus running in time on Monday for me to get there on time. I said good-bye to uncle Jack, and cousin Jack, and Inza gave me a ride to the bus. Patty came to see me off when I left. I made it to the airport and got on a Douglas DC 9. It was a big plane and the first time I was ever on one. I had a window seat on the right side just behind the wings. I looked it all over and seen it had two jet engines on my side. We had about a twenty minute wait then had to fasten our seat belts. I watched us take off from the window and shortly after I noticed a lot of smoke coming from the outside engine. It turned to be a very black smoke and shortly after I believe I seen flames, then the pilot told us over the speakers that we lost one engine and had to circle back and land. He had to go way up and make a large circle and wait for landing instructions.

He told us what was happening all the way and did say that we were in no danger and he could fly this with just two engines, but I was not happy about that then thought about the other people on board. We did land and were asked to get off. The flight instructor told us that there was not another flight going out today to our destiny and we would have to wait while they changed the engine. The captain said he thought a bird flew into the engine. We flew over Alcatraz Island where there are a lot of birds. I went to the rest room in the front and there was a pilot coming out and asked him how fast we were flying. He said an average of five hundred and fifty miles per hour. I had a lot of time to think and I was glad I had a window seat. I did cry most of the way home and hid my face against the window. We did not land at La-Guardia until almost dark and lost three hours in the time change. I called the garage and asked John to pick me up at the Danbury bus terminal. I walked in to see Ed and Margaret and told them I would talk to them in the morning. I went to my room and suffered all night because I was afraid I would have another nightmare. I did fall asleep and awoke late and sat with Margaret. I told her Bonnie killed herself and she said, "Oh! my God," then said, "I remember what you told me about your nightmare." She then asked when it happened and I said about two years ago. She said, "No! That is about when you had that bad dream. How did she do it?" and I said, "I did not ask and I never want to know," because my dream was not just a coincidence and I know I was there. I didn't want to talk about it anymore and I wanted to leave. I did not call Sherry I just went to her house and knocked on her door. She came to the door not knowing it was me, then threw her arms around me and said, "Oh my God, you're home." I put my arms around her, then picked her up then kissed her. I was more happy to see her than I thought I would be, and asked if I could take her to work. She said, "You came just in time. I thought you weren't coming home until Wednesday."

I said," I missed you so much I had a nervous breakdown."

She said, "You're kidding."

I said, "I'm not kidding and I did have a break down. My nerves just couldn't handle all the problems."

She said "Why, what, what happened?" I didn't know what to say and told her a very close friend killed herself. She asked, "Is that why your eyes are swollen?"

I said, "I guess," and she held me without talking. I dropped her off and told her, I will be here at ten tonight." I went back to my room because I was still drained of life and hurt very badly inside. I know I must see Sherry as much as possible to keep my mind occupied because I may try to join Bonnie. I went home and talked with Margaret because, I could always talk candid with her and I did explain what happened. I said, "I must have known when it happened and Bonnie must have found a way to tell me but I must also find a way to tell her I never stopped loving her."

I started to cry again and Margaret said, "I'm so very sorry."

I said I don't know what to say to Sherry because I really can't love anyone right now because I did promise Bonnie I would love her until my last breath. Margaret said, "Al, you must forget her and put this in your past You told me it wasn't your fault and now you're taking the blame. She seen I was still crying and left me alone. I laid there a while and went to work, but couldn't concentrate on what I was doing and my thoughts were out of harmony with reality. I couldn't separate the happiness I had with Bonnie with what I have now. There must be a way I could put this behind me and go forward. I know Sherry is trying to understand me and I do believe that she does love me. I know if I try she may be the answer and the only girl that has not hurt me in anyway. She is always there when I need her, but I don't know if what I feel for her is love, contentment or just an excuse to hide my blame. My mind has been contaminated with evil and is in a state of consternation. I do believe that I am developing a schizophrenic personality and feel I have not been granted the right to offer my love to anyone that rightfully belongs to Bonnie. I believe she has giving her life because of the love she had for me and I should not be so free with what I feel still controls my heart and soul. I have worked every night until after midnight and at times all night. Jacky has become very close to me and stays with me most of the time. He is the closest friend I have ever had and the only person that I told the complete story to, but he just repeated what Margaret told me. He also had a tragedy in his family. When I first opened my service station, his oldest brother Bob worked for me part time just to help me out, but due to a failed love affair he also took his life. I know now while looking back the suffering he went through and rose to the point where he could not accept it. This also raises a concern in my own life.

I have not seen Sherry all week, and promised her that we would go out Saturday wherever she wanted then to go. For some reason, right now I don't want to see her and I just mourn for Bonnie, but I know I can't do this forever and what would happen if I lost Sherry. It is three thirty and I am on my way home. I wanted to talk with Ninny and Goldy (my aunts), so I said I was on my way. I took Sherry with me and they were happy to meet her. We all talked for a long time and we were all happy to be together. They really liked Sherry and told me to hang on to her. I said, "I intend to, because she's my inspiration and life support," then we talked about my business and Uncle Jack. Goldy said he told his son, John, that I was not working hard enough and I shouldn't have a girlfriend taking me away all the time. I told them I work seventeen hours a day, until two or three on Saturday and I only take some Sundays off.

Goldy was Jack's wife until she got a divorce. She said, "He is impertinent and too hard to live with." I asked her if she knew anything about the antique gun and sword he was going to sell for me because I could never get a straight answer from him. She told me he sold them and that is where he got the money to buy his new car. I was shocked but not surprised, she told me to never say she told me and I promised I wouldn't. I became very sad and wondered why my complete life was so susceptible to this constant misery.

I took Sherry home and we sat in the car. She said that she didn't want to tell me this before because I appeared to be upset since I went to California but she should explain now. She said that Charley Hyatt, whom is the resident State Police Officer, gave her a ride home while I was gone and tried to take her out. We both knew him very well and he was a friend of mine when he raced at the race track in Danbury. She didn't mind him giving her a ride to her home and never expected this because he is married. She told him she was going with me but he insisted he really wanted to make love to her. During her conversation with him, he told her he would "run my ass out of town" if he had to. After she told him no, he was still waiting on her road for her because he knew she walked to work. I told her, "Just don't get into his car anymore because he just wants to use you, and I will take care of it." This did nothing to help me from my mood, but we did stay and loved each other. I thanked her for telling me and went home.

The Twin Oaks Motel was just a short ways from my garage and I have noticed Charley going there with the Police Car late at night so I made a plan. I borrowed an infrared camera and Jacky and I went to the Motel and parked as if we were customers and I took a customer's car because he may recognize mine. We waited two nights and he did not show but I knew he didn't know about my plan because I did not tell anyone. The third night we got what we wanted and he had a different girl with him. I took several pictures and made sure I had one of him helping her out of the cruiser. I had them developed and they were not very clear but you could identify him and the registration of his vehicle. I saved these but I still took Sherry to work to avoid any future confrontations.

The first two nights when I took her home I noticed him waiting along her road home. I thought this would be the end of this, but when I had to pick up parts at the parts store in town and was driving a customer's car, he spotted me, then turned around and followed me but I was able to get to the parts store. I pulled in and he stopped along side me with his emergency lights on. He asked me for my license and gave me a ticket for driving with defective equipment. I said Charley, "What in the fuck are you doing? I can't believe this."

He was very cocky and said, "I'm gonna nail your ass every time I see you." I took the citation and walked to the Ford garage where I worked before. It was just a block from where the car was parked so I walked. I explained what happened to Lee and asked if he would give the car an inspection and please note this time on it. I did not drive the car there and he had his mechanic drive it in and completed a full inspection. I went back to work and did not tell anyone about what happened, but I went to Troop A in Ridgefield, then showed the chief the citation and the inspection report with an explanation of what led to this. I also supplied the pictures that I had. I don't know what happened but I didn't see him again and he was no longer the resident state cop.

Sherry said, "Boy, that was smart."

I said, "I don't know what happened to him because we were good friends before this. I have many friends with the state police and I like and respect them." We had two resident state police officers in Brookfield and I liked them very much and would play cards with them. They were Al Kosalowski and Sy Conrad. Well, I believe I did justice and have no regrets about it.

Sherry and I still date but it just isn't as it was before and I couldn't give her the love and affection she deserved. I could see she was lost for words and didn't know what to say. She was very loving and caring but I knew if I wanted to keep her I would have to yield to her needs and desires. I tried to settle my thoughts and dilute my past to think of her. I held, kissed and asked her what she wanted to do or go. I have not taken her anywhere lately and have ignored her. I tried to apologize and she said, "Love is never having to say you're sorry." I told her I really loved her because I knew I would be very lost without her. I could feel that she wanted to be loved because she looked at me sadly and said, "I didn't want to tell you before, but we'll have to try again. I did get my friend last week," and I said, "Honey, I'm very sorry to hear that, but practice makes perfect." I tried to get in a good mood by laughing and tickling her then played with her. She had her skirt on and looked so cute so I told her she looked beautiful. She pushed me towards the door very carefully and straddled me with her legs and said, "What's wrong?"

I said, "I'm sorry but I've been laughing so hard and don't think we could do anything this way." With all my problems and thoughts of Bonnie I felt that I was becoming more imperturbable and just wanted to hold her. I asked her to get up and change places with me so she grabbed the small cushion that was left in the car and put it behind her head then pulled me on top of her. It seems that I do feel better because I do realize how much I love her and helped clear my mind. This is when my brain lets her own me and I love these moments not so much for sex but for the ability to have feelings for her that are trapped inside me. I want so very much to make love and think about her a lot but when I'm alone I seem to lose the power of love. I was able to get comfortable, then move to her command but I forgot how much I did enjoy her. I was happy she does force me at times because it was just what I needed to quiet my thoughts and relax me. I felt so good being here with her this way because right now I didn't have a worry in the world.

I thanked her for loving me and said, "I do love you with all my heart." We sat a long time talking about us which made me really want and need a baby. I believe that would be my salvation but after all the times I have tried and no one became pregnant. I do fear that I will never have my own children, which is in parallel with everything else I wanted so much. I did not tell her this because I don't want to lose her now but I will tell her before we get married. I took her home then went home myself and fell asleep. I slept much better and believe I could think better also. I did go back to work and we were very busy so I worked late every night.

I haven't seen Sherry all week, but I promised I would take her to Pleasure Beach this Sunday. We left early that morning and stayed until dark. While we were on our way home but still in Bridgeport the water pump went bad on and the engine over heated. The bearing blew apart and the fan belts also came off. I waited until it cooled down then drove it a short way from a Diner then parked it. We walked to the diner and I called John. Jacky was still at the garage and had his girlfriend with him but he said he would come with John. John, Jacky and his girlfriend Jane did come. I left Sherry, Jane and Jacky at the diner and John and I went to try to fix the car. We changed the pump, then started the car. John had to go home because he lives in Danbury and this took nearly two hours. I went back to the diner to get them, then I dropped Jacky and Jane off.

I took Sherry home, but things didn't seem right because she did not sit close to me. I thought it was because we had someone with us. When she got out of the car she started to walk to the house and I asked her, "What about my kiss?" She came back and gave me a small one. I felt there must be something wrong and went home and fell asleep but the next day Jacky told me that Sherry was all over this guy at the diner. He also heard the conversation when she asked him to pick her up and she wanted to go out with him. I thanked him for telling me and did not say anymore. That answered my question why I didn't get a kiss last night. I thought it was over and I fell in the dumps once again. I waited all week for her to call and at least tell me why, but she never did.

I started to work all the time and favored the race drivers with their work. I started to modify all their racing transmissions and developed the name of being the best in this area. I didn't care if I was because I just wanted to stay busy. Sherry has not called since then and I was so confused I forgot to order gas this week. We are going to run out of regular before the next delivery, so I planned to use the power steering pump on my car to pump about three hundred gallons of high test gas from one tank into the regular. I would only be losing a few cents a gallon, but it will keep my customers happy. I attached the hoses to the pump and into the gas tanks, then started the motor and it was working very well. To make the story short, I was so down with life I forgot to tighten the hose clamp. The hose popped off and I tried to grab it but with the engine running it exploded and I was in flames. I was in the hospital and was released with both my hands bandaged and could not drive. The only thing that saved me was when a customer wrapped a rain coat around be to subdue the fire.

Thinking back during the fire

There are four four-thousand gallon gas tanks in the ground that are full of fumes now and if they ignited it would cause more damage than four bombs so I was lucky that I was able to pull the hoses away. I was still numb and didn't notice the skin falling off my arms and hands. But just then my face, chest and hands started to hurt with indescribable pain. I ran to put cold water on me and the firemen came. The car was in flames and they ran to extinguish that and water down the ground near the underground gas tanks. The ambulance came and took me to the hospital, but first I asked the fire company if they would close the garage and turn off the power.

I searched my mind about what went wrong with my relations with Sherry. Her leaving me isn't what hurt the most but it's that everything I ever want or love I seem to lose for some reason. This pain is worst than my burns because my burns will heal. I could not drive or even open a door. The next morning I went to the garage at eight o'clock with Ed because he drives past my garage when he goes to work. I would just be there when they needed advice. I had my car towed to the junk yard because I never wanted to see it again. The load of gas did come and things were normal except for me. I fell into a depression and had problems dealing with life again. I know now while looking back at the fire that I was not thinking properly because I never tightened the clamp on the hose and that's why it came off. My mind was preoccupied with Sherry and I was very careless. I believe now that I am being punished for the murder of Dorothy's mother and Bonnie. I do know I was the direct cause which makes me very depressed and I must find something to occupy my mind. After a few days the doctor took the bandage off my left hand and re-bandaged my right hand. I lost a lot of skin and he said it was only the epidermis left, but at least I could drive now. I bought a fifty-nine Ford, it is black and white and it drives very well, but it is a standard shift which makes it hard for me to drive. There wasn't much I could do and stayed depressed but I don't blame it all on Sherry because I knew I did not offer the love that I should have and something in my mind was always holding me back.

I have not tried to see her and I have not seen her walking because I am never there at that time. I do miss her very much and would like to see her again. I would like to know the truth because it may help me in the future. It is now September and it is starting to get cold, but I don't go home every night. I sleep here, then go home in the afternoon to shower and change. I'm leaving work early because I want to see if Sherry is working and see who she is going with. When I got there she was still in the store, but I could see she cut her hair because it is curly and looks different. I don't want her to see me looking, but I know she noticed me driving past. I went to Al Pat's thinking that I'll go back at ten o'clock when she gets out. I don't know why I'm doing this and know I shouldn't. I drove past and noticed she was standing where she did when I used to pick her up. I rode around the block and drove past again without looking at her. She was still there and I wanted to know who was picking her up. Just past her there was a girl that I knew before and will take a long shot to see if she needs a ride. I did not look at Sherry at all and stopped, then motioned for the girl to come over to my car. I didn't remember her name but she did come over and asked if she remembered me.

She answered, "Yes, and you were always snotty with me."

I said, "I'm sorry, but I need a favor and I'll make it up to you." I asked her if she needed a ride, but she said her dad would be here in about fifteen minutes to get her. I said, "Would you please do me a favor and just sit in the car?" She asked why. I said, "I'll tell you when you get in." She did get in and I told her not to look, but "I want to see who picks that girl up," while pointing at Sherry. "I don't want her to think I'm here because of her and I need a reason to be here."

She said, "You guys are all alike," and I said, "Not really, I'm bad luck to everyone that goes out with me." Sherry walked to the other side of the street and then towards her home. I waited for her to get out of sight and thanked the girl for what she did. I wondered why Sherry was waiting there and left when I didn't stop. Maybe she thought I would stop to pick her up and she lost her regular ride. I waited long enough for her to get almost home so I could see if she was going home. I drove home past her walking and didn't want her to see me look. She watched me go past her and down the road to my house. I went in and told Margaret I was going up to see my sister. I went up and she was playing her guitar. I was there about twenty minutes and the phone rang so Arlean answered it. I picked up her guitar and played, "I'm Gonna Knock on Your Door" because I did believe it was Sherry on the phone, but did not ask who it was then I heard Arlean say, "It's for Al," and she handed me the phone. I did not take it, but asked who it was and she said, "It's Sherry."

"Tell her I'm busy and will call her back."

She talked for a while longer and Arlean said, "You should call her because she sounds very sad."

I said, "Why should I call her after what she did to me?"

Arlean said, "We all make mistakes."

I waited at least a half hour anyway before I called her and she answered on the first ring. I asked what she wanted and she said, "I want to say I'm sorry."

I said, "Love is never having to say you're sorry, do you remember that?"

She said in sad voice, "Yes. Could you please come over?" I said I was too tired now but I'd call her tomorrow. She said, "Will you please, because I'll wait for your call." I did not say anymore and hung up. I was excited that she called and there was nothing more I wanted than to be with her, just to hold her and forgive her, but I knew if this happened once I could never trust her. I cared too much about her and knew I would just be hurt more. I felt I should never go back but I would be good to know the truth or at least listen to what she tells me and I will have to take it from there. I got up early and drove past her house then went to work. I had trouble trying to evaluate her calling me now after thinking, *how could you leave someone you say you love without even saying good-bye?*

I'm confused and need time to think because I haven't heard from her in over a month, but wonder how much could she have cared. I missed her every day and if I knew that she would have talked to me, I would have called in a second. I am not blaming her and if she doesn't care for me any longer she has that right to leave, but let's be truthful. I think back when my car broke down in Bridgeport and what she did at the diner. She did this in front of my friends and that was the only way I knew. She never said anything to me, she just stopped with no reason. Was our affair just a fling or a challenge and was I just being used? Before I moved to California I was very popular with the girls and many of them wanted to go out with me. She said she knew me from before and watched me play at Jossey's. I did not have that personality now and was a loner. I did not want to be noticed by anyone and just wanted her now. I never kept eye contact with any girl that looked at me in an inviting way. I had those problems before and do not want to relive them. I know I still love her and will fall to her as prey, but I know I can't let her control me through my weakness. It is two o'clock and I could leave but I am afraid of the consequences before me because of my past experience.

The Fast Side of Life

I sat at my desk and was looking at some auto magazines when I noticed a new model Ford. It is a fast back, two-door racing car that they are going to use at the Daytona Raceway. I read that style wouldn't be released to the public until next April. I wanted to kill time so I went to see my friend Bill Mortel at Mortel Buick. I knew he had friends working at the Detroit assembly line and wanted to know more about this car. He was in his office and I went in to see him. I showed him the magazine and the car I wanted. I was joking with Bill and said, "I want that one," but I called the Ford Dealer and they said it was a half-year model and couldn't be sold until after April fifteenth of next year. Bill said this is true of a Ford Dealer as a new car but as a General Motors dealer, he may be able to buy it and sell it to me as used and it would be legal and he said he would check on it.

I was so excited I forgot about Sherry and it is four o'clock now. I went home and when I passed her house she was just walking towards her door. It looked as if she was walking in, but she did notice me going past. I waved to her with just a friendly wave and continued home. I took a shower, changed my clothes and went up to my sister's. I walked in and Sherry was there, she must have walked down while I was in the shower. She met me at the door and asked how I was. I said I was just fine. I went to sit on the couch and she sat next to me. She asked what I had planned and I said I don't make plans anymore. She looked at me and said, "Could we please go somewhere, because I would like to talk." I really wanted to hold her and never let go but I was afraid.

Her eyes appeared to show some honesty and I said, "Where would you like to go?"

She said, "New York state to get drunk," and I said, "My, what a change." I looked at her without answering and could see that she was different. She wasn't the same girl that I was dating before. She cut her hair short, had it frosted and wore makeup, which she never did before. She did look very nice and I don't think she thought we would ever get together again so I knew she didn't do this for me. This really confused me and I thought I should not go

346

back with her. I know every time I went back in my past I ended up with more problems and I am concerned now.

I asked, "Why do you want to get drunk?" and she looked at me and said, "I want to drown my mistakes." I did not answer or remark because my mind was searching for an analytical answer. I feel now that there were too many changes and he must have dropped her but I don't know what she wants from me. I may be wrong but I don't think it is I that she wants. I could not walk out of her life without even a phone call and expect her to take me back.

She wondered why I haven't answered yet and said, "Well?" I said that we could go somewhere and talk, but I know now that I have lost my trust with her. I do still love her and will give her this opportunity because this may lead me to an answer I need to know. I said, "I'm hungry. Where would you like to go?"

She answered, "It doesn't matter, anywhere you want." I just went to the Sycamore Drive-In and on the way she did not sit right next to me, but did sit close as if she wanted me to pull her over.

I asked, "What do you want to talk about?" She turned toward me with eyes wide open and she would look from one eye to the other. This is what she did when we first went out. I really wanted to hold and kiss her because I did miss her very much.

She said, "I'm sorry, I don't know what happened to me and I did miss you very much but was afraid to call you. I thought you would not talk to me and that would hurt me more." She moved close, then kissed me on the cheek and had her head on my shoulder. My heartbeat was faster and I knew that this is what I needed. I needed her to be close to me so I could feel her body next to mine. I said to myself, *Take advantage of the moment because it may not permanent.*

I just drove without talking and waited for her to lift her head, then said, "I'll go out with you, but I won't let you hurt me anymore than you already have."

She said, "I never wanted to hurt you."

I interrupted and said, "How could you say that? You climbed all over some guy at the diner while you were with me in front of my friends and you asked him to go out with you. You leave me without even saying good-bye and I was just a nobody to you then. What would you do if I did that to you.?"

She said, "I know it looks bad, but please understand."

I said, "I don't understand and there is no excuse when you really love someone. Until this happened I would have given my life for you."

She said, "You wouldn't know?" and I said, "No! I was hurt too much by what you did but I know I must live with it and I have learned to." She said in a sad voice, "You don't love me?"

347

I said, "I love you more than life itself, but what does that have to do with anything now?" I don't know how I said this and I really didn't want to right now but I said, "I believe it's over between us. It was you that broke it off and why should it matter to you how I feel?"

She answered, "Because I know I still love you, but since we are talking about this could you please tell me what really happened in California?" I asked her why and she said, "I don't know how to say this, but you have not been the same since then." I was lost for words and knew she may have been right.

I said, "What do you mean?" but while looking at the look she had, something happened to my mind. A sudden headache came upon me and all I could see was Bonnie pleading for me to stay. It was almost as if I had her here with me. I looked at her and said, "I'm sorry, but it's a long story."

She said, "I don't care, will you please tell me?" I didn't know how to tell her and I thought the truth may break us up for good. I tried to make it appear not to be important and told her that my last girlfriend committed suicide. She said, "Why?"

I didn't have time to think up something to say so I said, "Because I left her, and I feel responsible for her death."

She said, "You still love her, don't you?"

I said, "I just feel guilty, but I do know that I love you."

She said, "But Al, you're never happy anymore and the only time I see you smile or laugh is when we are having sex. She just looked at me awaiting a logical answer then said, "Will you ever get over her?" I did not answer her and for the first time I knew she was right. I started to hurt again, but not just for Bonnie but her also. I thought to myself that I have messed up every girl that I have ever went with. I believe that she hurt now and must believe that I will always have this problem.

I turned the car around and said "New York State is a good idea." We went there to a bar I haven't been before and we both ordered drinks. I cannot believe this, I'm almost twenty four and they asked me for my ID, Sherry is four years younger and they didn't ask her. We sat there for a long time and I said very little. We both had a few drinks by now and were feeling pretty good. After thinking about it I felt that I may have been that way when I first came back but not lately. I said, "I don't understand because I have built my life around you since then." We both wanted a child and spoke about owning our own home. "I tried to spend every minute I could with you so I don't believe it is my fault." I said, "Maybe it would be good for you to date other guys and I will date other girls for a while."

She said, "I couldn't take seeing you out with another girl. Who is that girl you had in your car? I did see you go past me and thought you wanted to see me when I was standing there waiting for you. You ignored me, then you just drove past and went with her."

I interrupted her and said, "It was you that left me, don't try and blame me." I did not say anymore, but I felt I had enough to drink and said maybe we should go home then asked for our check and we left. When we got into the car and she sat real close to me but before I could start the car she put her lips on mine and kissed me as when we first went out. My mind went blank and I did not stop her nor did I want to.

I had what I missed so much and did not volunteer any assistance because she knew what she wanted and I left it up to her. My lips were getting sore and I asked her if we could leave. I started to go and she said, "I don't want to go home, I want to make love," but she didn't have to tell me that. She already had her hand on it. I was driving towards home and remembered my friend Henry had a one-room shack where he sold split wood. He would stay there all day sometimes selling wood for fire places and was never there at night. I drove there because it is on our way home and not out of the way. There were no cars around and I found the key where he said it would be. I opened the door and could not find a light but the outside street light was plenty of light. She started to kiss me and I did join in. She got on top of me and kissed me, I tried to get up and she pushed me back down and stayed on top. I was excited as I ever was and rolled over and got on top. I gave her all that she wanted then turned over on my side. We got dressed and went to Al Pat's for breakfast, then I took her home. We were both very tired but I had to go to work.

After work, I went to my sister's. Again, I picked up the guitar and started to play it because one of my old school friends asked me if I would play at a party he was having. I told him I haven't played in a long time but I would consider it. I was just practicing and asked my sister if she wanted to play with me there and she said she would. Sherry walked in, so I put the guitar down and asked her if she wanted to get some food. I didn't want to go to Al Pat's so I went to Fabs Hot Dog Stand. They have all kinds of fast foods there and it's where most of the kids hang out. I did notice that she was friendlier with other guys than before and I noticed that she was making eye contact with one the most and he was staring at her also. I did not feel comfortable and told her I wanted to go home. On the way she said, "I don't have to go home now," and I said, "And where would you like to go?"

She said, "Just out, anywhere." I said I would rather wait until tomorrow but she said, "Yes, but why can't we go out tonight? After seeing the way she was with other guys I knew I was just asking for trouble. I told her was am tired but would still like to wait until tomorrow and I would pick her up at work.

I went home and thought about our relation and didn't know what to do because I felt that the hurt that I had, did destroy most of the love I had for her. I know that all I had left was the fear of losing her but I got to the point of accepting it. I did pick her up but didn't want to take her anywhere that we knew people because I didn't want to be embarrassed again. We decided to go to the amusement park Saven Rock in New Haven. I could see that things were not as before and she was not that loving girl that I knew before. I tried to be extra nice but could see she was not with me today.

During the day she wanted to do different things and she wanted to see a gypsy fortune teller. She wanted to be alone and I did not go in with her, but when she came out I also went in alone. I had my fortune read and the lady said I had some sad days coming and she asked if that was my girlfriend. I told her just a short while ago we had planned on getting married. She just smiled and said, "Not with her." I don't believe in fortune tellers but I did believe her because she just talked with Sherry so I just tried to be myself.

We finished for the day and she wanted to go home. It appeared that we had little to talk about so I just took her home. I pulled into her yard and was dark and we just sat there for a minute. I was lost for words and waited for her to say something, but it seems that every time I get depressed I could only think of Bonnie. She was never progressive but always left it up to me and we could go places without sex running our lives. She opened her door to get out and I just kept quiet. She looked at me and I gave her a kiss but didn't say good night, but instead I said good bye and wondered why I lose everyone I love. The future no longer bears any promises and based on my previous relations it seems inevitable. I don't know what to do and I'm afraid to fall in love again. Until now I left every girl that loved me and I believe this is what I am being punished for but I may not ever know. Maybe I am prudent and naive but how can I change, and is it too late? I have always been able to commingle with people and have always been complaisant with everyone I went with. But I believe that coming from a broken family, with so many heartaches and only bad memories, has impaired my knowledge to give love.

It was still early so I went to see Bill Mortel and he told me he could get me this car but the only one they had was one that was set up for Daytona Race track. I asked how we could get it if it was made for Daytona. He said, "For some reason it did not pass all the tests and you will have to take it with no guarantee," and I asked why. He said, "It's not designed for the road because it has too much power," and I said, "Yes, I want it." He filled out the buyer's agreement and all necessary papers and applied for a loan with the General Motors Acceptance Corporation and I was approved. He got me this car for just a little more than if I bought a regular one. I asked when I would have it and he said next week. Buying this fast car brings back memories of my very bad accident I had with my Jaguar that was modified to the limit and it came in first place at the Grand Prix races in France.

I Almost Killed My Friend

I was invited to play at a house party that was sponsored by some friends I went to high school with. It was a very nice house that is located on Lake Candlewood. We had two other guitar players there but I took the floor most of the time. Not because I was better and as a matter of fact they were more experienced than I was. But, as always, everyone appears to like my style better. I don't just play lead nor rhythm, but a combo of both which gives the effects of two or more players. Many more people attended than were expected and the law prohibits the sale of alcoholic beverages after eight p.m. The party went very strong and everyone was having so much fun. They were singing, dancing and I was happy that everyone behaved so well. I was on the stage at midnight and was told that we were out of beer and almost all alcohol. I finished my number then went to talk with Herby the host. We were already under the weather and I consumed a lot of Vodka. I am not a heavy drinker and only drink casually but the party was going to well to end. I allowed Herby to coach me to drive to the nearest Tavern to fetch some more. It was twelve thirty a.m. now and the place was seventeen miles away. He knew I had the fastest car so we left but only traveled about eight miles. I was reaching speeds to exceed one hundred miles per hour on all back roads. I was an excellent driver and had race track experience but the alcohol took away my keen instincts. I entered a sharp corner at a ridiculous speed and my rear tires drove over a patch of wet leaves. The curve went ninety degrees to my left and my car slid to the right and I could not pull it away from the long row of guard rail. The impact tore down the complete row of guard rails while I was still fighting to pull it to the left.

I was still at full power to try and pull it through but when I ran out of guard rails my car did what I was asking. It quickly caught traction and my car dove across the road into a ledge, then bounced off and settled back on the right side of the road. I looked for Herby and he was missing along with my passenger door. I noticed that most of the right side of my car was missing. I walked up the road calling for Herby but it was dark and I could not find him. Another motorist noticed the accident and stopped to the right where I first hit the rails. The lights illuminated the area where Herby was laying and I could hear him moaning. I went to pick him up but must have been intoxicated because when I tried to pick him up the door would follow him. I started to kick the door off and someone slapped me in the face and pulled me away. It was a woman and she finally got Herby up but he was in very much pain. She flagged the next auto that came by and sent him for an ambulance and the police. Another car stopped and noticed me then came over. It was another kid from the party and no one told us that he left earlier to get the booze. He had several cases of beer and some quarts of whisky. I asked him to grab me a bottle of liqueur and he asked why but I said please so he did get it for me. I opened it and poured about half on the ground then just took some in my mouth and spit it out. He asked, "Why did you do that?" I said when the police come I will tell them that this was when I started drinking because I was so upset. This was they can't cite me for a D.W.I. He said, "That's pretty smart," then the police and ambulance came. I appeared not to be hurt but they took Herby to the hospital because the door handle punctured his stomach and was caught under his ribs. They said he lost a lot of blood and I'm sure I didn't help the situation either. The car was a total wreck and I had it towed to the farm. So there it is, you got it all and could see that I was also a stupid kid at times.

The Beginning of the
Wild Side of Life

Bill called me from Mortel Buick and told me that my car was delivered to a Ford Agency in Stanford and I would have to go there to drive it back. There policy is to safety check every new car, which they did but the mechanic said it was awesome to drive. He said he was brave and just hit the gas and the front wheels came off the ground. That is why the manager won't let anyone drive it. I went that night and signed the documents that I did receive the vehicle and left. I had Jack Rothe with me and his brother drove us there. Since the car was designed for racing it had a two hundred mile an hour odometer that really didn't fit the dash, but it also had a comparable oil pressure and temperature gauge. They asked me if I wanted to replace them with original equipment and I said, "No, I like them." Jacky and I left but I did burn out to impress the mechanic. I drove very slowly through Stanford but when I approached the straightaway I punched it, the wheels did come up so I eased on the gas but it was just seconds and I was traveling over one hundred fifty miles per hour. My heart was in my throat and I was so happy. Jacky said he was a little scared because he said the pressure forced him against the seat and he couldn't move and I said I also experienced that.

After driving so fast, seventy miles per hour seemed slow but I passed a state police officer and recognized him. It was Charles Dirienzo, whom I admired but knew he would have to give me a citation. I did not want to embarrass him so I just took it above a speed I knew he could never reach and was far off the road before he knew where I went. I did slow down and continued back to the garage while Jacky and I looked it all over. I think he was as excited as I was and said, "I have never seen anyone outrun a state cop before. I said there probably would be a lot more. I checked all the service points and found that the engine oil was almost empty. I thought the dealer did not check it, so I filled it. I drove it the following day and we took it to a bridge where we would normally race because it was just a quarter mile long. Without really tying I punched it and did it in thirteen seconds at one hundred forty miles per hour. I could have done better but when the front end came up so high it scared me and I let up for a second. The next day I checked the oil again and it was very low again. I knew there was a problem and called Bill. He instructed me to return it to the dealer and he would call them. Jacky and I returned it that night and left it there. It was there for a week when Bill called me and said it was ready but the mechanic wanted to speak with me. I went there the next day and did have the opportunity to speak with him. He said, "I've never seen anything like this." This engine was blueprinted and has a roller tappet cam shaft which I have never seen before. He was more excited than I was and I had to ask him, "What about the oil."

He said, "I called Dear Borne, Michigan and they told me this car was set up for a quarter mile track and they use only one compression ring and no oil rings on the pistons." He said, "I also found that this body is mostly aluminum," then said, "My God, this is something." He was still talking, but I thanked him for the information and left. I was so very happy because I knew I was the only one that have this type of car on the highway.

After it was broke in properly, we tried it out again on the bridge and this time I tried to see what it would really do. I had traction problems because I had regular rear tires on it but I still reached one hundred seventy miles per hour in eleven seconds. After this I drove the highways as if I owned them. Then one time I entered the highway 184 at speeds over one hundred miles per hour and there was a state police trooper traveling in the same direction. I didn't have time to look but I believe it was Jimmy Bocsh. I knew I couldn't slow down so I took it to excessive speeds and drove into New York State, which was just seven miles away. I took Rte. Twenty-two and drove home that way. I was beginning to love this life and I was never caught but I knew it had to end. Word got around that I had this car and the police started to watch me everywhere I went. One day when I was leaving work I was stopped by a local state police officer, so I pulled off the road and he came to my door. I said, "Can I help you?" and he said, "Yea, do you mind if I just look at your car?"

I asked why and he said, "I hear a lot about it and I am interested in seeing why it's so fast. He was very friendly but I did not recognize him, so I got out of my car to show him. I opened the hood and had to remove the two safety pin locks up through it, so the hood could never blow off. He looked and could see the 427 C. I. D. engine with twin eleven hundred C.F.M.. Holley Carburetors and the air cleaner with just a top and bottom and the sides all open to match the air scoops in the hood. He kept looking and I found that he was a race driver also but drove on a quarter mile oval track. He looked under it and noticed the traction bars that went from the differential to just behind the front wheels. After looking it all over he said, "My God, I never seen anything like this and I have been racing cars for years." He thanked me then gave me a lecture and said, "Don't ruin what you have because you are getting a bad name. They are waiting for you and will get you, even if they have to put up road blocks."

I said, "I know all about road blocks," and thanked him. I said, "Could you do me a favor and call the office? Tell them I am all through playing and I will obey the law from here on." I thanked him and we shook hands. I knew I had to cool it and was lucky this far because I knew they all knew my car now. I said, "I will really try but it is so hard to drive this car slow." I really became to love speed and would race only on the back roads. Then all the race drivers started to hang out with me. There was Bob Scribner, Nick Bates, Bones Stevens, Cliff Beardsley, Andy Sapinaro, Duffy Wills, John Mead and so many more. One night we were racing on I84 on a long stretch but I was not racing so I volunteered to be blocker. I would block all traffic during the race which was maybe one minute. Just as they started to race a state police car came towards me at a high rate of speed. I did not have time to move so he drove in to the medium and slid about three hundred feet sideways but he did pull it out and got back on the road. I noticed it was Jimmy Bosch so I just left and took all the back roads back to New Milford. I pulled into a sandwich shop just north of town and parked in front of the door. Jacky was with me as always and Jimmy Bosch spotted my car and flew in. He jumped out of his cruiser and drew his revolver and came to my door. I had the window down but he didn't say a word. He just tapped his revolver on the top of my door with the barrel of his gun and was shaking mad. He still hadn't said a word and I became worried because the gun was pointed at me while he had his finger on the trigger. He finally spoke and said, "If you ever do that again I will shoot to kill." I did not answer, and then he left.

It is March now and I was told that my uncle was coming back to run the garage. I never expected this but he was still the president. I picked him up at the airport with my fifty nine Ford and brought him home. My red Ford was parked along side of the garage and on the second day he was here he asked me, "Who owns that car?" I said I did and we had a big argument over it. He said I had no right spending any money without asking him.

I said, "It is all right for you to steal the money from my gun and sword," and I walked out. I went back that night with Bob and Jacky then loaded all my tools and equipment in to my van. I moved my homemade car to a friend's house and took my two Fords to my sister's house. Arlean just moved to a very large place. It was a resort that was not used any longer and they were caretakers there. There was two homes, a guest house, and a recreation hall with sixteen bed rooms over the main floor that had a walkway around and above the dance floor and the party room. I moved my things there and moved in to live here. My uncle called me and said he was having me arrested for taking my tools because he said he owned everything I had.

I told him to do what he had to but I was never coming back. I then ran a transmission shop from my van and would go to the dealers place, then rebuild them. This was a good setup and I was making money with no overhead. During the time that I was at the garage I overhauled some diesel engines for the trucking companies and was offered part time jobs driving for them if I wanted.

Turning Over in a Loaded Tractor Trailer

I took the job and was driving one or two days a week for Joe Calorie from Providence, Rhode Island, who hauled for Kimberly Clark Corporation located here in New Milford. I also volunteered to be a substitute driver for Victory and Palmer lines in this area. Between my own business and driving the tractor trailer I was working too hard and was not getting any sleep after driving truck all night then working at my job. Then a driver had a heart attack so I was called for a substitute to take a load to Springfield, Mass. For some reason the weather dropped to below zero and I went home to get one hour sleep before I left. I oversleep and was more than two hours late. I left home then went to Kimberly Clark and got the tractor trailer. I was driving very fast and was going around a sharp curve on to the bridge right here in town. I did not check to see if my front brake was off because we do not use the front tractor brakes in the winter, but whoever drove it last used it for some reason. There was a New Milford policeman, Carlton Day just crossing the bridge at that time. I stepped on the brake and without warning the truck jack knifed, then flipped over. I missed the cop only by inches but he was able to avoid a collision with me and was able to come over and tried to assist me. I had Jacky with me and the truck went over on my side. He was scared and tried to push the door up to get out but was standing on me. I was yelling at him but we were finally able to get out. The policeman Carl said he never seen anything turn over so fast. Driving most of my life I knew just what happened. By leaving the front brake valve on and the air tank was not drained of water which condenses from normal use. This allowed the left front brake diaphragm to fill with water and freeze. When I released the brake the left front brake stayed locked. This is what jack knifed the truck and the speed turned it over.

Carl understood and I did not receive a citation. I called the wrecker service and they had one of the largest wreckers in the area. While they tried to lift the tractor and trailer back on its wheels I went to get another tractor to move the trailer. When I got back the rig was still on its side. It was very heavy and they changed the wrecker to a tree next to South worth Auto Dealer and pulled it from the ground. I told them I would unhook the tractor and they could pull it forwards, away from the trailer and pick them up separately. Another wrecker came and still could not lift them both, so they took my advice and it worked. I had the tractor towed to the garage and I pulled the trailer back to K. C. After this I only made a few runs and decided not to do any more. My life was getting worse and I just didn't care anymore. I had the fastest car around and I just raced for money. I was making money but I was spending it on traffic violations. My driving privilege was suspended but I drove anyway and didn't care. I was tired of what I was doing and finally opened my eyes that I was on the wrong road.

I went to the Exxon Station that advertised for a mechanic and met Frank and his son, Junior. They hired me to start the next day so I worked very hard and he told me that I was the best mechanic he ever had work for him. His son Junior and I became like brothers and we were always together. Every afternoon we would go to the bowling alley for lunch and bowl for a while. I met the owner of the concession stand and we became very close friends. His name is Serge Bertaglia and has dozens of trophies from professional boxing, bowling and other sports. He taught Junior and I how to spot bowl and fitted our ball for us. We both were very good and we played on a team. I still did not have my driving license and Serge said he could have it back for me in a few weeks. One night just as I was leaving to go home, a state policeman was parked across the road and was watching me. I couldn't leave and did not have a ride because Frank and Junior had left, so I kept working. I waited until four thirty a.m. before he left and I quickly left to go home. I knew he could not come back in time to see me leave and once I was on the road he could never catch me. I drove onto the back road home and it was just before day break.

I was driving towards the underpass that I go under every day and just before this is a dirt road on the left. I was stopped by a large light coming towards me. It was a ball that was larger than a basket ball and it came within fifty feet from my car, then stopped. I watched it and it appeared as if it was spinning very fast. It was a white orange color with a blue glow. I got out of my car then walked towards it and it seemed to have an influence on me. I was very interested to know what it was and when I walked towards it, it would move away from me at the same distance then I would stop and it stopped. We did this several times and then it went very fast towards the intersection where the dirt road meets on the left. It stopped again and I went to it again but could not get close which I wanted. It went up the side road about one hundred feet this time and it stopped again. I walked up to it again then got within twenty five feet from it and just watched.

I could see for sure that it was spinning very fast and was more bluish now. I did not dare get any closer because I could feel my hair being pulled towards it so watched it for a moment because I wanted to understand it more. I tried to get a little closer but it went almost straight up at a very high rate of speed then disappeared. I stood there for a while and nothing else happened but I am very happy I did get to see this. I drove on home and on the way I thought about it. I believe it was a ball of highly charged ions which the energy is incredible and in the billions of volts. It must have a positive field charge with little or no nucleus or a neutron nucleus with a low rate of current which develops it own magnetic and gravitational field. My own field of radiation was creating enough force to expel it away from me, but I don't know what made it go up and could only speculate. I believe that the speed of rotation controls the amount of the polarity and when it approached the positive earth field the speed increased. It then created a greater positive field, which repelled it from the earth gravity. I am still excited and wish I had a camera. Today is Saturday and I am late for work and I had the only key because Junior was not here. Frank broke the window to open this morning and I explained why I was late. He did understand and I told him I would have my license back this Wednesday. Three months have gone by and Junior is in the U.S. Marines now and I miss him. We were almost like brothers and we are very busy now because Frank fired his other mechanic. I am doing a great amount of transmission overhauls and we had to add on another bay.

I do have my license now and I have changed my life around. I do not drink or race any more but I still have a very fast car and every now and then I will blow the carbon out of it. I do not go bowling as much but I do go there for lunch when I can. The summer has gone by and I am still very busy, but have not gone out with anyone since Sherry although I do see her some times and we are still friends. Her little girl Laura is very cute and I know she is not mine although she has my hair and eye color. It is the middle of September now and I have been playing (acting) at the Brookfield Playhouse for the last four months. I started in "Cat on a Hot Tin Roof" and just finished playing in "Oklahoma". I really enjoy it but it takes a lot of my time. I did meet a few girls here that I like but they are just my real good friends. Frank has me just about running this place now and he does not have to come in as much. I am very close to his complete family and go flying with his brother Dick. He has four brothers, we are all friends and I work for them when they are in a jam. I was leaving for lunch and a gentleman approached me and asked if he could join me to lunch.

The Break I Have Been Waiting For

He is a Texaco Representative and I was recommended by the Chevrolet Dealer that I mentioned earlier when I operated their body shop for a while before I went to California. They are building a new service station in New Milford and it is located in the most strategic area in town. It is on the main thoroughfare and the exit to Kimberly & Clark Company. He told me that I am the first person that he approached because of my credibility and knowledge. I agreed that I will accept their offer when he told me it would take two more months to complete and this would give Frank time to replace me. I have gone past the site several times and I did like it but I thought I could never afford it. We agreed they will start me on credit but I will have to pay for all the permits and licenses. It is a three-bay garage with a parts room a front office and a rear office and small lounge and it has two acres of property. It is in compliance with all regulations and I am allowed to do any kind of repairs even diesel. I also have the permits to sell automobiles. I am very happy and Frank did not want me to leave but he does understand. Junior was hurt in the Marine and was discharged with a knee problem and he is back now. I hate to see a family fight but Frank always teases Junior because he didn't do anything while he was in the Marines and Frank has a purple heart for bravery. Junior does not like this and he feels bad.

I try to tell him that's just a father boasting and don't worry about it. I have just one more week here and Frank and his family with all his brothers had a party for me at Frank's house. That is the nicest thing that was ever done for me and I had tears in my eyes. They tricked me into going to his house and it was a complete surprise. I really don't want to leave but this is what I wanted all my life. I applied for all my permits and license but my friend Howard Moraghan who is my lawyer helped me get them soon and without question. I will open to the public on February sixth, nineteen sixty five. The deal I have with Texaco is my rental is twenty-six hundred dollars per month and I receive credit of one cent per gallon for the first twenty five thousand gallons of gas I sell and one point nine percent thereafter. I liked this because I knew I could sell much more. During this time my sister's husband Frank wanted to become my partner and I did allow this to come to pass. I assumed he would share equal responsibility and I could have some time off. I was to operate the Mechanical Department and he would manage the gasoline sales. I open for business at six a.m. and close at midnight.

Texaco came in then installed a sign thirty feet high and the Texaco letters were six by five feet in size. It was very nice but the Ford dealer was right behind my building and their parking came within twenty feet from my new sign. Lee was the previous owner of this dealership and sold it to Pete Rittman. Kurt, the gentleman that bought the new T bird from Lee when I worked there (the one that had a knock and oil leak that I fixed), well, he ordered a new one from Ford next door and it was parked in their yard near my new sign. The day it came in we had a bad storm and my sign blew down, crushing his new T-Bird even before he seen it so we again meet by accident. After that Texaco installed a new one but it is seventy feet tall and is vertical. It was installed with the base twenty feet in the ground with cement and I had no more problems. The rest of the week went fine and my partner would pump gas when he wasn't working at his other job but I was here from six a.m. until midnight. I had plenty of expenses but still had to buy more tools. I have two car lifts, a one is a two post, the other is a single post and this is just what I need. I ran a few ads in the local news papers and have a transmission special, then I dropped the gas prices below all of the other dealers.

I was surprised when a friend came to visit. It was Andy Vasaturo, with whom I played with at the Play House. He said that the club wanted to have a party for all the members and needed a place to hold it. He knew all about the place I was staying at and asked me if I could help them. I said, "The place needs a lot of work. There is no electric or heat and it will have to be cleaned up." I said, "I just opened my new business here and I am very busy."

He said, "Please?" and I said, "Only if I could get some help." I went home that night and Arlean told me that Sherry was coming to visit and she wanted me to be nice to her. I said, "I have nothing against her, and I just talked with her a few days ago." Shortly after, Sherry came in with her daughter, Laura and she really is a cute kid. She is just a year old now and the same age as Arlean's daughter, Tina. I was supposed to go back to work but I called Frank and told him to close up. I found out that she never got married and broke up with him. She is living with an old friend of mine now.

Arlean told me they wanted to go out for a while and asked if I would baby sit. I said, "As long as Sherry doesn't mind."

Then Sherry said, "I would love for you to." I agreed and they left. The kids were awake and we really had fun. I played with them for hours and learned how to change their diapers. I just loved these kids and wished they were mine because I am partial to little girls. I was with them for about four hours and it seemed as if it was one but they did fall asleep. They came home about eleven p.m. and Sherry asked how Laura was. I said, "You're going to leave her here."

She said, "No way," then asked why.

I said, "I had so much fun with them. I had them each on one knee and they were pulling my hair and my nose. They had me laughing so hard, I just love them both."

Sherry just looked at me and said, "You always did love kids," and I am sure she remembered when I asked her to have one with me.

I quickly forgot our past relation and talked with Arlean. I told her about the party for the club house and she said, "Yes, please have it here."

I said, "But it needs so much cleaning and other work." Sherry did not wait, but said, "I will help you clean it," and I said, "Thank you, that would be a great help." I told her I would be here Saturday afternoon and all day Sunday.

She said, "I will be here early and spend some time with Arlean until you get here." I really don't know how I feel now but I was happy to have her help me but I knew I did love her before and this did bring back memories.

I went to work the next day and looked at the newspaper. I could see that once again my business hit the newspapers and I made headlines with a full cover story. They also put a full-sized picture of me and my station on the front page. The other gas stations are mad at me, but that's business and every day I'm getting new customers from K C and local residents. The lower prices are really helping and increased my bay work also. I am very happy with my business and my life is the best since I left Bonnie. I still think about her and wish she could see that I did make it. I do not know why she didn't wait and she could be here now. I know I must stop thinking about her and I have tried but she will not let me go. I know she was the love of my life and the only one that I cannot forget. It has been long enough now and many hurt hours have passed, but I do realize she is gone and would want me to move in to the future. I believe I am on the right road now and must make the best of my life without her.

I worked very hard this morning so I could leave early to get ready for the party. Sherry was there when I got there and she went with me to the dance hall. She already had a broom, some washcloths, and a pail of hot water. I said, "My God, you're all ready."

She said, "I told you I would help you." We entered the building and I had to move many things but she started to sweep the heaviest first. She cleaned the rest of the day and only took one break for a drink. I attached the temporary electric service from the outside panel on the house. The heating system couldn't be fixed in time, so I planned to get a coal burner just for that weekend. It wasn't very cold yet, but nights were chilly. I came back to the main room and seen how much she had done. I didn't say anything then but thought that she would have made a very good wife.

I thanked her and said, "I am very surprised about how much you have done." She just smiled and we walked back to the house. I had to go back to work and closed the garage, then I came back home. Sherry was still there and Arlean had to give her a ride home. I did not offer because I did not know how I felt so I watched Tina while Arlean took her home. She was there early Sunday but I don't know how she got there. I didn't know if she was going with someone but I did not ask. We both went back to work in the dance hall and by day's end she had almost everything cleaned.

I told her not to worry about the upper floor because we really don't need it. She had to leave soon so I thanked her again then went to repair some water pipes. It was getting dark but I needed water to the bathrooms. I shut all the water valves except those and had to repair some leaks. I had water now to the bathrooms, all the lights fixed and working so all I needed was the stove. They already left so I just went back to the garage to close up. I did not see Sherry all week but she was there again on Saturday when I got home at two p.m. She said she was ready to start work but she asked if she could come to the party. I said, "You better come after all you have done." She smiled and we talked about what was happening. I said, "There are ninety six people invited and I have a caring outfit bringing all the food, so I need a some long tables to serve the food and electric outlets for the food warmers." I said, "At first we will have some finger foods until everyone shows up. I told them it will start at six, but be here by seven." She appeared to be happy because she was coming and I was happy because she really is a good person. We still had three weeks before the party and we were almost ready with the hall, thanks for the help I got from Sherry.

I went back to work and had to get caught up because I am the only mechanic and one week a month I have to manage the gas service. Monday night is our slowest night and I am always here alone until closing. It was just about eight o'clock p.m. when this white Chevy drove in for gas. I waited on them and washed the windshield on the driver's side, then asked the gentleman what he wanted and he said, "Fill it up." I started to fill the gas, then cleaned the rear window, then went to the passenger side windshield. I noticed a young blonde starting at me and I recognized her from a time I gave her a ride home and asked her for a date to go to the Drive In Theater. I found that she was fourteen years old so I never went back. I remember she was very friendly then, but I did not say anything. I finished with the gas and went for change, but I could see she still stared at me until they left. Some young guy was driving, but she was not sitting close to him and I wondered why she was looking at me that much. I noticed that she hadn't changed much, but maybe a little older. She was very good looking and reminded me of Bonnie. I was sitting at my front desk preparing the daily records when the phone rang. I answered it and a girl said, "Do you know who this is?"

I said, "Yeah, you just left here and got gas with your husband."

She said, "He's not my husband, and how did you know it was me?"

I said, "I knew before you left that I would hear from you." I heard a baby crying and said, "Go take care of your kid."

She replied, "Oh, I'm babysitting for a friend." She said, "Don't hang up," and she went to care for the child. She came right back and we talked in between customers for nearly a half hour. I asked her how she got my phone number and she said, "You have it advertised with your name above your door, it's an easy number to remember 8818, because the complete town uses the same prefix."

I said, "Sure, you could call me anytime." I was happy that I hired another employee because it was getting busy and I couldn't get any bay work done. Gary is going to pump gas for me every weeknight and Frank works. I started a lot of promotions with coupons, green stamps and buy one and get one free. I became very busy and had to hire a mechanic and another gas attendant. Jolene did call me tonight, then called me every night. I finally got the nerve to go see her. She lives only a mile away and I told her I was leaving now. I drove my Ford with the racing engine that still had the racing slicks (tires) on the rear. I drove to her house and pulled across the street and got stuck in the mud because we had a lot of rain lately.

I got out of my car and walked towards her and she looked so beautiful. I didn't know what to say but, "You look very nice," then said, "Could I use your phone?" She led me to the phone and I noticed a little baby sleeping in the middle of the floor. It was cold in here and I could see she was covered with grown-up jackets. Her long blonde hair told me she is a girl and she was so beautiful, I wanted to pick her up and just hold and love her. I turned to look at Jolene and I felt an attraction as I did once before. I believe it is love at first sight. I didn't have to ask because she said they ran out of heating oil and were waiting for some. While I waited for the wrecker I looked things over and felt that there is something wrong. I didn't know what to say but I said, "I will call you when I get back to the garage." John Michaud brought the four wheel drive pickup that I just bought along with a tow chain. On my way back I couldn't believe what I just seen. My mind went back to when I was a child with just old coats to cover with and it was always cold in our house. Then I thought about sleeping on the floor with Bonnie. I said, "I must look into this." When I talked to her before, she gave me her phone number and told me to only call her after three p.m. and not on weekends. I did not ask her why, but I believe I know now. I called her as soon as I got back and said, "There's something wrong and I want you to tell me, please."

She said, "I was too embarrassed to tell you, but this is my daughter." She did not have any oil or any money to pay for it. She said she stilled owed them and they wouldn't extend their credit any further. She started to tell me, but started crying then continued saying, "I don't have any formula for the baby and I am giving her just milk." I could have started to cry myself.

I asked her for her address and house number and said, "I will call you right back." I called Layton fuel and told him to fill the fuel tank and bill me for it. I also told him to please start the furnace and make sure it is working properly when you leave. He said he would do it right away, then I called her then told her he was on his way and I would be there in a little while. I went to the store and picked up two cases of baby formula and took it to her. When I got there I said, "That was your husband in the car."

She said, "Yes," then had tears in her eyes and said, "I wish I never married that bastard." I didn't say anymore because I just wanted to grab her and tell her, 'I love you and will help you,' but I felt like crying so I left. I did not call her because I don't know how she feels after telling me the truth, but she did call as usual. I was excited but very confused because my mind went back to Bonnie and I wondered what her baby would look like and I would probably love it also. I felt very strange and wondered if I should involve myself because she is married and has a child with her husband. This was impeding my ability to concentrate on my business because I thought about her all the time. I talked with her every night and became comfortable with our relations because I knew some way she would be mine and she would be with me as Bonnie was. Things were going very well, but I had another breakdown in my life. My partner Frank was just told by Arlean that she wanted a divorce and that just about destroyed him. There was nothing I could do about it but after trying I just stayed out of it. He became a big problem at the garage, because he was crying to all my customers about it, and many cane to me and complained that they have their own problems. It became unbearable and we had to separate. After many discussions and arguments, I finally bought his share. All the finances were from me, but I owed him for his time he worked. I paid him and we parted as friends. Everything turned out fine and I was doing very well and late Friday Jolene came in with her friend. She had June in a bassinet and she was awake.

I asked if I could pick her up and Jolene said, "Yes."

I reached to pick her up and as soon as I did she said, "Dada." I held her and almost started crying, because I waited for those words for so long. I just held her and knew how much I loved her. I knew I wanted her to be mine, then wished that I could take her from this life to give her what I never had and give her everything she may ever need. For some reason there was an immediate attraction for this baby, and I felt it was because of wanting to see Bonnie's. This brought me so much closer to Jolene and I knew she doesn't love her husband. After hearing the complete story he didn't deserve Jolene or the baby. He showed no affection for either one and didn't know his child was freezing and going hungry. She told me he only cared about himself. I could see this became my life's dream and I wanted this to be my family. I thought, *How could such a little child have so much influence on me?* I began to worry if I could trust my own feelings and wondered what another downfall would do to me. I became afraid of the future again because my life has been immutable, and I believe I should become more impassive. She is married and this child that I love so much is not mine to have. I said to myself, *Do I have the right to interfere, and if I do what will happen?*

The next morning my friend Art Assarito called and asked if I wanted to go flying with him, so I told him I would be there in a few minutes. My sister Arlean was there so I asked her to call Jolene so I could speak with her. She did, then I took the phone. She said she was out of cigarettes, so I told her I would fly over her house and drop them off. I met Dick and he flew over Lake Candlewood, then towards New Milford. I took the controls then because I wanted to fly over my garage to take an aerial picture of it because I had a new idea for advertisement. I flew it at about three hundred feet while Dick took the pictures. I started to climb but Dick was being funny and killed the engine. This is a single engine plane so I hit the start button but it wouldn't start. I was losing altitude very fast and hit the ether injector and it started, but was loaded with fuel so I still didn't have full power that I needed for the climb. I went full rudder to the right away from the power lines then headed towards the valley. I tell you I wouldn't want to be standing on the light poles when I went over them. I was scared shitless, but Dick was laughing and said, "You did a good job, and you're learning." I could have killed him. Then I flew over Jolene's house and again went to about three hundred feet but I held my hand on the switch.

Dick said, "Why, don't you trust me?" and I said, "Hell no, not after what you just did." I seen her out on the road and dropped her cigarettes, and then Dick took over. He flew over the river and was heading straight for the Boardman Bridge, then dropped down just above the water. The bridge is only about thirty feet above the water, but he flew under it. I was a little scared but I wouldn't let him know it. I knew he could fly well because he was a crop duster. I went back to work and was happy to be back on the ground.

Jolene called me every day and I knew we loved each other. She said, "I have to come see you and will try to get there this Friday, about three thirty." I was very excited and really wanted to see her. I was waiting all day Friday and at four o'clock her girlfriend brought her here. She had June with her and I had a chance to see her again. She came inside so no one could see her from the road and we talked while I held June. It was getting dark and she said she had a surprise for me. I asked what and she said she was staying with me until ten o'clock. I was happy but scared, then her girlfriend took June with her. I didn't want to stay here so we took a ride. I didn't know where to go but I knew my brother just bought a new house just a few miles from here. We went to his house and parked into the driveway. There wasn't anyone home so we sat in the car but not long before our lips went together. I loved and kissed her and this was the first time I felt this way since Bonnie. We started just loving and I found we were making love right here in the car. I don't know how it happened or who started it but I was happy just as we are. I just know this is one of the happiest moments in my life.

Somehow I took her home, but I can't remember if we even talked, because I think we both just thought about what we did. I drove her to her house and believed that I found someone equal in my heart and will replace the only girl that I really ever loved. After this night I had no doubt but I would have to marry her. I was so very much in love and she was my complete life now. I know with her and June I would never want for anything else. I went home and went to bed but started to think about Bonnie and the time in the bathroom when she was beating on her stomach only because I said I would hate it. I know these were the words that made her take her life. It hurts now because June may be the answer, because I do know now that I could love a child regardless of the mother's conception.

I did not choose to love June unilaterally, but we chose each other when she called me "Daddy". I am just sad because of my pride and hatred for an unjust cause. I went to work and was sad all day until Jolene called me and I was very happy again because she said she wanted to leave home right away. I asked when and she said tomorrow so I was there just after three o'clock to get my new family, my wife, my child, and my dreams. I did not have a place for us to live but at the time it didn't appear to be important. Material things didn't seem to matter as long as we were together. She took her blankets and pillows and we went to the guest house at Arlean's. I took her and June to the second floor and fixed the blankets on the floor. She told me she left a note at her house telling her husband Joe that she left and would not be back. We also had June's formula and baby food, but nothing for Jolene. I went back to work but later that day brought some food, drinks and other things she would need. I stayed with them for a while, then had to go to work.

I was at work for just a short while when Jolene called me from Arlean's phone. She said that Arlean seen me bring something here and wondered why I was going in there. She went there and heard June so went up and found them. Arlean told her that she could stay there with her and had a place for June, but she would have to sleep with me. I only had a twin bed, but that was plenty large enough for her and I. I was happy and just loved my sister but we were always very close. Jolene was very happy but she worried about her husband Joe, because he started to follow me a lot. Arlean had a large black wig and Jolene would wear it when we went out, but I believe that Joe caught on to it and followed me ever where. But I had my Ford and it was no problem losing him. To cover my tracks I asked Sherry to ride around with me. She did and I would take her to lunch often and I was glad we remained friends. This did confuse him and he stopped following me. I just loved living with them and was never happier. June and I were inseparable and she was a ball of love and fun. Jolene and I did sleep together and making love with her was just as if I was with Bonnie, always on the floor or in the car. But it wasn't long after that Bonnie was almost completely out of my thoughts.

Jolene told me that she had to talk with Joe because she wanted to get some money to pay for June's things. I said, "You don't have to," but she said she still wanted to, and she would tell him she wanted a divorce. She had her girlfriend take her and went to the bowling alley where he worked. His mother was there and said she wanted to hold June, but she took her out the door while Joe held Jolene from trying to get her back. She slapped him and got away, but his mother had already left. Jolene called the police, but after they came they told her there was nothing they could do because it was a family relations matter. She called me and I was almost in tears and told her to please come here. She did but she was crying and I told her I would hire the best lawyer there was. Everyone knew that she was with me so I gave her a job as secretary and she was with me all the time now.

I hired a lawyer from her home town. She had to meet with family relations and because of her young age and because she didn't have a place of her own to live, they granted rights to Joe's parents. She was awarded visitation rights, but just for Sundays. We fought to get June back soon because life was very lonely without her and we both were very sad. Jolene decided to move in with her brother Harvey and his wife, Cindy. They lived in Newtown and it was twenty some odd miles from my garage. I only see her and stay with her over night there. She did smoke so I would bring her cigarettes, things she needed and gave her a lot of clothing on her birthday. She was very happy to have clothes that she always wanted and this did remind me of Bonnie. I have lost so much of the hurt and feel so much more secure with life now.

After closing my garage, she was in town with her girlfriend so she came and stayed with me. I had a nice bunk in my back office and we stayed all night making love but she did not reach a climax. I tried very hard and then she told me she never did. Her husband told her she wasn't supposed to and she became to believe it. She said he would do it for a few minutes and he was satisfied but didn't care about her and always left her that way. During our night I explained that she should have an orgasm and she should try. I think it was blocked in her mind and that was the problem. I took her to her brother's house and was back in time to open the garage. I worried about that all day and knew she couldn't be happy until she enjoys all that life has to offer. I told her that next Sunday we were going to do it until it happened because I wanted her to think about it all week and it may help. When I was with Dot and Jen I always thought that sex would help keep you together and it was some kind of bond. But I do realize that it does not matter at all because it only relieves pressure for the moment and I know that since I left Bonnie it didn't seem to be the same. I know it didn't help Jen because she needed it more after I left and I don't think it mattered with whom she did it with.

Love is nothing you should forget in a few months, but I also believe you must do it at the right time. Since she has moved away I started to develop a fear that I may also lose her so I don't want her to be away from me very long.

But her lawyer said it would not be a good idea if we lived together right now. It is Saturday night and we just went to Jimmy's Hot Dog Stand in Monroe and had some food. I talked about tomorrow a lot. She was very excited and we went back to her house. We did not have a bed so we slept on the floor as Bonnie and I did. There were too many similarities that kept taking me back to Lamont. I fell asleep looking at her and she was already sleeping. The blue eyes, blond hair and sleeping on a blanket on the floor was not helping and I fell asleep thinking about Bonnie in her bathroom that horrible day.

I awoke early, then went to work and I did not want to work late because of my promise but for some reason I did get much more excited as the day went by. I just couldn't wait to be with her and wanted to go there now. I left at seven p.m., then went to see her and we both took a shower but not together. We went back to Jimmy's, had a dinner, and then we went parking. We went down this long back road where I know no one ever goes and it goes down to our old farm. It was a nice moonlit night and we could see each very well. I kissed her in every way I knew, massaged her body and made her wait as I explained what I was going to do. We started and I did everything I could think of, but did not stop. It took a while and everything happened just as I thought but I think she was just as scared as happy. She was completely satisfied and more excited than I imagined, which made me very happy. We hugged and talked about what we did, then we went home. I am laying here with her, but I do believe I love her as much as I did Bonnie and feel about the same as I did with her. I have not asked her to marry me yet and I hope she does want to. I know I love June more than anything else in my life and I pray that we get her back soon because I have not felt the same ever since they took her from us. I was very happy then and did not think about my past as much. I went to work this morning and I'm much happier then usual. I have a better outlook on life and my business is doing very well. Our gas average is near sixty thousand gallons per month, which is double their expectations.

Jolene said she wanted me to give her brother a job. He appeared to be a very good kid and I liked him. I knew I could trust him, so I did hire him and he would open the business so I could come in late sometimes. Things went very well for the next few weeks and I was becoming happier while gaining more confidence with my life. Friday nights are the busiest time here with gas so I never leave before midnight and get home about one a.m. after making my deposit. This night I did not feel well and went home at ten p.m. When I arrived at our house there was no one there so I took a ride back to Danbury. I stopped at the gas station where Cindy always gets her gas and asked the attendant if she was here tonight. He told me she was here earlier with the blond that's always with her and they had two guys with them. I was just punched in the mouth again and didn't know what to do, but I do want to see her and explain what is going on. I waited along the road home because it was still early and they still have two hours before they expect me to come home. I had to wait for about an hour when I seen the car heading towards her home. I pulled out but they recognized my car and drove very fast to try to get away. She pulled into a driveway and I waited for near an hour for them to come out.

I did not want to drive in there because I did not want to get into a fight. I have too much to lose now, but I did drive in after that wait and found it was a short cut to another road. I did not know that and I just went straight to her house. They drove in just before I did and were walking into the house. I got out of my car, then stood there. Jolene just stood in her doorway and did not say anything so I asked her to come here. She did and I asked her why. She said, "I didn't do anything and Cindy just picked up two hitch hikers."

I said, "You picked them up before ten and took them home at one?"

She said, "They weren't with me, I was sitting in front with Cindy." I was still lost and couldn't buy what she told me because I was so hurt, so I turned to get into my car and left.

She did not try to stop me so I went back to the garage and said, *Here I go again.* I tried to sleep and asked myself why, because I treated her the best that I possibly could and gave her everything she wanted. I may have gotten a little sleep but I was still numb and opened the garage. Harvey, Jolene's brother, also works at K.C. and went to work at ten last night. He came here to work when he left there but I didn't say anything. Jolene did call twice today, but I said I was too busy to talk now.

I had a few of my things there and I left at three to get them. When I got there she met me at the door and I asked if I could go into the house to get my things. She asked me why. I said, "I'm leaving," and she asked where I was going. I said, "Anywhere but here."

Then her eyes filmed over and she said, "Why? I didn't do anything. Please don't go." She held onto me and started crying and I could feel the same hurt all over again when Bonnie was crying. I became . . . I don't know what, but I pulled her into my arms and all I could see was the last time when I was with Bonnie when she was pleading for me not to leave her. I look back now and know I could have prevented her ultimate decision. Tears began to run down my face and I knew that was the mistake of my life. Jolene is holding me while my mind is spinning and I don't know what to do. I know how much

I love her and I didn't want to hurt anymore like I did last night, today or in the past. I really didn't want to leave but I didn't know if I should stay. Being very confused, I broke her grip on me and went back to my car. I sat there and seen she was watching to see what I am going to do. I put my hands on the steering wheel and buried my face in them. I did not cry anymore, but I am all choked up and she came to the car, then got in the passenger door.

She didn't say anything for a while and said, "You must believe me." I did not answer, but she came over and held me. I stayed for a while without talking because I wanted to be able to breathe better.

I turned towards her, held her for a minute and said, "I have to go to work now, but I will come back tonight so we could talk." I went back to work and said to myself, *I don't care what she tells me, I know I will never trust her as much as I did.* I fought with myself the rest of the day and thought about Bonnie. I thought about how Sherry left me and I knew I should have never gone back with her then. Something wanted me to go back to hold and kiss her like never before, but something also told me not to go back there at all. I knew that I really didn't have to go back and Harvey could bring my things to me, but somehow I thought I should listen to the truth if she does tell me but I will never know. I did leave early and my employee Gary said he would close up for me. I left my safe unlocked and told him to put everything in it and lock it. When I got there I sat in the car, then she came out and said, "Come on in." She was without color and I knew she was bothered by the way I felt.

I did go in and sat by her while she explained it to me again and it was the same as it was told last night. I looked in her eyes and could see the sadness, then told her I believed her. She grabbed me and held me very tightly, then said, "I would never cheat on you." She said she was hungry and asked if we could go to Jimmy's, so I took her there. I was very tired and I couldn't get out of this mood because I still was not happy. I believe my mind is becoming impervious to thought, and I can only improvise now. I looked at her when she wasn't looking. I knew I really didn't want to lose her but I still have this problem that I can't forget, because my mind went back to the gas station where Cindy got her gas. These two guys were with them at ten o'clock but I don't know how long before this and they were with them until one o'clock. I said, *why? And what happened during that time, because it could have been all that day, and she did not call me at all.* My thoughts did change me and I did not know how to act. I said to myself, *It's got to be my fault, but what am I doing wrong? I have had a problem with every girl I've gone out with and every affair has been immutable but no one can tell me.* We started to go back home and she asked if we could go to the same spot we were Sunday night. I did go there but wasn't really in the mood for sex, but she found a way to get me excited and we did make love. I did feel this girl was confused and had problems in her life also. After this I felt that we would be together for a while so I will try everything to keep her happy.

The week went by and everything was fine. Harvey is going to open for me so I could sleep in late tomorrow. I always kept the bays open on Sundays, but decided to close them for a while. I did sleep late, but was awaken by her father and I heard him say to Jolene, "You didn't have to sleep with him. I could have satisfied you."

I heard her say, and called her father by his first name, "Harvey, why are you like that? I'm your daughter and I want to marry him." I made believe I was sleeping, because I could not handle what I just heard and my brain became impregnated with hate and fear. If I get up I know I will kill him because I thought about what happened to Bonnie, but this was worse, it was her father. I waited until he left and I got up very upset and told Jolene I heard what was said. She started crying, than told me she watched him have sex with her sister and felt very bad, but didn't know what to do about it. I said, "Do you wonder why this kid is so fucked up and was pregnant when she was fourteen?" I said right after that, "This whole world is fucked up." I held her in my arms then said, "Don't worry, I will take care of you and June and you will never need anyone again.

I believe we did become close again, and I needed her more now than ever. I went to work on Monday, but I was still shaking with anger and fear. I said, "When is this all going to end, and what kind of a world am I living in?" I had money now and searched the papers for an apartment, and then we found one in Marble dale. Jolene moved there and she did get her visitation rights with June. She was little but she did remember me and seemed very happy. I was so happy to see her again and knew I would never leave Jolene because I just loved both of them and was happy to have June with us again, even if it is only on Sunday. I was not supposed to live there, so I drove a different car and I parked behind the house, but I did stay with her every night.

The summer went by and it is fall now. Our lawyer said the divorce was coming up in court and I should go with her, then he took my financial report to have it ready. I looked in the newspaper for a home and I did find a small house on Candlewood Lake. I always wanted to live near the water, so I called the Real Estate Broker. He said he would handle all the paper work and my application was accepted. I took Jolene there and she did like it but it only had one bedroom and I said I would add on right away. I bought it and we moved in and started to live together there. Her lawyer called and said the hearing for the divorce was coming up and I should have a financial report ready. I asked him when and he said it was on the calendar in ten days. The divorce did go through and we did get full custody of June. My life finally became as I always dreamed and I was the happiest ever. June's father had rights to take her every Sunday, but he very seldom did, and his mother was the only one who would take her. He was ordered by the court to pay child support and was always behind, so I asked the court for an adoption application. I did adopt her and her father didn't appeal it at all. I finally had my beloved family and this is the happiest day of my life. We then planned to get married and set the date.

Meanwhile, I started to put on the additions to add another bedroom and again I had to drive in the stakes for the foundation. My mind did go back to when Bonnie was helping me, but I was able to put that into proper perspectives and completed the bedroom in record time without missing much time at work. We had a one car garage that I turned it into a large dining room and added on to the kitchen also. We had a nicely sized home now and it was on the lake. We were very happy and got along very well. I would take June out with me on Sundays while Jolene made our dinner.

We always had dinner at home on Sundays because she made a very good meal and she turned out to be a very good cook. We did try and have another child but with no luck. It was getting near Christmas and I haven't given her an engagement ring yet but we both agreed not to get things we need for the house or garage, because they were really for both of us and things we needed anyway. I did buy her a diamond ring because I love her and she never had one before, so I wanted to surprise her. I didn't want to put it in a small box because she would have known, so I went to Sears and was able to get an automatic dishwasher box. I took it to the garage and put concrete blocks in it to make it the weight of a dishwasher and I tied the ring crisscrossed in the middle. I wrapped it and waited for Christmas, then we got a big Christmas tree. June helped decorate it and we had a lot of fun because she was so excited and that made my life worthwhile. I bought Jolene a lot of other things also and we got everything June would want plus some real nice clothes but we all couldn't wait for Christmas. Jolene never drove before, so I did teach her to drive and I bought her a Volkswagen because it was very easy to drive. I also showed her how to drive in snow, ice, and high speed on corners. I demonstrated with my race car how to pull it out of a spin and when to use the gas, brake or both in sequence. This is how she learned to drive and was real good.

Today is Saturday and tomorrow is Christmas so I left the garage at five p.m. Harvey had to help me carry in the ring and put it next to the tree because it is very heavy. We have company coming for dinner tomorrow, so we stayed home and got everything ready tonight. June was sleeping while we wrapped all her presents and I couldn't wait to see her reactions in the morning. We finished all we had to do then put all the presents under the tree, then went to sleep. June woke us in the morning early, she was so very excited and said, "Mommy, Daddy, come quick because Santa was here." We got up and I took pictures of June, Jolene, and all the presents, then watched Jolene open her box and she was not happy when she read "dishwasher" on the box but did not say anything. She opened the box and took out the ring, then jumped up and down and said, "I love it," but this is exactly how Bonnie acted when I gave her, her ring.

I was sad for just a short while, but seeing everyone so happy I forgot about it and watched her put on her ring. It fit perfectly and I was happy because I had trouble getting her ring size without her suspecting it. The only time I really did think about Bonnie was when I added on the extra rooms. I remembered her when I drove in the stakes. I did not have Jolene help me then because I thought it may be bad luck. The winter went by very fast and we all were very happy. I bought the biggest television I could find and we stayed home to watch it a lot. We bought all the furniture we needed and bought June her own bed; but we saved her crib, hoping we would need it again. We then planned our wedding and had a garden wedding at her grandmothers. Just our family and close friends came and June was the ring bearer. We had many pictures taken and when I looked at them, her in that beautiful wedding gown and me in my tuxedo, I knew this was the happiest moment and times in my life. It is now May first and June's birthday is on the sixth. I plan to take her to some nice places and then next week we are leaving for California for a two week vacation. I am driving my Ford so we could make good time but I made no plans to go near Bonnie's house. I believe I have satisfied my conscience that it was not my fault. I firmly believe it was the action conducted by non professional law enforcement officers. We are going to Cheyenne, Laramie in Wyoming and spend one day there, then go to Yellowstone National Park for two days. When we arrived we watched Old Faithful and all the other fountains then went to Yellowstone Lake. From there we went through Idaho to Spokane, Washington and, of course, Moses Lake. I wanted to show them where I lived here and the lake, then I took Ninety-Nine South to the volcano crater and spent some time there.

While we were there June had to go potty, but all they have are outhouses with just a hole. It is open, so you could look straight down hundreds of feet, and June screamed when she looked down. She would not go there and she called it the "hole potty". She talked about it for a long time and it really scared her. We followed route ninety nine to Bend, Oregon, where the movie "The Birds" was filmed. We arrived there after ten p.m. I was almost out of gas and couldn't find a gas station. I found a hotel that was opened and asked the desk clerk for help. He told me that there was nothing open, but I could look for the local police officer. There was only one on duty and I would probably find him in the supermarket parking lot. While I was looking for him I developed a feeling that there was a gas station open about ten miles further.

I just had enough gas to get there, but having June with us we decided to wait for the officer. I drove to the supermarket and found the police car. I noticed he did have an occupant, but I knocked on the window anyway. He rolled the window down a little way and I explained my problem to him. I noticed he had a female with him and he said he would meet me at the only gas station in town. We waited for forty five minutes before he came. He had a key to the station and explained he would have to charge me a fee for his involvement, which I didn't mind. I felt this was a strange town and the female was not with him now. I paid for the gas and his services, then left. His fee was more than the price of the gas but we were on the road again.

We drove about ten miles and there was a Shell gas station that is open twenty four hours a day. It was the place I seen in my mind and Jolene asked how I knew. I answered her, "I don't know, I just seen it in my mind, and it had to be a premonition. This area appeared very familiar and I must have been here before but not in this lifetime. We continued into Klamath Falls and I took Rte. 199 from Klamath Falls at Grants pass to California. We found a Motel in Crescent City, then went to Eureka. I have never seen fog so thick that you could feel it. I drove the rest of the day and wanted to see the coast. We left Route 101 and went to Route One and I thought I seen fog before. I was forced to drive one to five miles an hour and it took well into the afternoon to get to the Red Wood National Park.

We spent the night and next day here because Jolene and June were very excited. We all had a lot of fun here, although I have been here several times before, but they loved it. We went into the tree houses, then bought toys and knickknacks but I must say that Route One, "the coastal route", is the most scenic route I have ever seen and we enjoyed the ride in the daylight, but I would not care to drive here in the dark again. We crossed the Golden Gate Bridge, then stopped in Chinatown for dinner. I took them for a ride through San Francisco on the trolleys and stayed at a motel. We got an early start and went through Sacramento, then back on highway fifty to the Rocky Mountains into Reno. We stopped in Lake Tahoe and stayed here for the night, then left for Las Vegas. They never believed it was this nice and we took June to Circus Circus. She was very excited and so was Jolene

They watched the trapeze and all the acts, then we took her on the Revolving Bar and had lunch. We enjoyed all the sights we could, then went to Lake Mead. The water is about eighty degrees, but it felt cool because it is very hot here today so we spent all day here swimming it the lake. The food was the best we ever had and we said, "We are coming back here more often." We went back to Circus Circus and heard about the accident with Ann Margaret. That made me very sad because she was so good and beautiful. We then drove almost nonstop to South Dakota and stayed in the Bad Lands. It was very interesting and we stayed at a motel overnight so we could stay for another day. After this we were tired of traveling, so we headed straight home. On the way home June was very restless and kept whining and wouldn't stop, so at a rest area I took her over my knee and spanked her lightly. She stopped whining but it hurt me more than it did her. It hurt more as we drove on, because I could hear her say in a low voice, "My daddy spanked me," and she kept frowning. We did make it home and everything is fine now but that was the first time I ever spanked her. I was still hurt and said I will never do that again.

June is three years old and every Sunday I would take her to the airport. There is a fence in front of the run way and we would watch the planes fly over us. She loved it so much, so I took her in a helicopter, it was an all glass one with no doors and she was strapped to my lap. I cannot believe how excited she is and she said, "I want to tell Mommy that we went up and we went down in a airplane." It was so much fun and I was so very proud to take her places. She had long, golden blond hair and she could sit on it.

Every place we went people would come to look and talk to her. I was very proud to say, "She is my daughter." Everything was really great in my life now and Jolene wanted to help me. We fixed the back office for June to have a place to play when she was there and Jolene started to prepare all my records. I talked about her pumping gas and she said she would, so I checked with the state and it was legal. Jolene talked to Arlean and they decided to do it together. I called Texaco and asked them if they could help me with a promotion. They agreed and in the next few days the salesman brought me red Texaco Fire Chief Suits. They had a Red Fire Hat with a speaker system and they looked so nice. I knew no one else had female gas attendants so I called the local news papers and it was headlines on one half of the front page.

The girls started the day the news was out, our yard was packed, and I had the highest sales in town. They pumped gas all summer and we stayed very busy so I ran another promotion for a joke. It read "Topples Girls at South End Texaco this weekend." I had June and Arlean's daughter Tina, who was also three, at the station with no tops on. It was funny, but a lot of people were mad and said they weren't coming anymore. We still take every Sunday off so Jolene, June and I would go somewhere. We went to Great Adventure, Palisades Park, Howe Caverns, Catskills, Danbury Race track, and all the fairs. We really enjoyed life and one day a movie group came in.

They were buying gas at the time and noticed June then asked if we would be interested in letting her be in a movie. I asked Jolene first. We found it was about ecology and was being filmed in Ridgefield, which is only twenty five miles from here. We said yes and while we were talking they asked if I could help them. They needed a wagon that looked very old and it would be towed behind a model A Ford. I said, "I don't think you will find one around here," but I said I could make one. I explained what I would do and would have it ready for the film. I bought a used twelve foot flat trailer and welded supports to hold the side boards, and then I used some old slabs that we had from our saw mill. It had to be safe because about twelve kids had to ride in it. It was very safe and I sprayed the slabs with clear lacquer paint to avoid splinters. They really loved it and I donated it to them. We became good friends and they would have me do all there auto service when they were in the area. June did go with them and did make that movie, but the last time she went she cried and pleaded to me that she didn't want to go anymore after this time. I would not force her to do anything she didn't want and it hurt me to see here plead with me. I believed it was because she was shy and told her she didn't have to do anything that bothered her that much. We enrolled her into acrobats and ballet and shortly after that Jolene and I joined classes in tap dancing, waltzing and modern jazz. We ended up doing several shows at schools, play houses and Halls. We had a lot of fun and really enjoyed it. June was very good in her Ballet, Acrobatics and also played in a lot of school plays.

Later that year, the movie crew came back here. I had my guitar in the office and the girl with them asked me who played it. I said, "I do, I'm the best." and she said, "I believe it, because everything you do has to be perfect."

I said, "That's me," and she asked if I would play something. I did and just played my special.

She said, "Boy, you weren't kidding, were you?" We started talking and she asked if I would be interested in playing in a movie.

I said, "Yes, I wanted this all my life." Then she told me that Burl Ives was making a movie in Tennessee and she could get me a part in it. I asked Jolene, but she pleaded with me not to so I said, "You and June are the most important things in my life," and I decided not to. It became spring again, but we had a rough winter and the worst in history. The snow had drifted forty feet high from the heavy winds. I headed for my garage before it got real bad but just barely made it because I had to drive through high snow drifts and when I got there the snow was drifted above all my vehicles and I had to go under the snow to find my Jeep with a snow plow. When I found it I had a lot of trouble getting into it. I could only get the door open enough to reach in and roll the window down. I then crawled in and I had to go back and forth to try and make an opening in the snow so I could see where to plow. Lucky near the road the wind cleared the snow down to a foot and I was able to start there. I found that I was the only gas station open. There was a State of Emergency and only emergency vehicles were allowed on the highways. My gas attendant was able to walk to work because he lived less than one half mile away and handled the gas pumps for the snow plows because they could only get gas from me. With the high drifting, our state equipment could not handle the high snow and we had to import trucks equipped with snow blowers from Canada. I could get home for three days and I operated Bulldozers for the town to open some roads.

When we finally did get the roads open I went home to see my family. I could not stay long because I was one of the few that had a wrecker and there were so many cars buried in the snow, some were abandoned and were hit by the plow trucks so I would have to tow them in. I also had to finish plowing my own place and it was very hard because I couldn't see where the cars were and when I did find one I had to clean it off and tow it out of the way. I did not get straightened out for about two weeks. Anyway, after that storm I wanted to live closer, so I bought a much bigger house that was on the lot my Dad promised me but I had to buy it from someone else. The house was thirty by fifty feet and had a full basement. I kept my house in Danbury and rented it to a friend of Jolene's.

I added on and completed the basement for living quarters also. I installed a wet bar and had a revolving wall with a bookcase on one side. I had a switch to turn it for just a straight wall for parties. This room is twenty four by thirty and has sliding glass doors to the rear lawn. I had Wagner Pools install a thirty thousand gallon gunite pool in-ground. I had a regulation diving board, waterslide, and a cast iron furnace to heat it. I built a brick barbecue by the pool and built one in our dining room. Our dining room is twenty four by fourteen feet and we have table settings for twelve. I kept the pool heated until January first. We were doing very well and we all seemed to be happy. But my biggest dream came true because Jolene said she was pregnant. I just held her and tears came to my eyes because I always thought that I could never have children. It was a boy and we named him Mark and I passed cigars with "It's a boy" all over town. I was so happy and he was so beautiful. I fixed up the lounge as I did for June and had Mark with us all the time. (To Be Continued)

This story appears to have a happy ending but only because I had no knowledge of what was to come. It appears I was born under a dark star and this road of life becomes narrower as I find my life in parallel with previous encounters. I reiterate my opening statement that we must always prepare ourselves for future ramifications of bewilderment. For much of the habitants it may be life of happiness but for us few we find ourselves in a world of uncertainties. Am I at fault, was it the fact that I came from a broken family, was mentally and physically tortured beyond belief, did a curse fall upon me or was it all the above. You may find the answers in the following episode.

SECOND EDITION, BITTER SWEET "ALL IN ONE LIFETIME"
Author / Owner
Al Duhan
Phone 860-946-7429
hightechinnovations@yahoo.com